COMPLETE WARRIOR™
A Player's Guide to Combat for All Classes
ANDY COLLINS, DAVID NOONAN, ED STARK

ADDITIONAL DESIGN
JESSE DECKER

DEVELOPMENT TEAM
MICHAEL DONAIS (LEAD), ANDREW J. FINCH,
RICHARD BAKER, DAVID ECKELBERRY

EDITORS
DALE DONOVAN, KIM MOHAN

MANAGING EDITOR
KIM MOHAN

DESIGN MANAGER
ED STARK

DEVELOPMENT MANAGER
ANDREW J. FINCH

DIRECTOR OF RPG R&D
BILL SLAVICSEK

VICE PRESIDENT OF PUBLISHING
MARY KIRCHOFF

PROJECT MANAGER
MARTIN DURHAM

PRODUCTION MANAGER
CHAS DELONG

ART DIRECTOR
DAWN MURIN

COVER ARTIST
WAYNE REYNOLDS

INTERIOR ARTISTS
BRENT CHUMLEY, ED COX, WAYNE ENGLAND,
REBECCA GUAY-MITCHELL, JEREMY JARVIS,
DOUG KOVACS, GINGER KUBIC, JOHN AND
LAURA LAKEY, DAVID MARTIN,
DENNIS CRABAPPLE MCCLAIN,
MATT MITCHELL, STEVE PRESCOTT,
WAYNE REYNOLDS, DAVID ROACH,
MARK SMYLIE, BRIAN SNODDY, RON SPENCER,
JOEL THOMAS

GRAPHIC DESIGNER
DAWN MURIN

GRAPHIC PRODUCTION SPECIALIST
ANGELIKA LOKOTZ

IMAGE TECHNICIAN
JASON WILEY

ORIGINAL INTERIOR DESIGN
SEAN GLENN

Sources: *Sword and Fist* by Jason Carl; *Tome and Blood* by Bruce R. Cordell and Skip Williams; *Defenders of the Faith* by Rich Redman and James Wyatt; *Masters of the Wild* by David Eckelberry and Mike Selinker; *Song and Silence* by David Noonan and John Rateliff; *Oriental Adventures* by James Wyatt; *Epic Level Handbook* by Andy Collins, Bruce R. Cordell, and Thomas M. Reid; various *Dragon* magazine issues and contributors including Andy Collins, Monte Cook, and Kolja Liquette.

Based on the original DUNGEONS & DRAGONS® rules created by Gary Gygax and Dave Arneson, and the new DUNGEONS & DRAGONS game designed by Jonathan Tweet, Monte Cook, Skip Williams, Richard Baker, and Peter Adkison.

U.S., CANADA, ASIA, PACIFIC,
& LATIN AMERICA
Wizards of the Coast, Inc.
P.O. Box 707
Renton WA 98057-0707
Questions? 1-800-324-6496

EUROPEAN HEADQUARTERS
Wizards of the Coast, Belgium
T Hofveld 6d
1702 Groot-Bijgaarden
Belgium
+322-467-3360

620-17664-001-EN
9 8 7 6 5 4 3 2
First Printing: December 2003

Visit our website at www.wizards.com/dnd

Contents

Introduction

The *Complete Warrior* book is a rules accessory for the DUNGEONS & DRAGONS® Roleplaying Game. It is primarily a player resource focusing on new options and expanded rules for D&D players who want to create or advance martial characters. DMs can use this book as a resource for creating or optimizing their own creations.

MARTIAL CHARACTERS

So what is a martial character? The authors of this book define a martial character as any character that focuses his or her development on improving his or her combat capabilities, particularly those capabilities that emphasize melee or ranged combat over spellcasting, skill use, or other abilities common to a D&D character. (For brevity in some places throughout this book, including its title, martial characters are referred to as warriors. In this context, "warrior" does not refer to a member of the warrior NPC class described in the *Dungeon Master's Guide*—although a character with levels in that class could be considered a martial character and could benefit from the material in this book just as any other character might.)

Again, though, this doesn't mean that if you're playing a wizard you should don plate armor and start hefting a greatsword. This book details options for non-"fighter-types" who want to maximize their combat effectiveness. Spellcasting warriors, skill-using soldiers, and holy (or unholy) combatants of all types can find resources within these pages. If you're playing a rogue who'd like to improve her chances to hit, or a sorcerer who might like to withstand a few more points of damage, this book is for you.

THE COMPLETE WARRIOR

This book contains information for players and DMs, showcasing new and interesting options for characters and creatures utilizing the D&D combat rules. Players can read through the entire book without hesitation—DMs can use the material to generate their own surprises without any help!

Classes (Chapter 1): This chapter introduces three new character classes: the arcane hexblade, the honorable samurai, and the dexterous swashbuckler. Each class provides an alternative for players interested in "a different kind of fighter." And, in keeping with the theme of alternatives, this chapter concludes with some variant rules for existing classes, including variant rangers and paladins.

Martial Prestige Classes (Chapter 2): A large number of prestige classes are presented here, all with a focus on being better in combat. Whether you're playing a fighter, a wizard, a cleric, or even some sort of strange monstrous character, you should find a prestige class here that appeals to you.

Supplemental Rules (Chapter 3): This chapter includes compilations of new feats and spells as well as some other rules systems you might not expect in a book for warrior-types. Fighting spellcasters should enjoy the section on guardian familiars, and the chapter also discusses new uses for skills such as Concentration, Perform, and Knowledge.

Fantasy Warfare (Chapter 4): A book for martial characters wouldn't be complete without a chapter on warfare. We look at historical warfare and fantasy warfare with a more modern slant. Here are suggestions and rules for war-oriented adventures as well as advice on running a wartime campaign. Players should find the sections on magic items and warrior organizations useful, and both DMs and players can use the section on the warrior pantheon.

SOURCES

This book includes material from other sources, including *Dragon* magazine, web articles previously published on the Wizards of the Coast website, and earlier works like *Sword and Fist*. Much of this material has been picked up and revised based on feedback and comments from D&D players and DMs all around the world. We hope you like the changes we made to the prestige classes, feats, and other elements of the game as well as the large amount of brand-new material you'll find in these pages.

Remember, however, that DUNGEONS & DRAGONS is *your* game. If you've been playing with a particular prestige class or feat that we've picked up and revised, we hope you'll look at the new version and see why we made the changes—but you *don't* have to play with the revised material if you don't want to. The Dungeon Master, as always, should make the final call about what material belongs in his or her game, and if you've been playing with an older version of something that appears in this book and you're having fun doing it, don't worry about making a change. We think all the changes we've made are for the best, but it's your game, after all.

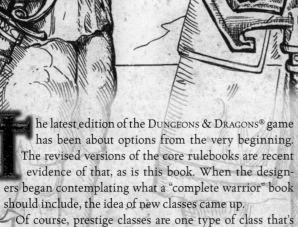

The latest edition of the DUNGEONS & DRAGONS® game has been about options from the very beginning. The revised versions of the core rulebooks are recent evidence of that, as is this book. When the designers began contemplating what a "complete warrior" book should include, the idea of new classes came up.

Of course, prestige classes are one type of class that's gotten a lot of attention since the concept was introduced in the *Dungeon Master's Guide*. However, new character classes haven't been given the same amount of exposure in D&D® accessories produced by Wizards of the Coast.

This chapter remedies that lack of attention to some degree with the presentation of three new character classes for the game. Following those class descriptions are new variant versions of the paladin and ranger classes, specifically designed for low-magic, warrior-centered campaigns and without the ability to cast spells.

HEXBLADE

Combining the dynamic powers of martial prowess and arcane might, the hexblade presents a deadly challenge to opponents unused to such a foe.

Adventures: Hexblades adventure for personal gain, whether that gain is power, prestige, wealth, or all the above.

Characteristics: The hexblade balances talents in combat and arcane spellcasting. At lower levels, the hexblade relies on melee ability augmented by his special power to curse his enemies. As he gains experience, he becomes capable of casting a limited number of spells while his curse ability becomes more potent and he gains the ability to warp the normal laws of probability. He can also draw upon the service of a familiar to further augment his abilities.

Alignment: The style of the hexblade tends to be selfish, sometimes even cruel, though it is by no means limited to evil characters. Still, even the friendliest hexblade is at best neutral. Hexblades may be tyrannical or free-minded, disciplined or creative, and thus have no particular bent toward law or chaos.

Religion: Most hexblades aren't very pious, relying on their own talents rather than counting on a deity to protect them. Those who revere a deity often choose Wee Jas (deity of death and magic) or Boccob the Uncaring (deity of magic). Some particularly evil hexblades venerate Nerull (deity of death) or Vecna (deity of secrets).

Background: Like that of the sorcerer, the power of the hexblade often displays itself at an early age, frequently in the form of unexplained accidents or other incidents of bad luck experienced by those around the budding hexblade. Though the hexblade is ultimately a self-taught character, many receive rudimentary training from another arcane spellcaster, such as an older hexblade, sorcerer, wizard, or bard, before setting off on their own.

Unlike sorcerers, hexblades share a unique bond. Though two hexblades who meet in a tavern or apothecary won't necessarily strike up a lasting friendship, it is rare for two hexblades to oppose one another unless great personal gain is on the line.

Races: As with sorcerers, most hexblades are humans or half-elves. Those few gnomes who enjoy a cruel twist to their levity may take up the tradition. Elves wishing to mix magic and warfare more often become fighter/wizards. Dwarves and halflings rarely exhibit the self-centered behavior common among hexblades.

Among the savage humanoids, hexblades may be found as leaders or advisors.

Other Classes: Hexblades tend to get along best with other classes whose members look out for themselves before others, including rogues, rangers, and barbarians. They avoid paladins and other characters dedicated to the service of good or other high-minded ideals. Hexblades sometimes feel jealous of the sorcerer's superior arcane talents, and they shun wizards as weak book-learners.

Role: Though a capable melee combatant, the hexblade relies on opportunistic use of his spells and special abilities to augment this role in the group. A hexblade with the proper skill selection can make a fine leader for a group comfortable with his style.

GAME RULE INFORMATION

Hexblades have the following game statistics.

Abilities: Charisma controls many of the hexblade's special powers, including his spellcasting. Strength is important for him because of its role in combat. Dexterity and Constitution both contribute to the hexblade's long-term survival.

Alignment: Any nongood.

Hit Die: d10.

Class Skills

The hexblade's class skills (and the key ability for each skill) are Bluff (Cha), Concentration (Con), Craft (Int), Diplomacy (Cha), Intimidate (Cha), Knowledge (arcana) (Int), Profession (Wis), Ride (Dex), and Spellcraft (Int). See Chapter 4 in the *Player's Handbook* for skill descriptions.

Skill Points at 1st Level: (2 + Int modifier) × 4.

Skill Points at Each Additional Level: 2 + Int modifier.

Class Features

All of the following are class features of the hexblade.

Weapon and Armor Proficiency: Hexblades are proficient with all simple and martial weapons, and with light armor but not with shields. Because the somatic components required for hexblade spells are simple, a hexblade can cast hexblade spells while wearing light armor without incurring the normal arcane spell failure chance. However, like any other arcane spellcaster, a hexblade wearing medium or heavy armor or using a shield incurs a chance of arcane spell failure if the spell in question has a somatic component (and most do). A multiclass hexblade still incurs the normal arcane spell failure chance for arcane spells derived from other classes.

Hexblade's Curse (Su): Once per day, as a free action, a hexblade can unleash a curse upon a foe. The target must be visible to the hexblade and within 60 feet. The target of a hexblade's curse takes a –2 penalty on attacks, saves, ability checks, skill checks, and weapon damage rolls for 1 hour thereafter. A successful Will save (DC 10 + 1/2 hexblade's class level + hexblade's Cha modifier) negates the effect.

TABLE 1–1: THE HEXBLADE

Level	Base Attack Bonus	Fort Save	Ref Save	Will Save	Special	— Spells per Day —			
						1st	2nd	3rd	4th
1st	+1	+0	+0	+2	Hexblade's curse 1/day	—	—	—	—
2nd	+2	+0	+0	+3	Arcane resistance	—	—	—	—
3rd	+3	+1	+1	+3	Mettle	—	—	—	—
4th	+4	+1	+1	+4	Summon familiar	0	—	—	—
5th	+5	+1	+1	+4	Bonus feat, hexblade's curse 2/day	0	—	—	—
6th	+6/+1	+2	+2	+5	—	1	—	—	—
7th	+7/+2	+2	+2	+5	Greater hexblade's curse	1	—	—	—
8th	+8/+3	+2	+2	+6	—	1	0	—	—
9th	+9/+4	+3	+3	+6	Hexblade's curse 3/day	1	0	—	—
10th	+10/+5	+3	+3	+7	Bonus feat	1	1	—	—
11th	+11/+6/+1	+3	+3	+7	—	1	1	0	—
12th	+12/+7/+2	+4	+4	+8	Aura of unluck 1/day	1	1	1	—
13th	+13/+8/+3	+4	+4	+8	Hexblade's curse 4/day	1	1	1	—
14th	+14/+9/+4	+4	+4	+9	—	2	1	1	0
15th	+15/+10/+5	+5	+5	+9	Bonus feat	2	1	1	1
16th	+16/+11/+6/+1	+5	+5	+10	Aura of unluck 2/day	2	2	1	1
17th	+17/+12/+7/+2	+5	+5	+10	Hexblade's curse 5/day	2	2	2	1
18th	+18/+13/+8/+3	+6	+6	+11	—	3	2	2	1
19th	+19/+14/+9/+4	+6	+6	+11	Dire hexblade's curse	3	3	3	2
20th	+20/+15/+10/+5	+6	+6	+12	Aura of unluck 3/day, bonus feat	3	3	3	3

At every four levels beyond 1st (5th, 9th, 13th, and 17th) a hexblade gains the ability to use his curse one additional time per day, as indicated on Table 1–1. Multiple hexblade's curses don't stack, and any foe that successfully resists the effect cannot be affected again by the same hexblade's curse for 24 hours.

Any effect that removes or dispels a curse eliminates the effect of a hexblade's curse.

Arcane Resistance (Su): At 2nd level, a hexblade gains a bonus equal to his Charisma bonus (minimum +1) on saving throws against spells and spell-like effects.

Mettle (Ex): At 3rd level and higher, a hexblade can resist magical and unusual attacks with great willpower or fortitude. If he makes a successful Will or Fortitude save against an attack that normally would have a lesser effect on a successful save (such as any spell with a saving throw entry of Will half or Fortitude partial), he instead completely negates the effect. An unconscious or sleeping hexblade does not gain the benefit of mettle.

Familiar: Beginning at 4th level, a hexblade can obtain a familiar. Doing so takes 24 hours and uses up magical materials that cost 100 gp. A familiar is a magical beast that resembles a small animal and is unusually tough and intelligent. The creature serves as a companion and servant.

The hexblade chooses the kind of familiar he gets. As the hexblade advances in level, his familiar also increases in power. Treat the hexblade as a sorcerer of three levels lower for determining the familiar's powers and abilities (see the Familiars sidebar on page 52 of the *Player's Handbook*).

If the familiar dies or is dismissed by the hexblade, the latter must attempt a DC 15 Fortitude saving throw. Failure means he loses 200 experience points per hexblade level; success reduces the loss to one-half that amount. However, a hexblade's experience point total can never go below 0 as the result of a familiar's demise or dismissal. A slain or dismissed familiar cannot be replaced for a year and day. A slain familiar can be raised from the dead just as a character can be, but it does not lose a level or a point of Constitution when this happy event occurs.

A character with more than one class that grants a familiar may have only one familiar at a time.

A hexblade

Spells: Beginning at 4th level, a hexblade gains the ability to cast a small number of arcane spells, which are drawn from the hexblade spell list (see Chapter 3). He can cast any spell he knows without preparing it ahead of time, just as a sorcerer can (see page 54 of the *Player's Handbook*).

To learn or cast a spell, a hexblade must have a Charisma score equal to at least 10 + the spell level (Cha 11 for 1st-level spells, Cha 12 for 2nd-level spells, and so forth). The Difficulty Class for a saving throw against a hexblade's spell is 10 + the spell level + the hexblade's Cha modifier.

Like other spellcasters, a hexblade can cast only a certain number of spells of each spell level per day. His base daily spell allotment is given on Table 1–1. In addition, he receives bonus spells per day if he has a high Charisma score (see Table 1–1: Ability Modifiers and Bonus Spells, page 8 of the *Player's Handbook*). When Table 1–1 indicates that the hexblade gets 0 spells per day of a given spell level (for instance, 1st-level spells for a 4th-level hexblade), he gains only the bonus spells he would be entitled to based on his Charisma score for that spell level.

The hexblade's selection of spells is extremely limited. A hexblade begins play knowing no spells, but gains one or more new spells at certain levels, as indicated on Table 1–2. (Unlike spells per day, his Charisma score does not affect the number of spells a hexblade knows; the numbers on Table 1–2 are fixed.)

Upon reaching 12th level, and at every third hexblade level after that (15th and 18th), a hexblade can choose to learn a new spell in place of one he already knows. In effect, the hexblade "loses" the old spell in exchange for the new one. The new spell's level must be the same as that of the spell being exchanged, and it must be at least two levels lower than the highest-level hexblade spell the hexblade can cast. For instance, upon reaching 12th level, a hexblade could trade in a single 1st-level spell (two spell levels below the highest-level hexblade spell he can cast, which is 3rd) for a different 1st-level spell. At 15th level, he could trade in a single 1st-level or 2nd-level spell (since he now can cast 4th-level hexblade spells) for a different spell of the same level. A hexblade may swap only

Illus. by W. England

a single spell at any given level, and must choose whether or not to swap the spell at the same time that he gains new spells known for the level.

Through 3rd level, a hexblade has no caster level. At 4th level and higher, his caster level is one-half his hexblade level.

Table 1–2: Hexblade Spells Known

Level	Spells Known 1st	2nd	3rd	4th
1st	—	—	—	—
2nd	—	—	—	—
3rd	—	—	—	—
4th	2[1]	—	—	—
5th	2	—	—	—
6th	3	—	—	—
7th	3	—	—	—
8th	4	2[1]	—	—
9th	4	2	—	—
10th	4	3	—	—
11th	4	3	2[1]	—
12th	4	4	3	—
13th	4	4	3	—
14th	4	4	4	2[1]
15th	4	4	4	3
16th	4	4	4	3
17th	5	4	4	4
18th	5	5	4	4
19th	5	5	5	4
20th	5	5	5	5

1 Provided the hexblade has sufficient Charisma to have a bonus spell of this level.

Bonus Feat: At 5th level, and every five levels thereafter (10th, 15th, and 20th), a hexblade gains a bonus feat, which must be selected from the following list: Combat Casting, Greater Spell Focus (enchantment, necromancy, or transmutation only), Greater Spell Penetration, Spell Focus (enchantment, necromancy, or transmutation only), Spell Penetration.

Greater Hexblade's Curse (Su): When a hexblade attains 7th level, the penalty on attacks, saves, ability checks, skill checks, and weapon damage rolls incurred by a target of the hexblade's curse becomes –4 instead of –2.

Aura of Unluck (Su): Once per day, a hexblade of 12th level or higher can create a baleful aura of misfortune. Any melee or ranged attack made against the hexblade while this aura of unluck is active has a 20% miss chance (similar to the effect of concealment). Activating the aura is a free action, and the aura lasts for a number of rounds equal to 3 + the hexblade's Charisma bonus (if any).

At 16th level and higher, a hexblade can use his aura of unluck twice per day. A 20th-level hexblade can activate this aura three times per day.

Dire Hexblade's Curse (Su): When a hexblade attains 19th level, the penalty on attacks, saves, ability checks, skill checks, and weapon damage rolls incurred by a target of the hexblade's curse becomes –6 instead of –4.

Ex-Hexblades

A hexblade who becomes good-aligned loses all hexblade spells and all supernatural class abilities. His familiar becomes a normal animal and leaves the hexblade's service as soon as possible. He may not progress any farther in levels as a hexblade. He retains all the other benefits of the class (weapon and armor proficiencies and bonus feats).

Human Hexblade Starting Package

Armor: Studded leather (+3 AC, armor check penalty –1, speed 30 ft., 20 lb.).

Weapons: Longsword (1d8, crit 19–20/×2, 4 lb., one-handed, slashing).

Skill Selection: Pick a number of skills equal to 3 + Int modifier.

Skill	Ranks	Ability	Armor Check Penalty
Bluff	4	Cha	—
Ride	4	Dex	—
Knowledge (arcana)	4	Int	—
Intimidate	4	Cha	—
Diplomacy	4	Cha	—
Spellcraft	4	Int	—
Spot (cc)	2	Wis	—
Listen (cc)	2	Wis	—

Feat: Weapon Focus (longsword).

Bonus Feat (Human): Improved Initiative.

Gear: Backpack with waterskin, one day's trail rations, bedroll, sack, flint and steel. Hooded lantern, 3 pints of oil. Quiver with 20 arrows.

Gold: 6d4 gp.

SAMURAI

Known for their matchless bravery and strict code of honor, the samurai were the noble soldiers of feudal Japan. In a fantasy setting, the samurai brings that courage and honor to the service of a lord, general, or other leader. The reputation of samurai for being tenacious in combat often precedes them in battle, and their mere presence is often enough to make dishonorable enemies slink away in the darkness.

Adventures: Samurai undertake quests and other adventures at the behest of their lord, who often uses mid- to high-level samurai as troubleshooters. A samurai might be ordered to defend a village beset by bandits, to lead allies in battle, or to hunt down and duel a rival who has stained the lord's honor.

Characteristics: Wielding their signature katana (bastard sword) and wakizashi (short sword) simultaneously, samurai are as potent in melee as a fighter, although they are less versatile. Their adherence to the code of bushido is intimidating to their foes, and the fixed stare of a samurai can unnerve most opponents.

Alignment: Almost every aspect of a samurai's life is ruled by the code of bushido, which demands total obedience to one's lord, bravery in the face of utmost peril, and honor and respect to superiors, peers, and lessers alike. Samurai are always lawful, stoic in demeanor, and implacable when matters of honor and justice are concerned.

Religion: In a fantasy world, some samurai worship no deity, instead relying on the code of bushido for guidance on moral and ethical issues. Others gravitate to the worship of deities of law, honor, and justice, such as Heironeous and St. Cuthbert. Some evil samurai find the tyrannical teachings of Hextor acceptable.

Background: Samurai are traditionally of noble birth, although folk tales are replete with samurai who were orphans adopted by noble families or foot soldiers who showed outstanding bravery in battle. Becoming a samurai means untold hours learning to use the katana and wakizashi, lessons in manners and etiquette, and relentless instruction in the tenets of bushido.

Races: The clan-based, lawful society of the dwarves would make a good match for samurai culture. Elves' long lives and sense of history could lead them down the samurai's path. Most halflings wander too much to make effective samurai, and gnomes show no particular affinity for the class. Least likely of all are half-orcs, who rarely attain a high enough station in civilized society to become samurai.

Other Classes: Because both classes live their lives according to a code of behavior, samurai tend to get along well with paladins, although samurai are sometimes puzzled when paladins ask, "Is this the right thing to do?" (A typical samurai's response might be "You dishonor the lord by questioning his orders.") Monks are likewise admired for their strict training regimen and self-discipline. Samurai also get along well with fighters, especially if they have served in an army, and bards whose art reflects appropriate themes. Barbarians are tolerated with only a thin veneer of politeness, as are rogues who focus on larceny and other dishonorable activities.

Role: With heavy armor and a razor-sharp blade in each hand, samurai are front-line melee combatants. They also benefit from a series of abilities that give morale penalties to their foes. In addition, because they are trained in matters of etiquette, samurai make good negotiators and spokesmen.

GAME RULE INFORMATION

Samurai have the following game statistics.

Abilities: Strength is of paramount importance to the sword-wielding samurai, and Dexterity and Constitution help him survive in the midst of battle. Many of the samurai's other class features depend on Charisma—a samurai's force of personality can make his enemies quake in fear.

A samurai

Alignment: Any lawful.
Hit Die: d10.

Class Skills

The samurai's class skills (and the key ability for each skill) are Concentration (Con), Craft (Int), Diplomacy (Cha), Intimidate (Cha), Knowledge (history) (Int), Knowledge (nobility and royalty) (Int), Ride (Dex), and Sense Motive (Wis). See Chapter 4 in the *Player's Handbook* for skill descriptions.

Skill Points at 1st Level: (2 + Int modifier) × 4.

Skill Points at Each Additional Level: 2 + Int modifier.

Class Features

All of the following are class features of the samurai.

Weapon and Armor Proficiency: A samurai is proficient with all simple and martial weapons, and with all types of armor, but not with shields.

Daisho Proficiency (Ex): In melee combat, a samurai favors the katana (a masterwork bastard sword) and the wakizashi (a masterwork short sword). Many samurai receive an heirloom set of these two blades, known as the daisho. Because a samurai is trained in their use, he gains Exotic Weapon Proficiency (bastard sword) as a bonus feat.

Two Swords as One (Ex): At 2nd level, a samurai has learned to wield the katana and wakizashi together. He is treated as having the Two-Weapon Fighting feat when wielding a katana and wakizashi, even if he does not meet the prerequisites for that feat.

Kiai Smite (Ex): Once per day, a samurai of 3rd level or higher can give a great cry during combat that invigorates him. When a samurai shouts (a free action), his next attack gains a bonus on the attack roll and the damage roll equal to his Charisma bonus (minimum +1).

As a samurai gains levels, he can make a kiai smite more often.

Iaijutsu Master (Ex): By 5th level, a samurai has become adept at iaijutsu, a fighting technique that concentrates on

Illus. by S. Prescott

Table 1–3: The Samurai

Level	Base Attack Bonus	Fort Save	Ref Save	Will Save	Special
1st	+1	+2	+0	+0	Daisho proficiency
2nd	+2	+3	+0	+0	Two swords as one
3rd	+3	+3	+1	+1	Kiai smite 1/day
4th	+4	+4	+1	+1	—
5th	+5	+4	+1	+1	Iaijutsu master
6th	+6/+1	+5	+2	+2	Staredown
7th	+7/+2	+5	+2	+2	Kiai smite 2/day
8th	+8/+3	+6	+2	+2	Improved Initiative
9th	+9/+4	+6	+3	+3	—
10th	+10/+5	+7	+3	+3	Mass staredown
11th	+11/+6/+1	+7	+3	+3	Improved two swords as one
12th	+12/+7/+2	+8	+4	+4	Kiai smite 3/day
13th	+13/+8/+3	+8	+4	+4	—
14th	+14/+9/+4	+9	+4	+4	Improved staredown
15th	+15/+10/+5	+9	+5	+5	—
16th	+16/+11/+6/+1	+10	+5	+5	Greater two swords as one
17th	+17/+12/+7/+2	+10	+5	+5	Kiai smite 4/day
18th	+18/+13/+8/+3	+11	+6	+6	—
19th	+19/+14/+9/+4	+11	+6	+6	—
20th	+20/+15/+10/+5	+12	+6	+6	Frightful presence

drawing his weapon and striking a foe in one fluid motion. He is treated as having the Quick Draw feat, but only when he draws his katana or wakizashi.

Staredown (Ex): At 6th level, a samurai becomes able to strike fear into his foes by his mere presence. He gains a +4 bonus on Intimidate checks and can demoralize an opponent (as described in the Intimidate skill description, page 76 of the *Player's Handbook*).

Improved Initiative (Ex): At 8th level, the samurai has practiced iaijutsu techniques used in ritual duels between two samurai, and he is able to anticipate when any enemy will attack. He now has the Improved Initiative feat.

Mass Staredown (Ex): At 10th level, a samurai has sufficient presence that he can cow multiple foes. Using a Intimidate check, the samurai can demoralize all opponents within 30 feet with a single standard action.

Improved Two Swords as One (Ex): At 11th level, a samurai's prowess with the katana and wakizashi improves. He is treated as having the Improved Two-Weapon Fighting feat when wielding a katana and wakizashi, even if he does not meet the prerequisites for the feat.

Improved Staredown (Ex): At 14th level, even a glance from the hard eyes of a samurai is enough to give his foes pause. The samurai can demoralize opponents within 30 feet as a move action, not a standard action.

Greater Two Swords as One(Ex): At 16th level, fighting with a katana and wakizashi becomes second nature for a samurai. He is treated as having the Greater Two-Weapon Fighting feat when wielding a katana and wakizashi, even if he does not meet the prerequisites for that feat.

Frightful Presence (Ex): A 20th-level samurai's bravery, honor, and fighting prowess have become legendary. When the samurai draws his blade, opponents within 30 feet must succeed on a Will save (DC 20 + samurai's Cha modifier) or become panicked for 4d6 rounds (if they have 4 or fewer Hit Dice) or shaken for 4d6 rounds (if they have from 5 to 19 Hit Dice). Creatures with 20 or more Hit Dice are not affected. Any foe that successfully resists the effect cannot be affected again by the same samurai's frightful presence for 24 hours.

Ex-Samurai

A samurai who ceases to be lawful or who commits an act of grave dishonor loses all samurai class features that depend on Charisma or Charisma-based checks. Minor embarrassments don't count, but major breaks with the code of bushido do. Acts that could lose a samurai his status include disobeying an order from a superior officer or feudal lord, fleeing in cowardice from an important battle, being caught in a major lie or other breach of integrity, and appallingly rude behavior. A disgraced character may not progress any farther as a samurai. He regains his class features the ability to advance in the class if he atones for his violations (see the *atonement* spell, page 201 of the *Player's Handbook*), assuming the feudal lord offers a chance at redemption. (Some feudal lords demand ritual suicide as the only act that cleanses the stain of dishonor.)

Like a member of any other class, a samurai may be a multiclass character, but multiclass samurai face a special restriction. A samurai who gains a level in any class other than samurai may never again raise his samurai level, though he retains all his current samurai abilities. The way of the samurai demands constant adherence to the code of bushido. Samurai may sometimes take levels in particular prestige classes without violating this code. The kensai and the knight protector (both in this book) and the dwarven defender (in the *Dungeon Master's Guide*) are three such examples. The Dungeon Master may designate other prestige classes as available to a samurai.

Some disgraced samurai take levels in the ronin prestige class (described in Chapter 2 of this book), which gives them a chance to regain their lost class features.

Human Samurai Starting Package

Armor: Scale mail (+4 AC, armor check penalty –4, speed 20 ft., 30 lb.).

Weapons: Bastard sword (1d10, crit 19–20/×2, 6 lb., one-handed, slashing).

Short sword (1d6, crit 19–20/×2, 2 lb., light, piercing).

Shortbow (1d6, crit ×3, range inc. 60 ft., 2 lb., piercing).

Skill Selection: Pick a number of skills equal to 3 + Int modifier.

Skill	Ranks	Ability	Armor Check Penalty
Craft (calligraphy)	4	Int	—
Diplomacy	4	Cha	—
Intimidate	4	Cha	—
Knowledge (history)	4	Int	—
Knowledge (nobility and royalty)	4	Int	—
Ride	4	Dex	—
Sense Motive	4	Wis	—

Feat: Weapon Focus (bastard sword).

Bonus Feat (Human): Combat Reflexes.

Gear: Backpack with waterskin, one day's trail rations, bedroll, sack, flint and steel. bullseye lantern and 1 pint oil, 20 arrows.

Gold: 2d4 gp.

SWASHBUCKLER

The swashbuckler embodies the concepts of daring and panache. Favoring agility and wit over brute force, the swashbuckler excels both in combat situations and social interactions, making her a versatile character indeed.

Adventures: Swashbucklers adventure for a variety of motivations, based on their alignment and background. Some seek to right injustices, while others seek only fame and fortune. All swashbucklers, however, share a tendency to leap into action when the call comes, regardless of their personal views.

Characteristics: The swashbuckler combines skill and finesse with sheer combat prowess. Though swashbucklers can't dish out quite as much damage as a typical fighter or barbarian, they tend to be more agile and mobile than most melee combatants. When she can pick her battles carefully, a swashbuckler becomes a very deadly opponent (not to mention hard to pin down). Swashbucklers also hold their own in social situations, unlike most fighters.

Alignment: Like rogues, swashbucklers tend to be diverse in their outlooks, and thus in their alignments. Those who chafe under societal restrictions tend to be chaotic, while those who uphold honorable traditions may well be lawful.

Religion: Most swashbucklers pay at least some small amount of homage to Olidammara (deity of thieves), since that deity is renowned as being lucky. Lawful or chivalrous swashbucklers may revere Heironeous (deity of valor) or even St. Cuthbert (deity of retribution). Swashbucklers who choose the open road over a fixed residence often worship Fharlanghn (deity of roads).

Background: Many swashbucklers come from affluent backgrounds, but anyone valuing finesse over force can become a swashbuckler, regardless of background. A common shared element among swashbucklers' backgrounds is life in an urban environment, whether the back alleys of a slum or the cultured halls of royalty.

Swashbucklers tend to see other swashbucklers as rivals rather than allies, even when sharing similar goals. The swashbuckler's need for attention often outweighs her better judgment, leading either to friendly competition or even outright distrust and antipathy.

Races: Swashbucklers are most often humans, elves, or half-elves. Humans and half-elves tend to have the daring nature required of a swashbuckler, and the natural grace of elves makes them well suited for the class. Halflings and gnomes often have the temperament to become a swashbuckler, though their slower speed works against them. Dwarves tend to prefer fighting in heavy armor with big weapons, and thus rarely become swashbucklers.

Among the savage humanoids, swashbucklers are virtually unknown.

Other Classes: Swashbucklers prefer to work with other quick, lightly armored characters. They get along best with rogues and bards, and appreciate the agility and combat talents of the monk (though chaotic swashbucklers may chafe at the monk's ascetic nature). Lawful good swashbucklers often share the paladin's honorable nature, but otherwise the classes tend to clash in their approach to life. Swashbucklers have no particular distaste for spellcasters, and they appreciate the utility of a cleverly chosen, well-timed spell. They don't interact with barbarians, druids, or rangers very often, since these characters tend to prefer natural settings to the typical urban environment of the swashbuckler.

Role: The swashbuckler is an able melee combatant, particularly when paired with a fighter or rogue. She can also make a fine party leader or spokesperson, thanks to her access to Charisma-based skills.

GAME RULE INFORMATION

Swashbucklers have the following game statistics.

Abilities: The lightly armored swashbuckler depends on a high Dexterity for her Armor Class, as well as for many class skills. High Intelligence and Charisma scores are also hallmarks of a successful swashbuckler. Strength is not as important for a swashbuckler as it is for other melee combatants.

Alignment: Any.

Hit Die: d10.

A swashbuckler

Illus. by G. Kubic

Class Skills

The swashbuckler's class skills (and the key ability for each skill) are Balance (Dex), Bluff (Cha), Climb (Str), Craft (Int), Diplomacy (Cha), Escape Artist (Dex), Jump (Str), Profession (Wis), Sense Motive (Wis), Swim (Str), Tumble (Dex), and Use Rope (Dex). See Chapter 4 in the *Player's Handbook* for skill descriptions.

Skill Points at 1st Level: (4 + Int modifier) × 4.
Skill Points at Each Additional Level: 4 + Int modifier.

TABLE 1–4: THE SWASHBUCKLER

Level	Base Attack Bonus	Fort Save	Ref Save	Will Save	Special
1st	+1	+2	+0	+0	Weapon Finesse
2nd	+2	+3	+0	+0	Grace +1
3rd	+3	+3	+1	+1	Insightful strike
4th	+4	+4	+1	+1	—
5th	+5	+4	+1	+1	Dodge bonus +1
6th	+6/+1	+5	+2	+2	—
7th	+7/+2	+5	+2	+2	Acrobatic charge
8th	+8/+3	+6	+2	+2	Improved flanking
9th	+9/+4	+6	+3	+3	—
10th	+10/+5	+7	+3	+3	Dodge bonus +2
11th	+11/+6/+1	+7	+3	+3	Grace +2, lucky
12th	+12/+7/+2	+8	+4	+4	—
13th	+13/+8/+3	+8	+4	+4	Acrobatic skill mastery
14th	+14/+9/+4	+9	+4	+4	Weakening critical
15th	+15/+10/+5	+9	+5	+5	Dodge bonus +3
16th	+16/+11/+6/+1	+10	+5	+5	—
17th	+17/+12/+7/+2	+10	+5	+5	Slippery mind
18th	+18/+13/+8/+3	+11	+6	+6	—
19th	+19/+14/+9/+4	+11	+6	+6	Wounding critical
20th	+20/+15/+10/+5	+12	+6	+6	Dodge bonus +4, grace +3

Class Features

All of the following are class features of the swashbuckler.

Weapon and Armor Proficiency: Swashbucklers are proficient with all simple and martial weapons, and with light armor. Some of the swashbuckler's class features, as noted below, rely on her being no more than lightly armored and unencumbered.

Weapon Finesse (Ex): A swashbuckler gains Weapon Finesse as a bonus feat at 1st level even if she does not qualify for the feat.

Grace (Ex): A swashbuckler gains a +1 competence bonus on Reflex saves at 2nd level. This bonus increases to +2 at 11th level and to +3 at 20th level. A swashbuckler loses this bonus when wearing medium or heavy armor or when carrying a medium or heavy load.

Insightful Strike (Ex): At 3rd level, a swashbuckler becomes able to place her finesse attacks where they deal greater damage. She applies her Intelligence bonus (if any) as a bonus on damage rolls (in addition to any Strength bonus she may have) with any light weapon, as well as any other weapon that can be used with Weapon Finesse, such as a rapier, whip, or spiked chain. Targets immune to sneak attacks or critical hits are immune to the swashbuckler's insightful strike. A swashbuckler cannot use this ability when wearing medium or heavy armor or when carrying a medium or heavy load.

Dodge Bonus (Ex): A swashbuckler is trained at focusing her defenses on a single opponent in melee. During her action, she may designate an opponent and receive a +1 dodge bonus to Armor Class against melee attacks from that opponent. She can select a new opponent on any action. This bonus increases by +1 at every five levels after 5th (+2 at 10th level, +3 at 15th, and +4 at 20th). A swashbuckler loses this bonus when wearing medium or heavy armor or when carrying a medium or heavy load.

If the swashbuckler also has the Dodge feat, she need not designate the same target for this ability as for the Dodge feat. (If she designates the same target, the bonuses stack.)

Acrobatic Charge (Ex): A swashbuckler of 7th level or higher can charge in situations where others cannot. She may charge over difficult terrain that normally slows movement or allies blocking her path. This ability enables her to run down steep stairs, leap down from a balcony, or to tumble over tables to get to her target. Depending on the circumstance, she may still need to make appropriate checks (Jump or Tumble checks, in particular) to successfully move over the terrain.

Improved Flanking (Ex): A swashbuckler of 8th level or higher who is flanking an opponent gains a +4 bonus on attacks instead of a +2 bonus on attacks. (Other characters flanking with the swashbuckler don't gain this increased bonus.)

Lucky (Ex): Many swashbucklers live by the credo "Better lucky than good." Once per day, a swashbuckler of 11th level or higher may reroll any failed attack roll, skill check, ability check, or saving throw. The character must take the result of the reroll, even if it's worse than the original roll.

Acrobatic Skill Mastery (Ex): At 13th level, a swashbuckler becomes so certain in the use of her acrobatic skills that she can use them reliably even under adverse conditions. When making a Jump or Tumble check, a swashbuckler may take 10 even if stress and distractions would normally prevent her from doing so.

Weakening Critical (Ex): A swashbuckler of 14th level or higher who scores a critical hit against a creature also deals 2 points of Strength damage to the creature. Creatures immune to critical hits are immune to this effect.

Slippery Mind (Ex): When a swashbuckler reaches 17th level, her mind becomes more difficult to control. If the swashbuckler fails her save against an enchantment spell or effect, she can attempt the save again 1 round later at the same DC (assuming she is still alive). She gets only this one extra chance to succeed at a certain saving throw.

Wounding Critical (Ex): A swashbuckler of 19th level or higher who scores a critical hit against a creature also deals 2 points of Constitution damage to the creature. (This damage is in addition to the Strength damage dealt by the swashbuckler's weakening critical class feature.) Creatures immune to critical hits are immune to this effect.

Half-Elf Swashbuckler Starting Package

Armor: Studded leather (+3 AC, armor check penalty –1, speed 30 ft., 20 lb.).

Weapons: Rapier (1d6, crit 18–20/×2, 2 lb., one-handed, piercing).

Dagger (1d4, crit 19–20/×2, 1 lb., light, piercing or slashing).

Shortbow (1d6, crit ×3, range inc. 60 ft., 2 lb., piercing).

Skill Selection: Pick a number of skills equal to 4 + Int modifier.

Skill	Ranks	Ability	Armor Check Penalty
Bluff	4	Cha	—
Climb	4	Str	–1
Diplomacy	4	Cha	—
Jump	4	Str	–1
Tumble	4	Str	–1
Use Rope	4	Dex	—
Spot (cc)	2	Wis	—
Listen (cc)	2	Wis	—

Feat: Weapon Focus (rapier).

Gear: Backpack with waterskin, one day's trail rations, bedroll, sack, flint and steel, hooded lantern, 3 pints of oil, quiver with 20 arrows.

Gold: 6d4 gp.

VARIANT: PALADINS AND RANGERS WITHOUT SPELLCASTING

The paladin and ranger in the *Player's Handbook* are hybrid classes, in that they combine martial talents with spellcasting and other abilities. To make these classes fit better into a warrior-focused campaign, consider using the following variants that trade the classes' spellcasting powers for other extraordinary, supernatural, or spell-like abilities. In general, these variant classes give up the versatility of daily spell selection in exchange for more powerful or reliable special abilities.

VARIANT PALADIN

This variant paladin gains all the normal class features of the paladin, with the following changes and additions:

Spells: The paladin does not gain the ability to cast divine spells.

Blessed Weapon (Su): Any melee weapon wielded by a paladin of 6th level or higher is treated as good-aligned for the purpose of overcoming damage reduction.

Divine Might (Su): At 11th level and higher, the paladin can use a standard action to add a +4 bonus to her Strength, Wisdom, or Charisma score. This ability may be used once per day, and its effect lasts for 1 minute per class level.

Tend to Mount (Su): A paladin of 13th level or higher who uses her lay on hands ability to heal her mount cures 5 points of damage per point of healing spent. In addition, the paladin may use her lay on hands ability to end any one of the following adverse conditions affecting her mount, at the cost of 5 points of healing per condition unless otherwise noted: ability damage (costs 1 point per ability point

restored), blinded, confused, dazed, dazzled, deafened, diseased, exhausted, fatigued, feebleminded, insanity, nauseated, sickened, stunned, or poisoned.

The paladin can remove adverse conditions at the same time that she heals damage, but any points of healing spent to end adverse conditions don't also cure hit point damage.

Holy Sword (**Sp**): At 16th level, a paladin gains the ability to use *holy sword* once per day, as a caster whose level is equal to one-half the paladin's class level.

VARIANT RANGER

The variant ranger gains all the normal class features of the ranger, with the following changes and additions.

Spells: The ranger does not gain the ability to cast divine spells.

Fast Movement (Ex): At 6th level, the ranger's base land speed increases by 10 feet. This benefit applies only when he is wearing no armor, light armor, or medium armor and not carrying a heavy load.

Nature's Blessing (Su): At 11th level and higher, the ranger can use a standard action to add a +4 bonus to his Constitution, Dexterity, or Wisdom score. This ability may be used once per day, and its effect lasts for 1 minute per class level.

Healing Touch (**Sp**): Once per day, a ranger of 13th level or higher can use either *neutralize poison* or *remove disease*, as a caster whose level is equal to one-half the ranger's class level.

Freedom of Movement (**Sp**): A ranger of 16th level or higher can use *freedom of movement* on himself once per day, as a caster whose level is equal to one-half the ranger's class level.

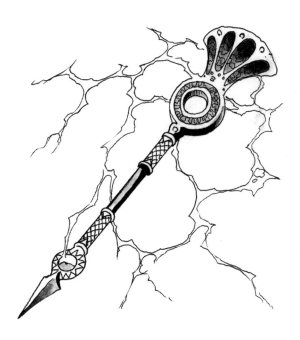

Illus. by W. Reynolds

This chapter presents a host of prestige classes geared toward combat and martial themes. As mentioned throughout this book, these prestige classes aren't simply for fighters—or even just members of the game's martial classes (fighters, paladins, monks, rangers, and barbarians). Many of these classes incorporate aspects of other classes in their requirements and class abilities, and more than a few should appeal to characters of any class.

PICKING A PRESTIGE CLASS

If you're looking for a prestige class—either for your current player character or as an NPC for a campaign you're running—review the descriptions of each prestige class in this chapter before choosing one. Also review the prestige class's requirements. Many of these prestige classes have high base attack bonus requirements, or they require a number of combat-oriented feats for admission. If you want to build a character hoping to achieve entry in one of these classes, you have to plan.

You also need to decide what you would like to do with your character. Since we have already narrowed

the focus of this book to combat-oriented prestige classes, that narrows things down somewhat. What sort of combat specialist do you want this character to be? Refer to Table 2–1 on the next page for some helpful suggestions. Terms used on the table are defined in the following text.

Good Guys/Bad Guys: Members of these groups define themselves by their alignment and their outlook on the world first, their other abilities second. Their strengths reflect their alignment choices, and roleplaying one of these characters means putting attitude first. The cavalier, justiciar, and kensai fall into both the "good guy" and "bad guy" categories, because the alignment requirement for those classes does not preclude such characters from being either good or evil.

Melee: A character belonging to one of these prestige classes is skilled at fighting in close quarters. He or she generally has a good amount of hit points, a high base attack bonus, and often little or no restriction on armor choices, unless the character, like the monk, focuses on mobility rather than toe-to-toe fighting.

Mounted: These characters prefer to ride into and out of combat and often have abilities that improve the capabilities of their mounts or other abilities related to riding.

Nemesis: When a character chooses to fight a particular kind of foe in preference to any other, that enemy becomes a nemesis. These prestige classes heighten a character's existing abilities, but at the expense of narrowing the character's focus. Members of these classes are often very good at fighting a particular kind of foe, but they lose some of their general utility.

Ranged: Masters of archery, thrown weapons, or other ranged attacks fall into this category. While any fighter can become good with a bow or javelin, members of these prestige classes gain additional benefits, sometimes at the expense of other attributes. Ranged weapon users tend to be less concerned with Armor Class and hit points and more focused on increasing their number of attacks, precisions, and damage per shot.

Spellcaster: Combat-oriented divine and arcane spellcasters fall into this group, as well as members of classes that don't actually cast spells, but instead have a considerable number of spell-like abilities. Some are just dabblers, casting spells from a small list or gaining a few spell-like abilities; a few are hybrids that blend physical combat with mystic spells, and a few others are pure spellcasters that give up very little in spellcasting to pick up a few combat-ready abilities.

Terrain: If a character spends most or all of his adventuring time in a particular environment, a terrain-oriented prestige class gives him an edge. The class's features focus on improving the character's abilities in that terrain, but don't help him much when he leaves that terrain behind.

Weapon Specialist: Members of these prestige classes usually pick one or two weapons (or sometimes a type of weapon, usually one considered suboptimal) to truly focus their efforts on. They become very good at their chosen weapons and sometimes gain abilities beyond the norm. Sometimes this means sacrificing other abilities, but often it simply means a sacrifice of flexibility.

THE MARTIAL PRESTIGE CLASSES

These classes follow the format presented in the *Dungeon Master's Guide*. Each class has a name and a description—both

of which can be modified to suit your own campaign without any serious impact to the class at all.

Most of these classes have combat-oriented requirements. The fastest way into each of them usually involves picking up one or more levels in the fighter, paladin, ranger, barbarian, or monk class. More than a few have requirements that can most easily be met by dabbling in a few other classes, too—rogue levels often make skill requirements easier to meet, and spellcasting requirements are usually met by picking up a few levels in the wizard, sorcerer, druid, or cleric class.

If you choose to adjust the requirements for one of these martial classes, do so carefully. Each class has been balanced against projected levels of entry. The bear warrior, for example, has a base attack bonus requirement of +7, meaning that even the martial classes don't meet that requirement until at least 7th level. This is because the bear warrior gains the ability to transform into a bear, an ability normally reserved for high-level spellcasters and druids.

The skill points gained at each level for each class were determined based primarily on the class's focus. A class whose strengths lie in many special abilities, learned feats, or spellcasting seldom has a high number of skill points. Those that need more skills, such as the master thrower, who values mobility, or the dark hunter, who needs skills to track his quarry, have more skill points per level. None of these classes are heavy skill-users, however; their focus is, again, on combat.

When you review the class features for each prestige class, note that they all use either the best or near-best attack progression, but only a few have more than one good saving throw category. This is another balancing factor. Combat-oriented characters need to be able to hit their opponents in combat, but sometimes a good offense means a poorer defense . . . at least as far as saving throws go. Since these are prestige classes, however, it's quite likely that your character has above-average saving throws (after multiclassing) in at least two categories. Examine the requirements to determine which classes your character has to invest in and how the saving throws stack with each other.

TABLE 2–1: PRESTIGE CLASS GROUPINGS

Group	Prestige Classes
Bad guys	cavalier, eye of Gruumsh[1], justiciar, kensai, ravager, Thayan knight[1]
Good guys	cavalier, darkwood stalker[1], hunter of the dead, justiciar, kensai, knight of the Chalice, knight protector, Purple Dragon knight
Melee	bear warrior, bladesinger[1], cavalier, dervish, drunken master, frenzied berserker, gnome giant-slayer[1], invisible blade, knight protector, nature's warrior, ravager, reaping mauler, ronin, tattooed monk, warshaper
Mounted	cavalier, halfling outrider[1]
Nemesis	dark hunter, darkwood stalker[1], gnome giant-slayer[1], hunter of the dead, knight of the Chalice, occult slayer
Ranged	hulking hurler[2], master thrower, master of the unseen hand, Order of the Bow initiate
Spellcaster	bladesinger[1], knight of the Chalice, mindspy, rage mage, spellsword, stonelord, tattooed monk, war chanter
Terrain	dark hunter, stonelord[1]
Weapon specialist	bladesinger[1], cavalier, dervish, drunken master, exotic weapon master, hulking hurler[2], eye of Gruumsh[1], kensai, master thrower, Order of the Bow initiate, reaping mauler

1 Race requirement.
2 Size requirement.

Every aspect of each prestige class is meant to balance with every other. You should not only be able to find a few prestige classes that appeal to you (as a player or as a DM), but combinations that work extraordinarily well together or in conjunction with the character classes from the *Player's Handbook* or Chapter 1 of this book. The combination of classes that qualifies you for a prestige class at the lowest possible character level is not always the most effective one, though it is a place to start.

If you're interested in building your own martial prestige classes, refer to the *Dungeon Master's Guide*.

Meeting Class Requirements: It's possible for a character to take levels in a prestige class and later be in a position where the character no longer qualifies to be a member of the class. An alignment change, levels lost because of character death, or the loss of a magic item that granted an important ability are examples of events that can make a character ineligible to advance farther in a prestige class.

If a character no longer meets the requirements for a prestige class, he or she loses the benefit of any class features or other special abilities granted by the class. The character retains Hit Dice gained from advancing in the class as well as any improvements to base attack bonus and base save bonuses that the class provided.

BEAR WARRIOR

Many people, particularly those in "uncivilized" regions of the world, revere bears as symbols of the warrior's strength and battle prowess. By adopting the bear as a totem anima, warriors of these people hope to tap into some of the bear's strength. Bear warriors, through a special relationship with bear spirits, literally adopt a bear's strength in the rage of battle, actually transforming into bears while they fight.

Only characters who can already tap into a spiritual power of rage can heighten that power to become bear warriors. Most bear warriors are barbarians, but other multiclass characters sometimes become bear warriors. Characters with another prestige class that grants a rage or frenzy ability occasionally adopt this class.

NPC bear warriors are usually the champions of barbarian tribes, rustic villages, or warlike temples. They lead other warriors not through discipline and order, but by the inspiring example they present.

Hit Die: d12.

Requirements

To qualify to become a bear warrior, a character must fulfill all the following criteria.

Base Attack Bonus: +7.
Feats: Power Attack.
Special: Rage or frenzy ability.

Class Skills

The bear warrior's class skills (and the key ability for each skill) are Climb (Str), Handle Animal (Cha), Intimidate (Cha), Jump (Str), Listen (Wis), Ride (Dex), Survival (Wis), and Swim (Str).

Skill Points at Each Level: 4 + Int modifier.

TABLE 2–2: THE BEAR WARRIOR

Level	Base Attack Bonus	Fort Save	Ref Save	Will Save	Special
1st	+1	+2	+0	+0	Bear form (black)
2nd	+2	+3	+0	+0	—
3rd	+3	+3	+1	+1	Scent
4th	+4	+4	+1	+1	—
5th	+5	+4	+1	+1	Bear form (brown)
6th	+6	+5	+2	+2	—
7th	+7	+5	+2	+2	Rage +1/day
8th	+8	+6	+2	+2	—
9th	+9	+6	+3	+3	—
10th	+10	+7	+3	+3	Bear form (dire)

Class Features

All of the following are class features of the bear warrior prestige class.

Weapon and Armor Proficiency: Bear warriors gain no proficiency with any weapon or armor.

Bear Form (Su): A bear warrior can transform into a bear (similar to the *polymorph* spell) while in a rage or frenzy. His only limit on the number of times per day he can assume a bear form is the number of times per day he enters a rage or frenzy, and the bear warrior returns to his own form once the rage or frenzy ends. The bear warrior retains the normal +2 bonus on Will saves and –2 penalty to Armor Class while raging, but the ability score bonuses granted by rage or frenzy are replaced by Strength, Dexterity, and Constitution bonuses appropriate to the bear form taken (see below). As normal for *polymorph*, the bear warrior gains the bear form's physical qualities (including size, movement, natural armor bonus, natural weapons, space, and reach), as well as any extraordinary special attacks possessed by the form (such as improved grab in the brown bear or dire bear form). The transformation lasts for the duration of the rage or frenzy.

Unlike with the *polymorph* spell, a bear warrior doesn't gain the bear's Strength, Dexterity, and Constitution scores when he takes bear form, nor does he regain any hit points when he transforms. However, his current hit points increase due to his new Constitution, as normal for a rage ability.

Any bear warrior can assume the form of a black bear once per day. While in black bear form, he gains a +8 bonus to Strength, a +2 bonus to Dexterity, and a +4 bonus to Constitution.

At 5th level, a bear warrior can assume bear form twice per day and can choose between black and brown bear forms. While in brown bear form, he gains a +16 bonus to Strength, a +2 bonus to Dexterity, and a +8 bonus to Constitution.

A bear warrior

1d4+4 each, 1 bite 1d6+8) or a brown bear (Large, +5 natural armor, +16 Str, +2 Dex, +4 Con, 2 claws 1d8+6 each, 1 bite 2d6+12, improved grab).

Improved Uncanny Dodge (Ex): Kurag cannot be flanked except by a rogue of at least 11th level.

Scent (Ex): Kurag has the scent special ability.

Rage (Ex): +4 to Str, +4 to Con, +2 on Will saves, −2 to AC for up to 8 rounds.

Trap Sense (Ex): Against attacks by traps, Kurag gets a +2 bonus on Reflex saves and a +2 dodge bonus to Armor Class.

Uncanny Dodge (Ex): Kurag can react to danger before his senses would normally allow him to do so. He retains his Dexterity bonus to Armor Class even when caught flat-footed.

Possessions: +2 greataxe, amulet of health +4, bracers of armor +2.

BLADESINGER

Bladesingers are elves who have blended art, swordplay, and arcane magic into a harmonious whole. In battle, a bladesinger's lithe movements and subtle tactics are beautiful, belying their deadly martial efficiency.

Multiclass fighter/wizards are the most obvious candidates for the prestige class, although any elf who can wield a martial weapon and cast arcane spells can become a bladesinger. Bladesinger ranger/wizards, rogue/wizards, and even bards are not unknown.

Bladesingers command great respect in most elf communities, and NPC bladesingers usually serve as itinerant guardians and champions of the elf community at large.

Hit Die: d8.

Requirements

To qualify to become a bladesinger, a character must fulfill all the following criteria.

Race: Elf or half-elf.

Base Attack Bonus: +5.

Skills: Balance 2 ranks, Concentration 4 ranks, Perform (dance) 2 ranks, Perform (sing) 2 ranks, Tumble 2 ranks.

Feats: Combat Casting, Combat Expertise, Dodge, Weapon Focus (longsword or rapier).

Spells: Able to cast arcane spells of 1st level.

Class Skills

The bladesinger's class skills (and the key ability for each skill) are Balance (Dex), Concentration (Con), Jump (Str), Knowledge (arcana) (Int), Perform (Cha), Spellcraft (Int), and Tumble (Dex).

At 10th level, a bear warrior can assume bear form three times per day and can choose between black, brown, and dire bear forms. While in dire bear form, he gains a +20 bonus to Strength, a +2 bonus to Dexterity, and a +8 bonus to Constitution.

Scent (Ex): At 3rd level, a bear warrior gains the scent special ability (see page 314 of the *Monster Manual*) while in bear or nonbear form.

Rage +1/Day (Ex): When a bear warrior attains 7th level, the number of times per day that he can enter a state of rage or frenzy increases by one. For example, a 7th-level barbarian/7th-level bear warrior can rage three times per day. If that character were to gain one more barbarian level, he could rage four times per day.

Sample Bear Warrior

Kurag Flint-Tooth: Human barbarian 7/bear warrior 5; CR 12; Medium humanoid; HD 12d12+36; hp 114; Init +2; Spd 30 ft.; AC 19, touch 12, flat-footed 17; Base Atk +12; Grp +16; Atk +18 melee (1d12+6/×3, +2 *greataxe*); Full Atk +18/+13/+8 melee (1d12+6/×3, +2 *greataxe*); SQ bear form 2/day, damage reduction 1/−, improved uncanny dodge, rage 2/day, scent, trap sense +2, uncanny dodge; AL CN; SV Fort +12, Ref +5, Will +7; Str 18, Dex 14, Con 17, Int 10, Wis 12, Cha 8.

Skills and Feats: Climb +16, Intimidate +14, Jump +16, Survival +16, Swim +13; Cleave, Combat Reflexes, Dodge, Improved Bull Rush, Power Attack, Track.

Bear Form (Su): While raging, Kurag can turn into a black bear (Medium, +2 natural armor, +8 Str, +2 Dex, 2 claws

Illus. by R. Guay-Mitchell

Skill Points at Each Level: 2 + Int modifier.

Class Features

All of the following are class features of the bladesinger prestige class.

Weapon and Armor Proficiency: Bladesingers gain no proficiency with any weapon. They gain proficiency with light armor but not with shields.

Spells per Day: At every odd-numbered level gained in the bladesinger class, the character gains new spells per day as if she had also gained a level in an arcane spellcasting class she belonged to before adding the prestige class. She does not, however, gain any other benefit a character of that class would have gained, except for an increased effective level of spellcasting. If a character had more than one arcane spellcasting class before becoming a bladesinger, she must decide to which class she adds the new level for purposes of determining spells per day.

Bladesong Style (Ex): When wielding a longsword or rapier in one hand (and nothing in the other), a bladesinger gains a dodge bonus to Armor Class equal to his class level, up to a maximum of her Intelligence bonus. If the bladesinger wears medium or heavy armor, she loses all benefits of the bladesong style.

Lesser Spellsong (Ex): When wielding a longsword or rapier in one hand (and nothing in the other), a bladesinger of 2nd level or higher can take 10 when making a Concentration check to cast defensively.

Song of Celerity (Ex): Once per day, a bladesinger of 4th level or higher may quicken a single spell of up to 2nd level, as if she had used the Quicken Spell feat, but without any adjustment to the spell's effective level or casting time. She may

Illus. by G. Kubic

only use this ability when wielding a longsword or rapier in one hand (and nothing in the other). At 8th level and higher, she can quicken a single spell of up to 4th level.

A bladesinger

Greater Spellsong (Ex): A bladesinger of 6th level or higher ignores arcane spell failure chances when wearing light armor.

Song of Fury (Ex): When a 10th-level bladesinger makes a full attack with a longsword or rapier in one hand (and nothing in the other), she can make one extra attack in a round at her highest base attack bonus, but this attack and each other attack made in that round take a –2 penalty. This penalty applies for 1 round, so it also affects attacks of opportunity the bladesinger might make before her next action.

Sample Bladesinger

Vilya Sorrowleaf: Half-elf wizard 6/fighter 2/bladesinger 4; CR 12; Medium humanoid; HD 6d4+6 plus 2d10+2 plus 4d8+4; hp 56; Init +1; Spd 30 ft.; AC 19 (15 without *mage armor*), touch 15, flat-footed 14; Base Atk +9; Grp +11; Atk +14 melee (1d6+2/18–20, *+2 rapier*); Full Atk +14/+9 melee (1d6+2/18–20, *+2 rapier*); SQ bladesong style, half-elf traits, lesser spellsong, low-light vision, song of celerity 1/day; AL CG; SV Fort +2, Ref +7, Will +11; Str 14, Dex 13, Con 12, Int 22, Wis 10, Cha 8.

Skills and Feats: Balance +7, Concentration +16, Diplomacy +1, Gather Information +1, Knowledge (arcana) +7, Listen +1, Perform (dance) +1, Perform (sing) +1, Search +7, Spellcraft +21, Spot +1, Tumble +15; Combat Casting, Dodge, Expertise, Extend Spell, Mobility, Spell Focus (enchantment), Spell Focus (evocation), Weapon Focus (rapier).

Bladesong Style (Ex): When wielding a longsword or rapier in one hand and nothing in the other, Vilya gains a +4 dodge bonus to Armor Class.

Half-Elf Traits (Ex): Immunity to magic *sleep* spells and effects; +2 racial bonus on saving throws against enchantment spells or effects; elven blood.

Table 2–3: The Bladesinger

Level	Base Attack Bonus	Fort Save	Ref Save	Will Save	Special	Spells per Day
1st	+1	+0	+2	+2	Bladesong style	+1 level of existing arcane spellcasting class
2nd	+2	+0	+3	+3	Lesser spellsong	—
3rd	+3	+1	+3	+3	—	+1 level of existing arcane spellcasting class
4th	+4	+1	+4	+4	Song of celerity (2nd)	—
5th	+5	+1	+4	+4	—	+1 level of existing arcane spellcasting class
6th	+6	+2	+5	+5	Greater spellsong	—
7th	+7	+2	+5	+5	—	+1 level of existing arcane spellcasting class
8th	+8	+2	+6	+6	Song of celerity (4th)	—
9th	+9	+3	+6	+6	—	+1 level of existing arcane spellcasting class
10th	+10	+3	+7	+7	Song of fury	—

Lesser Spellsong (Ex): Vilya can take 10 when making a Concentration check to cast defensively.

Low-Light Vision (Ex): Vilya can see twice as far as a human in starlight, moonlight, torchlight, and similar conditions of poor visibility. He retains the ability to distinguish color and detail under these conditions.

Song of Celerity (Ex): Vilya may quicken a spell of up to 2nd level without any adjustment to the spell's level or casting time, if wielding a longsword or rapier in one hand and nothing in the other.

Wizard Spells Prepared (4/6/5/4/2; save DC 16 + spell level, 17 + spell level for enchantments and evocations as indicated below by asterisks): 0—*dancing lights, detect magic, light, ray of frost*; 1st—*charm person*, mage armor, magic missile, shield* (2), protection from evil*; 2nd—*bear's endurance, bull's strength, cat's grace, daze monster*, invisibility*; 3rd—*deep slumber*, fireball*, haste, lightning bolt**; 4th—*confusion*, stoneskin*.

Spellbook: 0—all; 1st—*charm person*, identify, mage armor, magic missile, magic weapon, protection from evil, shield, sleep**; 2nd—*bear's endurance, bull's strength, cat's grace, darkvision, daze monster*, invisibility, knock, Melf's acid arrow, resist energy, scorching ray, see invisibility, web*; 3rd—*clairaudience/clairvoyance; deep slumber*, dispel magic, fireball*, fly, haste, hold person*, greater magic weapon, invisibility sphere, lightning bolt*, protection from energy, suggestion**; 4th—*charm monster*, confusion*, dimension door, enervation, greater invisibility, ice storm, Otiluke's resilient sphere*, polymorph, scrying, stoneskin, wall of fire*.

Possessions: +2 rapier, spellbook, headband of intellect +4, spell component pouch, 250 gp diamond dust.

CAVALIER

Representing the ultimate in mounted warfare, the cavalier is the quintessential knight in shining armor. The charge of the cavalier is among the most devastating offensive weapons any culture can hope to field.

Most cavaliers belong to the upper social class or nobility of a society. The cavalier dedicates his life to the service of a higher authority, such as a noble or sovereign, deity, military or religious order, or a special cause. His is a hereditary honor that comes with the price of lifelong service to his monarch, country, or other object or entity. The cavalier is expected to participate in any wars or other armed conflict in which his lord or cause is engaged. Cavaliers in service to other nobles often serve their master beyond the battlefield as well, performing such duties as their skills, and their noble lord, see fit.

The cavalier often pursues such selfless goals as the eradication of evil and chaos from the world, and justice for all the subjects of his land. He can also be a bully and a braggart who uses his status and privileges to pursue only his own self-aggrandizement.

Hit Die: d10.

Requirements

To qualify to become a cavalier, a character must fulfill all the following criteria.

Alignment: Any lawful.

Base Attack Bonus: +8.

Skills: Handle Animal 4 ranks, Knowledge (nobility and royalty) 4 ranks, Ride 6 ranks.

Feats: Spirited Charge, Weapon Focus (lance), Mounted Combat, Ride-By Attack.

A cavalier

Class Skills

The cavalier's class skills (and the key ability for each skill) are Diplomacy (Cha), Handle Animal (Cha), Intimidate (Cha), Knowledge (nobility and royalty) (Int), Profession (Int), and Ride (Dex).

Skill Points at Each Level: 2 + Int modifier.

Class Features

All of the following are class features of the cavalier prestige class.

Illus. by M. Smylie

TABLE 2–4: THE CAVALIER

Level*	Base Attack Bonus	Fort Save	Ref Save	Will Save	Special
1st	+1	+2	+0	+2	Special mount, mounted weapon bonus (lance) +1, Ride bonus +2, courtly knowledge
2nd	+2	+3	+0	+3	Deadly charge 1/day, mounted weapon bonus (sword) +1
3rd	+3	+3	+1	+3	Burst of speed
4th	+4	+4	+1	+4	Deadly charge 2/day, Ride bonus +4
5th	+5	+4	+1	+4	Mounted weapon bonus (lance) +2
6th	+6	+5	+2	+5	Deadly charge 3/day, full mounted attack, mounted weapon bonus (sword) +2
7th	+7	+5	+2	+5	Ride bonus +6
8th	+8	+6	+2	+6	Deadly charge 4/day
9th	+9	+6	+3	+6	Mounted weapon bonus (lance) +3, Ride bonus +8
10th	+10	+7	+3	+7	Unstoppable charge 5/day, mounted weapon bonus (sword) +3

*Special: Cavalier class levels stack with paladin levels for determining the characteristics of a paladin's mount.

Weapon and Armor Proficiency: Cavaliers are proficient with all simple and martial weapons, all types of armor, and shields.

Special Mount **(Sp):** A cavalier's class levels stack with any paladin levels the character may have for determining the characteristics of a paladin's mount.

Mounted Weapon Bonus (Ex): A cavalier gains a competence bonus on his attack roll when using the indicated weapon while mounted. For the lance, this bonus starts out at +1 at 1st level and increases by +1 every four levels thereafter. For the sword, this bonus starts out at +1 at 2nd level and increases by +1 every four levels thereafter.

Ride Bonus (Ex): A cavalier gains a competence bonus on Ride checks. This bonus starts out at +2 and improves to +4 at 4th level, +6 at 7th level, and +8 at 9th level.

Courtly Knowledge (Ex): A cavalier adds his class level to his Knowledge (nobility and royalty) checks as a competence bonus.

Deadly Charge (Ex): When mounted and using the charge action, a cavalier of 2nd level or higher may declare a "deadly charge" before making his attack roll (thus, a failed attack ruins the attempt). If he hits, he deals triple damage with a melee weapon (or quadruple damage with a lance). This ability does not stack with the benefit of the Spirited Charge feat.

Burst of Speed (Ex): At 3rd level and higher, a cavalier can urge his mount to greater than normal speed when charging. This ability doubles the maximum distance the mount can travel when making a charge, up to four times its speed. This ability can be used once per day without penalty to the mount. Each additional use of the ability in a single day requires the mount to make a DC 20 Will save immediately after the conclusion of the charge; failure results in the mount taking 2d6 points of damage.

Full Mounted Attack (Ex): At 6th level and higher, a mounted cavalier can make a full attack when his mount moves more than 5 feet but no farther than a single move action would carry it. The cavalier cannot combine this full attack with a charge.

Unstoppable Charge (Ex): When making a deadly charge, a 10th-level cavalier deals quadruple damage with a melee weapon (or quintuple damage with a lance).

Multiclass Note: A paladin who becomes a cavalier may continue advancing as a paladin.

Sample Cavalier

Willem the Bold: Human fighter 8/cavalier 2; CR 10; Medium humanoid; HD 10d10+10; hp 65; Init +2; Spd 20 ft. (25 ft. mounted); AC 24, touch 12, flat-footed 22; Base Atk +10; Grp +14; Atk +16 melee (1d8+6/19–20/×3, +1 lance) or +16 melee (1d8+6/19–20, +1 longsword); Full Atk +16/+11 melee (1d8+6/19–20 /×3, +1 lance) or +16/+11 melee (1d8+6/19–20, +1 longsword); SQ deadly charge 1/day, mounted weapon bonus (lance) +1, mounted weapon bonus (sword) +1, Ride bonus +2; AL CN; SV Fort +10, Ref +4, Will +6; Str 19, Dex 14, Con 13, Int 10, Wis 12, Cha 8.

Skills and Feats: Diplomacy +3, Handle Animal +4, Intimidate +10, Knowledge (nobility and royalty) +6, Ride +15; Improved Critical (lance), Improved Sunder, Mounted Combat, Power Attack, Ride-By Attack, Spirited Charge, Weapon Focus (lance), Weapon Specialization (lance), Weapon Focus (longsword), Weapon Specialization (longsword).

Deadly Charge (Ex): When mounted and using the charge action, Willem can declare a deadly charge that deals triple damage with a melee weapon (or quadruple damage with a lance).

Mounted Weapon Bonus (Lance) (Ex): Willem gains a +1 competence bonus on attacks with a lance while mounted.

Mounted Weapon Bonus (Sword) (Ex): Willem gains a +1 competence bonus on attacks with a sword while mounted.

Possessions: +1 lance, +1 longsword, +1 full plate, +1 heavy shield, +1 full plate barding, gauntlets of ogre power +2, heavy warhorse.

DARK HUNTER

Dark hunters specialize in hunting down and eliminating creatures in the dark, twisting caves of the Underdark, often protecting underground communities or those people who make their living under the earth (such as miners or hunters). They use stealth, ambush, and deception to single out foes and remove them one by one. A typical strategy is to locate the enemy, then hide against a nearby wall of earth or stone. The dark hunter then waits for her enemy to pass by, leaping out to attack when the target least expects it. A dark hunter uses her knowledge of underground terrain to find the best areas to create pits, cave-ins, and rockslides, often enabling her to eliminate the enemy without drawing her axe. If a dark hunter is outnumbered, she retreats into the darkness, hiding until she can pick off individual targets.

Because they spend so much time in the stark wilderness of caves and caverns, dark hunters are slightly ostracized by other members of society. Most individuals live among others of their own kind, so the rootless existence of the dark hunter seems like a social aberration. Still, great honor is to be found in protecting the clan from attack, so dark hunters are given respect. None of this concerns the individual, who cares little for what others think; she finds purpose in what she does every time she brings down another one of her enemies. She prefers to work alone, but also knows that cooperation with others has its advantages.

Rangers are the most likely characters to become dark hunters. Druids, rogues, and fighters are also common. Feral tribes of barbaric dwarves sometimes produce dark hunters, who track down their foes in silence and then explode into action once they ambush their prey. Half-orcs make excellent dark hunters, since they are often found on the fringes of society anyway.

Elves, with their abiding hatred of the drow, sometimes follow this path.

Hit Die: d8.

Table 2–5: The Dark Hunter

Level	Base Attack Bonus	Fort Save	Ref Save	Will Save	Special
1st	+1	+0	+2	+0	Improved stonecunning
2nd	+2	+0	+3	+0	Enhanced darkvision
3rd	+3	+1	+3	+1	Sneak attack +1d6
4th	+4	+1	+4	+1	Stone's hue
5th	+5	+1	+4	+1	Death attack

Requirements

To qualify to become a dark hunter, a character must fulfill all the following criteria.

Base Attack Bonus: +5.

Skills: Craft (trapmaking) 5 ranks, Knowledge (dungeoneering) 2 ranks, Move Silently 2 ranks, Survival 2 ranks.

Feats: Blind-Fight, Track.

Class Skills

The dark hunter's class skills (and the key ability for each skill) are Climb (Str), Concentration (Con), Craft (Int), Disable Device (Int), Hide (Dex), Knowledge (dungeoneering) (Int), Listen (Wis), Move Silently (Dex), Profession (Wis), Spot (Wis), Survival (Wis), Swim (Str), and Use Rope (Dex).

Skill Points at Each Level: 4 + Int modifier.

Class Features

All of the following are class features of the dark hunter prestige class.

Weapon and Armor Proficiency: Dark hunters gain no proficiency with any weapon or armor.

Improved Stonecunning (Ex): A dark hunter gains the stonecunning ability possessed by dwarves (see page 15 of the *Player's Handbook*), or, if the character already has the ability, she increases her bonus from +2 to

A dark hunter

+4 on checks to notice unusual stonework, such as sliding walls, stonework traps, new construction, unsafe stone surfaces, shaky stone ceilings, and the like. This bonus also applies on Search checks made to detect stonework traps.

Enhanced Darkvision (Ex): Dark hunters spend most of their lives in the darkest caverns they can find. As a dark hunter's skills improve, her almost mystical understanding of the deep caverns sharpens her inborn visual acuity. If a dark hunter does not already have darkvision when she attains 2nd level, she gains it at a range of 30 feet. If she already had darkvision, she adds 30 feet to the range. Once a dark hunter attains 4th level, her darkvision range increases by an extra 30 feet.

This bonus stacks with other natural or extraordinary abilities that improve darkvision, but it does nothing to improve magically granted darkvision.

Any condition that causes the character to lose her normal darkvision also causes the enhanced darkvision to fail.

Sneak Attack (Ex): If a dark hunter can catch an opponent when he is unable to defend himself effectively from her attack, she can strike a vital spot for extra damage. Any time the dark hunter's target would be denied his Dexterity bonus to AC (whether the target actually has a Dexterity bonus or not), the dark hunter's attack deals an extra 1d6 points of damage. Should a dark hunter score a critical hit with a sneak attack, this extra damage is not multiplied.

It takes precision and penetration to hit a vital spot, so ranged attacks can only count as sneak attacks if the target is within 30 feet.

With a sap or an unarmed strike, a dark hunter can make a sneak attack that deals nonlethal damage instead of lethal damage. She cannot use a weapon that deals lethal damage to deal nonlethal damage in a sneak attack, not even with the usual −4 penalty, because she must make optimal use of her weapon in order to execute the sneak attack.

A dark hunter can only sneak attack living creatures with discernible anatomies—undead, constructs, oozes, plants, and incorporeal creatures lack vital areas to attack. Any creature that is immune to critical hits is not vulnerable to sneak attacks. The dark hunter must be able to see the target well enough to pick out a vital spot and must be able to reach such a spot. A dark hunter cannot sneak attack while striking a creature with concealment or striking the limbs of a creature whose vitals are beyond reach.

If a dark hunter gets a sneak attack bonus from another source (such as rogue levels), the extra damage stacks.

Stone's Hue (Su): When within 5 feet of a stone or earth wall, a dark hunter can take on the coloration of the stone and may seem to blend into the surface of the wall. As long as the dark hunter is within 5 feet of the wall, she gains a +10 circumstance bonus on Hide checks and can successfully hide herself from view in the open without having anything to actually hide behind.

Death Attack (Ex): If a dark hunter studies her victim for 3 rounds and then makes a sneak attack with a melee weapon that successfully deals damage, the sneak attack has the additional effect of possibly either paralyzing or killing the target (dark hunter's choice). While studying the target, the dark hunter can undertake other actions as long as her attention stays focused on the target and the target does not detect the dark hunter or recognize the dark hunter as an enemy. If the victim of such an attack fails a Fortitude save (DC 10 + the dark hunter's class level + the dark hunter's Int modifier) against the kill effect, he dies. If the saving throw fails against the paralysis effect, the victim's mind and body become enervated, rendering him helpless and unable to act for 1d6 rounds plus 1 round per level of the dark hunter. If the victim's saving throw succeeds, the attack is just a normal sneak attack. Once the dark hunter has completed the 3 rounds of study, she must make the death attack within the next 3 rounds. If a death attack is attempted and fails (the victim makes his save) or if the dark hunter does not launch the attack within 3 rounds of completing the study, 3 new rounds of study are required before she can attempt another death attack.

Sample Dark Hunter

Baltha the Implacable: Dwarf ranger 5/dark hunter 5; CR 10; Medium humanoid; HD 5d8+15 plus 5d8+15; hp 75; Init +1; Spd 20 ft.; AC 17, touch 11, flat-footed 16; Base Atk +10; Grp +12; Atk +14 melee (1d8+3/17–20/, +1 *longsword*) or +12 ranged (1d4+1/19–20, +1 *elfbane hand crossbow*); Full Atk +14/+9 melee (1d8+3/17–20/, +1 *longsword*); or +12/+7 melee (1d8+3/17–20/, +1 *longsword*) and +11 melee (1d4+1/19–20, +1 *elfbane hand crossbow*); or +12 ranged (1d4+1/19–20, +1 *elfbane hand crossbow*); SA death attack, sneak attack +1d6; SQ animal companion, darkvision 90 ft., dwarf traits, favored enemy elves +4, favored enemy aberrations +2, improved stonecunning, stone's hue, wild empathy; AL N; SV Fort +8, Ref +9, Will +2; Str 15, Dex 13, Con 16, Int 12, Wis 10, Cha 6.

Skills and Feats: Craft (trapmaking) +14, Hide +14, Knowledge (dungeoneering) +14, Listen, +13, Move Silently +14, Spot +13, Survival +13; Blind-Fight, Endurance, Exotic Weapon Proficiency (hand crossbow), Improved Critical (longsword), Track^B, Two-Weapon Fighting, Weapon Focus (longsword).

Death Attack (Ex): If Baltha studies her victim for 3 rounds and then makes a sneak attack with a melee weapon, she can paralyze the victim for 1d6+5 rounds or kill the victim (Fortitude DC 16 negates).

Animal Companion (Ex): Baltha has a dire rat as an animal companion. Its statistics are as described on page 64 of the *Monster Manual*, except that Baltha can handle it as a free action (see page 36 of the *Player's Handbook*).

Combat Style (Ex): Baltha has selected two-weapon combat. She gains the Two-Weapon Fighting feat despite not having the requisite Dexterity score.

Dwarf Traits (Ex): +4 bonus on ability checks to resist being bull rushed or tripped; +2 bonus on saving throws against poison, spells, and spell-like effects; +1 bonus on attack rolls against orcs and goblinoids; +4 bonus to AC against giants; +2 bonus on Appraise or Craft checks related to stone or metal.

Favored Enemy (Ex): Baltha gains a +4 bonus on her Bluff, Listen, Sense Motive, Spot, and Survival checks when using these skills against elves. She gets the same bonus on weapon damage rolls against elves.

Against aberrations, she gains a +2 bonus on these skill checks and on weapon damage rolls.

Improved Stonecunning (Ex): Baltha has a +4 bonus on checks to notice unusual stonework, including stonework traps.

Stone's Hue (Su): Baltha gains a +10 circumstance bonus on Hide checks and can hide in plain sight when within 5 feet of a stone or earth wall.

Wild Empathy (Ex): Baltha can improve the attitude of an animal in the same way a Diplomacy check can improve the attitude of a sentient being. She rolls 1d20+3, or 1d20−1 if attempting to influence a magical beast with an Intelligence score of 1 or 2.

Possessions: +1 mithral breastplate, +1 longsword, +1 elfbane hand crossbow, potion of cure moderate wounds.

DARKWOOD STALKER

Elves and orcs are ancient foes, their enmity dating back to times before humans walked the land. Some elves train as elite hunters of the hated orcs. These hunters, called darkwood stalkers among the elves, pursue their age-old enemies with grim determination.

Darkwood stalkers usually come from the ranks of elf (or half-elf) rangers or rogues, although the rare elf barbarian can follow this path as well. Fighters and paladins make poor darkwood stalkers without gaining at least one level in ranger or rogue. Spellcasters rarely take up the mantle of the darkwood stalker, although druids willing to forego spellcasting can fit well into the order.

Most darkwood stalkers are affiliated with elven military units, although some are lone scouts or field agents.

Hit Die: d8.

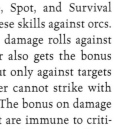
A darkwood stalker

Requirements

To qualify to become a darkwood stalker, a character must fulfill all the following criteria.

Race: Elf or half-elf.

Base Attack Bonus: +5.

Skills: Hide 5 ranks, Listen 5 ranks, Move Silently 5 ranks, Speak Language (Orc), Spot 5 ranks, Survival 5 ranks.

Feats: Dodge, Track.

Class Skills

The darkwood stalker's class skills (and the key ability for each skill) are Climb (Str), Craft (Int), Heal (Wis), Hide (Dex), Jump (Str), Knowledge (nature) (Int), Listen (Wis), Move Silently (Dex), Profession (Wis), Ride (Dex), Search (Int), Spot (Wis), Survival (Wis), Swim (Str), and Use Rope (Dex).

Skill Points at Each Additional Level: 4 + Int modifier.

Class Features

All of the following are class features of the darkwood stalker prestige class.

Weapon and Armor Proficiency: Darkwood stalkers gain no proficiency with any weapon or armor.

Ancient Foe (Ex): Due to his extensive study of orcs and training in the proper techniques for combating them, a darkwood stalker gains a +2 bonus on Bluff, Listen, Sense Motive, Spot, and Survival checks when using these skills against orcs. He gets the same bonus on weapon damage rolls against these creatures. A darkwood stalker also gets the bonus on damage with ranged weapons, but only against targets within 30 feet (the darkwood stalker cannot strike with deadly accuracy beyond that range). The bonus on damage does not apply against creatures that are immune to critical hits. At 4th, 7th, and 10th level, the darkwood stalker's bonus goes up by +2.

This bonus stacks with a favored enemy bonus (if any) acquired through ranger levels.

TABLE 2–6: THE DARKWOOD STALKER

Level	Base Attack Bonus	Fort Save	Ref Save	Will Save	Special
1st	+1	+2	+2	+0	Ancient foe +2
2nd	+2	+3	+3	+0	Uncanny dodge
3rd	+3	+3	+3	+1	Sneak attack +1d6
4th	+4	+4	+4	+1	Ancient foe +4, darkvision 30 ft.
5th	+5	+4	+4	+1	Improved uncanny dodge
6th	+6	+5	+5	+2	Sneak attack +2d6
7th	+7	+5	+5	+2	Ancient foe +6, darkvision 60 ft.
8th	+8	+6	+6	+2	Dodge critical
9th	+9	+6	+6	+3	Sneak attack +3d6
10th	+10	+7	+7	+3	Ancient foe +8, death attack

Uncanny Dodge (Ex): Starting at 2nd level, a darkwood stalker gains the ability to react to danger before his senses would normally allow him to do so. He retains his Dexterity bonus to Armor Class (if any) regardless of being caught flat-footed or struck by an invisible attacker. He still loses his Dexterity bonus to AC if immobilized.

If a darkwood stalker already had the uncanny dodge ability from another class, the character automatically gains improved uncanny dodge instead.

Sneak Attack (Ex): If a darkwood stalker can catch an opponent when she is unable to defend herself effectively from his attack, he can strike a vital spot for an extra 1d6 points of damage. For complete details on the sneak attack ability, see the description of the dark hunter earlier in this chapter.

Darkvision (Ex): Although stealthy and keen-eyed, the darkwood stalker is often at a disadvantage against orcs when fighting in the darkness. Long ago, elven sages developed a ritual to allow the most dedicated stalkers to overcome this disadvantage. Now, as they grow in experience, their night vision continually improves, eventually matching the darkvision of their hated foes. At 4th level, a darkwood stalker gains darkvision out to 30 feet, and at 7th level, the range increases to 60 feet. If the darkwood stalker already has darkvision as a racial ability, this ability does not increase it.

Improved Uncanny Dodge (Ex): At 5th level and higher, a darkwood stalker can no longer be flanked, since he can react to opponents on opposite sides of him as easily as he can react to a single attacker. This defense denies other characters the ability to use flank attacks to sneak attack him. The exception to this defense is that a rogue of at least four levels higher than the character can flank him (and thus sneak attack him).

If a darkwood stalker gains the uncanny dodge ability from another class, the levels from the classes that grant uncanny dodge stack to determine the minimum rogue level required to flank the character.

Dodge Critical (Ex): Although often more skilled than their orc foes, darkwood stalkers have seen too many battles won by one lucky blow from a falchion. At 8th level, a darkwood stalker becomes able to turn even the luckiest blow into a grazing strike. Once per day, a darkwood stalker can make a Reflex saving throw (DC 20 + the enhancement bonus, if any, possessed by the weapon) to turn a critical hit dealt upon him into a normal hit. The darkwood stalker must be aware of the attack and not flat-footed, and he must declare his attempt to reduce the effect of the critical hit before the damage from the hit is rolled.

Death Attack (Ex): If a 10th-level darkwood stalker studies a particular orc for 3 rounds and then makes a sneak attack with a melee weapon that successfully deals damage, the sneak attack has the additional effect of possibly killing the target. While studying the orc, the darkwood hunter can undertake other actions as long as his attention stays focused on the target and the target does not detect the darkwood stalker or recognize the darkwood stalker as an enemy. If the victim of such an attack fails a Fortitude save (DC 10 + the darkwood stalker's class level + the darkwood stalker's Wis modifier), he dies. If the victim's saving throw succeeds, the attack is just a normal sneak attack. Once the darkwood stalker has completed the 3 rounds of study, he must make the death attack within the next 3 rounds. If a death attack is attempted and fails (the victim makes his save) or if the darkwood stalker does not launch the attack within 3 rounds of completing the study, 3 new rounds of study are required before he can attempt another death attack.

Sample Darkwood Stalker

Nexal Ebonleaf: Elf ranger 5/darkwood stalker 8; CR 13; Medium humanoid; HD 5d8 plus 8d8; hp 59; Init +5; Spd 30 ft.; AC 23, touch 15, flat-footed 23; Base Atk +13; Grp +15; Atk +16 melee (1d8+2/19–20, longsword) or +23 ranged (1d8+5/19–20/×3, +3 composite longbow [+2 Str bonus]); Full Atk +16/+11/+6 melee (1d8+2/19–20, longsword) or +23/+18/+13 ranged (1d8+5/19–20/×3, +3 composite longbow [+2 Str bonus]) or +21/+21/+16/+11 ranged (1d8+5/19–20/×3, +3 composite longbow [+2 Str bonus]); SA sneak attack +2d6; SQ ancient foe, animal companion, darkvision 60 ft., elf traits, favored enemy orcs +4, favored enemy dragons +2, improved uncanny dodge, low-light vision, uncanny dodge, wild empathy; AL CG; SV Fort +10, Ref +15, Will +4; Str 14, Dex 20, Con 11, Int 10, Wis 12, Cha 8.

Skills and Feats: Climb +8, Hide +26, Listen +17, Move Silently +26, Spot +17, Speak Language (Goblin), Speak Language (Orc), Survival +9; Dodge, Endurance, Improved Critical (composite longbow), Point Blank Shot, Rapid Shot, Shot on the Run, Track[B], Weapon Focus (composite longbow).

Ancient Foe (Ex): Nexal gains a +10 bonus on his Bluff, Listen, Sense Motive, Spot, and Survival checks when using these skills against orcs. He gets a +10 bonus on weapon damage rolls against orcs. (These bonuses include the favored enemy bonus from the character's ranger levels.)

Animal Companion (Ex): Nexal has a wolf as an animal companion. Its statistics are as described on page 283 of the *Monster Manual*, except that Nexal can handle it as a free action (see page 36 of the *Player's Handbook*).

Combat Style (Ex): Nexal has selected archery. He gains the Rapid Shot feat without having to meet the normal prerequisites.

Dodge Critical (Ex): Once per day Nexal can attempt a Reflex save (DC 20 + weapon's enhancement bonus) to turn a critical hit into a normal hit.

Elf Traits (Ex): Immunity to magic *sleep* spells and effects; +2 bonus on saves against enchantments; entitled to a Search check when within 5 feet of a secret or concealed door.

Favored Enemy (Ex): Nexal gains a +2 bonus on his Bluff, Listen, Sense Motive, Spot, and Survival checks when using these skills against dragons. He gets the same bonus on weapon damage rolls against dragons. (His +4 bonus against orcs is accounted for in his ancient foe ability; see above.)

Improved Uncanny Dodge (Ex): Nexal cannot be flanked except by a rogue of at least 12th level.

Low-Light Vision (Ex) Nexal can see twice as far as a human in starlight, moonlight, torchlight, and similar conditions of poor visibility. He retains the ability to distinguish color and detail under these conditions.

A dervish

Uncanny Dodge (Ex): Nexal can react to danger before his senses would normally allow him to do so. He retains his Dexterity bonus to Armor Class even when caught flat-footed.

Wild Empathy (Ex): Nexal can improve the attitude of an animal in the same way a Diplomacy check can improve the attitude of a sentient being. He rolls 1d20+4, or 1d20−1 if attempting to influence a magical beast with an Intelligence score of 1 or 2.

Ranger Spells Prepared: 1st—*longstrider.*

Possessions: +3 *composite longbow* (+2 Str bonus), +1 *mithral breastplate,* +1 *buckler, cloak of elvenkind, boots of elvenkind, lesser bracers of archery,* masterwork longsword, 20 arrows.

DERVISH

Wild, exotic, and as dangerous as her whirling blades, the dervish epitomizes speed, quickness, and abandon. Her motions appear to be as random as they are graceful, but the steps of her lethal dance play out according to their own rhythm.

Nearly all dervishes belong to nomadic cultures. These nomads are not simple wanderers with no roots to call their own—they have their ancient traditions, and their societies simply do not consider permanent settlements an important part of their nature. They are gypsies, keeping their own traditions and forging their own familial and societal bonds while they move throughout the world. Often, these tribes adopt the attitudes and even some of the laws of the lands they live in—for the sake of expedience, if nothing else. The dervish treats fighting styles the same way. A dervish learns the dance of war as she grows up among her family and her tribe. She watches others as she travels, however, and brings new steps to the dance as she goes.

Fighters, rangers, and monks often take up the role of the dervish. Many paladins look at the wildness of the dance and assume it has some roots in chaos, but those who look past the seeming randomness can find things to learn. Barbarians seldom choose to learn the ways of the dance—the dervish depends on subtlety more than brute force. The way of the dervish has been known to appeal to some druids, bards, and even sorcerers—those who wish to learn a type of fighting that does not rely on heavy arms or armor find the class interesting.

Halflings and elves make good dervishes, and many nomadic halfling tribes have dervishes as their primary protectors.

NPC dervishes seldom wander without their tribes. They can be sent on missions, or serve as scouts in new lands, but the dervish is too important to the tribal unit to go off on her own for extended periods of time. Some dervishes balk at this responsibility, however, so exceptions to this rule do show up occasionally. A dervish found wandering alone is usually seeking new challenges and new knowledge.

Hit Die: d10.

Illus. by G. Kubic

Requirements

To qualify to become a dervish, a character must fulfill all the following criteria.

Base Attack Bonus: +5.

Skills: Perform (dance) 3 ranks, Tumble 3 ranks.

Feats: Combat Expertise, Dodge, Mobility, Weapon Focus (any slashing melee weapon).

Class Skills

The dervish's class skills (and the key ability for each skill) are Balance (Dex), Craft (Int), Escape Artist (Dex), Jump (Str), Listen (Wis), Perform (Cha), Profession (Wis), Swim (Str), and Tumble (Dex).

Skill Points at Each Level: 4 + Int modifier.

Class Features

All of the following are class features of the dervish prestige class.

Weapon and Armor Proficiency: Dervishes gain no proficiency with any weapon or armor.

AC Bonus (Ex): A dervish gains this bonus to Armor Class as long as she is wearing no armor or light armor and not carrying a shield. This bonus to AC applies even against touch attacks or when the dervish is flat-footed. She loses this bonus when she is immobilized or helpless, when she wears any armor heavier than light, when she carries a shield, or when she carries a medium or heavy load.

Dervish Dance (Ex): A dervish can become a whirling dancer of death a certain number of times per day. While in this dervish dance, she can take a full attack action (for melee attacks only) and still move up to her speed. However, the dervish must move a minimum of 5 feet between each attack when using this ability, and she cannot return to a square she just exited (though she may return to that square later during her full attack). The dervish is subject to attacks of opportunity while dancing, but may tumble normally as part of her move. A dervish prevented from completing her move is also prevented from finishing her full attack.

If a dervish wields a slashing weapon while in a dervish dance, she gains a bonus on her attack and damage rolls. This bonus is +1 at 1st level, and it increases by an extra +1 at every odd-numbered level thereafter.

A dervish may only perform a dervish dance while wielding a slashing weapon (she may use a double weapon, or multiple weapons, only if both ends of the weapon or all weapons are of the slashing type). She cannot perform a dervish dance in any armor heavier than light or if she is using a shield. While dancing, a dervish cannot use skills or abilities that involve concentration or require her to remain still, such as Move Silently, Hide, or Search. A dervish with the bardic music ability can, however, sing while she dances, and a dervish can also use the Combat Expertise feat while in a dance. A dervish cannot perform a dervish dance while under the effect of a rage or frenzy ability.

A dervish can perform a dervish dance only once per encounter. A dervish dance lasts 1 round for every two ranks of Perform (dance) that the character has. At the end of a dervish dance, the character becomes fatigued for the duration of the encounter (unless she is a 9th-level dervish, at which point this limitation no longer applies).

Movement Mastery (Ex): A dervish is so certain of her movements that she is unaffected by adverse conditions. When making a Jump, Perform (dance), or Tumble check, she may take 10 even if stress and distraction would normally prevent her from doing so.

Slashing Blades: A dervish treats the scimitar as a light weapon (rather than a one-handed weapon) for all purposes, including fighting with two weapons.

Fast Movement (Ex): At 2nd level and higher, a dervish gains an enhancement bonus to her speed. A dervish in any armor heavier than light or carrying a medium or heavy load loses this bonus.

Spring Attack: At 3rd level, a dervish gains the Spring Attack feat, even if she does not meet the prerequisites.

Dance of Death: At 4th level, a dervish gains the benefit of the Cleave feat while performing a dervish dance, even if she does not meet the prerequisites for the feat. She does not have to move 5 feet before making the extra attack granted by this ability.

Improved Reaction (Ex): When she attains 6th level, a dervish gains a +2 bonus on initiative rolls.

Elaborate Parry (Ex): When she attains 7th level, a dervish gains an extra +4 bonus to Armor Class when she chooses to fight defensively or use all-out defense in melee combat.

TABLE 2–7: THE DERVISH

Level	Base Attack Bonus	Fort Save	Ref Save	Will Save	AC Bonus	Special
1st	+1	+0	+2	+2	+1	Dervish dance 1/day, movement mastery, slashing blades
2nd	+2	+0	+3	+3	+1	Fast movement +5 ft.
3rd	+3	+1	+3	+3	+1	Spring Attack, dervish dance 2/day
4th	+4	+1	+4	+4	+1	Dance of death
5th	+5	+1	+4	+4	+2	Fast movement +10 ft., dervish dance 3/day
6th	+6	+2	+5	+5	+2	Improved reaction
7th	+7	+2	+5	+5	+2	Elaborate parry, dervish dance 4/day
8th	+8	+2	+6	+6	+2	Fast movement +15 ft.
9th	+9	+3	+6	+6	+3	Tireless dance, dervish dance 5/day
10th	+10	+3	+7	+7	+3	A thousand cuts

Tireless Dance: When a dervish reaches 9th level, the character no longer becomes fatigued for the duration of the encounter at the end of a dervish dance.

A Thousand Cuts (Ex): When a dervish reaches 10th level, once per day she may double the number of melee attacks she makes while performing a full attack action (whether in a dervish dance or not). If a dervish uses this ability in conjunction with her dervish dance, she can make up to two attacks between moves.

The dervish also gains the benefit of the Great Cleave feat with slashing weapons while performing a thousand cuts, even if she does not meet the prerequisites. She does not have to move 5 feet before making any extra attacks granted by this ability.

A dervish using this ability can receive an extra attack from the *haste* spell, but the bonuses provided by the spell do not stack with the bonuses granted by the class.

Sample Dervish

Zethara: Halfling fighter 7/dervish 10; CR 17; Small humanoid; HD 7d10+14 plus 10d10+20; hp 126; Init +6; Spd 35 ft.; AC 25, touch 18, flat-footed 21; Base Atk +17; Grp +20; Atk +28 melee (1d4+14 plus 1d6 fire/15–20, +2 *flaming scimitar*) or +23 ranged (1d6+8/×3, +1 *composite longbow* [+7 Str bonus]); Full Atk +28/+23/+18/+13 melee (1d4+14 plus 1d6 fire/15–20, +2 *flaming scimitar*); or +26/+21/+16/+11 melee (1d4+14 plus 1d6 fire/15–20, +2 *flaming scimitar*) and +26/+21 melee (1d4+10 plus 1d6 cold/15–20, +2 *frost scimitar*) (dervish dance); or +31/+31/+26/+26/+21/+21/+16/+16 melee (1d4+16 plus 1d6 fire/15–20, +2 *flaming scimitar*) and +31/+31/+26/+26 melee (1d4+14 plus 1d6 cold/15–20, +2 *frost scimitar*) (a thousand cuts and dervish dance); or +23/+18/+13/+8 ranged (1d6+8/×3, +1 *composite longbow* [+7 Str bonus]); SA dervish dance, a thousand cuts; SQ elaborate parry, halfling traits, slashing blades; AL CN; SV Fort +11, Ref +14, Will +10; Str 24, Dex 18, Con 14, Int 12, Wis 10, Cha 8.

Skills and Feats: Intimidate +9, Jump +27, Perform (dance) +14, Tumble +17; Combat Expertise, Dodge, Improved Critical (scimitar), Improved Two-Weapon Fighting, Mobility, Quick Draw, Spring Attack, Two-Weapon Fighting, Weapon Specialization (scimitar), Weapon Focus (scimitar).

Dervish Dance (Ex): Five times per day, Zethara can take a single move action and still make a full attack, but she must move 5 feet between each attack and cannot return to a square she just exited. She gains a +5 bonus on attack and damage rolls when performing the dervish dance with a slashing weapon.

A Thousand Cuts (Ex): Once per day, Zethara can double the number of melee attacks she makes, as noted in the full attack entry above.

Elaborate Parry (Ex): Zethara gains an extra +4 bonus to Armor Class when she fights defensively or uses all-out defense.

Halfling Traits (Ex): +2 morale bonus on saves against fear; +1 bonus on attack rolls with thrown weapons and slings.

Slashing Blades (Ex): Zethara treats the scimitar as a light weapon rather than a one-handed weapon.

Possessions: +2 *Small flaming scimitar*, +2 *Small frost scimitar*, +2 *Small mithral breastplate*, +1 *Small composite longbow* (+7 Str bonus), *gloves of Dexterity +4*, *belt of giant strength +6*, 20 arrows.

DRUNKEN MASTER

Martial arts students face a bewildering array of martial arts schools, each with its own adherents and detractors. However, few schools are as unusual—or as controversial—as drunken boxing. By weaving and staggering about as if inebriated, drunken boxers avoid many blows. Likewise, their stumbling, lurching attacks catch their opponents off guard. Moreover, when they actually imbibe alcohol, drunken masters can perform truly prodigious feats of strength and bravery.

This ability garners a drunken master little respect among adherents of other martial arts schools, because drunken boxing exacts a toll on its users. Drunken masters may remain intoxicated for hours after a fight, and they are often found half-asleep in taverns, mumbling incoherently. This flies in the face of other schools' ascetic principles. Members of rival schools must be wary—they never know when the tipsy lout at the bar is just a harmless thug, and when he is a nigh-unstoppable drunken master.

Monks form the backbone of the drunken boxing school. A monk loses some face with his original school or monastery for becoming a drunken master, but a brilliant display of drunken fighting can sometimes silence critics in one's former school. Members of other classes become drunken masters only rarely, although students often tell the tale of a barbarian from the north who became a phenomenal drunken master.

Prospective students are studied at a distance by other drunken masters, then treated to a display of the power of drunken boxing. If the student expresses enthusiasm for learning the new techniques, a group of drunken masters takes him or her from tavern to tavern, getting rip-roaring drunk, causing trouble, and passing along the first secrets of the technique. Those who survive the revelry are welcomed as new drunken masters.

NPC drunken masters are often found in taverns and bars. They rarely pick fights there, but are quick to come to the aid of someone overmatched in a tavern brawl. Most keep a low profile, although some are famous—or infamous—for the deeds they have performed while under the influence.

Hit Die: d8.

Requirements

To qualify to become a drunken master, a character must fulfill all the following criteria.

Skills: Tumble 8 ranks.

Feats: Dodge, Great Fortitude, Improved Unarmed Strike (or the monk's unarmed strike ability).

Special: Flurry of blows ability; evasion ability; must be chosen by existing drunken masters and survive a night of revelry among them without being incarcerated, poisoned, or extraordinarily embarrassed.

Class Skills

The drunken master's class skills (and the key ability for each skill) are Balance (Dex), Bluff (Cha), Climb (Str), Craft (Int), Escape Artist (Dex), Hide (Dex), Jump (Str), Listen (Wis), Move Silently (Dex), Perform (Cha), Profession (Wis), Swim (Str), and Tumble (Dex).

Skill Points at Each Level: 4 + Int modifier.

TABLE 2–8: THE DRUNKEN MASTER

Level	Base Attack Bonus	Fort Save	Ref Save	Will Save	Special
1st	+0	+2	+2	+0	Drink like a demon, improvised weapons
2nd	+1	+3	+3	+0	Stagger
3rd	+2	+3	+3	+1	Swaying waist
4th	+3	+4	+4	+1	AC bonus +1, improved improvised weapons
5th	+3	+4	+4	+1	greater improvised weapons
6th	+4	+5	+5	+2	Improved Feint
7th	+5	+5	+5	+2	Improved Grapple
8th	+6	+6	+6	+2	*For medicinal purposes*
9th	+6	+6	+6	+3	AC bonus +2, corkscrew rush, superior improvised weapons
10th	+7	+7	+7	+3	*Breath of flame*

Class Features

All of the following are class features of the drunken master prestige class.

Weapon and Armor Proficiency: Drunken masters gain no proficiency with any weapon or armor.

Drink Like a Demon (Ex): A drunken master's body handles alcohol differently from other people's. He can drink a large tankard of ale, a bottle of wine, or a corresponding amount of stronger alcohol as a move action. Every bottle or tankard of alcohol he consumes during combat reduces his Wisdom and Intelligence by 2 points each, but increases his Strength or Constitution (character's choice) by 2 points. A drunken master may benefit from a number of drinks equal to his class level. The duration of both the penalty and the bonus is a number of rounds equal to the character's drunken master level + 3.

Improvised Weapons (Ex): While bottles and tankards are a drunken master's preferred improvised weapons, he can use furniture, farm implements, or nearly anything else at hand to attack his foes. A drunken master's improvised weapon deals as much damage as his unarmed strike plus an extra 1d4 points. Most improvised weapons deal bludgeoning damage, although some (a broken glass bottle, for example) would deal piercing or slashing damage. When a drunken master rolls a natural 1 on an attack roll while using an improvised weapon, that weapon breaks apart and becomes useless.

Stagger (Ex): By tripping, stumbling, and staggering, a drunken master of 2nd level or higher can make a charge attack that surprises his opponents. This ability has two beneficial aspects: First, the charge need not be in a straight line, even though the character can still move up to twice his speed. Second, if a drunken master makes a DC 15 Tumble check before beginning a charge, his movement through threatened squares provokes no attacks of opportunity.

Swaying Waist (Ex): At 3rd level, a drunken master knows how to weave and bob during an attack, making him more difficult to hit. The character gains a +2 dodge bonus to Armor Class against any one opponent he chooses during his turn.

AC Bonus (Ex): At 4th level, a drunken master gains a +1 bonus to Armor Class. This bonus improves to +2 at 9th level.

Improved Improvised Weapons (Ex): A drunken master of 4th level or higher can use long improvised weapons (such as ladders) as reach weapons according to their length, and improvised weapons with many protrusions (such as chairs) provide a +2 bonus on opponents' disarm attempts. Finally, large objects with broad, flat surfaces (such as tables) can be upended to become improvised tower shields.

Greater Improvised Weapons (Ex): At 5th level and higher, a drunken master wielding an improvised weapon deals an extra 1d8 points of damage instead of 1d4.

Improved Feint (Ex): A drunken master who attains 6th level gains Improved Feint as a bonus feat even if he does not meet the prerequisites.

Improved Grapple (Ex): A drunken master who attains 7th level gains Improved Grapple as a bonus feat even if he does not meet the prerequisites.

For Medicinal Purposes **(Sp):** At 8th level, a drunken master gains the ability to convert a single alcoholic drink he has ingested into a single *potion of cure moderate wounds*, as if he had just drunk a dose of the potion. To use this ability, the character must be under the effect of an alcoholic drink (see Drink Like a Demon, above). When he converts one drink of alcohol into one dose of the potion, his ability scores change (+2 to Intelligence and Wisdom, –2 to Strength or Constitution) as if the duration of the alcohol's effect had expired. This ability can be used up to three times per day. It is a standard action that does not provoke an attack of opportunity.

Corkscrew Rush (Ex): A drunken master of 9th level or higher can perform this maneuver, leaping forward and twisting his body in midair as he attempts to head-butt an opponent. When making a charge attack he can, in addition to dealing normal damage, initiate a bull rush (without provoking an attack of opportunity). If the bull rush attempt succeeds, the opponent is stunned unless she makes a Will save (DC 10 + the drunken master's class level + the drunken master's Wis modifier). However, if the bull rush attempt fails, the drunken master lands prone in front of the opponent.

Superior Improvised Weapons (Ex): At 9th level and higher, a drunken master wielding an improvised weapon deals an extra 1d12 points of damage instead of 1d8.

Breath of Flame (Sp): A 10th-level drunken master can ignite some of the alcohol within his body and spew it forth from his mouth as a free action. This *breath of flame* deals 3d12 points of fire damage to all within the 20-foot cone, or half damage to those who make a Reflex save (DC 10 + the drunken master's class level + the drunken master's Con modifier). Each time a drunken master uses *breath of flame*, it consumes one drink's worth of alcohol from within his body, lessening the penalty to his Wisdom and Intelligence scores and reducing the bonus to his Strength or Constitution score (character's choice).

Multiclass Note: A monk who becomes a drunken master may continue advancing as a monk.

Sample Drunken Master

Kirin Kotellos: Human monk 5/drunken master 8: CR 13; Medium humanoid; HD 5d8+5 plus 8d8+8; hp 72; Init +2; Spd 40 ft., AC 20, touch 17, flat-footed 18; Base Atk +9; Grp +17; Atk +14 melee (1d10+4/19–20, unarmed strike) or +14 melee (1d6+7, *rod of the python*) or +12 ranged (1d8/ 19–20, +1 *light crossbow*); Full Atk +14/+9 melee (1d10+4/19–20, unarmed strike); or +13/+13/ +8 melee (1d10+4/19–20, unarmed strike); or +13/+8 melee (1d6+5, *rod of the python*) and +13 melee (1d6+3, rod of the python); or +12 ranged (1d8/19–20, +1 *light crossbow*); SA flurry of blows, ki strike (magic); SQ drink like a demon, evasion, purity of body, slow fall 20 ft., still mind; AL LG; Fort +15, Ref +14, Will +10; Str 19, Dex 14, Con 12, Int 10, Wis 14, Cha 8.

Skills and Feats: Balance +20, Bluff +7, Climb +20, Diplomacy +1, Intimidate +1, Jump +26, Tumble +20; Combat Reflexes, Dodge, Great Fortitude, Improved Critical (unarmed strike), Improved Feint, Improved Grapple, Mobility, Spring Attack, Stunning Fist, Weapon Focus (unarmed strike).

A drunken master

Flurry of Blows (Ex): Kirin may use a full attack action to make one extra attack per round with an unarmed strike or a special monk weapon at his highest base attack bonus, but this attack and each other attack made in that round take a –1 penalty apiece. This penalty applies for 1 round, so it affects attacks of opportunity Kirin might make before his next action. If armed with a kama, nunchaku, or siangham, Kirin can make the extra attack either with that weapon or unarmed. If armed with two such weapons, he uses one for his regular attack(s) and the other for the extra attack. In any case, his damage bonus on the attack with his off hand is not reduced.

Ki Strike (Su): Kirin's unarmed strike can deal damage to a creature with damage reduction as if the blow were made with a magic weapon.

Drink Like a Demon (Ex): Each drink Kirin takes during combat reduces his Wisdom and Intelligence by 2 points but increases either his Strength or his Constitution by 2 points for 11 rounds.

Evasion (Ex): If Kirin is exposed to any effect that normally allows him to attempt a Reflex saving throw for half damage, he takes no damage with a successful saving throw.

For Medicinal Purposes (Sp): Kirin can convert an alcoholic drink to a *potion of cure moderate wounds* three times per day.

Improvised Weapons (Ex): Kirin can use almost anything at hand to attack his foes. An improvised weapon deals 1d6 points of damage (type of damage depends on the weapon's shape). Long items have reach, and items with many protrusions give Kirin a +2 bonus on disarm attempts.

Purity of Body (Ex): Kirin has immunity to all diseases except for magical diseases such as mummy rot and lycanthropy.

Slow Fall (Ex): When within arm's reach of a wall, Kirin can use it to slow his descent while falling. He takes damage as if the fall were 20 feet shorter than it actually is.

Illus. by J. Jarvis

Stagger (Ex): Kirin doesn't need to move in a straight line when making a charge, and he can tumble through threatened squares to avoid attacks of opportunity during a charge.

Still Mind (Ex): +2 bonus on saving throws against spells and effects from the enchantment school.

Swaying Waist (Ex): Kirin gains a +2 dodge bonus against any one opponent he chooses during his turn. This benefit does not stack with the benefit of the Dodge feat.

Possessions: Rod of the python, +1 light crossbow, gauntlets of ogre power +2, ring of protection +1, cloak of resistance +2, bracers of armor +3, potion of good hope, 4 bottles of liquor, 10 bolts.

EXOTIC WEAPON MASTER

Characters of any race or background can become exotic weapon masters; the only real requirement is commitment and perseverance. Nevertheless, most exotic weapon masters are human, because members of that race have the most exposure to new cultures and thus the most opportunity to take up exotic weapons.

NPC exotic weapon masters often open training arenas or schools for those interested in learning to fight with unusual weapons or tactics. They often take levels in other prestige classes and can be found as champions or leaders among bands of warriors.

Hit Die: d10.

TABLE 2–9: THE EXOTIC WEAPON MASTER

Level	Base Attack Bonus	Fort Save	Ref Save	Will Save	Special
1st	+1	+2	+0	+0	Exotic weapon stunt
2nd	+2	+3	+0	+0	Exotic weapon stunt
3rd	+3	+3	+1	+1	Exotic weapon stunt

Requirements

To become an exotic weapon master, a character must fulfill the following criteria.

Base Attack Bonus: +6.

Skills: Craft (weaponsmithing) 3 ranks.

Feats: Exotic Weapon Proficiency (any exotic weapon), Weapon Focus (any exotic weapon).

Special: Races that have familiarity with an exotic weapon (such as the dwarf's familiarity with the dwarven waraxe and the dwarven urgrosh) are considered to have the Exotic Weapon Proficiency feat for the purpose of meeting the requirements for this class.

Class Skills

The exotic weapon master's class skills (and the key ability for each skill) are Craft (Int), Intimidate (Cha), and Profession (Int).

Skill Points at Each Level: 2 + Int modifier.

Class Features

All of the following are class features of the exotic weapon master prestige class.

Weapon and Armor Proficiency: Exotic weapon masters gain no proficiency with any weapon or armor.

Exotic Weapon Stunt (Ex): At each level, an exotic weapon master learns a special trick that he can use with any exotic weapon for which he has the Weapon Focus feat. He must select the trick learned when he gains the level, and once selected, the choice cannot later be changed. He can't select the same stunt more than once.

Close-Quarters Ranged Combat: A character who knows this stunt doesn't provoke an attack of opportunity when using an exotic ranged weapon.

Double Weapon Defense: When wielding an exotic double weapon with both hands, the character gains a +1 shield bonus to AC.

Exotic Reach: When wielding an exotic weapon with reach, the character may make an attack of opportunity against a foe that provokes such an attack even if the foe has cover (but not total cover).

Exotic Sunder: When wielding a one-handed or two-handed exotic weapon, the character deals an extra 1d6 points of damage on any successful sunder attempt.

Flurry of Strikes: When wielding an exotic double weapon or a spiked chain with both hands, the character can elect to use a full attack action to make a flurry of strikes. When doing so, he may make one extra attack in the round at his full base attack bonus, but this attack takes a –2 penalty, as does each other attack made in that round and until the exotic weapon master's next turn. The extra attack may be with either end of the double weapon.

Ranged Disarm: The character can make a disarm attempt even on a ranged attack. Such an attack provokes no attack of opportunity (except as normal for using a ranged weapon). For the purpose of this disarm attempt, treat the character's ranged weapon as a light weapon. If the character fails this disarm attempt, the defender can't attempt to disarm him.

Show Off: As a standard action, the character can display his mastery with an exotic weapon and confound his opponent. The character may make an Intimidate check against a single opponent within 30 feet that can see him, adding his base attack bonus to the result. If the result exceeds the opponent's modified level check (see the skill description on page 76 of the *Player's Handbook*), the opponent becomes shaken (–2 penalty on attack rolls, ability checks, and saving throws) for 1 round per class level of the exotic weapon master.

Stunning Blow: If the character has the Stunning Fist feat, he can utilize the feat while wielding an exotic melee weapon.

Throw Exotic Weapon: The character can throw an exotic weapon with no penalty on the attack roll, even if it isn't designed to be thrown (such as an orc double axe or a spiked chain). When he throws a double weapon, only one end of the weapon (character's choice) can strike the target. Exotic weapons thrown in this way have a range increment of 10 feet.

Twin Exotic Weapon Fighting: When wielding the same light exotic weapon in each hand, the character is treated as having the Two-Weapon Fighting feat. If he already has the feat, the penalties on attack rolls are lessened to –1 for both the primary hand and the off hand when fighting in this manner.

Trip Attack: The character can use a one-handed or two-handed exotic weapon to make a trip attack. If he is tripped during his own trip attempt, he can drop the weapon to avoid being tripped. If the exotic weapon already allows its wielder to make trip attacks, the character instead adds a +2 bonus on any trip attempt.

Uncanny Blow: When wielding a one-handed exotic melee weapon in two hands, the character can focus the power of his attack so that he deals extra damage equal to his Strength bonus ×2 instead of his Strength bonus ×1-1/2. If he has the Power Attack feat, he treats the weapon as two-handed for purposes of determining his bonus on damage rolls.

An exotic weapon master

Sample Exotic Weapon Master

Golgos Athroaka: Gnome fighter 6/exotic weapon master 3; CR 9; Small humanoid; HD 6d10+12 plus 3d10+6; hp 68; Init +1; Spd 20 ft.; AC 21, touch 12, flat-footed 20; Base Atk +9; Grp +8; Atk +16 melee (1d6+7/×3, +2 gnome hooked hammer) or +12 ranged (1d6+3/×3, masterwork composite longbow [+3 Str bonus]); Full Atk +16/+11 melee (1d6+7/×3, +2 gnome hooked hammer); or +12/+12/+12 melee (1d6+7/×3, +2 gnome hooked hammer) and +7 melee (1d4+4/×4, +2 gnome hooked hammer); or +12/+7 ranged (1d6+3/×3, masterwork composite longbow [+3 Str bonus]); SA double weapon defense, flurry of strikes; SQ gnome traits, show off; AL LE; SV Fort +10, Ref +4, Will +3; Str 17, Dex 12, Con 14, Int 13, Wis 10, Cha 8.

Skills and Feats: Climb +9, Craft (weaponsmithing) +12, Intimidate +9, Jump +1; Cleave, Combat Expertise, Improved Disarm, Improved Trip, Power Attack, Two-Weapon Fight-

ing, Weapon Focus (gnome hooked hammer), Weapon Specialization (gnome hooked hammer).

Double Weapon Defense (Ex): When wielding a gnome hooked hammer (or any other exotic double weapon) with both hands, Golgos gains a +1 shield bonus to AC.

Flurry of Strikes (Ex): As part of a full attack, Golgos can make an extra attack, with all of his attacks up to his next turn taking a –2 penalty.

Gnome Traits (Ex): +1 save DC for illusions, +2 bonus on saves against illusions, +1 bonus on attack rolls against kobolds and goblinoids, +4 dodge bonus to AC against giants, +2 bonus on Listen checks and Craft (alchemy) checks.

Show Off (Ex): As a standard action, Golgos can display his prowess with a weapon and make an Intimidate check, adding +9 to the result. If the result exceeds the opponent's modified level check, the opponent becomes shaken (–2 penalty on attack rolls, ability checks, and saving throws) for 3 rounds.

Possessions: +2 gnome hooked hammer, +1 full plate, Small masterwork composite longbow (+3 Str bonus), 20 arrows.

EYE OF GRUUMSH

Most people think they have seen the worst that orcs can breed when an orc barbarian comes raging over a hilltop—until they see a one-eyed orc barbarian come raging over a hilltop. This creature may well be an eye of Gruumsh, an orc so devoted to his evil deity that he has disfigured himself in Gruumsh's name.

In an epic battle at the dawn of time, the elven deity Corellon Larethian stabbed out Gruumsh's left eye. Filled with rage and hatred, the orc deity called for followers loyal enough to serve in his image. Those who heed this call are known as the eyes of Gruumsh. They sacrifice their right eyes instead of their left ones so that their impaired vision complements that of their deity. Thus, symbolically at least, eyes of Gruumsh can see what Gruumsh cannot. These living martyrs are some of the toughest orcs and half-orcs in the world.

Illus. by J. Jarvis

The eye of Gruumsh is a true prestige class in the sense that all orcs respect those who achieve it. If a candidate proves capable with the orc double axe and has no moral code to stand in the way of his service, only the test remains—to put out his own right eye in a special ceremony. This is a bloody and painful ritual, the details of which are best left undescribed. If the candidate makes a sound during the process, he fails the test. No consequences for failure exist, except that the candidate can never thereafter become an eye of Gruumsh—and he has lost an eye.

Barbarians gain the most value from this prestige class, since it encourages raging as a fighting style. Fighters, clerics, rangers, and even rogues also heed this calling. Some orc tribes whisper of barbarians from other races who have adopted this mantle. Of course, these may just be legends meant to inspire young orcs to jealous rage.

Hit Die: d12.

Requirements

To qualify to become an eye of Gruumsh, a character must fulfill all the following criteria.

Race: Orc or half-orc.
Alignment: Chaotic evil, chaotic neutral, or neutral evil.
Base Attack Bonus: +6.
Feats: Exotic Weapon Proficiency (orc double axe), Weapon Focus (orc double axe).
Special: The character must be a worshiper of Gruumsh and must put out his own right eye in a special ritual. None of the eye of Gruumsh's special abilities function if the character regains sight in both eyes.

Class Skills

The eye of Gruumsh's class skills (and the key ability for each skill) are Climb (Str), Intimidate (Cha), Jump (Str), Ride (Dex), Survival (Wis), and Swim (Str).

Skill Points at Each Level: 2 + Int modifier.

TABLE 2–10: THE EYE OF GRUUMSH

Level	Base Attack Bonus	Fort Save	Ref Save	Will Save	Special
1st	+1	+2	+0	+0	Blind-Fight, command the horde, rage
2nd	+2	+3	+0	+0	Swing blindly
3rd	+3	+3	+1	+1	Ritual scarring +1
4th	+4	+4	+1	+1	Blinding spittle 2/day
5th	+5	+4	+1	+1	Blindsight 5 ft.
6th	+6	+5	+2	+2	Ritual scarring +2
7th	+7	+5	+2	+2	Blinding spittle 4/day
8th	+8	+6	+2	+2	Blindsight 10 ft.
9th	+9	+6	+3	+3	Ritual scarring +3
10th	+10	+7	+3	+3	Sight of Gruumsh

Class Features

All of the following are class features of the eye of Gruumsh prestige class.

Weapon and Armor Proficiency: Eyes of Gruumsh gain no proficiency with any weapon or armor.

Blind-Fight: An eye of Gruumsh gains Blind-Fight as a bonus feat. In addition, he suffers no adverse effects from the loss of one of his eyes.

Command the Horde (Ex): An eye of Gruumsh can direct the actions of any nongood orcs or half-orcs that are within 30 feet of him and whose Hit Dice are lower than his character level. Those who follow the character's orders gain a +2 morale bonus on Will saves. Any eligible orc or half-orc who willingly goes against the eye of Gruumsh's directions loses this bonus immediately.

Rage (Ex): An eye of Gruumsh can fly into a rage just as a barbarian can, with all the same benefits and drawbacks (see page 25 of the *Player's Handbook*). An eye of Gruumsh's class levels stack with his barbarian levels (if any) for determining the number of times per day he can use his rage ability. Add together the character's levels in the eye of Gruumsh and barbarian classes and refer to Table 3–3: The Barbarian on page 25 of the *Player's Handbook* to determine the number of rages per day. For example, a 6th-level barbarian/2nd-level eye of

---

ORGANIZATION: THE EYES OF GRUUMSH

"The cycle of my father's people is a simple one. You kill, you get better at killing, and you kill again. Break the cycle, and you die."
—Krusk

Though orcs revere eyes of Gruumsh for their unique clarity of vision, the average eye of Gruumsh isn't particularly well qualified to think for an entire tribe—even though he often assumes leadership of a tribe early in his career. Thus, he relies on a cleric of Gruumsh for wise counsel. To discourage any unhealthy confusion among their followers about who is in charge, both the eye of Gruumsh and the cleric encourage war against other races at every opportunity.

Since eyes of Gruumsh seek to avenge Corellon Larethian's insult to their deity, most are so obsessed with the destruction of

elves that they attack any elven community on sight. Inspired by their leaders' rage, other orcs often throw themselves heedlessly at elven hordes.

Multiple eyes of Gruumsh usually don't work well together because they commonly have competing ideas about which course of action serves their deity best. Every few decades or so, however, several eyes of Gruumsh get the same idea in their heads—a crusade! (After all, a holy crusade involving hundreds of tribes under the command of dozens of eyes of Gruumsh is just the thing to inspire the younger generation to the deity's service.) When this occurs, the eyes of Gruumsh meet and declare truces between competing tribes by closing their functional left eyes all at once—thus blinding them to their own bickering. Then they go out and try to eradicate some other kind of creature.

Gruumsh could rage three times per day (the same as an 8th-level barbarian), while a 4th-level eye of Gruumsh with no levels in barbarian could rage twice per day (the same as a 4th-level barbarian).

Swing Blindly (Ex): An eye of Gruumsh's rage becomes more powerful when he reaches 2nd level, but at the cost of lowered defenses. The character adds an extra +4 to Strength while in a rage, but his Armor Class penalty goes from –2 to –4.

Ritual Scarring (Ex): Through frequent disfiguration of his own skin, an eye of Gruumsh's natural armor bonus improves by +1 at 3rd level (or to +1 if he didn't already have a natural armor bonus). This bonus increases by another +1 for every three eye of Gruumsh levels gained thereafter.

Blinding Spittle (Ex): An eye of Gruumsh of 4th level or higher can launch blinding spittle at any opponent within 20 feet. With a successful ranged touch attack (at a –4 penalty), he spits his stomach acid into the target's eyes. An opponent who fails a Reflex save (DC 10 + eye of Gruumsh's class level + eye of Gruumsh's Con modifier) is blinded until he or she can rinse away the spittle. This attack has no effect on creatures that don't have eyes or don't depend on vision. Blinding spittle is usable twice per day at 4th level and four times per day at 7th level.

Blindsight (Ex): At 5th level, an eye of Gruumsh gains blindsight (see page 306 of the *Monster Manual*) out to 5 feet. The range increases to 10 feet at 8th level.

Sight of Gruumsh (Ex): At 10th level, an eye of Gruumsh gains the ability to see the moment of his own death through his missing eye. This foreknowledge gives him a +2 morale bonus on all saving throws and Armor Class from then on. He also does not go unconscious when reduced to negative hit points; however, the character still dies at –10 hit points. (Whether or not the vision is accurate is irrelevant—the character believes it to be true.)

Illus. by W. England

Sample Eye of Gruumsh

Bara-Katal: Half-orc barbarian 6/eye of Gruumsh 4; CR 10; Medium humanoid; HD 6d12+12 plus 4d12+8; hp 85; Init +2; Spd 30 ft.; AC 20, touch 12, flat-footed 20; Base Atk +10; Grp +14; Atk +16 melee (1d8+7/19–20/×3, +1 *keen orc double axe*) or +13 ranged (1d8+5/×3, +1 *composite longbow* [+4 Str bonus]); Full Atk +16/+11 melee (1d8+7/19–20/×3, +1 *keen orc double axe*); or +14/+9 melee (1d8+5/19–20/×3, +1 *keen orc double axe*) and +14 melee (1d8+3/×3, +1 *orc double axe*); or +13/+8 ranged (1d8+5/×3, +1 *composite longbow* [+4 Str bonus]); SA blinding spittle 2/day; SQ command the horde, darkvision 60 ft., improved uncanny dodge, rage 3/day, ritual scarring, swing blindly, trap sense +2, uncanny dodge; AL CE; SV Fort +11, Ref +5, Will +4; Str 18, Dex 15, Con 14, Int 8, Wis 12, Cha 6.

Skills and Feats: Intimidate +7, Jump +18, Swim +7; Blind-Fight[B], Exotic Weapon Proficiency (orc double axe), Power Attack, Two-Weapon Fighting, Weapon Focus (orc double axe).

Blinding Spittle (Ex): Ranged touch attack (+7 bonus) with a range of 20 feet. Target must succeed on a Will save (DC 18 if Bara-Katal is raging, DC 16 if not) or be blinded until he or she can rinse away the spittle.

An eye of Gruumsh

Command the Horde (Ex): Bara-Katal provides a +2 morale bonus on Will saves by nongood orcs and half-orcs within 30 feet that have less than 10 HD, so long as those individuals follow Bara-Katal's directions.

Improved Uncanny Dodge (Ex): Bara-Katal cannot be flanked except by a rogue of at least 10th level.

Rage (Ex): +8 to Str, +4 to Con, +2 on Will saves, –4 to AC for up to 7 rounds. The swing blindly class feature (see below) imposes a greater AC penalty but grants a further +4 bonus to Strength for a total of +8.

Ritual Scarring (Ex): Bara-Katal has a +1 natural armor bonus to AC.

Swing Blindly (Ex): Bara-Katal gains an extra +4 to Strength while in a rage, but his Armor Class penalty is –4 instead of –2.

Trap Sense (Ex): Against attacks by traps, Bara-Katal gets a +2 bonus on Reflex saves and a +2 dodge bonus to Armor Class.

Uncanny Dodge (Ex): Bara-Katal can react to danger before his senses would normally allow him to do so. He retains his Dexterity bonus to Armor Class even when caught flat-footed.

Possessions: +1 keen/+1 orc double axe, +2 breastplate, +1 composite longbow (+4 Str bonus), 20 arrows.

FRENZIED BERSERKER

The random madness of the thunderstorm and the unpredictability of the slaadi come together in the soul of the frenzied berserker. Unlike most other characters, she does not fight to achieve some heroic goal or defeat a loathsome villain. Those are mere excuses—it is the thrill of combat that draws her. For the frenzied barbarian, the insanity of battle is much like an addictive drug—she must constantly seek out more conflict to feed her craving for battle.

Along the wild borderlands and in the evil kingdoms of the world, frenzied berserkers often lead warbands that include a variety of character types—and even other frenzied berserkers. Some such groups turn to banditry and brigandage; others serve as specialized mercenaries. Whatever their origin, such warbands naturally gravitate toward situations of instability and conflict, because wars and civil strife are their bread and butter. Indeed, the coming of a frenzied berserker is the most obvious herald of troubled times.

The frenzied berserker's path is unsuited for most adventurers—a fact for which the peace-lovers of the world can be thankful. Because of their traditional love for battle, orc and half-orc barbarians are the ones who most frequently adopt this prestige class, though human and dwarf barbarians also find it appealing. It might seem that elves would be good candidates because of their chaotic nature, but the elven aesthetic and love of grace are at odds with the frenzied berserker's devaluation of the self. Spellcasting characters and monks almost never become frenzied berserkers.

NPC frenzied berserkers often lead tribal warbands or raiders made up of fighters, barbarians, or other martial characters. Some fall in with humanoids and even giantish tribes, but not all frenzied berserkers turn their chaotic strength to evil. A few have found homes in small villages or in rural areas, acting as members of the settlement's defenses. Most people give even such well-intentioned frenzied berserkers a wide berth, however, and they often find themselves wandering as loners in the wilderness.

Hit Die: d12.

Requirements

To qualify to become a frenzied berserker, a character must fulfill all the following criteria.

Alignment: Any nonlawful.

Base Attack Bonus: +6.

Feats: Cleave, Destructive Rage*, Intimidating Rage*, Power Attack.

*New feats found in Chapter 3 of this book.

Class Skills

The frenzied berserker's class skills (and the key ability for each skill) are Climb (Str), Intimidate (Cha), Jump (Str), Ride (Dex), and Swim (Str).

Skill Points at Each Level: 2 + Int modifier.

TABLE 2–11: THE FRENZIED BERSERKER

Level	Base Attack Bonus	Fort Save	Ref Save	Will Save	Special
1st	+1	+2	+0	+0	Frenzy 1/day, Diehard
2nd	+2	+3	+0	+0	Supreme cleave
3rd	+3	+3	+1	+1	Frenzy 2/day
4th	+4	+4	+1	+1	Deathless frenzy
5th	+5	+4	+1	+1	Frenzy 3/day, improved power attack
6th	+6	+5	+2	+2	Inspire frenzy 1/day
7th	+7	+5	+2	+2	Frenzy 4/day
8th	+8	+6	+2	+2	Greater frenzy, inspire frenzy 2/day
9th	+9	+6	+3	+3	Frenzy 5/day
10th	+10	+7	+3	+3	Inspire frenzy 3/day, tireless frenzy, supreme power attack

Class Features

All of the following are class features of the frenzied berserker prestige class.

Weapon and Armor Proficiency: Frenzied berserkers gain no proficiency with any weapon or armor.

Frenzy (Ex): A frenzied berserker can enter a frenzy during combat. While frenzied, she gains a +6 bonus to Strength and, if she makes a full attack action, gains a single extra attack each round at her highest bonus. (This latter effect is not cumulative with *haste* or other effects that grant additional attacks.) However, she also takes a –4 penalty to Armor Class and takes 2 points of nonlethal damage per round. A frenzy lasts for a number of rounds equal to 3 + the frenzied berserker's Constitution modifier. To end the frenzy before its duration expires, the character may attempt a DC 20 Will save once per round as a free action. Success ends the frenzy immediately; failure means it continues. The effects of frenzy stack with those from any rage ability the character may have.

At 1st level, the character can enter a frenzy once per day. Thereafter, she gains one additional use per day of this ability for every two frenzied berserker levels she acquires (but she can't use the ability more than once in any encounter). The character can enter a frenzy as a free action. Even though this takes no time, she can do it only during her turn, not in response to another's action. In addition, if she takes damage from an attack, spell, trap, or any other source, she automatically enters a frenzy at the start of her next action, as long as she still has at least one daily usage of the ability left. To avoid entering a frenzy in response to a provoking effect, the character must make a successful Will save (DC 10 + points of damage taken since her last action) at the start of her next turn.

While frenzied, the character cannot use any Charisma-, Dexterity-, or Intelligence-based skills (except for Intimidate), the Concentration skill, or any abilities that require patience or concentration, nor can she cast spells, drink potions, activate magic items, or read scrolls. She can use any feat she has except Combat Expertise, item creation feats, or metamagic feats. She can use her special ability to inspire frenzy (see below) normally.

During a frenzy, the frenzied berserker must attack those she perceives as foes to the best of her ability. Should she run out of enemies before her frenzy expires, her rampage continues. She must then attack the nearest creature (determine randomly if several potential foes are equidistant) and fight that opponent without regard to friendship, innocence, or health (the target's or her own).

When a frenzy ends, the frenzied berserker is fatigued (–2 penalty to Strength and Dexterity, unable to charge or run) for the duration of the encounter.

A frenzied berserker

If the character is still under the effect of a rage ability, the fatigued condition does not apply until the rage ends—at which point the character is exhausted, not merely fatigued.

Diehard: A frenzied berserker gains Diehard as a bonus feat even if she does not meet the prerequisites.

Supreme Cleave: At 2nd level and higher, a frenzied berserker can take a 5-foot step between attacks when using the Cleave or Great Cleave feat. She is still limited to one such adjustment per round, so she cannot use this ability during a round in which she has already taken a 5-foot step.

Deathless Frenzy (Ex): At 4th level and higher, a frenzied berserker can scorn death and unconsciousness while in a frenzy. As long as her frenzy continues, she is not treated as disabled at 0 hit points, nor is she treated as dying at –1 to –9 hit points. Even if reduced to –10 hit points or less, she continues to fight normally until her frenzy ends. At that point, the effects of her wounds apply normally if they have not been healed. This ability does not prevent death from massive damage or from spell effects such as *slay living* or *disintegrate*.

Improved Power Attack: Beginning at 5th level, a frenzied berserker gains a +3 bonus on her melee damage rolls for every –2 penalty she takes on her melee attack rolls when using the Power Attack feat (or +3 for every –1 penalty if wielding a two-handed weapon other than a double weapon). This benefit does not stack with the normal effects of Power Attack.

Inspire Frenzy (Su): Beginning at 6th level, a frenzied berserker can inspire frenzy in her allies while she herself is frenzied. When she uses this ability, all willing allies within 10 feet of her gain the benefits and the disadvantages of frenzy as if they had that ability themselves. The frenzy of affected allies lasts for a number of rounds equal to 3 + the frenzied berserker's Constitution modifier, regardless of whether they remain within 10 feet of her.

A frenzied berserker gains one additional use of this ability per day for every two additional frenzied berserker levels she acquires, though the ability is still usable only once per encounter.

Greater Frenzy (Ex): Starting at 8th level, the character's bonus to Strength during a frenzy becomes +10 instead of +6.

Supreme Power Attack: A 10th-level frenzied berserker gains a +2 bonus on her melee damage rolls for every −1 penalty she takes on her melee attack rolls when using the Power Attack feat (or +4 for every −1 penalty if wielding a two-handed weapon other than a double weapon). This benefit does not stack with the effects of Power Attack or Improved Power Attack.

Tireless Frenzy: A 10th-level frenzied berserker no longer becomes fatigued after a frenzy, though she still takes the nonlethal damage for each round it lasts.

Sample Frenzied Berserker

Shanna Furiesdottr: Human barbarian 6/frenzied berserker 8; CR 14; Medium humanoid; HD 6d12+12 plus 8d12+16; hp 119; Init +1; Spd 20 ft.; AC 21, touch 11, flat-footed 21; Base Atk +14; Grp +19; Atk +21 melee (2d6+9/19–20, +2 *greatsword*) or +16 ranged (1d6+5, masterwork javelin); Full Atk +21/+16/+11 melee (2d6+9/19–20, +2 *greatsword*) or +16 ranged (1d6+5, masterwork javelin); SQ frenzy 4/day, rage 2/day; AL CN; SV Fort +13, Ref +5, Will +5; Str 20, Dex 13, Con 14, Int 10, Wis 12, Cha 8.

Skills and Feats: Climb +12, Intimidate +16, Jump +14, Ride +18, Swim +10; Cleave, Diehard[B], Dodge, Destructive Rage, Improved Sunder, Intimidating Rage, Power Attack.

Frenzy (Ex): When frenzied, Shanna gains a +10 bonus to Strength, and she gains a single extra attack at a +21 bonus if she makes a full attack action. She takes a −4 penalty to Armor Class and takes 2 points of nonlethal damage every round. The frenzy lasts for 5 rounds, or 7 rounds if she is also raging. If she takes damage and still has uses of greater frenzy remaining that day, she goes into greater frenzy as a free action during her next turn unless she succeeds on a Will save (DC 10 + points of damage). While in a frenzy, she must attack foes, or a random creature if no foes remain. She isn't considered disabled if she has 0 hit points or incapacitated below −1 hit point. Even if she's below −9 hit points, she doesn't die until the frenzy is over.

Improved Power Attack: Shanna gains a +3 bonus on her melee damage rolls for every −1 penalty she takes on the attack roll when using the Power Attack feat.

Improved Uncanny Dodge (Ex): Shanna cannot by flanked except by a rogue of at least 10th level.

Inspire Frenzy (Su): While she is frenzied, all allies within 10 feet of Shanna gain the benefits and disadvantages of frenzy unless they succeed on a DC 17 Will save. Their

frenzy lasts for 6 rounds (or 8 rounds if the frenzied berserker is raging), even if they move away from the frenzied berserker.

Rage (Ex): +4 to Str, +4 to Con, +2 on Will saves, −2 to AC for up to 7 rounds.

Trap Sense (Ex): Against attacks by traps, Shanna gets a +2 bonus on Reflex saves and a +2 dodge bonus to Armor Class.

Uncanny Dodge (Ex): Shanna can react to danger before her senses would normally allow her to do so. She retains her Dexterity bonus to Armor Class even when caught flat-footed.

Possessions: +2 greatsword, +1 mithral full plate, gauntlets of ogre power +2, amulet of natural armor +1, 4 masterwork javelins.

GNOME GIANT-SLAYER

In every gnome community, only a select few individuals of extraordinary courage take up the mantle of giant-slayer. Relying on a combination of agility, combat prowess, and pure craftiness, the gnome giant-slayer is the bane of all creatures who use their size to terrorize the small or weak. The champion of those far-too-often trampled underfoot, the gnome giant-slayer stands far taller than his stature would suggest. As the ultimate believers that "The bigger they are, the harder they fall," these doughty battlers actively seek out ogres, trolls, giants, and the like to slay. Some also utilize their training to take on other immense opponents, such as umber hulks, monstrous vermin, and even dragons.

Most gnome giant-slayers are fighters or rangers, although some paladins and clerics also take up the path of giant slaying. Rogues who favor looting the dens of ogres and the like also become giant-slayers. Monks make excellent giant-slayers. Arcane spellcasters rarely take up this class, since it largely depends on toe-to-toe interaction with immensely powerful creatures.

Gnome giant-slayer NPCs are often lauded as heroes or celebrities within gnome communities. They might serve as captains of the guard, trainers, or in other positions of authority. Some pass down their mantle from generation to generation, granting the bravest son or daughter a treasured nickname such as "Trollbane" or "Giant-Crasher." Those who work for their own purposes might still enjoy some measure of popularity but prefer to remain aloof from political venues in favor of pursuing personal gain. Of course, many look to adventure to prove their mettle; rare indeed is the gnome giant-slayer who hasn't bearded his share of trolls or fire giants in their very lairs.

Hit Die: d10.

Requirements

To qualify to become a gnome giant-slayer, a character must fulfill all the following criteria.

Race: Gnome.

Base Attack Bonus: +5.

Skills: Escape Artist 3 ranks, Speak Language (Giant), Tumble 3 ranks.

Feats: Dodge, Mobility, Spring Attack.

Class Skills

The gnome giant-slayer's class skills (and the key abilities for each) are Climb (Str), Craft (Int), Escape Artist (Dex), Hide (Dex), Intimidate (Cha), Jump (Str), Move Silently (Dex), Tumble (Dex), and Use Rope (Dex).

Skill Points at Each Level: 2 + Int modifier.

Table 2–12: The Gnome Giant-Slayer

Level	Base Attack Bonus	Fort Save	Ref Save	Will Save	Special
1st	+1	+2	+0	+0	Favored enemy (giant) +2
2nd	+2	+3	+0	+0	Crafty fighter
3rd	+3	+3	+1	+1	Slippery
4th	+4	+4	+1	+1	Favored enemy (giant) +4
5th	+5	+4	+1	+1	Close shot
6th	+6	+5	+2	+2	Fast movement
7th	+7	+5	+2	+2	Favored enemy (giant) +6
8th	+8	+6	+2	+2	Improved mobility
9th	+9	+6	+3	+3	Annoying strike
10th	+10	+7	+3	+3	Favored enemy (giant) +8, defensive roll

Class Features

All of the following are class features of the gnome giant-slayer prestige class.

Weapon and Armor Proficiency: Gnome giant-slayers have proficiency with all simple and martial weapons, with light and medium armor, and with shields.

Favored Enemy (Giant) (Ex): A gnome giant-slayer gains a +2 bonus on Bluff, Listen, Sense Motive, Spot, and Survival checks when using these skills against giants. He gets the same bonus on weapon damage rolls against giants. This benefit stacks with the ranger favored enemy class feature if giant is the ranger's favored enemy. This bonus increases by an extra +2 for every three gnome giant-slayer levels beyond 1st.

Crafty Fighter (Ex): At 2nd level, a gnome giant-slayer gains a +4 dodge bonus to his Armor Class against giants, or a +2 dodge bonus against any other (nongiant) creature at least two size categories larger than himself. This benefit is lost in any situation in which the gnome giant-slayer would lose his Dexterity bonus to Armor Class. He also loses this bonus in heavy armor.

Slippery (Ex): If a gnome giant-slayer of 3rd level or higher is grappled by a creature at least two size categories larger than himself, he can add his gnome giant-slayer level as a bonus on any checks (whether grapple checks or Escape Artist checks) made to escape grappling.

In addition, a gnome giant-slayer can move through an area occupied by a creature two size categories larger than he is. This doesn't apply against creatures that completely fill their area, such as a gelatinous cube. (Normally, a character can only move through an area occupied by another creature if it is at least three size categories larger than the character.)

Close Shot (Ex): At 5th level and higher, a gnome giant-slayer does not provoke attacks of opportunity from giants for using a ranged weapon while threatened by them.

Fast Movement (Ex): At 6th level, a gnome giant-slayer's base land speed increases by 10 feet. This benefit applies only when he is wearing no armor, light armor, or medium armor and not carrying a heavy load. Apply this bonus before modifying the giant-slayer's speed because of any load carried or armor worn.

Improved Mobility (Ex): At 8th level and higher, a gnome giant-slayer gains a +4 dodge bonus to his Armor Class when moving out of or within a giant's threatened area. As with all

A gnome giant-slayer toys with a hill giant before finishing her off.

dodge bonuses, this benefit stacks with the bonus granted by the Mobility feat.

Annoying Strike (Ex): Whenever a gnome giant-slayer of 9th level or higher damages a giant in melee, that giant is shaken for 1 round.

Defensive Roll (Ex): A 10th-level gnome giant-slayer can roll with a potentially lethal blow to take less damage from it than he otherwise would. Once per day, when he would be reduced to 0 or fewer hit points by damage in combat (from a weapon or other blow struck by a giant, not a spell or special ability), he can attempt to roll with the damage. To use this ability, he makes a Reflex saving throw (DC = damage dealt; the gnome giant-slayer adds his class level as a bonus on this saving throw). If the save succeeds, he takes only half damage from the blow; if it fails, he takes full damage. He must be aware of the attack and able to react to it in order to execute his defensive roll—if he is denied his Dexterity bonus to AC, he can't use this ability. Since this effect would not normally allow a character to make a Reflex save for half damage, the character's evasion or improved evasion ability (if applicable) does not apply to the defensive roll.

Sample Gnome Giant-Slayer

Seebo Schorrek: Gnome rogue 4/ranger 2/gnome giant-slayer 5; CR 11; Small humanoid; HD 4d6+8 plus 2d10+4 plus 5d10+10; hp 75; Init +4; Spd 20 ft.; AC 23, touch 16, flat-footed 23; Base Atk +10; Grp +8; Atk +14 melee (1d10+4/19–20, +1 *Small greatsword*) or +17 ranged (1d3+3, +1 *returning dart*); Full Atk +14/+9 melee (1d10+4/19–20, +1 *Small greatsword*) or +17 ranged (1d3+3, +1 *returning dart*) and +12 ranged (1d3+2, masterwork dart); or +15 ranged (1d3+3, +1 *returning dart*) and +15/+10 ranged (1d3+2, masterwork dart); SA sneak attack +2d6; SQ close shot, crafty fighter, evasion, favored enemy giants +6, gnome traits, low-light vision, slippery, spell-like abilities, trap sense +1, trapfinding, uncanny dodge; AL NG; SV Fort +10, Ref +12, Will +3; Str 14, Dex 18, Con 14, Int 8, Wis 12, Cha 10.

Skills and Feats: Craft (alchemy) +1, Escape Artist +10, Hide +16, Listen +12, Move Silently +12, Search +8, Spot +10, Tumble +15; Dodge, Mobility, Quick Draw, Rapid Shot, Spring Attack, Track[B].

Close Shot (Ex): Seebo does not provoke attacks of opportunity from a giant for using a ranged weapon in a space the giant threatens.

Combat Style (Ex): Seebo has selected archery. He gains the Rapid Shot feat without having to meet the normal prerequisites.

Crafty Fighter (Ex): Seebo has a +4 dodge bonus to his Armor Class against giants.

Evasion (Ex): If Seebo is exposed to any effect that normally allows him to attempt a Reflex saving throw for half damage, he takes no damage with a successful saving throw.

Favored Enemy (Ex): Seebo gains a +6 bonus on his Bluff, Listen, Sense Motive, Spot, and Survival checks when using

these skills against giants. He gets the same bonus on weapon damage rolls against giants.

Gnome Traits (Ex): +1 save DC for illusions, +2 bonus on saves against illusions, +1 bonus on attack rolls against kobolds and goblinoids, +4 dodge bonus to AC against giants, +2 bonus on Listen checks and Craft (alchemy) checks.

Low-Light Vision (Ex): Seebo can see twice as far as a human in starlight, moonlight, torchlight, and similar conditions of poor visibility. He retains the ability to distinguish color and detail under these conditions.

Slippery (Ex): Seebo can move through the space of a creature of at least Large size. He also gains a +5 bonus on grapple checks and Escape Artist checks when grappled by a foe of at least Large size.

Spell-Like Abilities: 1/day—*dancing lights, ghost sound, prestidigitation, speak with animals* (burrowing animal only). Caster level 1st; save DC 10 + spell level.

Trap Sense (Ex): Against attacks by traps, Seebo gets a +1 bonus on Reflex saves and a +1 dodge bonus to Armor Class.

Trapfinding (Ex): Seebo can use a Search check to locate a trap when the task has a DC higher than 20.

Uncanny Dodge (Ex): Seebo can react to danger before his senses would normally allow him to do so. He retains his Dexterity bonus to Armor Class even when caught flat-footed.

Possessions: +1 *returning dart*, +1 *Small greatsword*, +2 *Small chain shirt*, *gloves of Dexterity* +2, *ring of protection* +1, Small masterwork buckler, 5 masterwork darts.

HALFLING OUTRIDER

The seminomadic culture of the halfling race often results in sudden encounters with peril. To safeguard themselves, many halfling communities turn to their outriders, elite champions whose task it is to warn their fellows of, and protect them from, danger. The halfling outrider is naturally skilled in the arts of riding and scouting.

Most halfling outriders are fighters, rangers, druids, or rogues. All classes, however, can benefit from the Armor Class bonus and defensive riding capabilities of the class.

NPC halfling outriders are usually found performing their duties in the field, or relaxing in their off-duty hours. The presence of an outrider whether afield or at rest usually indicates that a halfling community cannot be far away.

However, some outriders feel the pull of adventure more strongly. These individuals leave behind their hearths and homes for a life of excitement on the road.

Hit Die: d8.

Requirements

To qualify to become a halfling outrider, a character must fulfill all the following criteria.

Race: Halfling.

Base Attack Bonus: +5.

Skills: Listen: 3 ranks, Ride 6 ranks, Spot 3 ranks.

Feats: Mounted Combat, Mounted Archery.

Class Skills

The halfling outrider's class skills (and the key ability for each skill) are Handle Animal (Cha), Listen (Wis), Ride (Dex), Spot (Wis), and Survival (Wis).

Skill Points at Each Level: 4 + Int modifier.

TABLE 2–13: THE HALFLING OUTRIDER

Level	Base Attack Bonus	AC Bonus	Fort Save	Ref Save	Will Save	Special
1st	+1	+1	+0	+2	+0	Mount, Alertness, Ride bonus
2nd	+2	+1	+0	+3	+0	Defensive riding
3rd	+3	+2	+1	+3	+1	Unbroken charge
4th	+4	+2	+1	+4	+1	Stand on mount
5th	+5	+3	+1	+4	+1	Leap from the saddle
6th	+6	+3	+2	+5	+2	—
7th	+7	+4	+2	+5	+2	Evasion
8th	+8	+4	+2	+6	+2	Full mounted attack
9th	+9	+5	+3	+6	+3	—
10th	+10	+5	+3	+7	+3	Quick turn

Class Features

All of the following are class features of the halfling outrider prestige class.

Weapon and Armor Proficiency: Halfling outriders gain no proficiency with any weapon or armor.

AC Bonus: A halfling outrider gains a dodge bonus to the character's Armor Class when she is mounted. This benefit is lost in any situation in which the character would lose her Dexterity bonus to Armor Class.

Mount: A halfling outrider gains a mount appropriate to the resources of her halfling community. Most halfling communities attempt to provide an outrider with a riding dog or a warpony. A halfling outrider may, of course, choose to find and train or purchase a more exotic mount. Standard tack and harness is also provided, though, again, the character may wish to purchase masterwork or magic gear.

Halfling outrider class levels stack with paladin, druid, and ranger levels for determining the characteristics of a paladin's mount or an animal companion.

Alertness: A halfling outrider gains Alertness as a bonus feat.

Ride Bonus: A halfling outrider gains a competence bonus equal to her class level on all Ride checks.

Defensive Riding (Ex): A halfling outrider of 2nd level or higher knows the tricks of defensive riding. If she does nothing else while mounted (she cannot attack when riding defensively), she gains a +2 bonus on Reflex saves and a +4 dodge bonus to Armor Class. In addition, her mount gains a +20 ft. bonus to its speed, a +2 bonus on all Will saves, and a +4 dodge bonus to its Armor Class.

Unbroken Charge (Ex): At 3rd level and higher, a mounted halfling outrider can charge through difficult terrain or squares occupied by friendly creatures by making a DC 15 Ride check.

Stand on Mount (Ex): At 4th level, a mounted halfling outrider becomes able to stand on her mount's back even during movement or combat, taking no penalties to actions while doing so, by making a DC 20 Ride check. While standing on her mount's back, a halfling outrider does not take any penalty for using a ranged weapon while her mount is taking a double move or running (see the Mounted Archery feat description, page 98 of the *Player's Handbook*).

Leap from the Saddle (Ex): A halfling outrider of 5th level or higher can dismount and land adjacent to her mount as a free action by making a DC 20 Ride check. If an opponent is in a square she threatens (after dismounting), she can make a melee attack against that opponent, taking a +2 bonus on the attack roll and a –2 penalty to Armor Class (just as if the character were making a charge). This ability is usable only if the mount is moving no faster than twice its speed.

Evasion (Ex): At 7th level, a halfling outrider gains the evasion ability. If she makes a successful Reflex saving throw against an attack that normally deals half damage on a successful save, she instead takes no damage. Evasion can be used only if the halfling outrider is wearing light armor or no armor. A helpless halfling outrider (such as one who is unconscious or paralyzed) does not gain the benefit of the ability.

While the halfling outrider is mounted, she confers this ability to her mount as well, and the mount is able to use the halfling outrider's Reflex save bonus or its own, whichever is higher.

If the character already has the evasion ability, she gains improved evasion instead, and her mount still receives the benefit of evasion as described above. Improved evasion works like evasion, except that while the character still takes no damage on a successful Reflex saving throw, she takes only half damage on a failed save.

Full Mounted Attack (Ex): At 8th level and higher, a halfling outrider may make a full attack when her mount moves more than 5 feet but no more than a single move action. The character cannot combine this full attack with a charge action.

Quick Turn (Ex): A 10th-level halfling outrider can make a DC 25 Ride check as a free action to force her mount to execute one change of direction during while running or charging (though the mount must still move at least 10 feet in a straight line after the turn to execute a charge). The turn may be up to 90 degrees, and the mount may make only one such turn per round. If the Ride check fails, the mount moves an extra 10 feet in a straight line and then loses the rest of its actions on this turn.

Sample Halfling Outrider

Altesia Coopersmith: Halfling ranger 5/halfling outrider 5; CR 10; Small humanoid; HD 5d8+10 plus 5d8+10; hp 56; Init +4; Spd 20 ft., 40 ft. when mounted; AC 22 (25 when mounted), touch 15, flat-footed 18; Base Atk +10; Grp +7; Atk +13 melee (1d6+2/×3, +1 lance) or +16 ranged (1d6+2/×3, +1

A halfling outrider

Combat Style (Ex): Altesia has selected archery. She gains the Rapid Shot feat without having to meet the normal prerequisites.

Defensive Riding (Ex): When doing nothing other than riding her boar, Altesia gains a +2 bonus on Reflex saves and a +4 dodge bonus to AC. The boar gains a +20-foot bonus to speed, a +2 bonus on Will saves, and a +4 dodge bonus to AC.

Favored Enemy (Ex): Altesia gains a +4 bonus on her Bluff, Listen, Sense Motive, Spot, and Survival checks when using these skills against magical beasts. She gets the same bonus on weapon damage rolls against magical beasts.

Against goblinoids, she gains a +2 bonus on these skill checks and on weapon damage rolls.

Halfling Traits (Ex): +2 morale bonus on saves against fear; +1 bonus on attack rolls with thrown weapons and slings.

Stand on Mount (Ex): Altesia can stand on her mount's back even during movement or combat, taking no penalties to actions while doing so, by making a DC 20 Ride check. While standing on her mount's back, Altesia does not take any penalty for using a ranged weapon while her mount is taking a double move or running.

Unbroken Charge (Ex): When mounted, Altesia can charge through difficult terrain or squares occupied by friendly creatures by making a DC 15 Ride check.

Wild Empathy (Ex): Altesia can improve the attitude of an animal in the same way a Diplomacy check can improve the attitude of a sentient being. She rolls 1d20+5, or 1d20+1 if attempting to influence a magical beast with an Intelligence score of 1 or 2.

composite longbow); Full Atk +13/+8 melee (1d6+2/×3, +1 lance) or +16/+11 ranged (1d6+2/×3, +1 composite longbow) or +14/+14/+9 ranged (1d6+2/×3, +1 composite longbow); SA leap from the saddle; SQ animal companion, combat style, defensive riding 2/day, favored enemy magical beasts +4, favored enemy goblinoids +2, halfling traits, stand on mount, unbroken charge, wild empathy; AL LG; SV Fort +10, Ref +15, Will +6; Str 12, Dex 18, Con 14, Int 8, Wis 12, Cha 10.

Skills and Feats: Climb +3, Hide +8, Jump –3, Listen +18, Move Silently +6, Ride +22, Search +7, Spot +16, Survival +9; Alertness[B], Endurance, Mounted Combat, Mounted Archery, Point Blank Shot, Rapid Shot, Ride-By Attack, Track[B].

Leap from the Saddle (Ex): If Altesia's mount is moving no faster than twice its speed, she can dismount as a free action with a DC 20 Ride check, then make a melee attack against a foe she threatens. She takes a +2 bonus on the attack roll and a –2 penalty to Armor Class (just as if she were making a charge).

Animal Companion (Ex): Altesia has a boar as an animal companion. Its statistics are as described on page 270 of the *Monster Manual*, except that Altesia can handle it as a free action (see page 36 of the *Player's Handbook*).

Possessions: +1 Small mithral breastplate, +1 Small composite longbow (+1 Str bonus), +1 Small lance, cloak of resistance +2, amulet of natural armor +1, Small masterwork greatsword.

HULKING HURLER

Usually brutish and always incredibly strong, hulking hurlers belong to those races of generously proportioned creatures who enjoy nothing more than wrenching boulders, trees, or even buildings free of their earthly bonds and throwing them at their foes. No one knows how this loose organization came into being, but there is no doubt that hulking hurlers make fearsome enemies.

Hulking hurlers usually come from the giant races, though a few members of other species learn the unusually focused skills of the organization. Those few hulking hurlers who advance in other classes first almost always come from fighter or barbarian backgrounds. NPC hulking hurlers sometimes serve as specialists in giant warbands, but they can also be found among smaller humanoids, serving the function of a sort of artillery unit.

Hit Die: d10.

TABLE 2–14: THE HULKING HURLER

Level	Base Attack Bonus	Fort Save	Ref Save	Will Save	Special
1st	+1	+0	+2	+0	Catch weapon, really throw anything
2nd	+2	+0	+3	+0	Two-handed hurl trick
3rd	+3	+1	+3	+1	Two-handed hurl trick

Requirements

To qualify to become a hulking hurler, a character must fulfill all the following criteria.

Base Attack Bonus: +5.

Feats: Point Blank Shot, Power Attack, Weapon Focus (any thrown weapon).

Special: Large size or larger.

Class Skills

The hulking hurler's class skills (and the key ability for each skill) are Climb (Str), Intimidate (Cha), Jump (Str), and Swim (Str).

Skill Points at Each Level: 2 + Int modifier.

Class Features

All the following are class features of the hulking hurler.

Weapon and Armor Proficiency: Hulking hurlers gain no proficiency with any weapon or armor.

Catch Weapon (Ex): A hulking hurler gains the Snatch Arrows feat even if he does not meet the prerequisites. He may catch weapons of his size or smaller (and hurl them back at the attacker immediately if he chooses).

Really Throw Anything (Ex): A hulking hurler gains the Throw Anything feat (described in Chapter 3 of this book) as a bonus feat. However, since a hulking hurler depends on brute strength more than skill, he can throw anything (not just weapons) he can lift as a light load. If the item is an improvised weapon, he takes a –2 penalty on his attack roll instead of the normal –4. Use the rules in Chapter 4 of this book to determine the amount of damage the thrown weapon does.

The range increment of a thrown weapon or improvised weapon wielded by a hulking hurler is 10 feet + 5 feet per size category the hulking hurler is beyond Large (this is a modification of the Throw Anything feat).

Two-Handed Hurl Trick (Ex): At 2nd level and again at 3rd level, a hulking hurler chooses one of the following tricks. In order to use any of these abilities, the hulking hurler must grip the weapon or improvised weapon in two hands and throw it as a full-round action.

Area Attack: The character makes an attack roll against a square the target creature occupies (AC 10) rather than the creature itself. Any creature in the square must succeed on a Reflex save (DC 10 + the hulking hurler's ranged attack bonus) or take full damage. This ability may only be used with a Huge or larger weapon.

Knockdown Blow: If the hulking hurler's attack hits and does damage to any creature of Medium or smaller size, the target is rendered prone.

Meteor Strike: As a full-round action, a hulking hurler deals extra damage equal to twice his Strength bonus on a successful hit with a thrown weapon.

Overburdened Heave: The hulking hurler can throw a weapon up to two sizes larger than his size category, or an item that weighs as much as his medium load (so a Large hulking hurler with a Strength score of 25 could heave a Gargantuan javelin or a rock weighing up to 533 pounds).

Ranged Power Attack: If the target is within 30 feet, the hulking hurler can use Power Attack with his thrown weapon.

Sample Hulking Hurler

Wellsy: Stone giant hulking hurler 3; CR 11; Large giant; HD 14d8+72 plus 3d10+18; hp 170; Init +3; Spd 30 ft.; AC 24, touch 12, flat-footed 21; Base Atk +13; Grp +25; Atk +20 melee (2d8+13, +1 *Large greatclub*) or +14 ranged (2d8+16, rock); Full

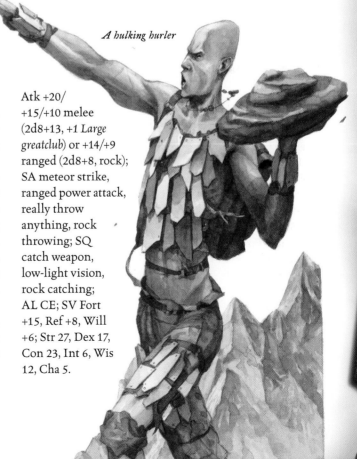

A hulking hurler

Atk +20/ +15/+10 melee (2d8+13, +1 *Large greatclub*) or +14/+9 ranged (2d8+8, rock); SA meteor strike, ranged power attack, really throw anything, rock throwing; SQ catch weapon, low-light vision, rock catching; AL CE; SV Fort +15, Ref +8, Will +6; Str 27, Dex 17, Con 23, Int 6, Wis 12, Cha 5.

Skills and Feats: Climb +9, Intimidate +0, Jump +8, Listen +4, Spot +7; Cleave, Improved Sunder, Point Blank Shot, Power Attack, Quick Draw, Snatch Arrows, Throw Anything, Weapon Focus (rock).

Meteor Strike (Ex): As a full-round action, Wellsy can add twice his Strength bonus on damage rolls when using a thrown weapon.

Ranged Power Attack (Ex): Wellsy can use the Power Attack feat with a thrown weapon if the target is within 30 feet.

Really Throw Anything (Ex): Wellsy can throw anything—weapon or not—weighing 692 pounds or less with a range increment of 10 feet. He takes only a –2 penalty on his attack roll if the thrown object is an improvised weapon.

Rock Throwing (Ex): Range increment 180 feet.

Catch Weapon (Ex): Wellsy can use the Snatch Arrows feat with any thrown weapon or projectile of Large size or smaller.

Low-Light Vision (Ex): Wellsy can see twice as far as a human in starlight, moonlight, torchlight, and similar conditions of poor visibility. He retains the ability to distinguish color and detail under these conditions.

Rock Catching (Ex): Wellsy can catch Small, Medium, or Large rocks (or projectiles of similar shape). Once per round, if he would normally be hit by a rock, he can make a Reflex save to catch it as a free action. The DC is 15 for a Small rock, 20 for a Medium one, and 25 for a Large one. (If the projectile provides a magical bonus on attack rolls, the DC increases by that amount.) Wellsy must be ready for and aware of the attack in order to make a rock catching attempt.

Possessions: Large +1 greatclub, 5 throwing rocks, 6 other items in his bag (see page 120 of the *Monster Manual*).

HUNTER OF THE DEAD

The hunter of the dead is the hated enemy of all undead. She spends each restless night tracking undead to their lairs and cleansing the land of their foul presence.

The hunter of the dead has many tools with which to fight such creatures. Her skill with arms is the match of any fighter's, but, to aid her in the hunt, she also possesses spells and special abilities that draw upon her connection with positive energy. Most hunters of the dead are clerics or paladins. Fighters, rangers, monks, druids, and barbarians also make excellent hunters of the dead, while rogues and bards add their subterfuge skills to create a foe that the undead never see coming. Sorcerers and wizards—especially those with a few levels of cleric or paladin—have many advantages when fighting undead, so they should never be discounted as potential hunters of the dead.

As NPCs, hunters of the dead are quiet loners, driven to think of little but their cause. They usually have some traumatic tale about what brought them to hate the undead, but few are willing to share it with those they meet as they wander from town to town. In places where spirits are particularly restless and the dead walk in numbers, hunters of the dead gather in secretive orders such as the House of Death to pool their strength and attack their foes together.

Hit Die: d8.

Requirements

To qualify to become a hunter of the dead, a character must fulfill all the following criteria.

Alignment: Any nonevil.

Base Attack Bonus: +5.

Skills: Knowledge (religion) 5 ranks.

Special: Able to turn undead.

Special: *Scar of Unlife:* The character must have lost one level or had an ability score point drained by an undead creature. Even if the loss is later offset by magic, this is the scar of unlife that all hunters of the dead carry.

Class Skills

The hunter of the dead's class skills (and the key ability for each skill) are Concentration (Con), Heal (Wis), Knowledge (religion) (Int), Profession (Wis), Ride (Dex), and Search (Int).

Skill Points at Each Level: 2 + Int modifier.

Class Features

All of the following are class features of the hunter of the dead prestige class.

Weapon and Armor Proficiency: Hunters of the dead gain no proficiency with any weapon or armor.

Spells: Beginning at 1st level, a hunter of the dead gains the ability to cast a number of divine spells. To cast a spell, a hunter of the dead must have a Wisdom score of at least 10 + the spell's level, so a hunter of the dead with a Wisdom of 10 or lower cannot cast these spells. Hunter of the dead bonus spells are based on Wisdom, and saving throws against these spells have a DC of 10 + spell level + the hunter of the dead's Wisdom bonus (if any). When the hunter of the dead gets 0 spells per day of a given spell level (for instance, 1st-level spells for a 1st-level hunter of the dead), she gains only the bonus spells she would be entitled to based on her Wisdom score for that spell level.

The hunter of the dead's spell list appears below; she has access to any spell on the list and can freely choose which to prepare. A hunter of the dead prepares and casts spells just as a cleric does (though a hunter of the dead cannot lose a spell to cast a *cure* spell in its place).

Detect Undead (Sp): At will, a hunter of the dead can use *detect undead* as if casting the spell of the same name.

Smite Undead (Su): Once per day, a hunter of the dead of 2nd level or higher can attempt to smite undead with one normal melee attack. She adds her Wisdom modifier (if positive) to her attack roll and deals 1 extra point of damage per level. For example, an 8th-level hunter of the dead armed with a longsword would deal 1d8+8 points of damage, plus any additional bonuses for Strength and magical effects that normally apply. If a hunter of the dead accidentally smites a creature that is not undead, the smite has no effect but it is still used up for that day. Note: A paladin/hunter of the dead can both smite evil and smite undead in the same day, potentially against the same target (if it's an evil undead).

Spurn Death's Touch (Ex): A hunter of the dead of 3rd level or higher applies her Wisdom modifier (if positive) as an additional bonus on all saving throws against effects and spells used by undead. This bonus stacks with the Wisdom modifier already applied to Will saves.

True Death (Su): Undead slain by a hunter of the dead of 5th level or higher, either by melee attacks or spells, can never rise again as undead. They are forever destroyed.

Extra Turning: At 6th level, a hunter of the dead receives Extra Turning as a bonus feat. This benefit allows the hunter to turn undead four more times per day than normal. It stacks with any turning ability the character has from another class.

Positive Energy Burst (Su): At the cost of two normal turning attempts, a hunter of the dead of at least 8th level can use a standard action to create a positive energy burst that deals 1d6 points of damage per class level to all undead creatures within 20 feet. Undead are allowed a Reflex save (DC 10 + the hunter's class level + the hunter's Cha modifier) for half damage.

A hunter of the dead

Sealed Life (Su): A 10th-level hunter of the dead cannot lose levels due to energy drain effects (although death still results in level loss, as do other level- or experience-draining effects).

Hunter of the Dead Spell List

Hunters of the dead choose their spells from the following list:

1st Level: *magic stone, magic weapon, cure light wounds, hide from undead, remove fear.*

2nd Level: *bull's strength, cure moderate wounds, continual flame, darkvision, lesser restoration, remove paralysis.*

3rd Level: *cure serious wounds, daylight, halt undead, protection from elements, searing light, speak with dead.*

4th Level: *cure critical wounds, death ward, disrupting weapon, freedom of movement, restoration.*

Sample Hunter of the Dead

Torga ("She Who Came Back") Ungart: Human paladin 5/ hunter of the dead 8; CR 13; Medium humanoid; HD 5d10+10 plus 8d8+16; hp 90; Init +0; Spd 20 ft.; AC 22, touch 10, flatfooted 22; Base Atk +13; Grp +18; Atk +21 melee (1d8+7, +2 *ghost touch heavy mace*) or +14 ranged (1d8+5/×3, masterwork composite longbow [+5 Str bonus]); Full Atk +21/+16/+11 melee (1d8+7, +2 *ghost touch heavy mace*) or +14/

TABLE 2–15: THE HUNTER OF THE DEAD

Level	Base Attack Bonus	Fort Save	Ref Save	Will Save	Special	Spells per Day			
						1st	2nd	3rd	4th
1st	+1	+2	+0	+0	*Detect undead*	0	—	—	—
2nd	+2	+3	+0	+0	Smite undead 1/day	1	—	—	—
3rd	+3	+3	+1	+1	Spurn death's touch	1	0	—	—
4th	+4	+4	+1	+1	—	1	1	—	—
5th	+5	+4	+1	+1	True death	1	1	0	—
6th	+6	+5	+2	+2	Extra Turning, Smite undead 2/day	1	1	1	—
7th	+7	+5	+2	+2	—	2	1	1	0
8th	+8	+6	+2	+2	Positive energy burst	2	1	1	1
9th	+9	+6	+3	+3	—	2	2	1	1
10th	+10	+7	+3	+3	Sealed life, Smite undead 3/day	2	2	2	1

+9/+4 ranged (1d8+5/×3, masterwork composite longbow [+5 Str bonus]); SA positive energy burst, smite evil 2/day, smite undead 1/day, turn undead 9/day; SQ aura of courage, aura of good, *detect evil, detect undead*, divine grace, divine health, lay on hands, special mount, spurn death's touch, true death; AL LG; SV Fort +14, Ref +7, Will +9; Str 20, Dex 10, Con 14, Int 8, Wis 15, Cha 14.

Skills and Feats: Jump +0, Knowledge (religion) +4, Ride +11; Divine Vengeance*, Extra Turning[B], Iron Will, Lightning Reflexes, Power Attack, Weapon Focus (mace).

*New feat described in Chapter 3 of this book.

Positive Energy Burst (Su): By expending two turning attempts as a standard action, Torga can deal 8d6 points of damage to all undead within 100 feet (Reflex DC 18 half).

Smite Evil (Su): Torga may attempt to smite evil with one normal melee attack. She adds +2 to her attack roll and deals 5 extra points of damage. Smiting a creature that is not evil has no effect but counts as a use of the ability for that day.

Smite Undead (Su): As smite evil, but it functions against undead and provides a +2 bonus on the attack roll, and a +8 bonus on the damage roll. Torga can use smite evil and smite undead in a single attack (against an evil undead creature) if she wishes.

Turn Undead (Su): Torga turns undead as a 2nd-level cleric.

Aura of Courage (Su): Torga is immune to fear (magical or otherwise). Allies within 10 feet of her gain a +4 morale bonus on saving throws against fear effects.

Aura of Good (Ex): Torga's aura of good (see the *detect good* spell) is equal to that of a 5th-level cleric.

Detect Evil **(Sp):** At will, as the spell of the same name.

Detect Undead **(Sp):** At will, as the spell of the same name.

Divine Grace (Su): Torga gains a +2 bonus on saving throws (already figured into the above statistics).

Divine Health (Ex): Torga is immune to all diseases, including magical diseases such as mummy rot and lycanthropy.

Lay on Hands (Su): Torga can cure 10 hit points of wounds per day.

Special Mount **(Sp):** Torga's special mount is a heavy warhorse (see page 45 of the *Player's Handbook*) that has +2 Hit Dice, a +4 bonus to natural armor, +1 Strength, and improved evasion. Torga has an empathic link with the mount and can share spells and saving throws with it. She can call her mount once per day for up to 10 hours as a full-round action.

Spurn Death's Touch (Ex): Torga gains a +2 bonus on saves against spells and effects from undead.

True Death (Su): Undead slain by Torga in melee or with spells can never again rise as undead.

Hunter of the Dead Spells Prepared (3/2/1/1; save DC 12 + spell level): 1st—*cure light wounds, hide from undead, magic weapon;* 2nd—*cure moderate wounds, lesser restoration;* 3rd—*daylight;* 4th—*death ward.*

Paladin Spells Prepared (1; save DC 12 + spell level): 1st—*bless weapon.*

Possessions: +2 *ghost touch heavy mace,* +1 *full plate,* +1 *heavy steel shield, periapt of Wisdom* +2, *cloak of Charisma* +2, *gauntlets of ogre power* +2, masterwork composite longbow (+5 Str bonus), 20 arrows.

INVISIBLE BLADE

Who is this fool who dares to challenge you in the arena? You brandish a greatsword, and he whips out a dagger. You unsheathe your longsword, and he throws off his armor. You advance menacingly, and he only smiles at you—a big, maniacal grin. Is he mad? Does he have a death wish? No, he is an invisible blade, and you have made the classic mistake of underestimating his prowess. As you fight, he seems almost relaxed, stepping lightly to the side, dodging your blows easily. His eyes note your every move, as though taking mental notes about your style. Then, in the split second when you lower your guard, he exploits your error, plunging his weapon into your heart.

Invisible blades are deadly fighters who prefer to use daggers and related weapons in combat. Their training and techniques with these weapons make them just as lethal as any well-armed fighter. Invisible blades enjoy cultivating misconceptions about the level of danger they present, and they relish any chance to demonstrate that the most unimposing weapons can be the most lethal. Thus, invisible blades are rarely impressed by how mighty their opponents appear.

An invisible blade specializes in fighting with the dagger, kukri, or punching dagger. He is not penalized for using other weapons with which he is proficient, but every class ability he possesses is tied into using one of these three weapons.

An invisible blade takes on a minotaur with his trusty pair of daggers.

The typical invisible blade was once a rogue, who chose this path because his sneak attack ability dovetailed nicely with the abilities of this prestige class. Bards and monks are also good candidates, as are barbarians, fighters, and rangers who are willing to exchange their arsenals of weapons for a less cumbersome approach. Clerics and druids seldom choose this class, perceiving its members as faithless, while paladins ironically view invisible blades as too self-absorbed. Sorcerers and wizards rarely become invisible blades because they don't appreciate the class's lack of offensive options and tight focus on weapon use.

NPC invisible blades are silently egotistical gladiators who regard their fighting style as superior to all other martial philosophies. They place enormous emphasis on making a single decisive strike, thereby hoping to end a bout in a single round. Most invisible blades pick up their skills in a guild. A few, however, learn from seasoned professionals who expect a potential gladiator to practice fanatically with the dagger until he can pass the required rite-of-passage combat (see Requirements, below).

Hit Die: d6.

Requirements

To qualify to become an invisible blade, a character must fulfill all the following criteria.

Skills: Bluff 8 ranks, Sense Motive 6 ranks.

Feats: Far Shot, Point Blank Shot, Weapon Focus (dagger, kukri, or punching dagger).

Special: The candidate must defeat a worthy opponent in single combat using one or more daggers, kukris, or punching daggers in any combination as his only weapons.

TABLE 2–16: THE INVISIBLE BLADE

Level	Base Attack Bonus	Fort Save	Ref Save	Will Save	Special
1st	+1	+0	+2	+0	Dagger sneak attack +1d6, unfettered defense
2nd	+2	+0	+3	+0	Bleeding wound
3rd	+3	+1	+3	+1	Dagger sneak attack +2d6, uncanny feint (move action)
4th	+4	+1	+4	+1	Feint mastery
5th	+5	+1	+4	+1	Dagger sneak attack +3d6, uncanny feint (free action)

Class Skills

The invisible blade's class skills (and the key ability for each skill) are Balance (Dex), Bluff (Cha), Climb (Str), Craft (Int), Escape Artist (Dex), Jump (Str), Hide (Dex), Innuendo (Cha), Listen (Wis), Move Silently (Dex), Perform (Cha), Profession (Wis), Sense Motive (Wis), Spot (Wis), and Tumble (Dex).

Skill Points at Each Level: 4 + Int modifier.

Class Features

All of the following are class features of the invisible blade prestige class.

Weapon and Armor Proficiency: Invisible blades gain no proficiency with any weapon or armor.

Dagger Sneak Attack (Ex): An invisible blade gains the sneak attack ability (see the description of the dark hunter, earlier in this chapter) if he does not already have it, but the extra damage applies only to sneak attacks made with a dagger, kukri, or punching dagger (the DM may allow other similar weapons). When making a sneak attack with one of these weapons, he deals an extra 1d6 points of damage at 1st level, and this increases to 2d6 at 3rd level and to 3d6 at 5th level. If he already has the sneak attack ability from a previous class, the applicable bonuses on damage rolls stack.

Unfettered Defense (Ex): An invisible blade benefits from an increased survival instinct during combat. Because of this sixth sense, he adds 1 point of Intelligence bonus (if any) per invisible blade class level to his Armor Class in addition to any other modifiers he would normally receive. If the invisible blade is caught flat-footed or is otherwise denied his Dexterity modifier to Armor Class, he also loses this bonus. Unfettered defense functions only when an invisible blade is not wearing armor and is armed with one or more daggers, kukris, or punching daggers as his only weapons.

Bleeding Wound (Ex): An invisible blade of 2nd level or higher who makes a successful dagger sneak attack can choose to deal a bleeding wound, sacrificing 1d6 points of the extra damage from the dagger sneak attack. Such an attack deals damage as normal in the round when the attack hits. Thereafter, the wound caused by the invisible blade's dagger bleeds for 1 point of damage per round. Multiple wounds from the weapon result in cumulative bleeding loss (two wounds for 2 points of damage per round, and so on). The bleeding can only be stopped by a DC 15 Heal check or the application of any *cure* spell or other healing spell (*heal*, *healing circle*, and so on). Creatures immune to sneak attack damage are immune to bleeding wounds as well.

Uncanny Feint (Ex): At 3rd level, an invisible blade gains the ability to feint in combat (see page 68 of the *Player's Handbook*) as a move action rather than a standard action. At 5th level, the character can feint in combat as a free action. An invisible blade can use uncanny feint only when armed with a dagger, kukri, or punching dagger.

Feint Mastery (Ex): At 4th level, an invisible blade armed with a dagger, kukri, or punching dagger becomes so sure of his ability to mislead opponents that he can take 10 on all Bluff checks when feinting in combat (see page 68 of the *Player's Handbook*), even if stress and distractions would normally prevent him from doing so.

Sample Invisible Blade

Tallis Cloudgather: Half-elf rogue 6/invisible blade 5; CR 11; Medium humanoid; HD 6d6+6 plus 5d6+5; hp 50; Init +4; Spd 40 ft.; AC 17, touch 16, flat-footed 17; Base Atk +7; Grp +8; Atk +13 melee (1d4+2/19–20, +1 *returning dagger*) or +14 ranged (1d4+2/19–20, +1 *returning dagger*); Full Atk +13/+8 melee (1d4+2/19–20, +1 *returning dagger*) or +14/+9 ranged (1d4+2/19–20, +1 *returning dagger*); SA bleeding wound, dagger sneak attack +6d6, feint mastery, sneak attack +3d6, uncanny feint; SQ evasion, half-elf traits, trap sense +2, trapfinding, uncanny dodge, unfettered defense; AL N; SV Fort +4, Ref +13, Will +3; Str 12, Dex 19, Con 13, Int 14, Wis 10, Cha 8.

Skills and Feats: Balance +6, Bluff +13, Climb +10, Diplomacy +5, Hide +27, Intimidate +1, Jump +28, Listen +9, Move Silently +18, Sense Motive +9, Spot +9, Tumble +20; Far Shot, Point Blank Shot, Weapon Finesse, Weapon Focus (dagger).

Bleeding Wound (Ex): Tallis can forgo 1d6 points of dagger sneak attack damage to inflict a wound that bleeds for 1 point of damage per round until the victim receives the benefit of a Heal check (DC 15) or magical healing. Multiple wounds result in cumulative bleeding. Creatures immune to sneak attack are immune to bleeding wounds as well.

Feint Mastery (Ex): When armed with a dagger, kukri, or punching dagger, Tallis can always take 10 on Bluff checks when feinting in combat.

Uncanny Feint (Ex): Tallis can feint in combat as a free action rather than a standard action.

Evasion (Ex): If Tallis is exposed to any effect that normally allows him to attempt a Reflex saving throw for half damage, he takes no damage with a successful saving throw.

Half-Elf Traits (Ex): Immunity to magic sleep spells and effects; +2 racial bonus on saving throws against enchantment spells or effects; elven blood.

Trap Sense (Ex): Against attacks by traps, Tallis gets a +2 bonus on Reflex saves and a +2 dodge bonus to Armor Class.

Trapfinding (Ex): Tallis can use a Search check to locate a trap when the task has a DC higher than 20.

Uncanny Dodge (Ex): Tallis can react to danger before his senses would normally allow him to do so. He retains his Dexterity bonus to Armor Class even when caught flat-footed.

Unfettered Defense (Ex): Tallis adds his +2 Intelligence bonus to his Armor Class when he is not wearing armor and is armed with one or more daggers, kukris, or punching daggers as his only weapons. If he is denied his Deterity modifier to AC, he loses this bonus.

Possessions: 2 +1 *returning daggers*, *headband of intellect +2*, *bracers of armor +1*, *cloak of elvenkind*, *boots of striding and springing*.

JUSTICIAR

Where there are laws, there are those who defy them, and where citizens live in fear of these lawbreakers, brave souls hunt them down. These are the justiciars. They don't do it for money; they don't do it for glory. They do it because it's a thankless job that needs to be done. It also happens to be a satisfying vocation to make a living by kicking the daylights out of a criminal who desperately deserves it.

Justiciars are generally solitary, relying on their own wits and skills. They are fearless and single-minded in pursuit of their prey and ruthlessly effective in combat. Innocence and alibi can be argued in front of a court, but pretty words don't change the facts of the case or absolve a criminal of guilt. A justiciar is not necessarily judge, jury, or executioner; often he simply sees to it that those people get the chance to do their jobs. When it is impractical to bring a miscreant to the hands of the law, or if the criminal resists, a justiciar doesn't hesitate to bring final justice to someone who deserves it. Some evil justiciars prefer torturing their prisoners into confessing before turning them in.

When faced with a difficult challenge, justiciars may team up with each other or with a posse of other characters to hunt those wanted by the law. The presence of one or more justiciars in a posse might come as a rude surprise to a group of individuals that have been robbing from the rich to give to the poor. . . .

Most justiciars begin as rangers. Some paladins also find being a justiciar in line with their ideology. Fighters often find enough reward in killing; bringing people back alive is typically more effort than they consider worthwhile. Conversely, many clerics are too forgiving to be justiciars; obvious exceptions include clerics of St. Cuthbert, as well as those of Hextor and certain other lawful evil deities. Rogues and bards, with their stealth-oriented skills, can be very effective in this class. Even the occasional druid, sorcerer, or wizard (especially diviners) enters the field, wielding spells as their weapons instead of steel.

Hit Die: d10.

Requirements

To qualify to become a justiciar, a character must fulfill all the following criteria.

Alignment: Any lawful.
Base Attack Bonus: +6.
Skills: Gather Information 5 ranks, Search 5 ranks, Survival 5 ranks.
Feats: Skill Focus (Gather Information), Track.

Class Skills

The justiciar's class skills (and the key ability for each skill) are Bluff (Cha), Climb (Str), Disguise (Cha), Gather Information (Cha), Heal (Wis), Hide (Dex), Intimidate (Cha), Jump (Str), Knowledge (Int), Listen (Wis), Move Silently (Dex), Open Lock (Dex), Ride (Dex), Search (Int), Sense Motive (Wis), Spot (Wis), Survival (Wis), Swim (Str), and Use Rope (Dex).

Skill Points at Each Level: 4 + Int modifier.

A justiciar

Class Features

All of the following are class features of the justiciar prestige class.

Weapon and Armor Proficiency: Justiciars gain no proficiency with any weapon or armor.

Bring 'em Back Alive (Ex): Whenever a justiciar attacks with a melee weapon, he can deal nonlethal damage with the weapon instead of lethal damage with no penalty on the attack roll. Normally, attempting to deal nonlethal damage with a weapon in this way incurs a –4 penalty on the attack roll.

Table 2–17: The Justiciar

Level	Base Attack Bonus	Fort Save	Ref Save	Will Save	Special
1st	+1	+0	+0	+2	Bring 'em back alive, nonlethal strike +1d6
2nd	+2	+0	+0	+3	Improved grapple, crippling strike
3rd	+3	+1	+1	+3	Exotic Weapon Proficiency (manacles), street savvy +2
4th	+4	+1	+1	+4	Nonlethal strike +2d6
5th	+5	+1	+1	+4	Hog-tie
6th	+6	+2	+2	+5	Street savvy +4
7th	+7	+2	+2	+5	Nonlethal strike +3d6
8th	+8	+2	+2	+6	Improved hog-tie
9th	+9	+3	+3	+6	Street savvy +6
10th	+10	+3	+3	+7	Intuition, nonlethal strike +4d6

Nonlethal Strike (Ex): A justiciar can make nonlethal strikes. Any time the character uses the bring 'em back alive ability and his target would be denied her Dexterity bonus to Armor Class (whether she actually has a Dexterity bonus or not) or when the justiciar flanks the target, the justiciar's attack deals an extra 1d6 points of nonlethal damage. This extra damage increases to 2d6 at 4th level, 3d6 at 7th level, and 4d6 at 10th level. Should the justiciar score a critical hit with a nonlethal strike, this extra damage is not multiplied.

A justiciar can use nonlethal strike only on a living creature with discernible anatomy—undead, constructs, oozes, plants, and incorporeal creatures are not subject to this extra damage. Also, creatures immune to nonlethal damage are immune to nonlethal strike damage. The justiciar cannot make a nonlethal strike against a creature with concealment.

Improved Grapple (Ex): At 2nd level, a justiciar receives Improved Grapple as a bonus feat even if he does not meet the prerequisites.

Crippling Strike (Ex): A justiciar of 2nd level or higher can make a nonlethal strike against an opponent with such precision that his blow weakens and hampers the opponent. When a justiciar damages an opponent with a nonlethal strike, that character also takes 1 point of Strength damage.

Exotic Weapon Proficiency (Manacles): Intimately familiar with the capture of criminals, justiciars have learned to do more with a pair of manacles than restrain a lawbreaker. A justiciar of 3rd level or higher can swing a pair of metal manacles in one hand as if they were a club without taking a penalty for using an improvised weapon. Masterwork manacles can be wielded as if they were a masterwork light flail.

Street Savvy (Ex): A justiciar of 3rd level or higher gains a circumstance bonus on Gather Information checks he attempts while in pursuit of a criminal. This bonus is initially +2 at 3rd level, and increases by an extra +2 every third level thereafter.

Hog-Tie (Ex): When a justiciar of 5th level or higher successfully pins an opponent while grappling, he can attempt to hog-tie the opponent (in addition to his other options; see

If You're Pinning an Opponent on page 156 of the *Player's Handbook*). A justiciar must have a rope, chain, or manacles in one hand to use this ability.

A justiciar can use this ability on an opponent of up to one size category larger than he is (for example, a halfling justiciar can attempt to hog-tie a Medium or smaller opponent). He can use the ability only against humanoid-shaped creatures (thus, most humanoids, monstrous humanoids, outsiders, and giants would qualify).

An attempt to hog-tie is resolved with an opposed check. The justiciar can make a Use Rope check instead of a normal grapple check, while the opponent makes either a grapple check or an Escape Artist check. If the justiciar succeeds, the opponent is hog-tied. If the opponent succeeds, the hog-tie attempt fails and the grapple continues.

If a justiciar successfully hog-ties an opponent, that person is considered bound and helpless. A bound opponent can attempt to escape by making an Escape Artist check opposed by the justiciar's Use Rope check (including his +10 bonus; see Bind a Character on page 86 of the *Player's Handbook*) or a Strength check (DC 23 for rope, DC 26 for chain or manacles, DC 28 for masterwork manacles) to break free.

Improved Hog-tie (Ex): A justiciar of 8th level or higher can make a hog-tie attempt without first pinning his opponent. Whenever a grapple is established, the justiciar can use an attack action to make a hog-tie attempt. Also, if the justiciar has the Quick Draw feat, he does not need to be holding the rope, chain, or manacles in his hand before making the attempt.

Intuition (Su): When hunting a specific person, a 10th-level justiciar can use a Survival check to determine in which direction the culprit might be found if the criminal is within 1 mile of the justiciar (DC 15 + target's HD). A justiciar can use this ability to determine the direction of anyone he has previously faced in combat if he or she is within range.

The DM should make this check secretly for the justiciar, since the character should not know if he failed the check because of the die roll or because the target is too far away. A justiciar can make this check once per day for any single target.

Multiclass Note: A paladin who becomes a justiciar may continue advancing as a paladin.

Sample Justiciar

Sharsek: Human ranger 6/justiciar 10; CR 16; Medium humanoid; HD 6d8+6 plus 10d10+10; hp 98; Init +2; Spd 30 ft.; AC 19, touch 12, flat-footed 17; Base Atk +16; Grp +26; Atk +25 melee (1d6+8/17–20, *+2 short sword*) or +23 melee (1d8+6, *dimensional shackles*) or +19 ranged (1d8+7, *+1 composite longbow* [+6 Str bonus]); Full Atk +25/+20/+15/+10 melee (1d6+8/17–20, *+2 short sword*); or +23/+18/+13/+8 melee (1d6+8/17–20, *+2 short sword*) and +22/+17 melee (1d6+4/17–20, *+1 short sword*); or +19/+14/+9/+4 ranged (1d8+7, *+1 composite longbow* [+6 Str bonus]); SA bring 'em back alive, crippling strike, improved hog-tie, nonlethal strike +4d6;

SQ animal companion, favored enemy humans +4, favored enemy goblinoids +2, intuition, street savvy, wild empathy; AL LN; SV Fort +9, Ref +10, Will +11; Str 22, Dex 14, Con 13, Int 9, Wis 14, Cha 10.

Skills and Feats: Gather Information +15, Intimidate +15, Search +8, Spot +11, Survival +21, Use Rope +21; Endurance, Exotic Weapon Proficiency (manacles), Improved Critical (short sword), Improved Grapple, Improved Two-Weapon Fighting, Point Blank Shot, Power Attack, Precise Shot, Quick Draw, Skill Focus (Gather Information), Track[B], Two-Weapon Fighting, Weapon Focus (short sword).

Bring 'em Back Alive (Ex): Sharsek can deal nonlethal damage with a melee weapon with no penalty on the attack roll.

Crippling Strike (Ex): When Sharsek makes a nonlethal strike (see below), he also deals 1 point of temporary Strength damage.

Improved Hog-Tie (Ex): Whenever Sharsek establishes a grapple against a Large or smaller humanoid-shaped creature, he can use an attack action to make a hog-tie attempt (a grapple check or Use Rope check opposed by the foe's grapple check or Escape Artist check). If he succeeds, the foe is bound and helpless.

Nonlethal Strike (Ex): When Sharsek deals nonlethal melee damage against a foe he is flanking or who would be denied her Dexterity bonus to Armor Class (whether she actually has a Dexterity bonus or not), Sharsek's attack deals an extra 4d6 points of damage. Only living creatures with discernible anatomy are subject to a subdual strike. The justiciar can't use subdual strike against creatures with concealment.

Animal Companion (Ex): Sharsek has a wolf as an animal companion. Its statistics are as described on page 283 of the *Monster Manual*, except that Sharsek can handle it as a free action and share spells if the companion is within 5 feet (see page 36 of the *Player's Handbook*).

Combat Style (Ex): Sharsek has selected two-weapon combat. He gains the Two-Weapon Fighting feat despite not having the requisite Dexterity score.

Favored Enemy (Ex): Sharsek gains a +4 bonus on his Bluff, Listen, Sense Motive, Spot, and Survival checks when using these skills against humans. He gets the same bonus on weapon damage rolls against humans.

Against goblinoids, he gains a +2 bonus on these skill checks and on weapon damage rolls.

Improved Combat Style (Ex): Sharsek has the Improved Two-Weapon Fighting feat despite not having the requisite Dexterity score.

Intuition (Su): When hunting a specific person, Sharsek can determine the direction of his quarry with a successful Survival check (DC 15 + target's HD) if the target is within 1 mile.

Street Savvy (Ex): Sharsek has a +6 circumstance bonus on all Gather Information checks made while in pursuit of a criminal.

Wild Empathy (Ex): Sharsek can improve the attitude of an animal in the same way a Diplomacy check can improve the attitude of a sentient being. He rolls 1d20+6, or 1d20+2 if attempting to influence a magical beast with an Intelligence score of 1 or 2.

Ranger Spells Prepared (2; save DC 12 + spell level): 1st— *animal messenger, magic fang.*

Possessions: +2 *short sword,* +1 *short sword,* +1 *composite longbow* (+6 Str bonus), +2 *mithral breastplate, belt of giant strength +4, dimensional shackles* (counts as masterwork manacles), *medallion of thoughts.*

KENSAI

The kensai masters body, mind, weapon, and will. He devotes his strength and his life to the service of a master or an ideal he accepts as greater than himself. Some kensai become masters in their own right, but even one who becomes an emperor sees himself as a servant of some higher power.

Most characters who become kensai aspire to the class from the beginning of their careers. Often, other kensai or elite military organizations train likely young men and women in the principles of service, the arts of war, and the purity of mind and body necessary to become a kensai. Even those who do not qualify at the end often become powerful adventurers.

A kensai can be a lone adventurer, serving an ideal or attempting to fulfill a lifetime goal. Some kensai swear fealty to great lords and rise to become trusted bodyguards, warlords, or leaders in the lord's service. Monks and paladins know the strenuous road a kensai must travel, and some tread that path. Fighters value the might of the kensai, and some clerics have been known to join their ranks. Few wizards or sorcerers achieve kensai status, and bards and barbarians find themselves particularly unsuited to service as a kensai. While it might be thought that a rogue would make a poor kensai, such characters are not unheard of and can be deadly adversaries.

Hit Die: d10.

Requirements

To qualify to become a kensai, a character must fulfill all the following criteria.

Alignment: Any lawful.

Base Attack Bonus: +5.

Skills: Concentration 5 ranks, Diplomacy 5 ranks, Ride 5 ranks.

Feats: Combat Expertise, Weapon Focus (any weapon).

Special: Must complete an oath of service (see sidebar) to either an overlord or an ideal.

Class Skills

The kensai's class skills (and the key ability for each skill) are Balance (Dex), Climb (Str), Concentration (Con), Craft (Int), Diplomacy (Cha), Intimidate (Cha), Jump (Str), Knowledge (local and nobility) (Int), Ride (Dex), and Sense Motive (Wis).

Skill Points at Each Level: 4 + Int modifier.

TABLE 2–18: THE KENSAI

Level	Base Attack Bonus	Fort Save	Ref Save	Will Save	Special
1st	+0	+0	+0	+2	Signature weapon
2nd	+1	+0	+0	+3	Power surge
3rd	+2	+1	+1	+3	—
4th	+3	+1	+1	+4	Ki projection
5th	+3	+1	+1	+4	Withstand
6th	+4	+2	+2	+5	—
7th	+5	+2	+2	+5	Ki projection
8th	+6	+2	+2	+6	Instill
9th	+6	+3	+3	+6	—
10th	+7	+3	+3	+7	Ki warlord

Class Features

All of the following are class features of the kensai prestige class.

Weapon and Armor Proficiency: Kensai gain no proficiency with any weapon or armor.

Signature Weapon (Su): The kensai chooses one of his weapons (it must be one for which he has the Weapon Focus feat) to become a signature weapon. Most kensai choose either a sword or bow for this weapon, but even a kensai's natural weapons can be chosen. If the weapon is a manufactured one, it must be of at least masterwork quality.

Upon qualifying for the class, a kensai gains the ability to establish a link with his signature weapon. The character focuses part of his life energy on the weapon, making it more effective in his hands and his hands alone.

SIGNATURE WEAPONS

Class Level	Weapon Bonus	Minimum XP Cost**
1st	+1	40
2nd	+2	160
3rd	+3	360
4th	+4	640
5th	+5	1,000
6th	+6*	1,440
7th	+7*	1,960
8th	+8*	2,560
9th	+9*	3,240
10th	+10*	4,000

* A weapon can't actually have an enhancement bonus higher than +5, but it can have special abilities that are the equivalent of additional bonuses. Use these lines on the table to determine the XP cost when special abilities are added to a signature weapon. *Example:* A 6th-level kensai who has a masterwork longsword can imbue it with the power to be a *+5 keen longsword* at a cost of 1,440 XP, since the keen special ability is equivalent to a +1 bonus.

** The XP cost presented here assumes that the weapon being imbued does not already have an enhancement bonus. If it does, the cost to imbue it with additional power is reduced. For instance, if a kensai has a *+1 longsword* and wants to imbue it with the power to be a *+3 longsword*, he may do so by paying the difference in XP cost between creating a +1 weapon and a +3 weapon (360 minus 40, or 320 XP).

The process for imbuing a signature weapon with power is a simple one. The character must find a quiet, safe spot to meditate (and pray, for those kensai who serve deities) for 24 hours. At the end of this meditation, the kensai sacrifices a number of experience points, essentially shifting some of his

OATH OF SERVICE

A kensai's oath of service must be sworn in front of witnesses and must be upheld for the kensai to continue advancing in levels. Typical oaths include swearing service to a powerful lord of the kensai's alignment, to an organization with the same alignment and goals of the kensai, to the kensai's deity, or even to an ideal or principle the kensai upholds.

These oaths are not trivial, and prospective kensai who attempt to enter the prestige class with broad oaths or ones deliberately easy to fulfill find themselves spurned and cannot join the class at all, even if they meet the other requirements.

A kensai who breaks his oath, for whatever reason, loses access to his kensai special abilities and must receive an *atonement* spell from a cleric or druid of his alignment to get them back and to continue advancing in the kensai class. A kensai must also strictly adhere to his alignment. A kensai who intentionally and seriously violates his alignment also breaks faith and endures the same negative effects.

This dual requirement can pose a serious conundrum at times. If a lawful good kensai swears service to a lord who then orders the kensai to perform an evil act, the kensai is caught between his oath and his alignment. He must violate one to fulfill the other, and either way he needs to atone. If the kensai chooses his alignment, he can break his oath, gain *atonement*, and swear

a new oath (often one relating to "correcting" his former lord). He can then advance as a kensai again. If the kensai chooses his lord, he changes alignment and must gain *atonement* from, in this case, an evil cleric.

A kensai who changes his alignment from lawful loses his kensai abilities and cannot advance further in this class until he gains *atonement* and switches his alignment back to lawful.

Fulfillment of the Oath of Service: If a kensai fulfills an oath of service, or if the terms of the oath no longer apply (for example, if a kensai swears service to a king who then dies of old age, or if a kensai swears to defeat an enemy power and then in the course of adventuring defeats it), the kensai must reflect and then swear a new oath. In general, a kensai can be "between oaths" for no more than one week per class level. A kensai who does not swear a new oath before the grace period expires is treated as if he broke his oath of service.

DM Note: The idea of the oath of service does not exist to punish a player who chooses to roleplay a kensai, but to challenge that player. The kensai is a powerful prestige class, and the oath of service is one of the costs that goes along with it. You should work with the player to come up with an oath that fits into your campaign—one that provides the player with roleplaying opportunities and you with a hook you can use to motivate the entire party.

life force into his signature weapon. The signature weapon then becomes a magic weapon (if it wasn't already) and gains an enhancement bonus and/or special abilities. His current class level limits the amount of enhancement a kensai can place into his signature weapon. A kensai cannot create a signature weapon if doing so would cost enough experience points to reduce his character level.

Use the table on the previous page to determine XP costs and class level limits.

If the ritual is interrupted, it can be begun again at any time, but it must run for a full 24 hours for the signature weapon to be imbued. The kensai pays the XP cost as soon as the ritual has been completed.

A kensai's signature weapon has a caster level equal to the character's class level + 10.

Imbuing Double Weapons: A double weapon may be imbued, but both ends of the weapon must be paid for and imbued separately.

Imbuing Natural Weapons: The process for imbuing a kensai's natural weapons (such as his fists) is the same as for a manufactured weapon, except all of the kensai's natural weapons of one type are imbued at 100% of the cost + 10% per natural weapon. For example, a human kensai who has Weapon Focus (unarmed strike) may turn his fists into signature weapons for 120% of the XP cost. A six-armed kensai with a bite and tail attack would have to choose between fists, bite, and tail and pay either 160% of the cost (for six fists) or 110% of the cost (for the single bite or tail). A kensai who imbues a particular type of natural weapon must imbue all his natural weapons of that type (so a human kensai with two fists must imbue both fists). It takes 24 hours for a kensai to imbue one type of natural weapon, regardless of how many actual weapons of that type he possesses.

Losing a Signature Weapon: If a kensai's signature weapon is lost or stolen, the character must strive to recover it by any means that do not violate his oath or alignment. A kensai who knowingly abandons a signature weapon is treated as if he broke his oath of service (see the sidebar). A kensai who abandons a signature weapon and atones for the deed can begin to create a new signature weapon.

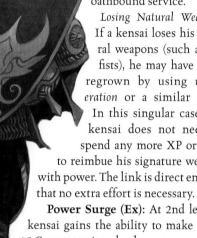

A kensai

If someone destroys a kensai's signature weapon, only the kensai can repair it. If enough is left of the weapon to salvage (the shattered shards of a sword, for example), the kensai can reforge the weapon as if he were using the Craft (weaponsmithing) skill to make a masterwork weapon. If he takes the reforged weapon and then meditates for 24 hours, he may pay the appropriate XP cost to restore his weapon to full strength.

Should nothing remain of the weapon, the kensai must begin anew with a weapon that has never before been imbued. The character, however, has not failed in his oath—the destruction of a kensai's weapon in service of his oath is not shameful, and other kensai are likely to show even more respect to a comrade whose weapon is destroyed in oathbound service.

Losing Natural Weapons: If a kensai loses his natural weapons (such as his fists), he may have them regrown by using *regeneration* or a similar spell. In this singular case, the kensai does not need to spend any more XP or time to reimbue his signature weapon with power. The link is direct enough that no extra effort is necessary.

Power Surge (Ex): At 2nd level, a kensai gains the ability to make a DC 15 Concentration check as a move action to focus his energy and spirit. If he succeeds, he gains +8 to his Strength for a number of rounds equal to one-half his class level. Each time after the first that a kensai successfully uses this ability in a single 24-hour period, the check DC increases by 5.

Ki Projection: At 4th level and higher, a kensai adds one-half his class level (round down) to any Bluff, Diplomacy, Gather Information, or Intimidate checks he makes. At 8th level and higher, the kensai adds his full class level to such checks.

A target that realizes it has been fooled by a kensai's successful Bluff check gains a +10 bonus on any check or saving throw involving the kensai's use of Bluff, Diplomacy, Gather Information, or Intimidate against that target in the future. The kensai can regain the creature's trust by changing its attitude from unfriendly to friendly (see Influencing NPC Attitudes, page 72 of the *Player's Handbook*).

Withstand (Ex): When a kensai of 5th level or higher is forced to make a Reflex save to avoid damage from an area effect spell (such as a *fireball*), he can make a Concentration check instead of a Reflex save to resist taking full damage. If a kensai has the evasion or improved evasion ability, those benefits apply on this Concentration check as well.

Instill (Ex): Once per day, a kensai of 8th level or higher may take a full-round action to make a Concentration check (DC 10 + target's HD or character level) to impart some of his own ability into a willing ally he can touch. The kensai then transfers some of his power to the ally: He subtracts up to 1 point per class level from his base attack bonus and/or any or all of his base save bonuses and transfers the same amount to the recipient. The kensai regains the instilled power 1 hour later, when it transfers back out of the ally. If the ally dies before the instilled power is transferred back, the kensai must make a Fortitude save (DC 5 + target's HD or character level) or die as well. If he succeeds, he immediately gets his instilled powers back.

Ki Warlord: When a kensai attains 10th level, he gains great notoriety and becomes known as a ki warlord. Other kensai of the same alignment revere the ki warlord, and even those of differing alignments treat him with some measure of respect. If the ki warlord has an NPC master, this master likely assigns the ki warlord more responsibility and authority within his domain (perhaps giving him a castle, monastery, or military school). If the ki warlord serves a deity, that deity may take a personal interest in giving the ki warlord more responsibility, perhaps actually contacting the ki warlord directly or through intermediaries and making the deity's wishes known.

In addition to this added responsibility, a ki warlord gains some tangible benefits. He has the right to petition other (lower-level) members of the prestige class for assistance on adventures or in the fulfillment of his oath. As long as a ki warlord's requests do not violate the other members' own oaths of service or alignment, lower-level kensai have a responsibility to assist a ki warlord in any reasonable manner—such as providing food and shelter, access to minor resources, and other things another character might have to barter for.

Ki warlords inspire those around them. When fighting within 30 feet of a ki warlord, allies gain a +1 morale bonus on Will saves, Concentration checks, and attack rolls. Lawful allies gain a +2 morale bonus on these checks.

Multiclass Note: A samurai, paladin, or monk who becomes a kensai may continue advancing in his original class.

Sample Kensai

Inscrutable Master Shen: Human monk 7/kensai 8; CR 15; Medium humanoid; HD 7d8 plus 8d10; hp 76; Init +3; Spd 50 ft.; AC 22, touch 18, flat-footed 19; Base Atk +13; Grp +14; Atk +22 melee (2d6+7, *+5 unarmed strike*); Full Atk +22/+17/+12 melee (2d6+7, *+5 unarmed strike*) or +21/+21/+17/+12 (2d6+7, *+5 unarmed strike*); SA flurry of blows, signature weapon, ki strike (magic), SQ evasion, instill, power surge, purity of body, slow fall 30 ft., still mind, wholeness of body, withstand; AL LG; SV Fort +7, Ref +10, Will +14; Str 12, Dex 16, Con 10, Int 13, Wis 16, Cha 8.

Skills and Feats: Balance +15, Concentration +18, Diplomacy +25, Gather Information +7, Intimidate +20, Jump +28, Ride +8, Tumble +23; Combat Expertise, Combat Reflexes, Dodge, Improved Disarm, Mobility, Spring Attack, Stunning Fist, Weapon Finesse, Weapon Focus (unarmed strike).

Flurry of Blows (Ex): Shen may use a full attack action to make one extra attack per round with an unarmed strike or a special monk weapon at his highest base attack bonus, but this attack and each other attack made in that round take a –1 penalty apiece. This penalty applies for 1 round, so it affects attacks of opportunity Shen might make before his next action. If armed with a kama, nunchaku, or siangham, Shen can make the extra attack either with that weapon or unarmed. If armed with two such weapons, he uses one for his regular attack(s) and the other for the extra attack. In any case, his damage bonus on the attack with his off hand is not reduced.

Signature Weapon (Su): Master Shen has imbued his fists, giving them a +5 enhancement bonus on attack and damage rolls.

Ki Strike (Su): Shen's unarmed strike can deal damage to a creature with damage reduction as if the blow were made with a magic weapon.

Evasion (Ex): If Shen is exposed to any effect that normally allows him to attempt a Reflex saving throw for half damage, he takes no damage with a successful saving throw.

Instill (Ex): Once per day, Shen can make a Concentration check (DC 10 + target's level or HD) as a full-round action to transfer up to 8 points of his base attack bonus and/or base save bonuses to the recipient for 1 hour. If the recipient dies, Shen must succeed on a Fortitude save (DC 5 + recipient's HD) or die as well.

Power Surge (Ex): Shen can make a Concentration check (DC 15, + 5 for each daily use beyond the first) to gain a +8 bonus to Strength for 4 rounds.

Purity of Body (Ex): Shen has immunity to all diseases except for magical diseases such as mummy rot and lycanthropy.

Slow Fall (Ex): When within arm's reach of a wall, Shen can use it to slow his descent while falling. He takes damage as if the fall were 30 feet shorter than it actually is.

Still Mind (Ex): Shen gains a +2 bonus on saving throws against spells and effects from the enchantment school.

Wholeness of Body (Su): Shen can cure up to 30 points of his own wounds per day, and he can spread this healing out over several uses.

Withstand (Ex): Shen can make a Concentration check rather than a Reflex save to avoid damage from an area effect spell.

Possessions: Bracers of armor +4, 4 javelins of lightning, monk's belt, ring of invisibility, masterwork longsword.

KNIGHT OF THE CHALICE

A knight of the Chalice is a member of an elite knightly organization devoted to fighting demons and other evil outsiders. Motivated by a pious hatred of these creatures that embody the principles of evil and routinely invade the Material Plane, knights of the Chalice learn tactics and gain special abilities to help them in their crusade.

A character who qualifies for entrance into the Order of the Chalice is typically a paladin/ ranger or a cleric/ranger. Characters with minimal levels as a ranger/cleric or ranger/paladin can qualify even if they have more levels in other classes— rogue, fighter, and even wizard or sorcerer. Wizards and sorcerers are rarely drawn to the order's crusade, and cannot qualify as knights until reaching high levels. Few monks or bards have enough dedication to exterminating demons to take up this class.

Knights of the Chalice are often lone crusaders, maintaining only loose connections to their order. NPC knights sometimes gather adventuring bands around themselves for combat support. A knight of the Chalice could become a temporary ally of a group of adventurers while the party is engaged in a campaign against a demon.

Hit Die: d10.

Requirements

To qualify to become a knight of the Chalice, a character must fulfill all the following criteria.

Alignment: Lawful good.
Base Attack Bonus: +8.
Skills: Knowledge (the planes) 5 ranks, Knowledge (religion) 10 ranks.
Spells: Able to cast divine spells, including protection from evil.

Class Skills

The knight of the Chalice's class skills (and the key ability for each skill) are Concentration (Con), Craft (Int), Diplomacy (Cha), Intimidate (Cha), Knowledge (the planes) (Int), Knowledge (religion) (Int), Profession (Wis), and Sense Motive (Wis).

Skill Points at Each Level: 2 + Int modifier.

Class Features

All of the following are class features of the knight of the Chalice prestige class.

Weapon and Armor Proficiency: Knights of the Chalice gain no proficiency with any weapon or armor.

Spells: Beginning at 1st level, a knight of the Chalice gains the ability to cast a number of divine spells. To cast a spell, a knight of the Chalice must have a Wisdom score of at least 10 + the spell's level, so a knight with a Wisdom of 10 or lower cannot cast these spells. Knight of the Chalice bonus spells are based on Wisdom, and saving throws against these spells have a DC of 10 + spell level + the knight's Wisdom modifier. When the knight gets 0 spells per day of a given spell level (for instance, 1st-level spells for a 1st-level knight), she gains only the bonus spells she would be entitled to based on her Wisdom score for that spell level.

A knight of the Chalice

The knight of the Chalice's spell list appears below; he has access to any spell on the list and can freely choose which to prepare. A knight of the Chalice prepares and casts spells just as a cleric does (though a knight cannot lose a spell to cast a cure spell in its place).

Fiendslaying (Ex): Knights of the Chalice gain a number of special benefits in combat with evil outsiders. A 1st-level knight of the Chalice gets a +1 competence bonus on attack rolls against evil outsiders. On a successful attack, she deals an extra 1d6 points of damage due to her expertise in combating these creatures. These bonuses increase as the knight advances in level, as shown on Table 2–19.

A 1st-level knight of the Chalice's +1 competence bonus also applies to Intimidate, Listen, Sense Motive, and Spot checks when she uses these skills against evil outsiders. She gets the same bonus on Will saving throws against attacks from evil outsiders, and on opposed ability checks she makes against evil outsiders.

These bonuses all stack with the knight's favored enemy bonus (if any).

Censure Demons (Su): Knights of the Chalice can censure demons, much as clerics turn undead. Rather than channeling positive energy, a knight of the Chalice channels energy from the celestial planes of lawful good.

When a knight of the Chalice uses this ability, any demon within 30 feet must succeed on a Will save (DC 10 + the knight of the Chalice's class level + the knight of the Chalice's Cha modifier) or be censured.

A censured demon whose Hit Dice are equal to or greater than twice the knight's class level is stunned by the knight's holy power for 1 round.

If a censured demon has fewer Hit Dice than twice the knight's class level, it is stunned and must succeed on a second Will save (same DC) or be sent back to its home plane as if it had been the subject of a *dismissal* spell. Only one demon may dismissed in this way by any single censure demons attempt; if more than one demon is required to make this second Will save, check for the demon with the lowest HD first.

A knight may attempt to censure demons once per day for every two class levels she possesses.

Courage of Heaven (Su): A knight of the Chalice of 2nd level or higher is immune to fear effects cast or created by evil outsiders. At 5th level and higher, a knight of the Chalice is also immune to enchantment spells and effects cast or created by evil outsiders, including charms and suggestions. At 8th level and higher, these immunities extend to all allies within 20 feet of the knight of the Chalice.

Consecrated Casting (Ex): When a knight reaches 4th level, spells cast by the character on evil outsiders become more difficult to resist. When the knight casts a spell that targets an evil outsider, add +2 to the knight's caster level check to overcome the target's spell resistance and +2 to the DC of any saving throw the spell allows.

Holy Aura **(Su):** A 10th-level knight of the Chalice has the ability to create a *holy aura* once per day that affects herself only. The aura's effect is as the spell cast by a 10th-level cleric, but it wards the knight against the attacks, spells, and mental influence of evil outsiders only, and only evil outsiders can be blinded if they strike the knight.

Multiclass Note: A paladin who becomes a knight of the Chalice may continue advancing as a paladin.

Knight of the Chalice Spell List

Knights of the Chalice choose their spells from the following list.

1st Level: *bless water, bless weapon, detect chaos, detect evil, divine favor, doom, endure elements, magic weapon, protection from evil, remove fear, summon monster I.*

2nd Level: *aid, align weapon, bull's strength, consecrate, endurance, resist elements, sound burst, spiritual weapon, summon monster II, undetectable alignment.*

3rd Level: *dispel magic, invisibility purge, magic circle against evil, magic vestment, prayer, protection from elements, searing light, shout, summon monster III.*

4th Level: *dimensional anchor, discern lies, dismissal, dispel evil, holy smite, greater magic weapon, lesser aspect of the deity, lesser planar ally.*

Sample Knight of the Chalice

Estrella Montenegro: Elf ranger 5/cleric 4/knight of the Chalice 6; CR 15; Medium humanoid; HD 5d8 plus 4d8 plus 6d10; hp 69; Init +1; Spd 20 ft., fly 40 ft.; AC 21, touch 10, flat-footed 21; Base Atk +14; Grp +19; Atk +21 melee (2d6+8/19–20, +1 evil outsider bane greatsword) or +17 ranged (1d8+6/×3, +1 composite longbow [+5 Str bonus]); Full Atk +21/+16/+11 melee

Table 2–19: The Knight of the Chalice

| Level | Base Attack Bonus | Fort Save | Ref Save | Will Save | Special | — Spells per Day — | | | |
						1st	2nd	3rd	4th
1st	+1	+2	+0	+0	Fiendslaying +1/+1d6	0	—	—	—
2nd	+2	+3	+0	+0	Censure demons, courage of heaven (fear)	1	—	—	—
3rd	+3	+3	+1	+1	Fiendslaying +2/+2d6	1	0	—	—
4th	+4	+4	+1	+1	Consecrated casting	1	1	—	—
5th	+5	+4	+1	+1	Courage of heaven (enchantment)	1	1	0	—
6th	+6	+5	+2	+2	Fiendslaying +3/+3d6	1	1	1	—
7th	+7	+5	+2	+2	—	2	1	1	0
8th	+8	+6	+2	+2	Courage of heaven (radius)	2	1	1	1
9th	+9	+6	+3	+3	Fiendslaying +4/+4d6	2	2	1	1
10th	+10	+7	+3	+3	Holy aura 1/day	2	2	2	1

(2d6+8/19–20, +1 *evil outsider bane greatsword*) or +17/+12/+7 ranged (1d8+6/×3, +1 *composite longbow* [+5 Str bonus]) or +15/+15/+10/+5 ranged (1d8+6/×3, +1 *composite longbow* [+5 Str bonus]); SA censure demons 3/day, fiendslaying +3/+3d6, turn undead 9/day; SQ animal companion, consecrated casting, courage of heaven (enchantment), courage of heaven (fear), elf traits, favored enemy evil outsiders +4, favored enemy undead +2, wild empathy; AL LG; SV Fort +16, Ref +11, Will +11; Str 20, Dex 12, Con 10, Int 10, Wis 13, Cha 14.

Skills and Feats: Concentration +7, Intimidate +8, Knowledge (the planes) +5, Knowledge (religion) +10, Listen +11, Sense Motive +9, Spot +11, Survival +9; Divine Vengeance*, Divine Vigor*, Endurance, Extra Turning, Power Attack, Rapid Shot, Track^B, Weapon Focus (composite longbow), Weapon Focus (greatsword).

*New feat described in Chapter 3 of this book.

Censure Demons (Su): Any demon within 30 feet of Estrella must succeed on a DC 18 Will save or be stunned for 1 round if it has 12 or more Hit Dice. A demon with 11 or fewer HD must succeed on a second DC 18 Will save or be sent back to its home plane (as the *dismissal* spell). Only one demon is dismissed per censure; check for the lowest Hit Die demon first.

Consecrated Casting (Ex): When Estrella casts a spell that targets an evil outsider, she receives a +2 bonus on any caster level check to overcome the target's spell resistance and a +2 bonus to the DC of any saving throw the spell allows.

Fiendslaying (Ex): Estrella has a +3 bonus on attack rolls against evil outsiders. On a successful attack, she deals an extra 3d6 points of damage. She also has a +3 competence bonus on Intimidate, Listen, Sense Motive, and Spot checks against evil outsiders, and a +3 bonus on Will saving throws and opposed ability checks against evil outsiders.

Animal Companion (Ex): Estrella has an eagle as an animal companion. Its statistics are as described on page 272 of the *Monster Manual*, except that Estrella can handle it as a free action and share spells if the companion is within 5 feet (see page 36 of the *Player's Handbook*).

Combat Style (Ex): Estrella has selected archery. She gains the Rapid Shot feat without having to meet the normal prerequisites.

Courage of Heaven (Su): Estrella is immune to fear effects and enchantment spells and effects cast or created by evil outsiders.

Elf Traits (Ex): Immunity to magic sleep spells and effects; +2 bonus on saves against enchantments; entitled to a Search check when within 5 feet of a secret or concealed door.

Favored Enemy (Ex): Estrella gains a +4 bonus on her Bluff, Listen, Sense Motive, Spot, and Survival checks when using these skills against evil outsiders. She gets the same bonus on weapon damage rolls against evil outsiders.

Against undead, she gains a +2 bonus on these skill checks and on weapon damage rolls.

Wild Empathy (Ex): Estrella can improve the attitude of an animal in the same way a Diplomacy check can improve the attitude of a sentient being. She rolls 1d20+7, or 1d20+3 if attempting to influence a magical beast with an Intelligence score of 1 or 2.

Cleric Spells Prepared (5/5/3; save DC 11 + spell level): 0—*detect magic* (2), *detect poison*, *light*, *read magic*; 1st—*divine favor, entropic shield, protection from evil*, *remove fear, shield of faith*; 2nd—*bear's endurance, bull's strength*, *lesser restoration*.

*Domain spell. Domains: Good (cast good spells at +1 caster level), Strength (1/day gain +4 bonus to Str for 1 round).

Knight of the Chalice Spells Prepared (2/1/1; save DC 11 + spell level): 1st—*bless weapon, detect evil*; 2nd—*align weapon*; 3rd—*magic circle against evil*.

Ranger Spells Prepared (1; save DC 11 + spell level): 1st—*delay poison*.

Possessions: +1 *evil outsider bane greatsword*, +1 *composite longbow* (+5 Str bonus), +3 *full plate*, *gauntlets of ogre power +2*, *winged boots*, *cloak of resistance +3*, 20 arrows.

KNIGHT PROTECTOR

The few, the proud, the knight protectors are martial characters dedicated to restoring the ideals of knightly chivalry before they fade forever. The protectors see moral decay everywhere they look in the world around them, brought on by a lapse in ethical behavior. Like paladins, knight protectors adhere to a rigid code of behavior that embraces such values as honor, honesty, chivalry, and courage. Unlike paladins, the first duty of knight protectors is to this code and the ideals for which it stands, rather than to a deity or a holy order. A protector is expected to display these ideals in all aspects of his behavior and throughout all his actions and deeds, however arduous they may be.

Many knight protectors come from backgrounds of honor and loyalty, such as other orders of chivalry or the service of a powerful master. Paladins and ex-paladins are the most common knight protectors, and clerics of lawful deities (such as St. Cuthbert or Heironeous) as well as fighters seeking a higher ideal often find much to appreciate in the knight protector's code of conduct. Members of most other classes, particularly spellcasters, lack either the interest or the dedication to pursue this path.

NPC knight protectors are often found wandering alone, looking for worthy people to protect or idealistic lords to serve. What little bond or organization exists between knight protectors is extremely strong—whether a knight protector was once a baron, a lowly liegeman, or a samurai, each feels a kinship to his compatriots and a longing for better days.

Hit Die: d10.

Requirements

To qualify to become a knight protector, a character must fulfill all the following criteria.

Alignment: Lawful neutral or lawful good.

Base Attack Bonus: +5.

Skills: Diplomacy 6 ranks, Knowledge (nobility and royalty) 4 ranks, Ride 6 ranks.

Feats: Armor Proficiency (heavy), Cleave, Great Cleave, Mounted Combat, Power Attack.

Class Skills

The knight protector's class skills (and the key ability for each skill) are Diplomacy (Cha), Intimidate (Cha), Knowledge (nobility and royalty) (Int), Ride (Dex), and Spot (Wis).

Skill Points at Each Level: 2 + Int modifier.

TABLE 2–20: THE KNIGHT PROTECTOR

Level	Base Attack Bonus	Fort Save	Ref Save	Will Save	Special
1st	+1	+0	+0	+2	Defensive stance +2, shining beacon
2nd	+2	+0	+0	+3	Best effort +2, Iron Will
3rd	+3	+1	+1	+3	Supreme cleave
4th	+4	+1	+1	+4	Defensive stance +3
5th	+5	+1	+1	+4	Best effort +3
6th	+6	+2	+2	+5	No mercy 1
7th	+7	+2	+2	+5	Defensive stance +4
8th	+8	+2	+2	+6	Best effort +4
9th	+9	+3	+3	+6	No mercy 2
10th	+10	+3	+3	+7	Defensive stance +5, retributive attack

Class Features

All of the following are class features of the knight protector prestige class.

Weapon and Armor Proficiency: Knight protectors gain proficiency with tower shields.

Defensive Stance (Ex): At the start of any turn when a knight protector is within 5 feet of an ally who has fewer Hit Dice than he does, the knight protector can transfer up to 2 points of Armor Class to the ally (making his own Armor Class worse by the same number). The maximum number of points he can transfer increases by 1 for every three levels beyond 1st.

Shining Beacon (Su): A knight protector is the physical and spiritual embodiment of high ideals. All his allies gain a +4 morale bonus on saves against fear effects when they stand within 10 feet of the character. If the knight protector is paralyzed, unconscious, or otherwise rendered helpless, his allies lose this bonus.

Best Effort (Ex): The daunting nature of the knight protector's goals often requires special focus of effort. Beginning at 2nd level, a knight protector gains a bonus on any one skill check he makes, once per day. The character must declare that he is using this ability before he makes the skill check. This bonus increases by 1 for every three levels beyond 2nd.

Iron Will (Ex): At 2nd level, a knight protector gains Iron Will as a bonus feat.

Supreme Cleave (Ex): Beginning at 3rd level, a knight protector can take a 5-foot step between attacks when using the Cleave or Great Cleave feat.

No Mercy (Ex): At 6th level, a knight protector gains the ability to make one extra attack of opportunity per round (as if he had the Combat Reflexes feat and a Dexterity modifier of +1). At 9th level and higher, the character can make as many as two extra attacks of opportunity per round. This benefit stacks with the benefit of the Combat Reflexes feat.

Retributive Attack (Su): If an ally of a 10th-level knight protector is rendered helpless or unconscious, the character can make a retributive attack against the creature that felled his ally. When making a retributive attack, the knight protector adds his Charisma bonus (if any) to his attack roll and deals an extra 10 points of damage on a successful hit.

A knight protector can make a number of retributive attacks per day equal to his Charisma bonus (minimum one), but never more than one per round. He may make more than one retributive attack against the same foe.

Multiclass Note: A paladin or samurai who becomes a knight protector may continue advancing in his original class.

Ex-Knight Protectors

A knight protector who willingly and knowingly violates the code for no adequate reason loses all supernatural class features of the prestige class and may no longer advance in levels as a knight protector.

Sample Knight Protector

Mathurin: Dwarf paladin 6/knight protector 10; CR 16; Medium humanoid; HD 6d10+12 plus 10d10+20; hp 120; Init +1; Spd 20 ft.; AC 26, touch 11, flat-footed 25; Base Atk +16; Grp +21; Atk +24 melee (1d10+7/×3, *+2 dwarven waraxe*) or +18 ranged (1d8+6/×3, *+1 composite longbow* [+5 Str bonus]); Full Atk +24/+19/+14/+9 melee (1d10+7/×3, *+2 dwarven waraxe*) or +18/+13/+8/+3 ranged (1d8+6/×3, *+1 composite longbow* [+5 Str

THE CODE OF THE KNIGHT PROTECTOR

A knight protector must be of lawful neutral or lawful good alignment, and must adhere to the order's code of conduct.

Support: The order supports its own. A knight protector can expect to receive room and board, as well as a mount with appropriate gear, from the order for as long as he remains in its ranks and adheres to the Code.

The Code:

Courage and enterprise in obedience to the order.

Defense of any mission unto death.

Respect for all peers and equals; courtesy to all lessers.

Combat is glory; battle is the true test of self-worth; war is the flowering of the chivalric ideal.

Personal glory above all in battle.

Death before dishonor.

A knight protector

Illus. by W. England

bonus]); SA retributive attack 3/day, smite evil 2/day, supreme cleave, turn undead 6/day; SQ aura of courage, aura of good, best effort +4, damage reduction 3/–, defensive stance +5, detect evil, divine grace, divine health, dwarf traits, lay on hands, no mercy 2, remove disease, shining beacon, special mount; AL LG; SV Fort +13, Ref +9, Will +13; Str 21, Dex 13, Con 14, Int 12, Wis 12, Cha 16.

Skills and Feats: Diplomacy +26, Knowledge (nobility and royalty) +5, Ride +20, Sense Motive +6, Spot +11; Cleave, Great Cleave, Iron Will[B], Mobility, Mounted Combat, Power Attack, Weapon Focus (dwarven waraxe).

Retributive Attack (Su): If one of Mathurin's allies is rendered helpless or unconscious, she can make a retributive attack against the creature that felled the ally, gaining a +3 bonus on the attack roll and dealing an extra 10 points of damage.

Smite Evil (Su): Mathurin may attempt to smite evil with one normal melee attack. She adds +3 to her attack roll and deals an extra 6 points of damage. Smiting a creature that is not evil has no effect but uses the ability for that day.

Supreme Cleave (Ex): Mathurin can take a 5-foot step between attacks when using the Cleave or Great Cleave feats.

Turn Undead (Su): As a 3rd-level cleric.

Aura of Courage (Su): Mathurin is immune to fear (magical or otherwise). Allies within 10 feet of her gain a +4 morale bonus on saving throws against fear effects.

Aura of Good (Ex): Mathurin's aura of good (see the *detect good* spell) is equal to that of a 6th-level cleric.

Best Effort (Ex): Mathurin can add a +4 bonus to any skill check once per day.

Defensive Stance (Ex): Mathurin can transfer up to 5 points of Armor Class to an ally within 5 feet, reducing her AC by the same amount.

Detect Evil (Sp): At will, as the spell of the same name.

Divine Grace (Su): Mathurin gains a +3 bonus on saving throws (already figured into the above statistics).

Divine Health (Ex): Mathurin is immune to all diseases, including magical diseases such as mummy rot and lycanthropy.

Dwarf Traits (Ex): +4 bonus on ability checks to resist being bull rushed or tripped; +2 bonus on saving throws against poison, spells, and spell-like effects; +1 bonus on attack rolls against orcs and goblinoids; +4 bonus to AC against giants; +2 bonus on Appraise or Craft checks related to stone or metal.

Lay on Hands (Su): Mathurin can cure 18 hit points of wounds per day.

No Mercy (Ex): Mathurin can make two extra attacks of opportunity per round.

Remove Disease (Sp): As the spell, once per week.

Shining Beacon (Su): All of Mathurin's allies within 10 feet gain a +4 morale bonus on saves against fear effects. If Mathurin is paralyzed, unconscious, or otherwise rendered helpless, her allies lose this bonus.

Special Mount (Sp): Mathurin's special mount is a heavy warhorse (see page 45 of the *Player's Handbook*) that has +2 Hit Dice, a +4 bonus to natural armor, +1 Strength, and improved evasion. Mathurin has an empathic link with the mount and can share spells and saving throws with it. She can call her mount once per day for up to 10 hours as a full-round action.

Paladin Spells Prepared (2; save DC 11 + spell level): 1st—*bless weapon, protection from evil.*

Possessions: +3 adamantine full plate, +2 heavy steel shield, +2 dwarven waraxe, +1 composite longbow (+5 Str bonus), belt of giant Strength +4, amulet of health +4, cloak of Charisma +2.

MASTER THROWER

"Only a master thrower would invent a new style of fighting that involves cleverly disarming herself." That's how many more traditional weapon masters think of master throwers. Indeed, many master throwers see those who dabble in thrown weapons the same way. If a character tosses away a hand axe, javelin, or dagger, he may end up facing his foe with bare hands. Unless one is a monk, one should avoid that situation at all reasonable costs.

Master throwers depend on quick reflexes, good planning, and, of course, deadly aim to survive in a world that values brute strength over clever tactics. Members of this prestige class establish a camaraderie that often overshadows alignment or cultural differences. This camaraderie won't prevent two master throwers from fighting each other if the need arises, but it does give those individuals an incentive to find peaceful—or at least nonlethal—ways of settling their differences. Some orders have developed sigils or small signs they can use to identify their members. Common sigils include a hand gripping a dagger by its point, or a whirling handaxe on a field of blue. Many master throwers make phantom throwing motions with their hands as they enter combat, watching their opponents to see if they return the sign.

NPC master throwers like to frequent cities and towns where they can demonstrate their abilities for others and pick up new tricks or pointers from specialists with different weapons. Since such demonstrations can be made against nonliving targets or in sport hunting, master throwers are often welcomed at fairs and celebrations, where they use their abilities to entertain. Some master throwers find service in the city guard or as personal protectors of the very rich.

Hit Die: d8.

TABLE 2–21: THE MASTER THROWER

Level	Base Attack Bonus	Fort Save	Ref Save	Will Save	Special
1st	+1	+0	+2	+0	Quick Draw, thrown weapon trick
2nd	+2	+0	+3	+0	Evasion
3rd	+3	+1	+3	+1	Thrown weapon trick
4th	+4	+1	+4	+1	Snatch Arrows
5th	+5	+1	+4	+1	Critical throw, thrown weapon trick

Requirements

To qualify to become a master thrower, a character must fulfill all the following criteria.

Base Attack Bonus: +5.
Skills: Sleight of Hand 4 ranks.
Feats: Point Blank Shot, Precise Shot, Weapon Focus (any thrown weapon).

Class Skills

The master thrower's class skills (and the key ability for each skill) are Bluff (Cha), Climb (Str), Concentration (Con), Craft (Int), Jump (Str), Perform (Cha), Profession (Int), Sleight of Hand (Dex), Spot (Wis), Tumble (Dex), and Use Rope (Dex).

Skill Points at Each Level: 4 + Int modifier.

Class Features

All of the following are class features of the master thrower prestige class.

Weapon and Armor Proficiency: Master throwers gain no proficiency with any weapon or armor.

Quick Draw: At 1st level, a master thrower gains the Quick Draw feat.

Thrown Weapon Trick (Ex): At 1st level and every two levels thereafter, a master thrower chooses one of the following thrown weapon tricks. Once chosen, the trick is a permanent part of the master thrower's repertoire and may not be exchanged. A master thrower cannot choose the same trick more than once. Each trick may only be used with a thrown weapon for which the character has taken Weapon Focus.

Deadeye Shot: The critical multiplier for any specific type of thrown weapon increases by one (for example, a hand axe has a critical multiplier of ×4 instead of ×3) when this ability is used. The benefit of this ability does not stack with any other effect that increases critical multipliers.

Defensive Throw: If a master thrower with this ability succeeds on a Concentration check (DC 10 + number of threatening foes) before attempting to attack with a thrown weapon while in a threatened square, her thrown weapon attacks don't provoke attacks of opportunity for 1 round. If the check fails, her opponents get attacks of opportunity as normal when she makes her attacks.

Doubletoss: A master thrower with this ability may, as a standard action, throw two weapons at one or two targets within 30 feet. The character may apply her full Strength bonus to each weapon (instead of one-half her Strength bonus for the off-hand weapon). The normal penalties for fighting with two weapons apply (see page 160 of the *Player's Handbook*).

Palm Throw: When using little thrown weapons (darts, shuriken, and daggers; the DM may allow other weapons), a master thrower with this ability may throw two of each weapon with a single attack roll. Damage for each weapon is resolved separately, but the master thrower does not apply her Strength bonus to either damage roll.

Sneaky Shot: Just before making a ranged attack, a master thrower with this ability can use a move action to make a Sleight of Hand check opposed by her target's Spot check. If she wins the opposed check, her opponent is denied his Dexterity bonus to Armor Class against the attack.

Trip Shot: A master thrower with this ability may use a thrown weapon to make a trip attempt against an opponent farther than 5 feet away. The character makes a normal attack against the opponent with a thrown weapon. If the attack succeeds, in addition to doing damage as normal, the master thrower makes a Dexterity check with a +4 bonus opposed by the opponent's Dexterity check or Strength check (whichever ability score has the higher modifier). Other modifiers may apply on this opposed check (see page 158 of the *Player's Handbook*). If the master thrower wins the opposed check, the opponent is tripped. The benefit of this ability does not stack with the benefit of the Improved Trip feat.

Tumbling Toss: When wearing light, medium, or no armor, a master thrower with this ability can hurl a single thrown weapon at any point during a tumbling attempt as a standard action. If the result of her Tumble check is 25 or higher, the master thrower does not provoke an attack of opportunity for making this attack regardless of how many opponents threaten her.

A master thrower

Two with One Blow: If a master thrower with this ability uses a thrown weapon to attack two opponents adjacent to each other, she may take a −4 penalty on the attack roll and attempt to hit both opponents at once. The attack may hit either, both, or neither opponent depending on the roll and the Armor Class of each opponent. Damage for each opponent is resolved separately. If the attack roll results in the threat of a critical hit, roll to confirm each critical hit separately.

Weak Spot: A master thrower can gain this ability only after reaching 5th level. When using a thrown weapon against a target of her size or larger, the character can make a ranged touch attack instead of a normal attack. If the attack hits, the master thrower does not apply her Strength bonus to the damage.

Evasion (Ex): At 2nd level, a master thrower gains the evasion ability. If she makes a successful Reflex saving throw against an attack that normally deals half damage on a successful save, she instead takes no damage. Evasion can be used only if the master thrower is wearing light armor or no armor. A helpless master thrower (such as one who is unconscious or paralyzed) does not gain the benefit of the ability.

If the character already has the evasion ability, he gains improved evasion instead. Improved evasion works like evasion, except that while the character still takes no damage on a successful Reflex saving throw, she takes only half damage on a failed save.

Snatch Arrows: A master thrower gains the benefit of the Snatch Arrows feat at 4th level, even if she does not meet the prerequisites.

Critical Throw (Ex): At 5th level, a master thrower gains the Improved Critical feat for any thrown weapon with which she has Weapon Focus.

Sample Master Thrower

Lessia Skyleaf: Gnome rogue 9/master thrower 5; CR 14; Small humanoid; HD 9d6 plus 5d8; hp 45; Init +6; Spd 30 ft.; AC 24, touch 19, flat-footed 24; Base Atk +11; Grp +8; Atk +19 melee (1d4+2/18–20, Small masterwork rapier) or +20 ranged (1d4+3/19–20, +1 *Small returning javelin*); Full Atk +19/+14/+9 melee (1d4+2/18–20, Small masterwork rapier) or +20/+15/+10 ranged (1d4+3/19–20, +1 *Small returning javelin*); SA defensive throw, sneak attack +5d6, sneaky shot, weak spot; SQ evasion, gnome traits, improved evasion, improved uncanny dodge, trap sense, trapfinding, uncanny dodge; AL CN; SV Fort +4, Ref +16, Will +4; Str 14, Dex 22, Con 10, Int 13, Wis 10, Cha 8.

Skills and Feats: Balance +6, Bluff +16, Concentration +11, Diplomacy +1, Disable Device +13, Hide +25, Intimidate +1, Jump −2, Move Silently +16, Open Lock +18, Search +11, Sleight of Hand +23, Tumble +23; Acrobatic, Improved Critical (javelin), Point Blank Shot, Precise Shot, Quick Draw, Snatch Arrows, Weapon Finesse, Weapon Focus (javelin).

Defensive Throw (Ex): If Lessia succeeds on a Concentration check (DC 10 + number of threatening foes) before attempting to attack with a thrown weapon while in a threatened square, her thrown weapon attacks don't provoke attacks of opportunity for 1 round.

Sneaky Shot (Ex): Just before making a ranged attack, Lessia can use a move action to make a Sleight of Hand check opposed by her target's Spot check. If she wins the opposed check, her opponent is denied his Dexterity bonus to Armor Class against the attack.

Weak Spot (Ex): When using a thrown weapon against a target of Medium size or larger, Lessia can make a ranged touch attack instead of a normal attack. If the attack hits, she does not apply her Strength bonus to the damage.

Evasion (Ex): If Lessia is exposed to any effect that normally allows her to attempt a Reflex saving throw for half damage, she takes no damage with a successful saving throw.

Gnome Traits (Ex): +1 save DC for illusions, +2 bonus on saves against illusions, +1 bonus on attack rolls against kobolds and goblinoids, +4 dodge bonus to AC against giants, +2 bonus on Listen checks and Craft (alchemy) checks.

Improved Evasion (Ex): If Lessia is exposed to any effect that normally allows her to attempt a Reflex saving throw for half damage, she takes no damage with a successful saving throw and only half damage on a failed save.

Improved Uncanny Dodge (Ex): Lessia cannot be flanked except by a rogue of at least 13th level.

Trap Sense (Ex): Against attacks by traps, Kurag gets a +2 bonus on Reflex saves and a +2 dodge bonus to Armor Class.

Illus. by J. Jarvis

Trapfinding (Ex): Lessia can use a Search check to locate a trap when the task has a DC higher than 20.

Uncanny Dodge (Ex): Lessia can react to danger before her senses would normally allow her to do so. She retains her Dexterity bonus to Armor Class even when caught flat-footed.

Possessions: 3 +1 *Small returning javelins,* 10 masterwork javelins, masterwork rapier, 5 shuriken, 3 darts, 2 daggers, *elven chain, gloves of Dexterity +2, quiver of Ehlonna, ring of force shield.*

MASTER OF THE UNSEEN HAND

Masters of the unseen hand delight in crushing their foes with invisible force, flinging massive objects into the sky, and disarming enemies with a single thought. Their mastery of the craft of telekinesis makes masters of the unseen hand potent and versatile combatants.

Originally a cabal of sorcerers who learned to push the limits of their telekinesis, the masters of the unseen hand are now a loose-knit group that includes outsiders and other creatures with the ability to use telekinesis.

Sorcerers are the most likely characters to become masters of the unseen hand, and some wizards take a level or two in the class as well. A significant minority of the order are creatures with the innate ability to use telekinesis, such as githyanki, ghosts, beholders, and even the occasional demon.

Because their abilities are suited to warfare, masters of the unseen hand are often found in the thick of the fighting, disarming opponents with telekinesis and using it to hurl them to the ground—or even high into the sky. Some hire themselves out as mercenaries, attaching themselves to a group of mid-level fighters who want to catch their foes by surprise.

Hit Die: d4.

TABLE 2–22: THE MASTER OF THE UNSEEN HAND

Level	Base Attack Bonus	Fort Save	Ref Save	Will Save	Special
1st	+1	+0	+0	+2	Improved caster level, versatile telekinesis
2nd	+2	+0	+0	+3	Telekinetic wielder, sustained concentration
3rd	+3	+1	+1	+3	Full attack telekinesis
4th	+4	+1	+1	+4	Improved violent thrust, telekinetic flight
5th	+5	+1	+1	+4	Fling skyward

Requirements

To qualify to become a master of the unseen hand, a character must fulfill all the following criteria.

Skills: Concentration 8 ranks.

Spells: Able to cast the *telekinesis* spell, or access to telekinesis as a spell-like or supernatural ability.

Class Skills

The master of the unseen hand's class skills (and the key ability for each skill) are Concentration (Con), Craft (Int), Intimidate (Cha), Knowledge (arcana) (Int), Profession (Wis), and Spellcraft (Int).

Skill Points at Each Level: 2 + Int modifier.

Class Features

All of the following are class features of the master of the unseen hand prestige class.

Weapon and Armor Proficiency: Masters of the unseen hand gain no proficiency with any weapon or armor.

Improved Caster Level (Ex): At 1st level, a master of the unseen hand begins his relentless focus on the power of telekinesis. He adds his levels in master of the unseen hand to his caster level (whether from actual spellcasting levels or determined by the spell-like ability) when using his telekinesis ability. For example, a 10th-level sorcerer/3rd-level master of the unseen hand casts *telekinesis* as a 13th-level caster, and a blue slaad who is a 2nd-level master of the unseen hand would use its *telekinesis* spell-like ability as a 10th-level caster.

Versatile Telekinesis (Ex): A master of the unseen hand learns to combine the three versions of the *telekinesis* spell or ability, switching from one to another as he likes. For instance, he can use sustained force for 2 rounds, then switch to combat maneuver, then return to using sustained force. The spell or spell-like ability ends after the first use of the violent thrust version, however, or if the master of the unseen hand is unable to maintain concentration.

Telekinetic Wielder (Ex): A master of the unseen hand develops the ability to wield weapons with his telekinetic power. By maintaining concentration on the combat maneuver version of *telekinesis*, a master of the unseen hand of 2nd level or higher can make a single attack with an unattended weapon or one he is holding, moving the weapon up to 20 feet before the attack. Resolve the attack as normal, except that the weapon's movement doesn't provoke attacks of opportunity. The master of the unseen hand's base attack bonus on this attempt is equal to his caster level plus his Intelligence modifier (if a wizard) or Charisma modifier (if a sorcerer or a creature with the *telekinesis* supernatural or spell-like ability). Any weapon-related feats the master of the unseen hand has (such as Weapon Focus and Power Attack) do not apply when he's telekinetically wielding a weapon.

The weapon wielded can be one the master of the unseen hand took from a foe on a successful disarm attempt.

Sustained Concentration (Ex): At 2nd level, a master of the unseen hand becomes adept at moving and fighting while maintaining his telekinesis ability. It only takes a move action, not a standard action, to use the sustained force version of *telekinesis* (or simply to maintain concentration so the ability doesn't end). The master of the unseen hand can even cast another spell while maintaining concentration on telekinesis, but doing so requires a successful Concentration check as if the caster were distracted by a nondamaging spell (Concentration check DC equal to the save DC of telekinesis). It still takes a standard action to use the combat maneuver or violent thrust versions of the ability, however.

Full Attack Telekinesis (Ex): At 3rd level, a master of the unseen hand is as skilled in telekinetic combat as a fighter is with melee combat. When using the combat maneuver version of *telekinesis* or wielding a weapon telekinetically, the master of the unseen hand can make a full attack, potentially attacking, bull rushing, disarming, grappling, or tripping more than once per round. Just as with nontelekinetic attacks, the master of the unseen hand gains an additional attack for every 5 points of base attack bonus above +1 (using caster level for base attack bonus as described in the *telekinesis* spell description).

Improved Violent Thrust (Ex): At 4th level, a master of the unseen hand's violent thrust version of *telekinesis* becomes more effective. He uses his caster level in place of his base attack bonus when making the attack roll, and he uses his Intelligence modifier (if a wizard) or Charisma modifier (if a sorcerer or a creature with the *telekinesis* supernatural or spell-like ability) as a bonus on damage rolls if he hurls weapons at the target. Finally, using a violent thrust no longer ends the telekinesis effect, but the master of the unseen hand can't make another violent thrust for 1d4 rounds.

Telekinetic Flight (Ex): A master of the unseen hand of 4th level or higher can use the sustained force version of *telekinesis* to lift himself and willing creatures into the air. With a move action, the master of the unseen hand can move 20 feet with perfect maneuverability and can move willing creatures as well. The master of the unseen hand doesn't have to move all the creatures he's lifting in the same direction, but any lifted creatures plummet to the ground if they move more than 40 feet from the master of the unseen hand. The master of the unseen hand can lift one Medium or smaller creature (carrying up to its maximum load) per three caster levels. A Large creature counts as two Medium creatures, a Huge creature counts as two Large creatures, and so forth. Unlike the form of flight granted by the *fly* spell, telekinetic flight ends immediately and abruptly if disrupted by dispel magic or a lapse in the master of the unseen hand's concentration. Without *telekinesis* to support them, creatures fall to the ground immediately, taking 1d6 points of damage per 10 feet fallen (maximum 20d6).

A master of the unseen hand

Fling Skyward (Ex): Rather than hurling a creature toward another target, a 5th-level master of the unseen hand can use the violent thrust version of *telekinesis* to hurl a creature straight up. A target is allowed a Will save (and spell resistance) to negate the effect. The master of the unseen hand can lift a creature into the air a maximum distance of 10 feet per caster level. At the beginning of the character's next action, the creature falls to the ground, taking 1d6 points of damage per 10 feet fallen. Unlike other times when a master of the unseen hand uses the violent thrust version of *telekinesis*, flinging a foe skyward immediately ends the telekinesis effect.

Sample Master of the Unseen Hand

Malik Orbius: Human sorcerer 12/master of the unseen hand 5; CR 17; Medium humanoid; HD 12d4+12 plus 5d4+5; hp 60; Init +2; Spd 30 ft.; AC 19, touch 14, flat-footed 17; Base Atk +11; Grp +10; Atk +11 melee (1d4/19–20, +1 *dagger*) or +14 ranged (1d4/19–20, +1 *dagger*); Full Atk +11/+6/+1 melee (1d4/19–20, +1 *dagger*) or +14 ranged (1d4/19–20, +1 *dagger*); SA fling skyward, full attack telekinesis, improved violent thrust, telekinetic wielder; SQ improved caster level, spell resistance 18, sustained concentration, telekinetic flight, versatile telekinesis; AL NG; SV Fort +10, Ref +11, Will +17; Str 8, Dex 14, Con 13, Int 10, Wis 12, Cha 23.

Skills and Feats: Bluff +21, Concentration +21, Diplomacy +8, Intimidate +13, Spellcraft +20; Craft Staff, Dodge, Extend Spell, Greater Spell Focus (transmutation), Greater Spell Penetration, Spell Focus (transmutation), Spell Penetration.

Fling Skyward (Ex): Malik can use the violent thrust version of *telekinesis* to hurl a creature as far as 170 feet straight up. The target can avoid being flung if it overcomes the attempt with spell resistance or if it succeeds on a DC 21 Will save. At the beginning of Malik's next action, it falls to the ground and take 1d6 points of damage for every 10 feet of distance. Flinging a foe skyward immediately ends the telekinesis effect.

Full Attack Telekinesis (Ex): When using the combat maneuver version of *telekinesis* or when wielding a weapon telekinetically, Mailk can make up to four attacks with a base attack bonus of +17/+12/+7/+2.

Improved Violent Thrust (Ex): Malik makes violent thrust attacks with an attack bonus of +23. If he hurls weapons at the target, each one deals an extra 6 points of damage. Using a violent thrust doesn't end his *telekinesis* spell, but he can't make another violent thrust for 1d4 rounds.

Telekinetic Wielder (Ex): Malik can make a single attack with an unattended weapon or one he is telekinetically holding, moving it up to 20 feet before the attack. He has a +23 base attack bonus and a +6 bonus on the damage roll.

Improved Caster Level (Ex): Malik casts *telekinesis* as a 17th-level caster.

Telekinetic Flight (Ex): Malik can make himself and four other Medium creatures fly at a speed of 20 feet with perfect maneuverability as a move action. The lifted creatures plummet if they move more than 40 feet away from Malik.

Sustained Concentration (Ex): Malik can use the sustained force version of *telekinesis* as a move action, or simply maintain concentration as a move action. If he casts another spell while still concentrating on *telekinesis*, he must succeed on a DC 23 Concentration check.

Versatile Telekinesis (Ex): Malik can switch between the three versions of the *telekinesis* spell at will. The spell ends when he stops concentrating on the spell or when its duration expires.

Sorcerer Spells Known (6/8/8/7/7/6/4; save DC 16 + spell level, DC 18 + spell level for transmutations): 0—*arcane mark, detect magic, detect poison, light, mage hand, message, open/close, ray of frost, resistance*; 1st—*charm person, feather fall, magic missile, shield, unseen servant*; 2nd—*bear's endurance, cat's grace, detect thoughts, scorching ray*; 3rd—*dispel magic, clairaudience/clairvoyance, fly, lightning bolt*; 4th—*charm monster, dimension door, enervation*; 5th—*telekinesis, teleport*; 6th—*Bigby's forceful hand.*

Possessions: Robe of the archmagi (white), cloak of Charisma +4, ring of protection +2, +1 dagger.

MINDSPY

Success in combat relies on anticipating your enemy's every move. A mindspy knows how easy that can be if you're privy to your foe's every thought. By reading the minds of her enemies, a mindspy knows exactly what they're going to do a fraction of a second before they do it. Eventually she learns to probe deeper, finding weak spots in her enemy's training.

Because the class relies utterly on *detect thoughts*, most mindspies are creatures who have it as a spell-like or supernatural ability usable at will, such as couatls, succubi, doppelgangers, ghaeles, myrmarchs, leonals, mind flayers, dark nagas, rakshasas, and green slaadi. Spellcasters sometimes take levels in the prestige class if they can cast detect thoughts frequently, or if they have a *helm of telepathy* to enable the mindspy's class features.

The most often encountered mindspies are elite mind flayer or doppelgangers. There is rumored to be a secretive order of couatl mindspies that roams the planes, hunting down evildoers.

Hit Die: d8.

Table 2-23: The Mindspy

Level	Base Attack Bonus	Fort Save	Ref Save	Will Save	Special
1st	+1	+0	+0	+2	Anticipate, combat telepathy, spherical detect thoughts
2nd	+2	+0	+0	+3	Faster mindscan
3rd	+3	+1	+1	+3	Multiple surface thoughts (two)
4th	+4	+1	+1	+4	Instant mindscan
5th	+5	+1	+1	+4	Multiple surface thoughts (four)

Requirements

To qualify to become a mindspy, a character must fulfill all the following criteria.

Base Attack Bonus: +3.

Skills: Concentration 8 ranks.

Spells: Able to cast the *detect thoughts* spell or to use *detect thoughts* as a spell-like ability.

Class Skills

The mindspy's class skills (and the key ability for each skill) are Bluff (Cha), Concentration (Con), Craft (Int), Intimidate (Cha), Profession (Wis), and Sense Motive (Wis).

Skill Points at Each Level: 2 + Int modifier.

Class Features

All of the following are class features of the mindspy prestige class.

Weapon and Armor Proficiency: Mindspies gain no proficiency with any weapon or armor.

Anticipate (Su): Because she is reading her foe's thoughts, a mindspy knows where she needs to block and how she needs to dodge before an attack from the foe arrives. In addition, a mindspy can detect weak points in a foe's defense by observing her enemy's thoughts. At 1st level, a mindspy can add 1 point of Charisma bonus (if any) per mindspy class level as a bonus to her Armor Class against attacks from a foe whose surface thoughts she is detecting (if the normal 3 rounds passes and the target fails its Will save) as well as an insight bonus on attack rolls against any foe whose surface thoughts she is detecting. If a mindspy is caught flat-footed or is otherwise denied her Dexterity bonus, she also loses this insight bonus to her Armor Class.

Combat Telepathy (Su): By reading her opponents' surface thoughts, a mindspy can anticipate their every move. She can make a Concentration check (DC 10 + damage taken during the previous round) at the beginning of her turn. If the mindspy succeeds, she can maintain concentration on *detect thoughts* as a free action. If the mindspy casts a spell or uses another spell-like ability, detect thoughts ends.

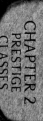

Spherical Detect Thoughts (Su): A mindspy can widen the area of her *detect thoughts* spell or ability into a sphere centered on her, rather than a cone. The radius of the sphere is equal to the length of the cone.

Faster Mindscan (Su): By 2nd level, a mindspy has become adept at tuning into others' thoughts quickly. In the round when she activates *detect thoughts*, she detects the presence or absence of thoughts and the Intelligence score of each thinking mind in the area. In the next round, she detects the surface thoughts of any one mind in the area.

Multiple Surface Thoughts (Su): A mindspy of 3rd level or higher can simultaneously detect the surface thoughts of any two creatures who fail their Will saves. This means that she gains anticipate bonuses against both of them. Once per round as a free action, she can choose new minds to listen in on. At 5th level, a mindspy can simultaneously detect the surface thoughts of four creatures.

Instant Mindscan (Su): At 4th level and higher, a mindspy can enter her enemies' minds at the speed of thought. She gains all the information from *detect thoughts* (presence or absence of minds, Intelligence scores, and surface thoughts) in the same round when she activates the spell or ability. The mindspy's enemies still get Will saves to keep their surface thoughts secret.

Sample Mindspy

Sanjakilar: Doppelganger sorcerer 3/mindspy 5; CR 11; Medium monstrous humanoid (shapechanger); HD 4d8+8 plus 3d4+6 plus 5d8+10; hp 72; Init +2; Spd 30 ft.; AC 16, touch 12, flat-footed 14; Base Atk +11; Grp +14; Atk +16 melee (1d6+4/19–20, +1 *short sword*); Full Atk +16/+11/+6 melee (1d6+4/19–20, +1 *short sword*), or +14/+9/+4 melee (1d6+4/19–20, +1 *short sword*) and +14 melee (1d6+2/19–20, +1 *short sword*); SA detect thoughts; SQ combat telepathy, change shape, immunity to sleep and charm effects; AL N; SV Fort +5, Ref +8, Will +12; Str 16, Dex 14, Con 14, Int 13, Wis 12, Cha 18.

Skills and Feats: Bluff +20, Concentration +17, Diplomacy +8, Disguise +13, Intimidate +6, Sense Motive +11; Combat Expertise, Combat Telepathy, Improved Feint, Two Weapon Fighting, Weapon Focus (short sword).

Anticipate (Su): Sanjakilar gains a +4 insight bonus on attack rolls against foes whose surface thoughts it is detecting, and the same bonus to Armor Class against attacks by such foes.

Detect Thoughts (Su): Sanjakilar can continuously use *detect thoughts* as the spell (caster level 18th; Will DC 16 negates). It can suppress or resume this ability as a free action.

Combat Telepathy (Su): By reading its opponents' surface thoughts, Sanjakilar can anticipate their every move. It can make a Concentration check (DC 10 + damage taken during the previous round) at the beginning of its turn. If the check succeeds, Sanjakilar can maintain concentration on *detect thoughts* as a free action. If Sanjakilar casts a spell or uses another spell-like ability, detect thoughts ends.

Change Shape (Su): Sanjakilar can assume any Small or Medium humanoid form or revert to its own form as a standard action. A change in form cannot be dispelled, but Sanjakilar would revert to its natural form if killed. A *true seeing* spell or ability reveals its natural form.

Instant Mindscan (Su): Sanjakilar gains all the information from *detect thoughts* (presence or absence of minds, Intelligence scores, and surface thoughts) in the same round when it activates the ability. Sanjakilar's enemies still get a Will save to keep their surface thoughts secret.

Multiple Surface Thoughts (Su): Sanjakilar can simultaneously detect the surface thoughts of four creatures within range who fail their Will saves. It can choose new minds to listen to once per round as a free action.

Spherical Detect Thoughts (Su): Sanjakilar can use *detect thoughts* within a 60-foot sphere centered on itself.

Skills: *Sanjakilar gets an extra +10 circumstance bonus on Disguise checks when using its change shape ability. If it can read an opponent's mind, it gets a further +4 circumstance bonus on Bluff and Disguise checks.

Sorcerer Spells Known (6/6; save DC 14 + spell level): 0—*detect magic, light, mage hand, message, read magic;* 1st—*expeditious retreat, mage armor, magic missile.*

Possessions: Two +1 *short swords, ring of feather fall.*

NATURE'S WARRIOR

Nature's warriors are defenders of the wild, protectors of the natural world . . . and often druids who have spent "too much time" in wild shape form. Members of this prestige class share a bond that transcends race and outside appearance.

When a character gains the ability to naturally shift into the form of a "lower animal," she sometimes gains a perspective on life that makes her envy this adopted form over her own. She may simply feel a stronger tie to nature while in animal (or elemental) form, or perhaps she longs for the power such forms give her. Certainly she begins to develop her abilities while in wild forms at the expense of the shape she was born in.

A mindspy

Many people consider nature's warriors to be loners or fanatics, even less a part of the world than the most solitary druid or ranger. Nature's warriors, however, tend to be very communal. They often communicate with each other—sometimes through animal messengers, or even face to face, when they can bring themselves to leave their territories—and they keep a careful watch on "civilization." Nature's warriors develop their animalistic instincts more strongly than the behavior associated with societal learning, and do have a tendency to come off as gruff or impatient with those who are not as "in tune" with nature as themselves. It is not uncommon for a nature's warrior to spend days or even weeks in a single animal or elemental form, or to shift from form to form regularly, without returning to whatever humanoid form she started with.

Virtually all nature's warriors begin as members of the druid class, but some members of other prestige classes or creatures with the wild shape ability have adopted this class. Many more militant druids—those with levels in fighter, barbarian, or ranger—find this class ideal for their purposes.

Hit Die: d10.

Requirements

To qualify to become a nature's warrior, a character must fulfill all the following criteria.

Alignment: Any neutral.

Base Attack Bonus: +4.

Skills: Knowledge (nature) 8 ranks, Knowledge (the planes) 2 ranks, Survival 8 ranks.

Feats: Track.

Special: Wild shape ability.

Class Skills

The nature's warrior class skills (and the key ability for each skill) are Diplomacy (Cha), Handle Animal (Cha), Intimidate (Cha), Jump (Str), Knowledge (nature) (Int), Listen (Wis), Survival (Wis), and Swim (Str).

Skill Points at Each Level: 2 + Int modifier.

TABLE 2–24: THE NATURE'S WARRIOR

Level	Base Attack Bonus	Fort Save	Ref Save	Will Save	Special
1st	+1	+2	+0	+0	Nature's armament, wilding
2nd	+2	+3	+0	+0	+1 level of existing divine spellcasting class
3rd	+3	+3	+1	+1	Nature's armament
4th	+4	+4	+1	+1	+1 level of existing divine spellcasting class
5th	+5	+4	+1	+1	Nature's armament

Class Features

All of the following are class features of the nature's warrior prestige class.

Weapon and Armor Proficiency: Nature's warriors gain no proficiency with any weapon or armor.

Spells per Day: At every even-numbered level gained in the nature's warrior class, the character gains new spells per day as if she had also gained a level in a divine spellcasting class she belonged to before adding the prestige class. If the character did not belong to a divine spellcasting class before attaining 2nd level in the prestige class, she gains a druid spellcasting level. In no case, however, does she gain any other benefit a character of that class would have gained, except for an increased effective level of spellcasting. If a character had more than one divine spellcasting class before becoming a nature's warrior, she must decide to which class she adds the new level for purposes of determining spells per day.

Nature's Armament (Su): Upon attaining an odd-numbered level in this prestige class, a nature's warrior may choose one of the following abilities. These abilities, unless otherwise noted, are only applicable while the nature's warrior is in wild shape form.

Armor of the Crocodile: The nature's warrior's natural armor bonus is improved by +1 per class level. This is an actual improvement, not an enhancement bonus.

Blaze of Power: While in fire elemental form, the nature's warrior is covered in a blaze of power, which functions as a warm fire shield at a caster level equal to her druid level (if any) plus her nature's warrior level.

Claws of the Grizzly: The nature's warrior gains a +3 bonus on damage when using her natural weapons.

Earth's Resilience: The nature's warrior gains damage reduction 3/—.

Nature's Weapon: The nature's warrior gains a +1 enhancement bonus on attack rolls when using her natural weapons, and her attacks are treated as magic weapons for the purpose of overcoming damage reduction.

Robe of Clouds: While in air elemental form, the nature's warrior may as a free action wreathe her body in mist and clouds for 1 minute per class level (or until she dismisses the effect). This gives her concealment, though it does not affect her ability to see or act at all.

Serpent's Coils: When in the form of a creature that normally has the improved grab ability, the nature's warrior gains a +4 bonus on all grapple checks and does damage equal to 1d8 + her Strength bonus after winning an opposed grapple check.

Water's Flow: To use this ability, the nature's warrior must be able to use wild shape to take the form of an elemental. Three times per day as part of a move action, the character may transform her body into a flowing rush of water. She may move at her base land speed while in this form but does not provoke attacks of opportunity while doing so. She may do nothing but move while in this form. At the end of her move, she immediately changes back into whatever form she was in prior to activating this ability. She may use this ability while not in wild shape form.

Wild Growth: The nature's warrior gains fast healing 1.

Wings of the Hurricane: If the nature's warrior is in an avian form or air elemental form, she increases her base fly speed by 30 feet and improves her maneuverability by one category (thus good maneuverability becomes perfect).

Wilding (Su): Nature's warrior class levels stack with druid levels (as well as levels in other prestige classes that allow these abilities to stack) to determine wild shape abilities and for wild empathy checks. For example, a druid 8/nature's warrior 3 would be considered an 11th-level druid for purposes of wild shape size, type, and frequency (she could assume wild shape form 4/day and could become a Tiny creature). She would add +11 for her class levels (instead of +8) to her wild empathy checks against animals and certain magical beasts.

Sample Nature's Warrior

Beshya: Female human druid 6/nature's warrior 4; CR 10; Medium humanoid; HD 6d8+12 plus 4d10+8; hp 69; Init +3; Spd 30 ft.; AC 20, touch 13, flat-footed 18; Base Atk +8; Grp +9; Atk +10 melee (1d6+2/18–20, *+1 scimitar*) or +12 ranged (1d4, masterwork sling); Full Atk +10/+5 melee (1d6+2/18–20, *+1 scimitar*) or +12/+7 ranged (1d4, masterwork sling); SA spells; SQ animal companion, armor of the crocodile, claws of the grizzly, nature sense, resist nature's lure, spontaneous casting, trackless step, wild empathy, wild shape 4/day, wilding, woodland stride; AL NG; SV Fort +11, Ref +6, Will +9; Str 12, Dex 16, Con 14, Int 10, Wis 16, Cha 8.

Skills and Feats: Concentration +11, Handle Animal +8, Knowledge (nature) +10, Knowledge (the planes) +2, Listen +9, Spot +12, Survival +14; Augment Summoning, Combat Casting, Spell Focus (conjuration), Track, Weapon Focus (scimitar).

Dire Wolf Shape: Beshya often uses wild shape to change into a dire wolf. This changes her statistics as follows: Init +2; Spd 50 ft.; AC 18, touch 11, flat-footed 16; Grp +19; Atk +14 melee (1d8+13, bite); Full Atk +14 melee (1d8+13, bite); SA trip; SV Fort +12, Ref +5, Will +9; Str 25, Dex 15, Con 17, Int 10, Wis 16, Cha 8.

Animal Companion (Ex): Beshya's animal companion is Grishka, a wolf (see below).

Armor of the Crocodile (Su): In wild shape form, Beshya gains a +4 bonus to her natural armor.

Claws of the Grizzly (Su): In wild shape form, Besyha gains a +3 bonus on damage rolls when using her natural weapons.

Nature Sense (Ex): Beshya gains a +2 bonus on Knowledge (nature) and Survival checks (already figured into the statistics above).

Resist Nature's Lure (Ex): Beshya gains a +4 bonus on saving throws against the spell-like abilities of fey.

Spontaneous Casting: Beshya can lose a prepared spell in order to cast any *summon nature's ally* spell of the same level or lower.

Illus. by W. England

A nature's warrior panics a couple of gnolls.

Trackless Step (Ex): Beshya leaves no trail in natural surroundings and cannot be tracked.

Trip (Ex) (Dire wolf shape only): If Beshya hits with her bite attack, she can attempt to trip her opponent (+11 check modifier) as a free action without making a touch attack or provoking an attack of opportunity. If the attempt fails, the opponent cannot react to trip her.

Wild Empathy (Ex): Beshya's wild empathy check is 1d20+9.

Wild Shape (Su): Beshya can turn herself into any Small, Medium, or Large animal and back again four times per day. This ability functions like the *polymorph* spell, except as noted here. The effect lasts for 6 hours, or until she changes back. Changing form is a standard action and doesn't provoke an attack of opportunity.

Wilding (Su): Beshya's druid levels and nature's warrior levels stack to determine wild shape abilities and wild empathy checks.

Woodland Stride (Ex): Beshya may move through any sort of undergrowth at her normal speed and without taking damage or suffering any other impairment. However, thorns, briars, and overgrown areas that have been magically manipulated still affect her.

Druid Spells Prepared (6/5/4/4/2; save DC 13 + spell level): 0—*cure minor wounds* (2), *detect magic, flare, light, resistance*; 1st—*cure light wounds* (2), *entangle, longstrider, speak with animals*; 2nd—*barkskin, bull's strength, flaming sphere, resist energy*; 3rd—*cure moderate wounds* (2), *greater magic fang, neutralize poison*; 4th—*air walk, flame strike*. Beshya casts spells as an 8th-level druid.

Possessions: +1 scimitar, +2 leather armor, +1 large wooden shield, gauntlets of Dexterity +2, ring of protection +1, boots of elvenkind, masterwork sling, 20 bullets, 20 silvered bullets.

Grishka: Wolf; Medium magical beast [augmented animal]; HD 6d8+15; hp 42; Init +3; Spd 50 ft.; AC 18, touch 12, flat-footed 16; Base Atk +4; Grp +6; Atk +7 melee (1d6+3, bite); Full Atk +7 melee (1d6+3, bite); SA trip; SQ animal companion abilities, low-light vision, scent; AL N; SV Fort +7, Ref +8, Will +3; Str 15, Dex 17, Con 15, Int 2, Wis 12, Cha 6.

Skills and Feats: Hide +2, Listen +7, Move Silently +5, Spot +5, Survival +1*; Alertness, Toughness, Track[B], Weapon Focus (bite).

*+4 racial bonus on Survival checks when tracking by scent.

Animal Companion Abilities: Link, share spells, evasion, devotion, 3 bonus tricks. Grishka is trained for hunting and also knows the tricks come, defend, and guard.

Scent (Ex): Grishka can detect approaching enemies, sniff out hidden foes, and track by sense of smell.

Trip (Ex): If Grishka hits with its bite attack, it can attempt to trip its opponent (+2 check modifier) as a free action without making a touch attack or provoking an attack of opportunity. If the attempt fails, the opponent cannot react to trip Grishka.

OCCULT SLAYER

The occult slayer is driven to confront any arcane or divine spellcaster who crosses her path. Occult slayers believe that mortals are too irresponsible to wield magic, and that those who dare to do so must be slain. Spellcasters who become occult slayers are considered to have seen the error of their ways—although they may still cast spells, they rely primarily on their battle prowess and their ability to resist magical effects to defeat their enemies.

The occult slayer comes into her own through exhaustive training. Every regimen she performs is an exercise that refines her anger against spellcasters into martial skill. Each occult slayer forms a preternatural bond with her masterwork weapon of choice, which serves as the instrument of her vengeance.

This prestige class is ideal for individuals who have been victimized by spellcasters and seek acceptable ways to oppose them. Most occult slayers begin their careers as fighters, although barbarians and rangers often take this path as well. Monks and rogues have also been known to embrace this calling, but bards and paladins find the occult slayer's preoccupation with spellcasters stifling. Clerics, druids, sorcerers, and wizards—the primary targets of occult slayers—tend not to adopt this prestige class, although such turnarounds are not without precedent.

NPC occult slayers seldom form organizations, because they have discovered that congregating in one place attracts spellcasters intent on making preemptive strikes against them. Instead, occult slayers discreetly meet from time to time to exchange information about spellcasting opponents they have targeted for matches. Otherwise, the occult slayer operates alone, traveling between venues in search of matches that involve spellcasters. Because of the inherent discretion that occult slayers display, a candidate for this prestige class must be chosen and trained by another occult slayer who is willing to share her secrets.

Hit Die: d8.

TABLE 2–25: THE OCCULT SLAYER

Level	Base Attack Bonus	Fort Save	Ref Save	Will Save	Special
1st	+1	+0	+0	+2	Magical defense +1, weapon bond
2nd	+2	+0	+0	+3	Vicious strike, mind over magic 1/day
3rd	+3	+1	+1	+3	Auravision, magical defense +2
4th	+4	+1	+1	+4	Mind over magic 2/day, nondetection cloak
5th	+5	+1	+1	+4	Blank thoughts, magical defense +3

Requirements

To qualify to become an occult slayer, a character must fulfill all the following criteria.

Base Attack Bonus: +5.

Skills: Knowledge (arcana) 4 ranks, Spellcraft 3 ranks.

Feats: Improved Initiative, Weapon Focus (any weapon).

Class Skills

The occult slayer's class skills (and the key ability for each skill) are Bluff (Cha), Craft (Int), Gather Information (Cha), Knowledge (arcana) (Int), Profession (Wis), Sense Motive (Wis), and Spellcraft (Int).

Skill Points at Each Level: 2 + Int modifier.

Class Features

All of the following are class features of the occult slayer prestige class.

Weapon and Armor Proficiency: Occult slayers are proficient with all simple and martial weapons and all armor and shields.

Magical Defense (Ex): An occult slayer's constant training in countering magic of all types manifests itself as a bonus on saving throws against spells or spell-like abilities. This bonus is +1 at 1st level, and it increases to +2 at 3rd level and to +3 at 5th level.

Weapon Bond (Su): An occult slayer must choose a particular weapon of at least masterwork quality as the focus of her power. Upon making her selection, she immediately forms a bond with the chosen weapon that imbues it with the force of her hatred for spellcasters. Thereafter, any successful attack she makes with that weapon against a spellcaster or a creature with spell-like abilities deals an extra 1d6 points of damage. If this particular weapon is lost or destroyed, the occult slayer loses the ability to deal   the extra damage until she

acquires and bonds with another weapon of the same kind of at least masterwork quality. The occult slayer must spend one day per character level practicing with the replacement weapon (and doing very little else—no adventuring) to create a new weapon bond.

Mind over Magic (Su): Starting at 2nd level, an occult slayer can cause a spell or spell-like ability targeted against her to rebound onto the originator as a free action. This ability otherwise functions as the *spell turning* spell (caster level equals the character's occult slayer level + 5). An occult slayer can use this ability once per day at 2nd level and twice per day at 4th level.

Vicious Strike (Ex): At 2nd level and higher, an occult slayer who readies an attack action to disrupt a spellcaster deals double damage if the attack hits.

Auravision (Su): At 3rd level, an occult slayer gains the ability to see magical auras at a range of up to 60 feet as a free action. This ability otherwise functions as the *detect magic* spell. The character cannot use this ability to determine anything but the number of magical auras present.

Nondetection Cloak (Su): Upon reaching 4th level, an occult slayer (and any gear she wears or carries) becomes more difficult to locate through divinations such as *clairaudience/ clairvoyance*, *locate object*, and other detection spells. The occult slayer gains magical protection from divinations equivalent to a nondetection spell (caster level equals the character's occult slayer level), except that it affects only the occult slayer and her possessions.

Blank Thoughts (Ex): At 5th level, an occult slayer can induce within herself a state of mental absence, thereby

An occult slayer hates spellcasters and has the ability to reflect their spells back upon them.

becoming immune to mind-affecting effects (charms, compulsions, patterns, phantasms, and morale effects). She can suppress or resume this ability as a free action.

Sample Occult Slayer

Harlech: Half-orc ranger 5/occult slayer 5; CR 10; Medium humanoid; HD 5d8+10 plus 5d8+10; hp 65; Init +3; Spd 30 ft.; AC 19, touch 13, flat-footed 16; Base Atk +10; Grp +12; Atk +13 melee (1d10+7/19–20, +1 *bastard sword*) or +16 ranged (1d8+6/×3, +2 *composite longbow* [+4 Str bonus]); Full Atk +13/+8 melee (1d10+7/19–20, +1 *bastard sword*) or +16/+11 ranged (1d8+6/×3, +2 *composite longbow* [+4 Str bonus]) or +14/+14/+9 ranged (1d8+6/×3, +2 *composite longbow* [+4 Str bonus]); SA vicious strike, weapon bond; SQ animal companion, auravision, blank thoughts, darkvision 60 ft., favored enemy elementals +4, favored enemy evil outsiders +2, magical defense +3, mind over magic 2/day, nondetection cloak, wild empathy; AL N; SV Fort +10, Ref +8, Will +6; Str 18, Dex 16, Con 14, Int 10, Wis 12, Cha 4.

Skills and Feats: Hide +11, Knowledge (arcana) +4, Listen +9, Move Silently +8, Sense Motive +6, Spellcraft +3, Spot +14, Survival +9; Combat Reflexes, Endurance, Improved Initiative, Point Blank Shot, Rapid Shot, Track^B, Weapon Focus (composite longbow).

Vicious Strike (Ex): Harlech deals double damage on attacks made as readied actions to disrupt spellcasters.

Weapon Bond (Su): Any hit Harlech scores with his composite longbow deals an extra 1d6 points of damage against a spellcaster or a creature with spell-like abilities.

Animal Companion (Ex): Harlech has an owl as an animal companion. Its statistics are as described on page 277 of the *Monster Manual*, except that Harlech can handle it as a free action and share spells if the companion is within 5 feet (see page 36 of the *Player's Handbook*).

Auravision (Su): Harlech can see magical auras within 60 feet as a free action, but can tell only the number of different auras, not their strength or school.

Blank Thoughts (Ex): Harlech can induce within himself a state of mental absence, thereby becoming immune to mind-affecting effects (charms, compulsions, patterns, phantasms, and morale effects). He can suppress or resume this ability as a free action.

Nondetection Cloak (Su): Harlech gains magical protection from divinations equivalent to a *nondetection* spell from a 5th-level caster, except that it affects only himself and his possessions.

Combat Style (Ex): Harlech has selected archery. He gains the Rapid Shot feat without having to meet the normal prerequisites.

Favored Enemy (Ex): Harlech gains a +4 bonus on his Bluff, Listen, Sense Motive, Spot, and Survival checks when using these skills against elementals. He gets the same bonus on weapon damage rolls against elementals.

Against evil outsiders, he gains a +2 bonus on these skill checks and on weapon damage rolls.

Magical Defense (Ex): Harlech gains a +3 bonus on saves against spells and spell-like effects.

Mind over Magic (Su): Harlech can reflect targeted spells back at their casters, as the *spell turning* spell from a 10th-level caster.

Wild Empathy (Ex): Harlech can improve the attitude of an animal in the same way a Diplomacy check can improve the attitude of a sentient being. He rolls 1d20+4, or 1d20+1 if attempting to influence a magical beast with an Intelligence score of 1 or 2.

Ranger Spells Prepared (1; save DC 11 + spell level): 1st— *longstrider*.

Possessions: +2 *composite longbow* (+4 Str bonus), +1 *bastard sword*, +1 *mithral breastplate*, 20 arrows.

ORDER OF THE BOW INITIATE

When asked, "What is Truth?," an initiate of the Order of the Bow picks up his bow, fires an arrow and, without saying a word, lets his mastery of the weapon serve as the gauge of the archer's progress along the way. By learning the meditative art of the Way of the Bow, the archer improves his discipline, precision, and spirituality. Order of the Bow initiates see their weapons as extensions of their being, and the use of a bow as a spiritual experience.

Fighters are the most common initiates of the Order of the Bow. Rangers, paladins, and even barbarians utilize these skills and philosophies as well. Some rogues and bards have been known to enter the order, but they are rare indeed.

NPC initiates are most often encountered teaching others the ways of archery or wandering the lands looking for true challenges for their skill.

Hit Die: d8.

TABLE 2–26: THE ORDER OF THE BOW INITIATE

Level	Base Attack Bonus	Fort Save	Ref Save	Will Save	Special
1st	+1	+0	+2	+2	Ranged precision +1d8
2nd	+2	+0	+3	+3	Close combat shot
3rd	+3	+1	+3	+3	Ranged precision +2d8
4th	+4	+1	+4	+4	Greater Weapon Focus
5th	+5	+1	+4	+4	Ranged precision +3d8
6th	+6	+2	+5	+5	Sharp-Shooting
7th	+7	+2	+5	+5	Ranged precision +4d8
8th	+8	+2	+6	+6	—
9th	+9	+3	+6	+6	Ranged precision +5d8
10th	+10	+3	+7	+7	Extended precision

Requirements

To qualify to become an Order of the Bow initiate, a character must fulfill all the following criteria:

Base Attack Bonus: +5.

Skills: Craft (bowmaking) 5 ranks, Knowledge (religion) 2 ranks.

Feats: Point Blank Shot, Precise Shot, Rapid Shot, Weapon Focus (longbow, shortbow, or the composite version of either).

Class Skills

The Order of the Bow initiate's class skills (and the key ability for each skill) are Climb (Str), Craft (Int), Knowledge (religion) (Int), Ride (Dex), Spot (Wis), and Swim (Str).

Skill Points at Each Level: 2 + Int modifier.

Class Features

All of the following are class features of the Order of the Bow initiate prestige class.

Weapon and Armor Proficiency: Order of the Bow initiates gain no proficiency with any weapon or armor.

Ranged Precision (Ex): As a standard action, an initiate may make a single precisely aimed attack with a ranged weapon, dealing an extra 1d8 points of damage if the attack hits. When making a ranged precision attack, an initiate must be within 30 feet of his target. An initiate's ranged precision attack only works against living creatures with discernible anatomies. Any creature that is immune to critical hits (including undead, constructs, oozes, plants, and incorporeal creatures) is not vulnerable to a ranged precision attack, and any item or ability that protects a creature from critical hits (such as armor with the fortification special ability) also protects a creature from the extra damage.

Unlike with a rogue's sneak attack, the initiate's target does not have to be flat-footed or denied its Dexterity bonus, but if it is, the initiate's extra precision damage stacks with sneak attack damage. Treat the initiate's ranged precision attack as a sneak attack in all other ways.

The initiate's bonus to damage on ranged precision attacks increases by +1d8 every two levels.

An initiate can only use this ability with a ranged weapon for which he has taken the Weapon Focus feat.

Close Combat Shot (Ex): At 2nd level, an initiate can attack with a ranged weapon while in a threatened square and not provoke an attack of opportunity.

Greater Weapon Focus (Ex): At 4th level, an Order of the Bow initiate gains the Greater Weapon Focus feat with

a single ranged weapon for which he has taken the Weapon Focus feat even if he has not attained 8th level as a fighter.

Sharp-Shooting: At 6th level, an initiate gains the Sharp-Shooting feat (see Chapter 3 of this book) even if he does not meet the prerequisites.

Extended Precision (Su): A 10th-level Order of the Bow initiate's senses and feel for "the shot" become so attuned that he may make ranged precision attacks (and sneak attacks, if he has the ability) at a range of up to 60 feet.

Sample Order of the Bow Initiate

Garrick Kuryana: Half-elf fighter 5/Order of the Bow initiate 8; CR 13; Medium humanoid; HD 5d10+5 plus 8d8+8; hp 77; Init +5; Spd 30 ft., 50 ft. when mounted; AC 19, touch 15, flat-footed 14; Base Atk +13; Grp +15; Atk +16 melee (2d6+4/19–20, +1 greatsword) or +23 ranged (1d8+10×3, +3 composite longbow [+2 Str bonus]) or +17 ranged (3d8+30/×3, +3 composite longbow [+2 Str bonus] with Manyshot); Full Atk +16/+11/+6 melee (2d6+4/19–20, +1 greatsword) or +23/+18/+13 ranged (1d8+8/×3, +3 composite longbow [+2 Str bonus]) or +21/+21/+16/+11 ranged (1d8+8/×3, +3 composite longbow [+2 Str bonus]) or +23/+18/+13 ranged (1d8+8×3, +3 composite longbow [+2 Str bonus]); SA ranged precision +4d8; SQ close combat shot, half-elf traits; AL NG; SV Fort +7, Ref +12, Will +8; Str 14, Dex 20, Con 13, Int 10, Wis 12, Cha 10.

Skills and Feats: Craft (bowmaking) +4, Intimidate +3, Knowledge (religion) +1, Ride +17, Spot +9; Greater Weapon Focus (composite longbow), Manyshot, Mounted Combat, Point Blank Shot, Precise Shot, Rapid Shot, Sharp-Shooting*, Weapon Focus (composite longbow), Weapon Specialization (composite longbow).

*New feat found in Chapter 3 of this book.

An Order of the Bow initiate

Ranged Precision (Ex): As a standard action, Garrick may make a single precisely aimed attack with a ranged weapon, dealing an extra 4d8 points of damage if the attack hits. When making a ranged precision attack, Garrick must be within 30 feet of his target. A ranged precision attack only works against living creatures with discernible anatomies. Any creature that is immune to critical hits (including undead, constructs, oozes, plants, and incorporeal creatures) is not vulnerable to a ranged precision attack.

Close Combat Shot (Ex): Garrick can attack with a ranged weapon while in a threatened square without provoking an attack of opportunity.

Half-Elf Traits (Ex): Immunity to magic sleep spells and effects; +2 racial bonus on saving throws against enchantment spells or effects; elven blood.

Possessions: +3 composite longbow (+2 Str bonus), +2 leather armor, +1 greatsword, lesser bracers of archery, gloves of Dexterity +2, 2 lesser arrows of undead slaying, 40 arrows, heavy warhorse.

PURPLE DRAGON KNIGHT

The famous Purple Dragons are regarded across the land as exemplars of disciplined, skilled, loyal soldiers. Their reputation is deserved partly because of the heroic actions of their leaders, the Purple Dragon knights.

Purple Dragon knights develop uncanny skills related to coordinating and leading soldiers. Most are fighters, rangers, or paladins, but a few bards, clerics, and rogues have been known to become Purple Dragon knights. Sorcerers and wizards tend to join the War Wizards, an elite brigade of fighting spellcasters allied with the Purple Dragons, while barbarians are too undisciplined, and druids and monks "lack the commitment" to measure up to the Purple Dragons' exacting standards.

In general, NPC Purple Dragon knights are responsible for leading the Purple Dragons on and off the battlefield. Player character knights either are retirees, special liaisons to the army, or recipients of honorary titles. A character's level in this prestige class is irrelevant to his rank in the military, although higher-ranked knights tend to be of higher level. It is not necessary to have this prestige class to serve in the Purple Dragons at large, or even to be an officer in their ranks. Likewise, a Purple Dragon knight might serve her entire career on "detached duty," away from the unit as a whole.

Hit Die: d10.

Requirements

To qualify to become a Purple Dragon knight, a character must fulfill all the following criteria.

Alignment: Lawful good, neutral good, lawful neutral, or neutral.

Base Attack Bonus: +5.

Skills: Diplomacy 1 rank or Intimidate 1 rank, Listen 2 ranks, Ride 2 ranks, Spot 2 ranks.

Feats: Mounted Combat, Negotiator.

Special: Membership in the Purple Dragons.

Class Skills

The Purple Dragon knight's class skills (and the key ability for each skill) are Climb (Str), Diplomacy (Cha), Handle Animal (Cha), Intimidate (Cha), Knowledge (local) (Int), Jump (Str), Ride (Dex), and Swim (Str).

Skill Points at Each Level: 2 + Int modifier.

TABLE 2–27: THE PURPLE DRAGON KNIGHT

Level	Base Attack Bonus	Fort Save	Ref Save	Will Save	Special
1st	+1	+2	+0	+0	Heroic shield, rallying cry
2nd	+2	+3	+0	+0	Inspire courage 1/day
3rd	+3	+3	+1	+1	Fear
4th	+4	+4	+1	+1	Inspire courage 2/day, oath of wrath
5th	+5	+4	+1	+1	Final stand

Class Features

All of the following are class features of the Purple Dragon knight prestige class.

Weapon and Armor Proficiency: Purple Dragon knights gain proficiency with tower shields.

Heroic Shield (Ex): A Purple Dragon knight can use the aid another action to give an ally a +4 circumstance bonus to Armor Class instead of the normal +2.

Rallying Cry (Su): Up to three times per day as a free action, a knight can utter a powerful shout that causes all allies within 60 feet to gain a +1 morale bonus on their next attack roll and increases their speed by 5 feet until the knight's next turn. Traditionally, this mind-affecting ability is used when a formation of soldiers is about to charge.

Inspire Courage (Su): This ability, gained at 2nd level, has the same effect as the bard ability of the same name. The knight makes an inspirational speech, bolstering her allies against fear and improving their combat abilities. To be affected, an ally must be able to hear the knight speak. The effect lasts for as long as the ally hears the knight speak and for 5 rounds thereafter. While speaking, the knight can fight but cannot cast spells, activate magic items by spell completion (such as scrolls), or activate magic items by magic word (such as wands). Affected allies receive a +2 morale bonus on saving throws against charm and fear effects and a +1 morale bonus on attack and weapon damage rolls. At 2nd level, a knight may use this ability once per day; at 4th level, she may use it twice per day.

Fear (Su): Once per day as a standard action, a knight of 3rd level or higher can evoke a fear effect (DC 10 + the knight's class level + the knight's Cha modifier) as the spell *fear*, using her class level as the caster level. Her allies are immune to the effect.

Oath of Wrath (Su): Once per day as a free action, a knight of 4th level or higher can select a single opponent within 60 feet and swear an oath to defeat him. For the duration of the encounter, the knight has a +2 morale bonus on melee attack rolls, weapon damage rolls, saving throws, and skill checks made against the challenged target.

The effect is negated immediately if the knight uses a full-round action to move away from the challenged opponent.

Final Stand (Su): Once per day, a 5th-level Purple Dragon knight can inspire his troops to a heroic effort, temporarily increasing their vitality. All allies within 10 feet of the knight gain 2d10 temporary hit points. This ability affects a number of creatures equal to the knight's class level + her Charisma modifier and lasts an equal number of rounds.

Multiclass Note: A paladin who becomes a Purple Dragon knight may continue advancing as a paladin.

Sample Purple Dragon Knight

Ardalis Brightflame: Half-elf paladin 5/Purple Dragon knight 5; CR 10; Medium humanoid; HD 5d10+5 plus 5d10+5; hp 65; Init +1; Spd 20 ft., 50 ft. when mounted; AC 24, touch 12, flat-footed 23; Base Atk +10; Grp +12; Atk +14 melee (1d8+3/19–20, +1 longsword) or +12 ranged (1d8+2/×3, masterwork composite longbow [+2 Str bonus]); Full Atk +14/+9 melee (1d8+3/19–20, +1 longsword) or +12/+7 ranged (1d8+2/×3, masterwork composite longbow [+2 Str bonus]); SA fear 1/day, smite evil 2/day, turn undead 5/day; SQ aura of courage, aura of good, detect evil, divine grace, divine health, final stand 1/day, half-elf traits, heroic shield, lay on hands, low-light vision, oath of wrath 1/day, rallying cry 3/day, special mount; AL LG; SV Fort +11, Ref +5, Will +5; Str 15, Dex 12, Con 12, Int 10, Wis 12, Cha 15.

Skills and Feats: Diplomacy +11, Gather Information +4, Listen +4, Search +1, Sense Motive +3, Spot +4, Ride +14; Mounted Combat, Negotiator, Ride-By Attack, Weapon Focus (longsword).

Fear (Su): Ardalis can invoke a fear effect (as the spell from a 5th-level caster; save DC 15). The knight's allies are immune to the effect.

Smite Evil (Su): Ardalis may attempt to smite evil with one normal melee attack. She adds +2 to her attack roll and

deals 5 extra points of damage. Smiting a creature that is not evil has no effect but uses the ability for that day.

Turn Undead (Su): As a 2nd-level cleric.

Aura of Courage (Su): Ardalis is immune to fear, magical or otherwise. Allies within 10 feet of her gain a +4 morale bonus on saving throws against fear effects.

Aura of Good (Ex): Ardalis's aura of good (see the *detect good* spell) is equal to that of a 5th-level cleric.

Detect Evil (Sp): At will, as the spell of the same name.

Divine Grace (Su): Ardalis gains a +2 bonus on saving throws (already figured into the above statistics).

Divine Health (Ex): Ardalis is immune to all diseases, including magical diseases such as mummy rot and lycanthropy.

Final Stand (Su): Once per day, up to seven allies within 10 feet of Ardalis gain 2d10 temporary hit points that last for 7 rounds.

Lay on Hands (Su): Torgga can cure 10 hit points of wounds per day.

Half-Elf Traits (Ex): Immunity to magic sleep spells and effects; +2 bonus on saving throws against enchantments; elven blood.

Heroic Shield (Ex): Ardalis can use the aid another action to give an ally a +4 circumstance bonus to Armor Class.

Lay on Hands (Su): Ardalis can cure 10 hit points of wounds per day.

Low-Light Vision (Ex): Ardalis can see twice as far as a human in starlight, moonlight, torchlight, and similar conditions of poor visibility. She retains the ability to distinguish color and detail under these conditions.

Oath of Wrath (Su): As a free action, Ardalis can swear to defeat a single opponent within 60 feet. She gains a +2 morale bonus on melee attack rolls, weapon damage rolls, saving throws, and skill checks made against the challenged target. The effect ends if she uses a full-round action to move away from the challenged opponent.

Rallying Cry (Su): As a free action, Ardalis gives each ally within 60 feet a +1 morale bonus on its next attack rolls and increases its speed by 5 feet until her next turn.

A Purple Dragon knight

Illus. by M. Smylie

Special Mount (**Sp**): Ardalis's special mount is a heavy warhorse (see page 45 of the *Player's Handbook*) that has +2 Hit Dice, a +4 bonus to natural armor, +1 Strength, and improved evasion. Ardalis has an empathic link with the mount and can share spells and saving throws with it. She can call her mount once per day for up to 10 hours as a full-round action.

Paladin Spells Prepared (1; save DC 12 + spell level): 1st—*bless weapon.*

Possessions: +1 *longsword,* +1 *full plate,* +1 *heavy steel shield,* masterwork composite longbow (+2 Str bonus), *cloak of Charisma* +2, *periapt of Wisdom* +2, *ring of protection* +1, 20 arrows.

RAGE MAGE

At first, it seems like a contradiction—an arcane spellcaster that "loses herself" in a blind fury. Yet, the rage mage makes for an interesting case, since her approach to magic is based on the primal passion of magic more than the studious quasi-scientific approach. The rage mage prestige class is sure to enliven any campaign, because it raises fascinating questions on the true nature of magic and magic use. But don't ask the rage mage to answer those questions herself—she's not interested in the "why," only the results.

A rage mage taps into the primal essence of magic, using her own natural anger and frenzy to channel the arcane power in flashy, flamboyant ways. Like the barbarian, the rage mage is often the product of a less civilized society. All rage mages must have at least some background as a barbarian (or some other class that grants a rage or frenzy ability), as well as training as a wizard, sorcerer, or—very rarely—a bard.

Rage mage NPCs are usually found working with barbarians. They tend to shy away from traditional spellcasters and avoid the colleges and guilds where such individuals usually gather.

Hit Die: d8.

Requirements

To qualify to become a rage mage, a character must fulfill all the following criteria.

Alignment: Any nonlawful.
Base Attack Bonus: +4.
Feat: Combat Casting.
Spells: Able to cast 2nd-level arcane spells.
Special: Rage or frenzy ability.

Class Skills

The rage mage's class skills (and the key ability for each skill) are Concentration (Con), Profession (Wis), Spellcraft (Int), and Survival (Wis).

Skill Points at Each Level: 2 + Int modifier.

Class Features

All of the following are class features of the rage mage prestige class.

Weapon and Armor Proficiency: Rage mages gain no proficiency with any weapon or armor.

Spells per Day: At every even-numbered level gained in the rage mage class, the character gains new spells per day as if she had also gained a level in an arcane spellcasting class she belonged to before adding the prestige class. In no case, however, does she gain any other benefit a character of that class would have gained, except for an increased effective level of spellcasting (but see spell rage, below). If a character had more than one arcane spellcasting class before becoming a rage mage, she must decide to which class she adds the new level for purposes of determining spells per day.

Spell Rage (Ex): A rage mage can cast spells while in a rage, as long as the spell's casting time is no more than 1 full round. When she casts a spell of the abjuration, conjuration, evocation, necromancy, or transmutation school while in a rage, the rage mage uses her character level as her caster level. This ability only works when the rage mage is in a spell rage.

While in a spell rage, a rage mage becomes reckless and loses her some of her ability to defend herself. She temporarily takes a –2 penalty to Armor Class. She can attempt Concentration checks to avoid having a spell disrupted, but can't use any other Charisma-, Dexterity-, or Intelligence-based skills (except for Balance, Escape Artist, Intimidate, and Ride) while in a spell rage.

A fit of rage lasts for a number of rounds equal to 3 + the character's Constitution modifier. A rage mage can end her rage voluntarily. At the end of the rage, the character is fatigued (–2 Strength, –2 Dexterity, can't charge or run) for the duration of the current encounter (unless the rage mage is 10th level, when this limitation no longer applies). A rage mage can only fly into a rage once per encounter, and only a certain number of times per day (determined by level).

TABLE 2–28: THE RAGE MAGE

Level	Base Attack Bonus	Fort Save	Ref Save	Will Save	Special	Spells per Day
1st	+0	+2	+0	+0	Spell rage 1/day	—
2nd	+1	+3	+0	+0	Overcome spell failure	+1 level of existing arcane spellcasting class
3rd	+2	+3	+1	+1	Rage +1 use/day	—
4th	+3	+4	+1	+1	—	+1 level of existing arcane spellcasting class
5th	+3	+4	+1	+1	Spell rage 2/day	—
6th	+4	+5	+2	+2	—	+1 level of existing arcane spellcasting class
7th	+5	+5	+2	+2	*Spell fury*	—
8th	+6	+6	+2	+2	Rage +1 use/day	+1 level of existing arcane spellcasting class
9th	+6	+6	+3	+3	Tireless rage	—
10th	+7	+7	+3	+3	*Warrior cry,* spell rage 3/day	+1 level of existing arcane spellcasting class

Entering a rage takes no time itself, but a rage mage can only do it during her action, not in response to somebody else's action.

Overcome Spell Failure (Ex): At 2nd level, a rage mage learns to ignore some of the restrictive nature of armor. Her arcane spell failure chance when wearing light or medium armor decreases by 10%.

Rage (Ex): A rage mage can enter a rage one additional time per day at 3rd level and another time per day at 8th level.

Angry Spell (Ex): Beginning at 5th level, when a rage mage casts a spell of the abjuration, conjuration, evocation, necromancy, or transmutation school while raging, the save DC for the spell increases by +2. At 10th level, this increase becomes +4.

Spell Fury **(Sp):** Upon reaching 7th level, a rage mage can quicken one spell of 4th level or lower (as if she had used the Quicken Spell feat), but without adjusting the spell's level or casting time. She may use this ability once during each rage.

Tireless Rage (Ex): At 9th level and higher, a rage mage no longer becomes fatigued at the end of her rage.

Warrior Cry **(Sp):** A 10th-level rage mage may scream out a cry once per day as a free action on her turn and gain the benefit of the *Tenser's transformation* spell, with one exception: She does not lose her spellcasting ability for the duration of this effect. The rage mage's caster level for the purpose of this effect is equal to her character level.

Sample Rage Mage

Kalya Spearblossom: Human sorcerer 6/barbarian 1/rage mage 7; CR 14; Medium humanoid; HD 6d4+18 plus 1d12+3 plus 7d8+21; hp 95; Init +1; Spd 40 ft.; AC 17, touch 11, flat-footed 16; Base Atk +9; Grp +10; Atk +11 melee (2d6+2/ 19–20, +1 greatsword); Full Atk +11/+6 melee (2d6+2/19–20, +1 greatsword); SA —; SQ overcome spell failure, rage 2/day, spell fury, spell rage 1/day; AL CN; SV Fort +11, Ref +6, Will +8; Str 13, Dex 12, Con 16, Int 8, Wis 10, Cha 22.

Skills and Feats: Concentration +19, Jump +7, Spellcraft +15; Combat Casting, Craft Magic Arms and Armor, Craft Staff, Spell Focus (evocation), Spell Focus (transmutation), Spell Penetration.

Overcome Spell Failure (Ex): Kalya's arcane spell failure chance when wearing light or medium armor decreases by 10%.

Rage (Ex): +4 to Str, +4 to Con, +2 on Will saves, –2 to AC for up to 8 rounds.

Spell Fury **(Sp):** Once per rage, Kalya can quicken a spell of 4th level or lower without adjusting the spell's level or casting time.

Spell Rage (Ex): Kalya can enter spell rage twice per day. This allows her to cast spells whose casting time is no more than 1 full round while in a spell rage, using her character level as her caster level. The spell rage lasts for 6 rounds, or until she wills it to end. Kalya is fatigued for the rest of the current encounter when her spell rage ends.

Sorcerer Spells Known (6/6/6/6/6/4; save DC 16 + spell level, 17 + spell level for evocation or transmutation spells, +4 during rage for abjuration, conjuration, evocation, necromancy, or transmutation spells): 0—*dancing lights, detect magic, detect poison, light, mage hand, message, read magic, resistance;* 1st—*cause fear, magic missile, protection from evil, shield, shocking grasp;* 2nd—*bear's endurance, invisibility, mirror image, scorching ray, web;* 3rd—*flame arrow, fly, heroism, lightning bolt;* 4th—*fear, ice storm, polymorph;* 5th—*cone of cold, teleport.*

Possessions: +1 greatsword, staff of fire, +2 mithral chain shirt, cloak of Charisma +4, amulet of health +2.

RAVAGER

Feared by many and understood by few, the infamous ravager is an individual who has dedicated himself to the service of Erythnul, deity of slaughter. Living a life of violence and savagery, the ravager seeks to spread this deity's malignant influence wherever he goes, never resting long in one place, lest the forces of good and law pursue him.

Ravagers who come from the ranks of fighters and barbarians find that the ravager's offensive capabilities enhance their combat skills, while wizard, sorcerer, cleric, and druid ravagers find that their ability to cause terror in their foes is a very useful defensive measure. Ravagers spend much of their time with others of their kind, roaming the land in small, close-knit warbands, striking unsuspecting communities without warning, and retiring back into the wilderness to plan their next terrible raid. Sometimes the clergy of Erythnul commands a lone ravager to undertake some mission or project that obliges the ravager to join up with other individuals, but such alliances are usually temporary and must be managed carefully, lest they lead to quarrels or worse.

NPC ravagers are usually encountered in small warbands of from two to six individuals, but sometimes a lone ravager may be encountered when undertaking a special mission.

All ravagers are readily identified by the bizarre and fearsome facial tattoos they wear to mark themselves as Erythnul's instruments.

Hit Die: d10.

TABLE 2–29: THE RAVAGER

Level	Base Attack Bonus	Fort Save	Ref Save	Will Save	Special
1st	+1	+2	+0	+0	Pain touch 1/day
2nd	+2	+3	+0	+0	Aura of fear 10 ft. 1/day
3rd	+3	+3	+1	+1	Cruelest cut 1/day
4th	+4	+4	+1	+1	Pain touch 2/day
5th	+5	+4	+1	+1	Aura of fear 20 ft. 2/day
6th	+6	+5	+2	+2	Cruelest cut 2/day
7th	+7	+5	+2	+2	Pain touch 3/day
8th	+8	+6	+2	+2	Aura of fear 30 ft. 3/day
9th	+9	+6	+3	+3	Cruelest cut 3/day
10th	+10	+7	+3	+3	*Visage of terror*

Requirements

To qualify to become a ravager, a character must fulfill all the following criteria.

Alignment: Chaotic evil or neutral evil.

Base Attack Bonus: +5.

Skills: Intimidate 3 ranks, Knowledge (religion) 3 ranks, Survival 4 ranks.

Feats: Improved Sunder, Power Attack.

Special: Must survive the ravager initiation rites (see the sidebar).

Class Skills

The ravager's class skills (and the key ability for each skill) are Intimidate (Cha), Knowledge (religion) (Int), Move Silently (Dex), Profession (Int), and Ride (Dex).

Skill Points at Each Level: 2 + Int modifier.

Class Features

All of the following are class features of the ravager prestige class.

Weapon and Armor Proficiency: Ravagers gain no proficiency with any weapon or armor.

Pain Touch (Su): Erythnul teaches that life is pain, and so is the touch of a ravager. A ravager can make an unarmed touch attack that deals 1d8 points of damage + 1 point per ravager level. Weapon attacks also transmit the pain of Erythnul, but only at the rate of 1d4 extra points of damage + 1 point per ravager level. The ravager can make one additional pain touch attack for every three levels beyond 1st.

Aura of Fear (Su): Enemies within 10 feet of a ravager of 2nd level or higher take a –2 morale penalty on all saving throws for as long as they remain within range. This ability is usable a number of times per day as given on the table. Each use lasts for a number of rounds equal to 3 + the ravager's Charisma modifier. The range of this aura increases at 5th level to 20 feet, and then again at 8th level to 30 feet.

Cruelest Cut (Ex): When a ravager reaches 3rd level, his familiarity with pain and fear grant him a cruel precision

A ravager

with his melee attacks. The character must declare he is making a cruelest cut attempt before he makes a melee attack (thus, a failed attack roll ruins the attempt). If he strikes

RAVAGER RITES

Individual ravagers are often perceived as dangerous loners but, in actuality, each belongs to a tight-knit warband. The initiation of a potential ravager into a warband (and into the prestige class) is brutally violent.

When a prospective member approaches a warband and makes his intention to join known, the ravagers' standard tactic involves attacking him en masse. The warband's lowest-ranked members (usually anywhere between six to sixteen warriors, rogues, or fighters with individual levels between 2nd and 6th) come out first and try their best to kill the newcomer. Should the newcomer survive an arbitrary period of time (usually between 3 and 10 rounds, depending on how well the newcomer appears to be fighting and the cruelty or interest of the

warband's leader), he is allowed to join the warband.

Should the newcomer actually want to progress in the ravager prestige class, he must undergo a second rite: the fire sacrifice. The candidate waits on his knees, praying to Erythnul (or a similar deity) to fill his heart with hate and malice. Other members of the warband acquire a suitable sacrificial victim (preferably human, but in a pinch any humanoid will do). The would-be ravager must sacrifice the victim in accordance with the unholy rites of the deity, which always involve bloodletting followed by burning the sacrifice alive. Following this cruel and horrific act, the warband applies a distinctively repulsive set of tattoos to the applicant's face that forever marks him as a true ravager. Once the ceremony is complete, the only way to leave the warband is to die.

successfully, he deals 1d4 points of Constitution damage to the target, in addition to any other damage the attack may cause. A ravager can use cruelest cut once per day for every three levels he has attained, but may only make one cruelest cut attempt per round.

Visage of Terror (**Sp**): A 10th-level ravager has plumbed the true depths of horror and hopelessness. Once per day, he can trigger a spell-like ability similar to the arcane spell *phantasmal killer* (save DC 10 + the ravager's class level + the ravager's Cha bonus) as a standard action. To the foe the ravager selects, he seems to take on the visage of what the target fears most. In all other respects, this ability functions as the spell described in the *Player's Handbook*.

Sample Ravager

Narrik Weepingscar: Half-orc barbarian 5/ravager 6; CR 11; Medium humanoid; HD 5d12+10 plus 6d10+12; hp 88; Init +2; Spd 40 ft.; AC 18, touch 12, flat-footed 18; Base Atk +11; Grp +15; Atk +17 melee (1d8+5/×3, +1 *battleaxe*) or +12 ranged (1d8+4/×3, masterwork composite longbow [+4 Str bonus]); Full Atk +17/+12/+7 melee (1d8+5/×3, +1 *battleaxe*), or +13/+8/+3 melee (1d8+5/×3, +1 *battleaxe*) and +13 melee (1d8+3/×3, +1 *battleaxe*), or +12/+7/+2 ranged (1d8+4/×3, masterwork composite longbow [+4 Str bonus]); SA cruelest cut 2/day, pain touch 2/day; SQ aura of fear 2/day, darkvision 60 ft., improved uncanny dodge, rage 2/day, trap sense +1, uncanny dodge; AL CE; SV Fort +11, Ref +5, Will +3; Str 18, Dex 14, Con 14, Int 10, Wis 10, Cha 10.

Skills and Feats: Intimidate +14, Jump +13, Knowledge (religion) +4, Ride +8, Survival +8; Improved Sunder, Power Attack, Two Weapon Fighting, Weapon Focus (battleaxe).

Cruelest Cut (Ex): If Narrik declares he is using cruelest cut before making an attack, and the attack strikes successfully, he deals an extra 1d4 points of temporary Constitution damage.

Pain Touch (Su): Narrik's melee touch attack deals 1d8+6 points of damage. He can also use pain touch through a melee weapon, dealing 1d4+6 points of damage.

Aura of Fear (Su): Enemies within 20 feet of Narrik take a –2 morale penalty on saving throws as long as they remain within range. The effect lasts for 3 rounds each time Narrik uses this ability.

Improved Uncanny Dodge (Ex): Narrik cannot be flanked except by a rogue of at least 9th level.

Rage (Ex): +4 to Str, +4 to Con, +2 on Will saves, –2 to AC for up to 7 rounds.

Trap Sense (Ex): Against attacks by traps, Narrik gets a +1 bonus on Reflex saves and a +1 dodge bonus to Armor Class.

Uncanny Dodge (Ex): Narrik can react to danger before his senses would normally allow him to do so. He retains his Dexterity bonus to AC even when caught flat-footed.

Possessions: Two +1 *battleaxes*, +1 *breastplate*, *gem of brightness*, *cloak of resistance* +1, masterwork composite longbow (+4 Str bonus), 20 arrows, heavy warhorse.

REAPING MAULER

Truly wise adventurers are always wary of unarmed opponents, for such adversaries are usually more than they seem. Such an opponent might even be a reaping mauler—the worst nightmare of a character who depends on weapon skills to win. Anyone who dares to wield a weapon against a reaping mauler had better make use of it quickly, because the opportunity won't last long.

Reaping maulers are the back-breakers, the limb-twisters, and the neck-snappers among pit fighters. Grapplers of the highest order, they wear nothing heavier than light armor in combat to maximize their flexibility, and they use no weapons to achieve their gruesome victories, for they prefer the intimacy of a barehanded kill. A reaping mauler wants to be close enough to taunt his opponent with whispers while crushing the life out of it, to smell its fear, and to watch the despair creep over its face when the opponent realizes just how useless its weapons are during a grapple.

Most of those attracted to the reaping mauler prestige class are fighters, but it is not uncommon for barbarians or rangers to embrace this path. Monks have natural ability in this direction, but the class sometimes feels too chaotic for such a character. Paladins and clerics have also been known to dabble in this prestige class, treating the combat style as both good, hearty sport and a means to render opponents unconscious without killing them. Druids sometimes become reaping maulers to enhance their ability to tame animals by hand, and even rogues occasionally adopt the class. Bards, sorcerers, and wizards usually lack the physical strength to be good candidates for the class, but they respect reaping maulers for their obvious spell-disrupting abilities.

NPC reaping maulers are burly, rowdy individuals who carry themselves with an air of invulnerability. When it comes to the simple pleasures of life—drink and food—they believe the world exists for their convenience. In a reaping mauler's mind, there is no problem that can't be solved with brawn. If something can be taken by force, he feels that it must naturally belong to him, and rarely does anyone openly oppose this concept.

Hit Die: d10.

TABLE 2–30: THE REAPING MAULER

Level	Base Attack Bonus	Fort Save	Ref Save	Will Save	Special
1st	+1	+2	+2	+0	Improved Grapple, Mobility
2nd	+2	+3	+3	+0	Adept wrestling +1
3rd	+3	+3	+3	+1	Counter grapple, sleeper lock
4th	+4	+4	+4	+1	Adept wrestling +2
5th	+5	+4	+4	+1	Devastating grapple

Requirements

To qualify to become a reaping mauler, a character must fulfill all the following criteria.

Base Attack Bonus: +5.

Skills: Escape Artist 5 ranks, Tumble 5 ranks.

Feats: Clever Wrestling*, Improved Unarmed Strike.

Special: The candidate must have defeated at least three opponents one size category larger than himself with his bare hands.

*New feat found in Chapter 3 of this book.

Class Skills

The reaping mauler's class skills (and the key ability for each skill) are Climb (Str), Craft (Int), Escape Artist (Dex), Intimidate (Cha), Jump (Str), Perform (Cha), Profession (Wis), Swim (Str), and Tumble (Dex).

Skill Points at Each Level: 2 + Int modifier.

Class Features

All of the following are class features of the reaping mauler prestige class.

Weapon and Armor Proficiency: Reaping maulers gain no proficiency with any weapon or armor.

Improved Grapple (Ex): When wearing light armor or no armor, a reaping mauler gains the benefit of the Improved Grapple feat, even if he does not meet the prerequisites.

Mobility (Ex): When wearing light armor or no armor, a reaping mauler gains the benefits of the Mobility feat, even if he does not meet the prerequisites.

Adept Wrestling (Ex): Beginning at 2nd level, a reaping mauler who is wearing light armor or no armor gains a +1 bonus on all grapple checks and opposed Dexterity or Strength checks. This bonus increases to +2 at 4th level.

Counter Grapple (Ex): When grappling or pinned, a reaping mauler of 3rd level or higher wearing light armor or no armor can attempt either a grapple check or an Escape Artist check opposed by his opponent's grapple check to free himself as normal. If he fails the check he has chosen, he can immediately attempt the other check as a free action.

Sleeper Lock (Ex): At 3rd level, a reaping mauler learns how to render an opponent unconscious with pressure. If the character pins his opponent while grappling and maintains the pin for 1 full round, the opponent must make a Fortitude save (DC 10 + the reaping mauler's class level + the reaping mauler's Wis modifier) at the end of the round or fall

unconscious for 1d3 rounds. A creature with no discernible anatomy has immunity to this effect.

Devastating Grapple (Ex): If a 5th-level reaping mauler pins his opponent while grappling and maintains the pin for 3 consecutive rounds, the opponent must make a Fortitude save (DC 10 + the reaping mauler's class level + the reaping mauler's Wis modifier) at the end of the third round or die. A creature with no discernible anatomy is immune to the effect of this ability.

Illus. by S. Prescott

A reaping mauler

Sample Reaping Mauler

Jorrick Shardcarver: Dwarf rogue 5/fighter 2/reaping mauler 5; CR 12; Medium humanoid; HD 5d6+10 plus 2d10+4 plus 5d10+10; hp 80; Init +2; Spd 20 ft.; AC 19, touch 12, flat-footed 19; Base Atk +10; Grp +21; Atk +17 melee (1d6+6, *+1 armor spikes*) or +13 ranged (1d8+5/×3, masterwork composite longbow [+5 Str bonus]); Full Atk +17/+12 melee (1d6+6, *+1 armor spikes*) or +13/+8 ranged (1d8+5/×3, masterwork composite longbow [+5 Str bonus]); SA devastating grapple, sleeper lock, sneak attack +3d6; SQ adept wrestling, counter grapple, dwarf traits, evasion, trap sense, trapfighting, uncanny dodge; AL CN; SV Fort +10, Ref +10, Will +3; Str 20, Dex 14, Con 14, Int 10, Wis 13, Cha 6.

Skills and Feats: Balance +3, Bluff +6, Diplomacy +0, Escape Artist +10, Hide +9, Intimidate +9, Jump +5, Listen +9, Move Silently +9, Spot +9, Search +8, Tumble +11; Clever Wrestling, Dodge, Improved Grapple, Improved Unarmed Strike, Mobility, Power Attack, Stunning Fist, Weapon Focus (armor spikes).

Devastating Grapple (Ex): If Jorrick pins his opponent while grappling and maintains the pin for 3 consecutive rounds, the opponent must make a DC 16 Fortitude save at the end of the third round or die.

Sleeper Lock (Ex): If Jorrick pins his opponent and maintains the pin for 1 full round, the opponent must make a DC 16 Fortitude save or fall unconscious for 1d3 rounds.

Adept Wrestling (Ex): Jorrick gains a +2 bonus on all opposed grapple checks (already added above) and opposed Dexterity or Strength checks.

Counter Grapple (Ex): When grappling or pinned, Jorrick can attempt either a grapple check or an Escape Artist check to free himself. If he fails the check, he can try the other check as a free action.

Dwarf Traits (Ex): +4 bonus on ability checks to resist being bull rushed or tripped; +2 bonus on saving throws against poison, spells, and spell-like effects; +1 bonus on attack rolls against orcs and goblinoids; +4 bonus to AC against giants; +2 bonus on Appraise or Craft checks related to stone or metal.

Evasion (Ex): If Jorrick is exposed to any effect that normally allows him to attempt a Reflex saving throw for half damage, he takes no damage with a successful saving throw.

Stunning Fist (Ex): DC 17 Fortitude save or be stunned for 1 round; usable 3/day.

Trap Sense (Ex): Against attacks by traps, Jorrick gets a +1 bonus on Reflex saves and a +1 dodge bonus to Armor Class.

Trapfinding (Ex): Jorrick can use the Search skill to locate traps when the task has a DC higher than 20.

Uncanny Dodge (Ex): Jorrick can react to danger before his senses would normally allow him to do so. He retains his Dexterity bonus to Armor Class even when caught flat-footed.

Possessions: +2 *mithral chainmail* with +1 *armor spikes*, *gauntlets of ogre power +2*, *boots of speed*, masterwork composite longbow (+5 Str bonus), 20 arrows.

RONIN

When a samurai or other noble warrior is exiled from the service of his feudal lord, he may become a ronin—a masterless warrior cast adrift in the world, but still clinging to the remnants of his former life. Blade in hand, a ronin wanders from job to job, trying to stay one step ahead of his enemies—and the shame of his past.

The vast majority of ronin were once samurai; both game rules and theme tie the two classes together. As with the samurai class presented in Chapter 1 of this book, the ronin prestige class has its roots in feudal Japan, but it's an appropriate choice in any campaign world that includes an Asian-themed culture. "Ronin" is Japanese for "wave-man," and ronin tend to be inveterate wanderers. Even if an Asian setting isn't an important part of your campaign, a ronin character may be a traveler from a distant land, eager to put his dishonor behind him and live out his days in a land where no one knows the code of bushido.

Ronin are often found in the pay of less scrupulous feudal lords. Because they are trained in the art of war, they are prized as mercenaries. Those who hire a ronin should watch their employee closely. Almost every ronin has a failure of honor in his past; most involve a conflict with their former masters.

Hit Die: d10.

TABLE 2–31: THE RONIN

Level	Base Attack Bonus	Fort Save	Ref Save	Will Save	Special
1st	+1	+2	+0	+0	Infamy, sneak attack +1d6
2nd	+2	+3	+0	+0	Banzai charge
3rd	+3	+3	+1	+1	—
4th	+4	+4	+1	+1	Sneak attack +2d6
5th	+5	+4	+1	+1	Bonus feat
6th	+6	+5	+2	+2	—
7th	+7	+5	+2	+2	Sneak attack +3d6
8th	+8	+6	+2	+2	—
9th	+9	+6	+3	+3	Bonus feat
10th	+10	+7	+3	+3	Sneak attack +4d6

Requirements

To qualify to become a ronin, a character must fulfill all the following criteria.

Alignment: Any nonlawful.

Base Attack Bonus: +6.

Feats: Exotic Weapon Proficiency (bastard sword).

Special: Must have fled or been exiled from the service of a feudal lord, commonly for disobeying orders, displaying rudeness or cowardice at a crucial juncture, or failing in a crucial task.

Class Skills

The ronin's class skills (and the key ability for each skill) are Bluff (Cha), Craft (Int), Disguise (Cha), Intimidate (Cha), Knowledge (history) (Int), Knowledge (nobility and royalty) (Int), Ride (Dex), and Sense Motive (Wis).

Skill Points at Each Level: 2 + Int modifier.

Class Features

All of the following are class features of the ronin prestige class.

Weapon and Armor Proficiency: Ronins gain no proficiency with any weapon or armor.

Infamy: The ronin's reputation for dishonor—deserved or not—follows him everywhere. Whenever someone in a position of authority has heard of the ronin's past (usually through a DC 10 Gather Information or Knowledge [nobility and royalty] check), that person's attitude starts one category worse than usual, and the ronin takes a –4 circumstance penalty on all Charisma-based checks involving that person. The infamy penalty applies only if the authority figure knows the ronin's identity, so some ronin adopt pseudonyms or secret identities.

Sneak Attack (Ex): If a ronin can catch an opponent when she is unable to defend herself effectively from his attack, he can strike a vital spot for an extra 1d6 points of damage. This extra damage increases by 1d6 points every third level (+2d6 at 4th level, +3d6 at 7th level, +4d6 at 10th level). For complete details on the sneak attack ability, see the description of the dark hunter earlier in this chapter.

Banzai Charge (Ex): The ronin has cast away the code of bushido and at least a measure of his own honor, but his heart still remembers the thrill of bravery. When a ronin of 2nd level or higher charges into battle, he can accept a variable penalty to his Armor Class and take an equivalent bonus on the damage roll. The normal –2 AC penalty for charging still applies and counts toward the bonus, but the ronin cannot accept a penalty smaller than –2 or larger than his base attack bonus. For example, a 2nd-level ronin making a banzai charge could take a –8 penalty to AC in exchange for a +8 bonus on the damage roll.

Bonus Feat: The ronin's experience in battle has taught him many tricks and techniques. At 5th and 9th level, a ronin may choose one feat from the following list: Far Shot, Improved Precise Shot, Manyshot, Mounted Archery, Mounted Combat, Point Blank Shot, Precise Shot, Rapid Shot, Ride-By Attack, Shot on the Run, Spirited

A ronin

Charge, Trample. The ronin must still meet all the prerequisites for the bonus feat.

Former Samurai

Ronins who possess levels of samurai (that is to say, are now ex-samurai) regain some of their lost class features the more levels of samurai they possess; refer to the accompanying table for details. High-level ronins retain much of their bushido training, even if fate has dealt them a treacherous blow.

Sample Ronin

Urashima Tanoki: Human samurai 6/ronin 10; CR 16; Medium humanoid; HD 6d10+12 plus 10d10+20; hp 120; Init +1; Spd 20 ft.; AC 21, touch 11, flat-footed 20; Base Atk +16; Grp +22; Atk +24 melee (1d10+7 plus 1 Con/17–20, +1 *wounding katana*) or +18 ranged (1d8+6, masterwork composite longbow [+6 Str bonus]); Full Atk +24/+19/+14/+9 melee (1d10+7 plus 1 Con/17–20, +1 *wounding katana*); or +22/+17/+12/+7 melee (1d10+7 plus 1 Con/17–20, +1 *wounding katana*) and +22/+17 melee (1d6+4/17–20, +1 *ghost touch wakizashi*); or +18/+13/+8/+3 ranged (1d8+6, masterwork composite longbow [+6 Str bonus]); SA banzai charge, kiai smite 1/day, sneak attack +4d6; SQ iaijutsu master, staredown; AL N; SV Fort +14, Ref +6, Will +4; Str 22, Dex 12, Con 14, Int 10, Wis 8, Cha 16.

Skills and Feats: Bluff +13, Diplomacy +14, Intimidate +28, Ride +20; Cleave, Exotic Weapon Proficiency (katana), Improved Two-Weapon Fighting (katana and wakizashi only), Improved Critical

EX-SAMURAI RONIN ABILITIES

Samurai Level	Regained Abilities
1st–5th	The ronin regains any kiai smite class feature he once possessed as a samurai, and can use it just as any samurai can.
6th–10th	As above, plus the ronin regains any staredown class feature (staredown, mass staredown, improved staredown) he once possessed as a samurai, using it just as he did before he became an ex-samurai.
11th+	As above, plus an ex-samurai of this stature immediately gains a ronin level for each level of samurai he trades in. For example, a character who has thirteen levels of samurai can immediately become a 10th-level ronin with all abilities if he chooses to lose ten levels of samurai. The character level of the character does not change. However, with the loss of samurai levels, the character might lose some of the class features granted by the samurai class. Thus, an ex-samurai of 14th level could become a 4th-level ronin/10th-level samurai, but would lose the improved two swords as one, kiai smite 3/day, and improved staredown class features.

(katana), Improved Critical (wakizashi), Mounted Combat[B], Power Attack, Ride-By Attack[B], Weapon Focus (katana), Weapon Focus (wakizashi).

Banzai Charge (Ex): During a charge, Urashima can accept a penalty to his Armor Class and receive an equivalent bonus on the damage roll. The normal –2 AC penalty for charging still applies and counts toward the bonus; the ronin can accept a penalty as small as –2 or as large as –16.

Iaijutsu Master (Ex): Urashima is treated as having the Quick Draw feat when drawing his katana.

Infamy: Authorities who have heard of Urashima's past have attitudes that start one category worse than normal, and the ronin takes a –4 circumstance penalty on Charisma-based checks involving that person.

Kiai Smite (Ex): When Urashima shouts, his next attack gains a +3 bonus on the attack and damage rolls. If the target of the attack has immunity to fear or has an Intelligence score of 2 or lower, the kiai smite has no effect.

Staredown (Ex): Urashima gains a +4 bonus on Intimidate checks (included in the above statistics) and can demoralize an opponent (as described in the Intimidate skill description, page 76 of the *Player's Handbook*) within 40 feet.

Possessions: +1 wounding katana, +1 ghost touch wakizashi, +2 full plate, belt of giant Strength +4, cloak of Charisma +2, rod of enemy detection, masterwork composite longbow (+6 Str bonus).

SPELLSWORD

The dream of melding magic and weaponplay is fulfilled in the person of the spellsword. A student of both arcane rituals and martial techniques, the spellsword gradually learns to cast spells in armor with less chance of failure. Moreover, he can cast spells through his weapon, bypassing his opponent's defenses.

Despite the class's name, a spellsword can use any weapon or even switch weapons. "Spellaxe," "spellspear," and other appellations for this prestige class are certainly possible but not commonly used. The requirements for this prestige class make it most attractive to multiclass wizard/fighters or sorcerer/fighters, although bard/fighters can meet the requirements just as easily.

Feared by other martial characters because of his ability to use spells, and feared by spellcasters because of his ability to cast those spells while wearing armor, a spellsword often walks the world alone.

Hit Die: d8.

Requirements

To qualify to become a spellsword, a character must fulfill all the following criteria.

Base Attack Bonus: +4.

Skills: Knowledge (arcana) 6 ranks.

Feats: Proficiency with all simple and martial weapons and with all armor (heavy, medium, and light).

Spells: Able to cast 2nd-level arcane spells.

Special: Must have defeated a foe through force of arms alone, without recourse to spellcasting.

Class Skills

The spellsword's class skills (and the key ability for each skill) are Climb (Str), Concentration (Con), Knowledge (Int), Jump (Str), Profession (Wis), and Spellcraft (Int).

Skill Points at Each Level: 2 + Int modifier.

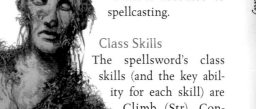

A spellsword

Illus. by B. Snoddy

Class Features

All of the following are class features of the spellsword prestige class.

Spells per Day: At every odd-numbered level, a spellsword gains new spells per day as if he had also gained a level in an arcane spellcasting class he belonged to before adding the prestige class. He does not, however, gain any other benefit a character of that class would have gained (improved chance of controlling or rebuking undead, metamagic or item creation feats, and so on), save for an increased effective level of spellcasting. If a character had more than one spellcasting

Table 2–32: The Spellsword

Level	Base Attack Bonus	Fort Save	Ref Save	Will Save	Special	Spells per Day
1st	+1	+2	+0	+2	Ignore spell failure 10%	+1 level of existing arcane spellcasting class
2nd	+2	+3	+0	+3	Bonus feat	—
3rd	+3	+3	+1	+3	Ignore spell failure 15%	+1 level of existing arcane spellcasting class
4th	+4	+4	+1	+4	*Channel spell* 3/day	—
5th	+5	+4	+1	+4	Ignore spell failure 20%	+1 level of existing arcane spellcasting class
6th	+6	+5	+2	+5	*Channel spell* 4/day	—
7th	+7	+5	+2	+5	Ignore spell failure 25%	+1 level of existing arcane spellcasting class
8th	+8	+6	+2	+6	*Channel spell* 5/day	—
9th	+9	+6	+3	+6	Ignore spell failure 30%	+1 level of existing arcane spellcasting class
10th	+10	+7	+3	+7	*Multiple channel spell*	—

class before becoming a spellsword, he must decide to which class he adds the new level for purposes of determining spells per day.

Ignore Spell Failure (Ex): Beginning at 1st level, a spellsword's hard work and practice at merging spellcraft with weaponplay starts to pay off. As an extraordinary ability, he ignores a portion of the arcane spell failure chance associated with using armor. This reduction starts at 10% and gradually increases to 30%, as shown on the class table. A spellsword subtracts the given percentage value from his total spell failure chance, if any. For instance, a character wearing scale mail and carrying a small shield normally has a spell failure chance of 30%, but this drops to only 20% for a 1st-level spellsword.

Bonus Feat: At 2nd level, a spellsword advances his art, gaining a bonus feat. This bonus feat must be either a metamagic feat or one drawn from the list of bonus feats allowed to a fighter (see Table 5–1 on page 90 of the *Player's Handbook*).

Channel Spell (**Sp**): At 4th level, a spellsword can channel any spell he can cast into his melee weapon. Using this ability requires a move action, and the spellsword uses up the prepared spell or spell slot just as if he had cast the spell. The channeled spell affects the next target that the spellsword successfully attacks with his weapon (saving throws and spell resistance still apply). Even if the spell normally affects an area or is a ray, it affects only the target. The spell is discharged from the weapon, which can then hold another spell. A spellsword can channel his spells into only one weapon at a time. Spells channeled into a weapon are lost if not used in 8 hours.

Multiple Channel Spell (**Sp**): A 10th-level spellsword can channel two spells into his melee weapon, using a move action to channel each one. Both channeled spells affect the next target the spellsword successfully attacks with his weapon, in the order the spells were placed into the weapon. As with the *channel spell* class feature, saving throws and spell resistance apply normally. Each time a spellsword uses *multiple channel spell*, two of his five *channel spell* uses per day are expended.

Sample Spellsword

Roland Wanderson: Human fighter 1/wizard 6/spellsword 6; CR 13; Medium humanoid; HD 1d10+1 plus 6d4+6 plus 6d8+6; hp 61; Init +5; Spd 20 ft.; AC 17, touch 11, flatfooted 16; Base Atk +10; Grp +12; Atk +15 melee (2d6+5/19–20, +2 greatsword); Full Atk +15/+10 melee (2d6+5/19–20, +2 greatsword); SA channel spell 4/day; SQ ignore spell failure 20%; AL CG; SV Fort +10, Ref +5, Will +10; Str 14, Dex 13, Con 12, Int 22, Wis 10, Cha 8.

Skills and Feats: Concentration +15, Decipher Script +12, Diplomacy +1, Intimidate +6, Knowledge (arcana) +20, Knowledge (nobility and royalty) +16, Knowledge (the planes) +18, Ride +5, Spellcraft +22; Craft Magic Arms and Armor, Combat Casting, Combat Expertise, Dodge, Improved Disarm, Improved Initiative, Scribe Scroll, Spell Penetration, Weapon Focus (greatsword).

Channel Spell (**Sp**): As a move action, Roland can channel a spell he has prepared into his sword, thus using up the spell as if it had been cast. The next creature he successfully hits with the sword is affected by the spell (saving throw and spell resistance applies). Only the target is affected by the spell, even if it's an area spell.

Wizard Spells Prepared (4/6/6/4/3/2; save DC 16 + spell level): 0—*detect magic* (2), *light*, *message*; 1st—*charm person*, *protection from evil*, *shield* (3); 2nd—*bear's endurance*, *bull's strength*, *daze monster*, *ghoul touch*, *scorching ray*, *web*; 3rd—*fireball*, *fly*, *haste*, *vampiric touch*; 4th—*contagion*, *enervation*, *stoneskin*; 5th—*hold monster*, *teleport*.

Spellbook: 0—all; 1st—*charm person*, *identify*, *mage armor*, *magic missile*, *magic weapon*, *protection from evil*, *shield*, *sleep*; 2nd—*bear's endurance*, *bull's strength*, *darkvision*, *daze monster*, *ghoul touch*, *invisibility*, *knock*, *Melf's acid arrow*, *resist energy*, *scorching ray*, *see invisibility*, *web*; 3rd—*clairaudience/clairvoyance*, *deep slumber*, *dispel*, *fireball*, *fly*, *greater magic weapon*, *haste*, *hold person*, *invisibility sphere*, *lightning bolt*, *protection from energy*, *vampiric touch*; 4th—*confusion*, *contagion*, *dimensional anchor*, *enervation*, *ice storm*, *Otiluke's resilient sphere*, *polymorph*, *scrying*, *stoneskin*, *wall of fire*; 5th—*baleful polymorph*, *cone of cold*, *hold monster*, *teleport*, *wall of force*.

Possessions: +2 greatsword, +1 mithral chainmail, headband of intellect +4, wand of magic missile (7th), spellbook, 250 gp of diamond dust.

STONELORD

Dwarves know more secrets about stone than anyone. They live and die among the stones, and the earth whispers to them—or at least to select individuals. These special dwarves are known as stonelords. They use their connection with the earth to draw from the infinite reserves of power within it to help them perform amazing feats.

Fighters are the most common stonelords, although dwarf paladins and rangers adopt the mantle as well. Though uncommon, dwarf rogues, clerics, and even the occasional wizard or sorcerer become stonelords.

NPC stonelords work in dwarven communities as protectors and leaders. Occasionally they work in groups, but even then, their varied backgrounds and chosen powers make them all very different.

Hit Die: d8.

TABLE 2–33: THE STONELORD

Level	Base Attack Bonus	Fort Save	Ref Save	Will Save	Special
1st	+1	+2	+0	+0	Earth's blood
2nd	+2	+3	+0	+0	Stone power
3rd	+3	+3	+1	+1	Stone shape
4th	+4	+4	+1	+1	Stone power
5th	+5	+4	+1	+1	Meld into stone
6th	+6	+5	+2	+2	Stone power
7th	+7	+5	+2	+2	Stone tell
8th	+8	+6	+2	+2	Stone power
9th	+9	+6	+3	+3	Earthquake
10th	+10	+7	+3	+3	Stone power

Requirements

To qualify to become a stonelord, a character must fulfill all the following criteria.

Race: Dwarf.

Base Attack Bonus: +5.

Skills: Craft (stoneworking) 6 ranks, Speak Language (Terran).

Feats: Endurance.

Special: The character must undergo an arduous ritual involving immersion in sacred loam, long fasting periods deep underground, and the ingestion of 1,000 gp worth of powdered gemstones. The gem type chosen is then the stonelord's totem gem, and she must carry that type of stone with her at all times to access the spell-like abilities she gains as a stonelord.

Class Skills

The stonelord's class skills (and the key ability for each skill) are Climb (Str), Concentration (Con), Craft (Int), Knowledge (Int), Profession (Wis), Spot (Wis), and Survival (Wis).

Skill Points at Each Level: 2 + Int modifier.

Class Features

All of the following are class features of the stonelord prestige class.

Weapon and Armor Proficiency: Stonelords gain no proficiency with any weapon or armor.

Earth's Blood (**Sp**): Once per day, a stonelord can take a standard action to heal her own wounds using a clump of mud. This ability heals a number of hit points equal to 1d8 + her stonelord class level.

Stone Power: At every even-numbered level, a stonelord can choose one ability from the following list of stone powers. No stone power can be chosen more than once. Unless otherwise noted, the stonelord uses her class level as the caster level for these effects (the save DCs are Constitution-based). Using one of these abilities is a standard action unless otherwise noted.

Earthgrip (**Sp**): Once per day, a stonelord with this ability can use *hold monster* on any target touching the ground. If the opponent is airborne or waterborne, the stonelord cannot affect the creature with the spell.

Earth Magic (**Su**): Once per day, a spell cast by a stonelord with this ability (assuming she can cast spells) is considered maximized as if prepared with the Maximize Spell feat, although the spell's level is unaffected. The spell's level cannot be higher than the class level of the stonelord. Using this ability is a free action.

Earth's Endurance (**Sp**): Once per day, a stonelord with this ability grants herself a boost to her Constitution score as if she were affected by a *bear's endurance* spell for 1 hour.

Earth's Strength (**Sp**): Once per day, a stonelord with this ability grants herself a boost to her Strength score as if she were affected by a *bull's strength* spell for 1 hour.

Earth Power (**Su**): Once per day, all melee attacks made in a single round by a stonelord with this ability gain a +2 bonus on the attack roll and deal an extra 2d6 points of damage on a successful hit. Using this ability is a free action.

Earth Shadows (**Su**): Once per day per class level, a stonelord with this ability can create a figment of a Medium earth elemental that appears in a flanking position adjacent to the stonelord's opponent for 1 round. This ability allows the stonelord to make flanking attacks (+2 to hit, can make a sneak attack if such ability is available) against that opponent during that round. Using this ability is a free action.

Gravity (**Sp**): Once per day, a stonelord with this ability can use a *slow* effect (as the spell).

Stoneskin (**Sp**): Once per day, a stonelord with this ability can give herself the benefit of a *stoneskin* spell (caster level equal to the stonelord's class level). The character must provide the material component as if she were actually casting the spell.

Summon Earth Elemental (**Sp**): Once per day, a stonelord with this ability can summon an earth elemental as if she had cast a *summon monster* spell. The size of the summoned earth elemental depends on the stonelord's class level, as follows: 1st–3rd, Small; 4th–6th, Medium; 7th–9th, Large; 10th, Huge.

Stone Shape (Sp): Once per day, a stonelord of 3rd level or higher can use a *stone shape* effect (caster level equal to the stonelord's class level).

Meld into Stone (Sp): Once per day per class level, a stonelord of 5th level or higher can use a *meld into stone* effect (caster level equal to the stonelord's class level).

Stone Tell (Sp): Once per day, a stonelord of 7th level or higher can speak with stone as if she had cast *stone tell* (caster level equal to the stonelord's class level).

Earthquake (Sp): Once per day, a stonelord of 9th level or higher can use an *earthquake* effect (caster level equal to the stonelord's class level).

Sample Stonelord

Chertia Granitegallow: Dwarf paladin 5/stonelord 8; CR 13; Medium humanoid; HD 5d10+10 plus 8d8+16; hp 90; Init +0; Spd 20 ft.; AC 19, touch 10, flat-footed 19; Base Atk +13; Grp +17; Atk +21 melee (1d10+7, *+3 greatclub*); Full Atk +21/+16/+11 melee (1d10+7, *+3 greatclub*); SA smite evil 2/day, turn undead 5/day; SQ aura of courage, aura of good, *detect evil*, divine grace, divine health, dwarf traits, earth power, *earth's blood, earth's endurance, earth's strength,* lay on hands, *meld into stone, special mount, stone shape, stone tell, stoneskin*; AL LG; SV Fort +10, Ref +3, Will +3; Str 18, Dex 10, Con 15, Int 10, Wis 12, Cha 14.

Skills and Feats: Craft (stoneworking) +12, Jump –7, Knowledge (dungeoneering) +12, Ride +3, Speak Language (Terran), Spellcraft +3; Endurance, Improved Bull Rush, Improved Sunder, Power Attack, Weapon Focus (greatclub).

Smite Evil (Su): Chertia may attempt to smite evil with one normal melee attack. She adds +2 to her attack roll and deals 5 extra points of damage. Smiting a creature that is not evil has no effect but counts as a use of the ability for that day.

Turn Undead (Su): As a 2nd-level cleric.

Aura of Courage (Su): Chertia is immune to fear (magical or otherwise). Allies within 10 feet of her gain a +4 morale bonus on saving throws against fear effects.

Aura of Good (Ex): Chertia's aura of good (see the *detect good* spell) is equal to that of a 5th-level cleric.

Detect Evil (Sp): At will, as the spell of the same name.

Divine Grace (Su): Chertia gains a +2 bonus on saving throws (already figured into the above statistics).

Divine Health (Ex): Chertia is immune to all diseases, including magical diseases such as mummy rot and lycanthropy.

Dwarf Traits (Ex): +4 bonus on ability checks to resist being bull rushed or tripped; +2 bonus on saving throws against poison, spells, and spell-like effects; +1 bonus on attack rolls against orcs and goblinoids; +4 bonus to AC against giants; +2 bonus on Appraise or Craft checks related to stone or metal.

Earth Power (Su): Once per day as a free action, Chertia can grant herself a +2 attack bonus and a +2d6 damage bonus on all attacks in a single round.

Earth's Blood (Sp): By using a clump of mud, Chertia can heal 1d8+8 points of damage to herself once per day.

Earth's Endurance (Sp): Once per day, Chertia can grant herself a +4 bonus to her Constitution score, as with a *bear's endurance* spell, that lasts for 8 minutes.

Earth's Strength (Sp): Once per day, Chertia can grant herself a +4 bonus to her Strength score, as with a *bull's strength* spell, that lasts for 8 minutes.

Lay on Hands (Su): Chertia can cure 10 hit points of wounds per day.

Meld into Stone (Sp): Eight times per day, Chertia can use a *meld into stone* effect (caster level 8th).

Special Mount (Sp): Chertia's special mount is a heavy warhorse (see page 45 of the *Player's Handbook*) that has +2 Hit Dice, a +4 bonus to natural armor, +1 Strength, and improved evasion. Chertia has an empathic link with the mount and can share spells and saving throws with it. She can call her mount once per day for up to 10 hours as a full-round action.

Stone Shape (Sp): Once per day, Chertia can use a *stone shape* effect (caster level 8th).

Stone Tell (Sp): Once per day, Chertia can use a *stone tell* effect (caster level 8th).

Stoneskin (Sp): Once per day, Chertia can gain the benefit of a *stoneskin* spell (damage reduction 10/adamantine until 80 points of damage are absorbed) for 80 minutes.

Paladin Spells Prepared (1; save DC 11 + spell level): 1st— *lesser restoration.*

Possessions: Maul of the titans, +1 full plate, gloves of Dexterity +2, cloak of Charisma.

TATTOOED MONK

Certain monastic orders bestow supernatural or spell-like powers on their members by inscribing magic tattoos on their skin. These tattooed monks shave their heads, speak in cryptic riddles and maxims, and—in many cases—travel the countryside furthering their quest for enlightenment by facing and conquering temptation.

The great majority of tattooed monks begin their careers as monks. A small number of fighters, druids, and even a few clerics adopt the tattooed monk prestige class. In general, tattooed monks are drawn almost exclusively from rural or wild regions, though more "civilized" individuals who gain the favor of the order are sometimes allowed to join.

The ranks of the tattooed monks are divided between worldly monks—those who believe that temptation can only be overcome if it is squarely faced—and ascetic monks, who rarely leave their mountaintop retreats. Player character tattooed monks are assumed to fall into the former category, but NPCs can be found in both roles. NPC tattooed monk often fulfill roles as philosophers and mystics, helping others find answers to esoteric questions and solutions to unusual problems.

Hit Die: d8.

TABLE 2–34: THE TATTOOED MONK

Level	Base Attack Bonus	Fort Save	Ref Save	Will Save	Special
1st	+0	+2	+2	+2	Monk abilities, tattoo
2nd	+1	+3	+3	+3	—
3rd	+2	+3	+3	+3	Tattoo
4th	+3	+4	+4	+4	—
5th	+3	+4	+4	+4	Tattoo
6th	+4	+5	+5	+5	—
7th	+5	+5	+5	+5	Tattoo
8th	+6	+6	+6	+6	—
9th	+6	+6	+6	+6	Tattoo
10th	+7	+7	+7	+7	—

Requirements

To qualify to become a tattooed monk, a character must fulfill all the following criteria.

Alignment: Any lawful.

Base Attack Bonus: +3.

Skills: Knowledge (religion) 8 ranks.

Feats: Endurance, Improved Grapple, Improved Unarmed Strike.

Class Skills

The tattooed monk's class skills (and the key ability for each skill) are Balance (Dex), Climb (Str), Concentration (Con), Craft (Int), Diplomacy (Cha), Escape Artist (Dex), Hide (Dex), Jump (Str), Knowledge (Int), Listen (Wis), Move Silently (Dex), Perform (Cha), Profession (Wis), Swim (Str), and Tumble (Dex).

Skill Points at Each Level: 4 + Int modifier.

Class Features

All of the following are class features of the tattooed monk prestige class.

Weapon and Armor Proficiency: Tattooed monks gain no proficiency with any weapon or armor.

Monk Abilities: A tattooed monk's class levels stack with his monk levels for determining his unarmed damage, AC bonus, and unarmored speed bonus.

Tattoo (Su or Sp): Tattooed monks gain their powers from the magic tattoos that eventually cover their bodies. A 1st-level tattooed monk has one tattoo and gains another tattoo at every odd-numbered level. A tattooed monk can choose his tattoos from among those described below. Note that three of the tattoos (centipede, crescent moon, and phoenix) have minimum class level requirements.

All tattoos are magical, and the abilities they bestow are supernatural (except for the crescent moon). A tattooed monk

A tattooed monk

in an *antimagic field* loses all benefits of his tattoos. Unless the effect of a tattoo is continuous, activating a tattoo is a move action that does not provoke an attack of opportunity.

Arrowroot: A character with this tattoo can heal wounds in another character by touch. Each day he can cure a total number of hit points equal to his Wisdom bonus × his class level. A tattooed monk cannot heal himself, but he may divide the curing among multiple recipients, and he doesn't have to use it all at once.

Bamboo: Once per day per tattoo he possesses, a character with this tattoo can add the number of tattoos he possesses as an enhancement bonus to his Constitution score. This benefit lasts for 1 round per class level.

Bat: Once per day per tattoo he possesses, a character with this tattoo can add the number of tattoos he possesses as an enhancement bonus to his Dexterity score. This benefit lasts for 1 round per class level.

Bellflower: Once per day per tattoo he possesses, a character with this tattoo can add his Charisma modifier as an enhancement bonus to any of his ability scores (including Charisma). This benefit lasts for 1 round per class level.

Butterfly: Once per day per tattoo he possesses, a character with this tattoo can add the number of tattoos he possesses as an enhancement bonus to his Wisdom score. This benefit lasts for 1 round per class level.

Centipede: Once per week, a character with this tattoo can use a shadow walk effect. This ability allows the tattooed monk to cross great distances, but he must end his journey on the Material Plane. A tattooed monk must be at least 5th level to gain this tattoo.

Chameleon: A character with this tattoo can use an alter self effect once per day per tattoo he possesses. This benefit lasts for 1 hour per class level.

Crab: A character with this tattoo gains damage reduction 2/magic. This damage reduction improves by 2 for each additional tattoo he possesses.

Crane: A character with this tattoo gains a gradual immunity to bodily decay. When a tattooed monk first gains this tattoo, he gains immunity to nonmagical diseases. When he gains his next tattoo (whatever it may be), he acquires immunity to poison as well. When he gains his next tattoo, he no longer takes ability score penalties for aging, and he cannot be magically aged. (Any aging penalties he may already have incurred remain in place.) Bonuses still accrue, and the tattooed monk still dies of old age when his time is up.

Illus. by G. Kubic

Chrysanthemum: Every hour that a character with this tattoo is in direct sunlight, he heals a number of hit points equal to his level. A *daylight* spell does not provoke this fast healing; the character must be exposed to real sunlight.

Dragon: Once per day per tattoo he possesses, a character with this tattoo can use fire breath as if he had drunk an *elixir of fire breath* (see page 255 of the *Dungeon Master's Guide*).

Dragonfly: Once per day, a character with this tattoo gains a dodge bonus to his AC equal to the number of tattoos he possesses. This benefit lasts for 1 round per class level.

Falcon: A character with this tattoo is immune to fear (magical or otherwise). Allies within 10 feet of his gain a morale bonus on their saving throws against fear effects equal to the tattooed monk's Charisma bonus (if any) plus the number of tattoos he possesses.

Lion: Once per day per tattoo he possesses, a character with this tattoo can smite a foe, gaining a +4 bonus on the attack roll and a bonus on the damage roll equal to his class level on a single melee attack. The tattooed monk must declare the smite before making the attack. A missed attack uses up the attempt.

Monkey: A character with this tattoo gains a +1 competence bonus per tattoo he possesses on all Balance, Climb, Escape Artist, Hide, Jump, Move Silently, Open Lock, Sleight of Hand, and Tumble checks.

Moon, Crescent: Once per day, a character with this tattoo can use ethereal jaunt as a spell-like ability. A tattooed monk must be at least 9th level to gain this tattoo.

Moon, Full: Once per day per tattoo he possesses, a character with this tattoo can gain a +2 luck bonus on a single attack roll, skill check, or ability check, as he calls on the power of the full moon. This ability cannot be used during daylight hours.

Mountain: A character with this tattoo can activate it to take on the immovability of a mountain for as much as 1 round per class level, gaining phenomenal durability though he cannot move from the spot where he stands. He gains a +4 bonus to his Constitution and Wisdom scores. The increase in Constitution increases the tattooed monk's hit points by 2 points per level, but these hit points go away when the ability's duration expires or when the character chooses to end it (a free action). These extra hit points are not lost first the way temporary hit points are. While using this ability, the tattooed monk takes a –20 penalty on any Dexterity-based skill checks. He is immune to bull rush and trip attacks. The tattooed monk may use this ability once per day per tattoo he possesses.

Nightingale: A character with this tattoo can heal wounds, either his own or others'. He can heal a number of hit points of damage equal to twice his current class level each day, and he can spread this healing out among several uses.

Ocean: A character with this tattoo never needs to eat, sleep, or drink.

Phoenix: A character with this tattoo gains spell resistance equal to his class level + 15. A tattooed monk must be at least 7th level to gain this tattoo.

Pine: A character with this tattoo gains the Remain Conscious feat.

Scorpion: Once per day per tattoo he possesses, a character with this tattoo can force an opponent attacking him to use his lowest ability score modifier instead of his Strength or Dexterity score modifier when making his attack roll. The character can activate this tattoo on his opponent's turn, but he must declare it before the success or failure of the attack is determined. The tattooed monk must be aware of the attack and not flat-footed in order to use this ability.

Spider: To use this tattoo, a character must have the Stunning Fist feat. Instead of a stunning fist attack, a character with this tattoo can make an attack that delivers a contact poison. The poison's save DC is equal to 10 + the tattooed monk's class level + his Con modifier. The poison's initial and secondary damage is 2 points of Constitution damage. Using this tattoo counts as one of the character's stunning fist attacks for that day.

Sun: Once per day per tattoo he possesses, a character with this tattoo can gain a +2 luck bonus on a single attack roll, skill check, or ability check, as he calls on the full power of the sun. This ability can only be used during daylight hours.

Tiger: Once per day per tattoo he possesses, a character with this tattoo can fight unarmed with a +1 bonus on all attack rolls and deal an extra 1d6 points of damage with a successful attack. This burst of martial arts ferocity lasts for 1 round per class level.

Tortoise: Once per day per tattoo he possesses, a character with this tattoo can use his class level as the number of ranks in a skill he does not possess for the purpose of one skill check. For example, a 4th-level tattooed monk with two tattoos can make up to two Use Magic Device checks as if he had 4 ranks in that skill. He adds his Charisma modifier to the skill check as usual.

Unicorn: A character with this tattoo gains the power of good fortune, usable once per day. This ability allows the tattooed monk to reroll one d20 roll that he has just made. The character must take the result of the reroll, even if it's worse than the original roll. The character must declare the reroll before the result of the original roll has been determined.

Wasp: Once per day per tattoo he possesses, a character with this tattoo can use *haste* on herself. The benefit lasts for 1 round per class level.

White Mask: A character with this tattoo is immune to *detect thoughts, detect lies,* and any attempt to magically discern his alignment. He gains a +10 bonus on all Bluff checks.

Multiclass Note: A monk who becomes a tattooed monk may continue advancing as a monk.

Sample Tattooed Monk

Akulya: Human monk 5/tattooed monk 7; CR 12; Medium humanoid; HD 5d8+5 plus 7d8+7; hp 66; Init +4; Spd 70 ft.; AC 21, touch 19, flat-footed 17; Base Atk +8; Grp +15; Atk +12 melee (2d8+2, unarmed strike); Full Atk +12/+7 melee (2d8+3, unarmed strike) or +11/+11/+6 melee (1d8+3, unarmed strike); SA flurry of blows, *ki* strike (magic); SQ crab tattoo, falcon tattoo, evasion, lion tattoo, phoenix tattoo, purity of body, slow fall 20 ft., still mind; AL LN; SV Fort +10, Ref +13, Will +11; Str 16, Dex 18, Con 12, Int 8, Wis 14, Cha 8.

Skills and Feats: Jump +36, Knowledge (religion) +15, Listen +21, Search +2, Spot +4, Tumble +21; Combat Reflexes, Dodge, Mobility, Endurance, Improved Grapple, Spring Attack, Stunning Fist, Weapon Focus (unarmed strike).

Flurry of Blows (Ex): Akulya may use a full attack action to make one extra attack per round with an unarmed strike or a special monk weapon at his highest base attack bonus, but this attack and each other attack made in that round take a –1 penalty apiece. This penalty applies for 1 round, so it affects attacks of opportunity Akulya might make before his next action. If armed with a kama, nunchaku, or siangham, Akulya can make the extra attack either with that weapon or unarmed. If armed with two such weapons, he uses one for his regular attack(s) and the other for the extra attack. In any case, his damage bonus on the attack with his off hand is not reduced.

***Ki* Strike (Su):** Akulya's unarmed strike can deal damage to a creature with damage reduction as if the blow were made with a magic weapon.

Crab Tattoo (Su): This tattoo provides Akulya with damage reduction 8/magic.

Falcon Tattoo (Su): This tattoo gives Akulya immunity to fear, and allies within 10 feet of his gain a +4 morale bonus on their saving throws against fear effects.

Evasion (Ex): If Akulya is exposed to any effect that normally allows his to attempt a Reflex saving throw for half damage, he takes no damage with a successful saving throw.

Lion Tattoo (Su): This tattoo gives Akulya the ability to smite a foe, gaining a +4 bonus on a single melee attack and a +7 bonus on the damage roll if the attack hits. He can make a smite attempt up to four times per day.

Phoenix Tattoo (Su): This tattoo provides Akulya with spell resistance 22.

Purity of Body (Ex): Akulya has immunity to all diseases except for magical diseases such as mummy rot and lycanthropy.

Slow Fall (Ex): When within arm's reach of a wall, Akulya can use it to slow his descent while falling. He takes damage as if the fall were 20 feet shorter than it actually is.

Still Mind (Ex): +2 bonus on saving throws against spells and effects from the enchantment school.

Possessions: Monk's belt, minor circlet of blasting, bracers of armor +2, gauntlets of ogre power +2, masterwork nunchaku.

THAYAN KNIGHT

While the Red Wizards of Thay are not opposed to blasting their opponents with deadly spells or shredding the minds of their enemies with dark magic, there are times when they need protectors who have mastered the art of swordplay. These protectors are the Thayan knights, familiar with magic and loyal to none but the tattooed mages.

The Thayan knights act as bodyguards and enforcers for the Red Wizards (see page 193 of the *Dungeon Master's Guide*). They lead common Thayan troops into battle and help guard the wizard enclaves. Although they are referred to as knights, they have no code of conduct, and the only rule that binds them is that their lives are worth nothing compared to the safety of the Red Wizards.

Almost all Thayan knights are fighters, although monks and rangers have been known to pursue this career. Barbarians are typically too reckless to concentrate on defense, and the Red Wizards consider other individuals too weak to perform the duties of a Thayan knight.

Hit Die: d10.

Requirements

To qualify to become a Thayan knight, a character must fulfill all the following criteria.

Race: Human.
Alignment: Any nongood.
Base Attack Bonus: +5.
Skills: Intimidate 2 ranks, Knowledge (arcana) 2 ranks, Knowledge (local Thay) 2 ranks.
Feats: Iron Will, Weapon Focus (longsword).
Special: Sworn allegiance to the Red Wizards of Thay.

Class Skills

The Thayan knight's class skills (and the key ability for each skill) are Bluff (Cha), Climb (Str), Craft (Int), Gather Information (Cha), Handle Animal (Cha), Intimidate (Cha), Jump (Str), Knowledge (arcana) (Int), Knowledge (Thay local) (Int), Profession (Wis), Ride (Dex), Spot (Wis), and Swim (Str).

Skill Points at Each Level: 2 + Int modifier.

TABLE 2–35: THE THAYAN KNIGHT

Level	Base Attack Bonus	Fort Save	Ref Save	Will Save	Special
1st	+1	+2	+0	+0	Horrors of Thay (+2 fear, +1 charm), zulkir's favor
2nd	+2	+3	+0	+0	Zulkir's defender
3rd	+3	+3	+1	+1	Fighter feat
4th	+4	+4	+1	+1	Horrors of Thay (+4 fear, +2 charm), final stand
5th	+5	+4	+1	+1	Zulkir's champion

Class Features

All of the following are class features of the Thayan knight prestige class.

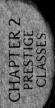

Weapon and Armor Proficiency:
Thayan knights gain proficiency with
tower shields.

Horrors of Thay (Ex): Because of
long exposure to the cruelty of her homeland, a Thayan
knight gains a +2 morale bonus on saving throws against
fear effects and a +1 morale bonus on saving throws against
charm effects. At 4th level, these bonuses increase to +4 and
+2, respectively. None of these bonuses apply against attacks
from Red Wizards.

Zulkir's Favor (Su): At 1st level, a Thayan knight under-
goes a long and painful tattooing ritual. A magic tattoo,
placed either on the back or the forehead, provides a +2
resistance bonus on Reflex saves. The tattoo also marks the
knight as someone loyal to the Red Wizards. The knight
automatically fails any
saving throw against a
mind-affecting spell cast
by a Red Wizard. When the tattoo is
visible, the knight gains a +2 morale
bonus on Intimidate checks as an extraordinary ability.

Zulkir's Defender (Ex): A Thayan knight of 2nd level or
higher gains a +2 morale bonus on attack rolls and damage
rolls against any creature that attacks her or that she has previously seen attack a Red Wizard.

Fighter Feat: At 3rd level, a Thayan knight may choose
any one feat except Weapon Specialization from the fighter
bonus feat list (see Table 5–1, page 90 of the *Player's Handbook*).

BEHIND THE CURTAIN:
WORLD-SPECIFIC PRESTIGE CLASSES

Creating prestige classes specific to your campaign setting is an
excellent way to give depth to the world and flavor to the prestige
class. Virtually all the prestige classes in this book come from
world-specific backgrounds but the designers made them more
generic to the implicit world of the Dungeons & Dragons game so
that you could fit them into your chosen campaign setting with
as little difficulty as possible. Prestige classes such as the bear
warrior and the tattooed monk, for example, were originally part
of the *Oriental Adventures* campaign sourcebook but have been
integrated into the core D&D experience.

The Thayan knight, however, is an example of a world-specific prestige class the designers chose not to make generic. It
is a prestige class taken from the Forgotten Realms *Campaign
Setting* and shows its roots clearly. The reason the designers
chose not to strip out this world flavor is twofold. First, it provides an excellent example of how a prestige class can reflect
the world and culture it belongs to; second, the Thayan knight
represents a classic fantasy archetype—the warrior-henchman
of a powerful wizardly cabal. Most D&D campaign settings have
cultures or organizations similar to the Red Wizards of Thay,
so even if you do not play in the Forgotten Realms setting, you
should have no difficulty customizing the Thayan knight to your
own game setting. To do so, look first at the requirements (the
Red Wizards are xenophobic, hence the racial requirement) and
then work your way down. While the Thayan knight's special
abilities have specific names, you should have no difficulty
establishing equivalents in your own campaign world.

Final Stand (Su): Once per day as a standard action, a Thayan knight of 4th level or higher can inspire her troops. Allies within 10 feet of the knight gain 2d10 temporary hit points. This ability affects a number of creatures equal to the knight's class level + the knight's Charisma modifier and lasts the same number of rounds.

Zulkir's Champion (Su): A 5th-level Thayan knight receives a large magic tattoo across her face, signifying her devotion to the protection of the Red Wizards. Once per day, she can add a +2 luck bonus on a single saving throw. This bonus can be taken after the die is rolled and after other modifiers have been applied to the roll. When the tattoo is visible, the knight gains a +4 morale bonus on Intimidate checks as an extraordinary ability.

Sample Thayan Knight

Bareris: Human fighter 5/Thayan knight 5; CR 10; Medium humanoid; HD 5d10+10 plus 5d10+10; hp 75; Init +1; Spd 20 ft.; AC 24, touch 12, flat-footed 23; Base Atk +8; Grp +12; Atk +14 melee (1d8+7/17–20, +1 longsword) or +11 ranged (1d8+7/×3, +1 composite longbow [+4 Str bonus]); Full Atk +14/+9 melee (1d8+7/17–20, +1 longsword) or +11/+6 ranged (1d8+7/×3, +1 composite longbow [+4 Str bonus]); SA —; SQ final stand, horrors of Thay, Zulkir's champion, Zulkir's defender, Zulkir's favor; AL LE; SV Fort +11, Ref +5, Will +4; Str 19, Dex 13, Con 14, Int 10, Wis 8, Cha 12.

Skills and Feats: Bluff +10, Diplomacy +3, Gather Information +3, Intimidate +20, Knowledge (arcana) +2, Knowledge (local, Thay +2, Spot +4; Cleave, Dodge, Improved Critical (longsword), Iron Will, Power Attack, Weapon Focus (composite longbow), Weapon Focus (longsword), Weapon Specialization (composite longbow), Weapon Specialization (longsword).

Final Stand (Su): Once per day as a standard action, Bareris can grant up to six allies within 10 feet of herself 2d10 temporary hit points each that last for 6 rounds.

Horrors of Thay (Ex): Bareris gains a +4 morale bonus on saving throws against fear effects and a +2 morale bonus on saves against charms.

Zulkir's Champion (Su): Once per day, Bareris gains a +2 luck bonus on a single saving throw; she can add the bonus after the die is rolled. She also gains a +4 morale bonus on Intimidate checks when the tattoo is visible (already figured into the statistics above).

Zulkir's Defender (Su): Bareris gains a +2 morale bonus on attack and damage rolls against any creature that attacks her or that she has observed attacking a Red Wizard.

Zulkir's Favor (Su): A magic tattoo on Bareris's forehead provides her a +2 resistance bonus on Reflex saves, but she automatically fails any saving throw against a mind-affecting spell cast by a Red Wizard.

Possessions: +1 longsword, +1 composite longbow (+4 Str bonus), +1 full plate, +1 heavy steel shield, gauntlets of ogre power +2, ring of protection +1, cloak of resistance +1, potion of cure moderate wounds, 20 arrows.

WAR CHANTER

The roar of battle, the screams of the dying, the howl of the warrior's cry . . . these are all notes in the music composed by the war chanter. His music flows across the battlefield like a raging torrent, catching friends and foes alike in its wake.

Bards of particularly militant mindsets become war chanters (giving up their spellcasting ability in the process), and among barbarians, war chanters are often the leaders or elite warriors of a tribe. The music of a war chanter inspires those around him and pushes them to greater heights of strength and deeds of valor.

Fighters and barbarians sometimes gain a few levels of bard in qualifying for this prestige class. Paladins and monks cannot join because of the alignment requirement, but members of both those classes respect the leadership and military qualities of the war chanter class.

NPC war chanters are usually leaders of small warbands. It is not unusual to see them as chief lieutenants in larger groups. They function best when surrounded by lesser allies, but can be encountered on their own as well.

Hit Die: d8.

TABLE 2–36: THE WAR CHANTER

Level	Base Attack Bonus	Fort Save	Ref Save	Will Save	Special
1st	+1	+2	+0	+0	Inspire toughness, war chanter music
2nd	+2	+3	+0	+0	—
3rd	+3	+3	+1	+1	Inspire recklessness
4th	+4	+4	+1	+1	—
5th	+5	+4	+1	+1	Combine songs
6th	+6	+5	+2	+2	—
7th	+7	+5	+2	+2	Inspire awe
8th	+8	+6	+2	+2	Singing shout
9th	+9	+6	+3	+3	—
10th	+10	+7	+3	+3	Inspire legion

Requirements

To qualify to become a war chanter, a character must fulfill all the following criteria.

Alignment: Any nonlawful.

Base Attack Bonus: +4.

Skills: Perform (sing) or Perform (oratory) 6 ranks.

Feats: Combat Expertise, Weapon Focus.

Special: Able to use the inspire courage bardic music ability.

Class Skills

The war chanter's class skills (and the key ability for each skill) are Balance (Dex), Climb (Str), Concentration (Con), Craft (Int), Diplomacy (Cha), Escape Artist (Dex), Gather Information (Cha), Intimidate (Cha), Jump (Str), Perform (Cha), Profession (Wis), Sense Motive (Wis), and Swim (Str).

Skill Points at Each Level: 4 + Int modifier.

Class Features

All of the following are class features of the war chanter prestige class.

Weapon and Armor Proficiency: War chanters gain no proficiency with any weapon or armor.

Inspire Toughness (Su): A war chanter with 9 or more ranks in Perform (sing) or Perform (oratory) can use her song or poetics to impart a kind of berserk resiliency on hher allies (including himself). To be affected, an ally must be able to hear the war chanter sing (or speak). The effect lasts for as long as the ally hears the war chanter sing and for 5 rounds thereafter. An affected ally receives +2 temporary hit points for every class level of the war chanter. At 6th level and higher, a war chanter also grants affected allies the benefit of the Diehard feat when using this ability.

War Chanter Music: War chanter music follows the same rules as bardic music (see page 29 of the *Player's Handbook*). War chanter levels stack with bard levels for the purpose of determining how often a character can use war chanter music or bardic music. War chanter levels do not stack with bard levels for determining which songs a bard has access to.

Inspire Recklessness (Su): A War chanter of 3rd level or higher with 12 or more ranks in any Perform skill can use her song or poetics to inspire an often dangerous, but very effective, ferocity in one of her allies within 60 feet (or in himself). The effect lasts for as long as the ally hears the war chanter sing and for 5 rounds thereafter. An affected ally (or the war chanter herself) is inspired to recklessness, gaining the ability to decrease her Armor Class by a number less than or equal to her base attack bonus and add the same number to her melee attack rolls as a morale bonus.

On her action, before making any attack rolls in a round, the affected character must choose to subtract a number from her Armor Class and add the same number to all melee attack rolls (this number may be 0). The penalty to Armor Class and the bonus on attack rolls apply until the character's next action.

Combine Songs (Su): A war chanter of 5th level or higher with 12 or more ranks in any Perform skill can combine two types of bardic music or war chanter music to provide the benefits of both (normal stacking rules for bonus types apply).

Inspire Awe (Su): A war chanter of 7th level or higher with 15 or more ranks in any Perform skill can inspire uneasiness, fear, or even terror in her foes. To be affected, a foe must be within 60 feet of the war chanter and must be able to hear the war chanter. Foes get a Will save (DC 10 + war chanter's class level + war chanter's Cha modifier) to resist the effect. The severity of the effect depends on the difference between the foe's Hit Dice and the war chanter's Hit Dice (character level). Subtract the foe's HD from the war chanter's HD and consult the following table.

The effect lasts for as long as the foe can hear the war chanter and 1 round thereafter. If a foe's hearing of the war chanter's song is interrupted, the foe needs to make another saving throw when he hears the war chanter's song again.

HD Difference	Effect
+10 or more	Foe is paralyzed with fear
+1 to +9	Foe is panicked
0 to −5	Foe is frightened
−6 or less	Foe is shaken

Singing Shout (Su): When a war chanter of 8th level or higher engages in battle, he often lets out a singing shout as a standard action. All allies (including herself) within a 60-foot radius who can hear the war chanter gain a +4 enhancement bonus to Strength for a number of rounds equal to one-half the class level of the war chanter.

Inspire Legion (Su): A 10th-level war chanter with 18 or more ranks in any Perform skill can unite her allies and make them fight better together. To be affected, an ally must be within 60 feet of the war chanter and must be able to hear the war chanter. Only allies who meet these requirements at the beginning of the song are affected, and an ally whose hearing is interrupted or who moves more than 60 feet away from the war chanter cannot rejoin the same song. The effect lasts as long as the affected characters can hear the war chanter and stay within range.

When the war chanter begins singing, determine the best base attack bonus among all the affected characters. All affected characters use this base attack bonus or the war chanter's character level as their base attack bonus for the duration of the effect. All affected characters gain a +2 competence bonus on damage rolls as well.

Sample War Chanter

Firreli the Bold: Half-elf bard 6/war chanter 7; CR 13; Medium humanoid; HD 6d6 plus 7d8; hp 53; Init +2; Spd 30 ft.; AC 20, touch 12, flat-footed 18; Base Atk +11; Grp +12; Atk +14 melee (1d6+2/18–20, +1 *rapier*) or +14 ranged (1d8, +1 *light crossbow*); Full Atk +14/+9 melee (1d6+2/18–20, +1 *rapier*) or +14 ranged (1d8, +1 *light crossbow*); SA —; SQ bardic knowledge 15, bardic music (including war chanter music) 13/day, combine songs, half-elf traits, low-light vision; AL CG; SV Fort +7, Ref +9, Will +6; Str 12, Dex 14, Con 10, Int 13, Wis 8, Cha 22.

Skills and Feats: Balance +3, Bluff +18, Concentration +7, Diplomacy +31, Gather Information +27, Intimidate +11, Jump +2, Knowledge (history) +6, Listen +9, Perform (sing) +25, Search +2, Sense Motive +6, Spellcraft +5, Spot +0, Tumble +10, Use Magic Device +18; Combat Expertise, Dodge, Improved Disarm, Mobility, Spring Attack, Weapon Focus (rapier).

Combine Songs (Su): Firreli can combine two types of bardic music or war chanter music at the same time, providing the benefits of both (subject to the normal stacking rules).

Countersong (Su): Firreli can counter magical effects that depend on sound by making a Perform check for each round of countersong. Any creature within 30 feet of her who is affected by a sonic or language-dependent magical attack may use Firreli's Perform check result in place of his or her saving throw if desired. Countersong lasts for 10 rounds.

Fascinate **(Sp):** Firreli can cause up to two creatures within 90 feet that can see and hear her to become *fascinated* with her (sit quietly, −4 penalty on skill checks made as reactions, such as Listen and Spot checks). Firreli's Perform check result is the opponent's Will save DC.

Half-Elf Traits (Ex): Immunity to magic *sleep* spells and effects; +2 bonus on saving throws against enchantments; elven blood.

Inspire Awe (Su): Foes within 60 feet of Firreli must make a DC 21 Will save or be paralyzed with fear if they have 3 HD or less, panicked if they have 4 to 12 HD, frightened if they have 13 to 18 HD, and shaken if they have 19 HD or more. The effect lasts for as long as the foe can hear Firreli and for 1 round thereafter.

Inspire Competence (Su): An ally within 30 feet who can see and hear Firreli gets a +2 competence bonus on skill checks.

Inspire Courage (Su): Allies (including Firrel who hear Firreli sing receive a +1 morale bonus on saves against charm and fear effects and a +1 morale bonus on attack rolls and weapon damage rolls.

Inspire Recklessness (Su): An ally within 60 feet who can hear Firreli can decrease his Armor Class by a number less than or equal to his base attack bonus and take the same number as a morale bonus on melee attack rolls. The effect lasts as long as Firreli sings and for 5 rounds thereafter.

Inspire Toughness (Su): Allies (including Firreli) who hear Firreli sing receive +14 temporary hit points and the

A war chanter

benefit of the Diehard feat, both of which last for as long as Firreli sings and for 5 rounds thereafter.

Low-Light Vision (Ex): Firreli can see twice as far as a human in starlight, moonlight, torchlight, and similar conditions of poor visibility. She retains the ability to distinguish color and detail under these conditions.

Suggestion **(Sp):** Firreli can make a *suggestion* (as the spell) to a creature she has already fascinated. A DC 17 Will save negates the effect.

Bard Spells Known (3/5/4; save DC 16 + spell level): 0—*detect magic, light, lullaby, message, read magic, summon instrument;* 1st—*charm person, cure light wounds, expeditious retreat, lesser confusion;* 2nd—*cure moderate wounds, heroism, hold person.*

Possessions: +3 chain shirt, +1 rapier, +1 light crossbow, cloak of Charisma +4, circlet of persuasion, masterwork buckler, handaxe, lyre, 10 bolts.

WARSHAPER

Most martial characters rely on manufactured gear such as a sword and a shield or natural endowments such as teeth and claws to survive on the battlefield. The warshaper finds those options sadly limiting, instead growing and evolving her own weapons and armor to suit the threat at hand. Blessed with the ability to change form at a moment's notice, warshapers delight in surprising their foes by growing massive claws, armored skin, or other unpleasant surprises.

Warshapers must have some ability to change their form, and many are shapechangers such as doppelgangers and lycanthropes. Wizards and sorcerers who know the *polymorph* spell can take levels in the prestige class, as can druids who have mastered the wild shape class feature.

Most warshapers can change their outward appearance in the blink of an eye, so they don't stand out among the ranks of their allies. It's not until the soldier you're fighting grows a tentacle and fangs that you know you have met a warshaper.

Hit Die: d8.

Requirements

To qualify to become a warshaper, a character must fulfill all the following criteria.

Race: Any (but see below).

Base Attack Bonus: +4.

Special: Must be able to change shape in one of the following five ways:

- Change shape supernatural ability (aranea, hound archon, barghest, doppelganger, rakshasa, slaad).
- Shapechanger subtype (lycanthropes, phasm).
- *Polymorph* as a spell-like ability (astral deva, planetar, solar, couatl, marilith, bronze dragon, gold dragon, silver dragon, efreeti, leonal guardinal, night hag, ogre mage, pixie).
- Able to cast the *polymorph* spell.
- Wild shape or similar class feature (bear warrior*, druid).

The alternate form ability (possessed by quasits, vampires, and others) is insufficient to become a warshaper.

*Prestige class from this book.

Class Skills

The warshaper's class skills (and the key ability for each skill) are Balance (Dex), Climb (Str), Concentration (Con), Craft (Int), Disguise (Cha), Escape Artist (Dex), Jump (Str), and Swim (Str).

Skill Points at Each Level: 2 + Int modifier.

TABLE 2–37: THE WARSHAPER

Level	Base Attack Bonus	Fort Save	Ref Save	Will Save	Special
1st	+0	+2	+0	+0	Morphic immunities, morphic weapons
2nd	+1	+3	+1	+1	Morphic body
3rd	+2	+3	+1	+1	Morphic reach
4th	+3	+4	+1	+1	Morphic healing
5th	+3	+4	+1	+1	Flashmorph/multimorph

Class Features

All of the following are class features of the warshaper prestige class. The class features function only when the warshaper is in a form other than her own (which for doppelganger and phasm warshapers is most of the time).

Weapon and Armor Proficiency: Warshapers gain no proficiency with any weapon or armor.

Morphic Immunities (Ex): A warshaper is adept at distributing her form's vital organs around her body to keep them safe from harm. Warshapers are immune to stunning and critical hits.

Morphic Weapons (Su): As a move action, a warshaper can grow natural weapons such as claws or fangs, allowing a natural attack that deals the appropriate amount of damage according to the size of the new form (see Table 5–1 on page

296 of the *Monster Manual*). These morphic weapons need not be natural weapons that the creature already possesses. For example, a warshaper *polymorphed* into an ettin (Large giant) could grow a claw that deals 1d6 points of damage, or horns for a gore attack that deals 1d8 points of damage.

If the warshaper's form already has a natural weapon of that type, the weapon deals damage as if it were one category larger. For example, a warshaper who used wild shape to become a dire wolf (Large animal) could grow its jaw and snout, enabling a bite attack that deals 2d6 points of damage (as a for Huge animal), not the normal 1d8.

A warshaper can change morphic weapons as often as it likes, even if it is using a shapechanging technique such as the *polymorph* spell or the wild shape class feature that doesn't allow subsequent changes after the initial transformation.

Morphic Body (Su): At 2nd level and higher, a warshaper can use its precise control over its form to make itself stronger and heartier. It gains +4 to Strength and +4 to Constitution.

Morphic Reach (Su): A warshaper of 3rd level or higher can suddenly stretch its limbs, neck, or other appendages outward, giving it 5 more feet of reach than the creature it's emulating. Unlike most creatures, warshapers don't appear to have a longer reach until they actually use it.

Morphic Healing (Su): At 4th level, a warshaper becomes able to change its form where wounds appear, creating smooth skin where once were wounds. The warshaper gains fast healing 2, and if it spends a full-round action and succeeds on a Concentration check (DC equal to the total damage it has sustained), it heals 10 points of damage.

Flashmorph/Multimorph (Su): A 5th-level warshaper gains one of two class features. If the warshaper has the ability to change form at will, such as from the change shape ability, the shapechanger subtype, or a *polymorph* spell-like ability, it gains the flashmorph class feature, allowing it to change form as a move action. If it casts the *polymorph* spell, has *polymorph* as a spell-like ability usable less often than at will, or has the wild shape class feature, it instead gains the multimorph class feature. Multimorph allows a warshaper to change forms multiple times during the duration of the spell, spell-like ability, or class feature that enables her to change form. For example, a wizard/warshaper could *polymorph* into a troll for 2 minutes, then change into a red dragon for 4 minutes, and then spend the rest of the spell's duration in the form of a hill giant. Each change requires a standard action, and only the first transformation heals the warshaper. If the warshaper changes into its natural form, the spell, spell-like ability, or use of wild shape ends.

Sample Warshaper

Koreya Stormgather: Halfling druid 10/warshaper 5; CR 15; Small humanoid; HD 10d8 plus 5d8; hp 68; Init +2; Spd 20 ft.; AC 22, touch 14, flat-footed 20; Base Atk +10; Grp +8; Atk +14 melee (1d4+4, +1 *Small quarterstaff*) or +16 ranged (1d6+3/×3, +1 *Small composite longbow* [+2 Str bonus]); Full Atk

+14/+9 melee (1d4+4, +1 *Small quarterstaff*) or +16/+11 ranged (1d6+3/×3, +1 *Small composite longbow* [+2 Str bonus]); SA —; SQ animal companion, halfling traits, morphic body, morphic healing, morphic immunities, morphic reach, morphic weapons, multimorph, resist nature's lure, trackless step, wild empathy; AL N; SV Fort +11, Ref +6, Will +14; Str 14, Dex 15, Con 10, Int 10, Wis 22, Cha 8.

Skills and Feats: Concentration +17, Handle Animal +9, Jump +0, Knowledge (nature) +12, Spellcraft +10, Survival +18; Martial Weapon Proficiency (composite longbow), Natural Spell, Power Attack, Spell Penetration, Track, Weapon Focus (claw).

A warshaper

Animal Companion (Ex): Koreya has a dire wolf as an animal companion. Its statistics are as described on page 65 of the *Monster Manual*, except that Koreya can handle it as a free action and share spells if the companion is within 5 feet (see page 36 of the *Player's Handbook*).

Halfling Traits (Ex): +2 morale bonus on saves against fear; +1 bonus on attack rolls with thrown weapons and slings.

Morphic Body (Su): Koreya gains a +4 bonus to Strength and a +4 bonus to Constitution when in animal form.

Morphic Healing (Su): In animal form, Koreya has fast healing 2. She can take a full-round action to make a

Concentration check (DC equal to the total damage she has sustained); a successful check heals 10 points of damage.

Morphic Immunities (Ex): When in animal form, Koreya is immune to stunning and critical hits.

Morphic Reach (Su): Koreya's reach when in animal form is 5 feet greater than normal for an animal of that kind.

Morphic Weapons (Su): As a move action, Koreya can grow claws, fangs, or other natural weapons that deal slam, bite, claw, or gore damage appropriate for the size of creature (see Table 5–1 on page 296 of the *Monster Manual*). If the animal form she takes already has a natural weapon of that type, it deals damage as if the creature were one size category larger.

Multimorph (Su): During each use of her wild shape ability (which lasts for 10 hours or until she changes back to elf form), Koreya can change form as many times as she likes, taking a standard action to do so. Only the first change heals Koreya.

Resist Nature's Lure (Ex): Koreya has a +4 bonus on saving throws against the spell-like abilities of fey.

Trackless Step (Ex): Koreya leaves no trail in natural surroundings and can't be tracked.

Wild Empathy (Ex): Koreya can improve the attitude of an animal in the same way a Diplomacy check can improve the attitude of a sentient being. She rolls 1d20+8, or 1d20+4 if attempting to influence a magical beast with an Intelligence score of 1 or 2.

Wild Shape (Su): Koreya can change into a Small, Medium, or Large animal and back again four times per day, as per the *polymorph* spell. Her morphic class features work only when she is in animal form.

Woodland Stride (Ex): Koreya may move through natural undergrowth at normal speed and without taking damage or suffering any other impairment.

Druid Spells Prepared (6/6/6/4/4/3; save DC 16 + spell level; she loses access to one 1st-, one 2nd-, and one 5th-level spell while in wild shape form, and the save DCs for her spells are 2 points lower): 0—*cure minor wounds, detect magic, detect poison, light, purify food and drink, read magic;* 1st—*cure light wounds, entangle, faerie fire, magic fang, obscuring mist, speak with animals;* 2nd—*barkskin, cat's grace, delay poison, gust of wind, lesser restoration, resist energy;* 3rd—*call lightning, daylight, greater magic fang, sleet storm;* 4th—*cure serious wounds, flame strike, ice storm, scrying;* 5th—*baleful polymorph, call lightning storm, cure critical wounds.*

Possessions: +1 *Small quarterstaff,* +1 *Small composite longbow* (+2 Str bonus), +3 *Small dragonhide breastplate, periapt of Wisdom +4, staff of swarming insects, ring of protection +1,* divine scroll of *find the path,* 20 arrows.

C lasses are the templates from which D&D characters are created, but it's the player's choice of feats, skills, domains, spells, and other supplemental rules that define and differentiate each PC. This chapter provides many new such options for the players of martial characters.

FEATS

The following collections of feats supplement those found in the *Player's Handbook* and other DUNGEONS & DRAGONS game products. When creating or advancing a character, you can choose to use these feats in addition to those presented elsewhere. Most of the feats presented here have prerequisites that must be met before you can choose them. The prerequisites can be met through options available in this book or the *Player's Handbook*.

In keeping with the theme of this book, these feats are oriented toward improving your character's combat abilities. They are not, however, only options for fighter characters but, rather, expand on the combat options of all the classes. Many of the feats here require class features or abilities not available to a character with levels in the fighter class only. Look for options that make your character's sneak attack, turning ability, stunning attacks, or other class features and skills more powerful or versatile.

CHOOSING FEATS

The DUNGEONS & DRAGONS game gives you a plethora of options for customizing your character. When designing or advancing a fighter-type character, you depend on feats to distinguish your character from others, and the fighter character class, as well as many fighter-oriented prestige classes.

You can adopt any number of strategies when choosing feats for your fighter-type character, and it would be impossible for the designers to anticipate them all. Still, here are a few suggestions.

Plan Ahead

You might not know at character creation, or even later on in your character's career, what path you want the PC to take. Whether you want your character to stay single-class, or experiment with multiclassing, or even head toward one of the many prestige classes presented here or elsewhere isn't a decision you have to make right away. However, you should always plan at least a level or two ahead to take advantage of the choices that are out there. Look at easy-entry feats (feats that have only one or two prerequisites, or prerequisites that follow the sort of character concept you want). Power Attack, for example, is a feat almost all fighter-types qualify for right away, and it leads to a group of other feats—Cleave, Great Cleave, Improved Sunder, and so on. If you want to be a "damage machine" character, you'll probably want to take Power Attack at some point.

Benefit Now

Power Attack, on the other hand, is also a great example of a feat you might want to wait at least a little while before taking. The feat is limited by your base attack bonus, and at low levels, that's a significant limit. Indeed, if you take Power Attack at 1st level and you don't have a phenomenal Strength score, you're mathematically hurting yourself. A good attack bonus does more for you at low levels than extra damage, since that extra damage does you no good if you don't hit your target.

That's where feats such as Weapon Focus come in. If you know you're going to be happy using a greatsword for a good part of your career, a +1 bonus on attack rolls at low levels is huge. Even if you're not sure you will always use a greatsword, if you plan on being in a fighter-oriented class for long, you have the feats to spare to make one or two wrong calls. Choose feats that you can use to good effect right

away, and you shouldn't be too disappointed if you change direction later.

Don't Pin Yourself Down

Once you have selected a feat, you can't undo that choice. Think about the repercussions to your character over the next few levels if you choose a feat that limits your options. Once you have decided you want to head in a particular direction, you can make a few adjustments and work your way there, as long as you haven't made too many contradictory choices. Building your character for two-weapon fighting and then deciding you really like some of the shield-using feats we put in this book leaves you with wasted choices.

Become Familiar with Class Abilities

The classes in the *Player's Handbook*, as well as prestige classes in the *Dungeon Master's Guide*, this book, and other books, often feature direct paths to quick, specific results. The cavalier (see Chapter 1 of this book), for example, is one of the best "knight in shining armor" mounted combat experts you're going to find. The master thrower makes thrown weapons a great choice, particularly for a dexterous, mobile character. The Order of the Bow ini-

Success in negotiation is all about give and take.

TABLE 3–1: GENERAL FEATS

Feat	Prerequisites	Benefit
Arcane Strike	Ability to cast 3rd-level arcane spells, base attack bonus +4	Sacrifice a spell for +1 on attacks and +1d4 damage per level of the spell
Arterial Strike	Sneak attack ability, base attack bonus +4	Trade 1d6 sneak attack damage for 1 point of damage per round
Axiomatic Strike	*Ki* strike (lawful), Stunning Fist	+2d6 unarmed damage against chaotic opponent
Clever Wrestling	Small or Medium size, Improved Unarmed Strike	Gain circumstance bonus to escape grapple or pin
Close-Quarters Fighting[1]	Base attack bonus +3	Use counterattack to resist grapple
Dash	—	Speed + 5 feet in light or no armor
Defensive Strike[1]	Dex 13, Int 13, Combat Expertise, Dodge	+4 bonus on attack roll after successful total defense
Defensive Throw	Dex 13, Combat Reflexes, Dodge, Improved Trip, Improved Unarmed Strike	Trip attempt after foe's attack misses
Destructive Rage	Rage or frenzy ability	+8 bonus on Strength checks to break objects
Earth's Embrace	Str 15, Improved Grapple or improved grab, Improved Unarmed Strike	Extra damage while pinning an opponent
Eagle Claw Attack	Wis 13, Improved Sunder, Improved Unarmed Strike	Add Wis modifier to damage against objects
Extend Rage[3]	Rage or frenzy ability	Rage lasts +5 rounds
Extra Rage[3]	Rage or frenzy ability	Number of rages per day increased by two
Extra Smiting[3]	Smite ability, base attack bonus +4	Number of smite attempts per day increased by two
Extra Stunning[3]	Stunning Fist, base attack bonus +2	Number of stunning attacks per day increased by three
Eyes in the Back of Your Head	Wis 13, base attack bonus +1	Opponents do not gain flanking benefit
Faster Healing	Base Fortitude save bonus +5	Heal hit points and ability damage faster than normal
Favored Power Attack	Favored enemy ability, Power Attack, base attack bonus +4	Trade attack bonus for damage at greater rate against favored enemies.
Fists of Iron	Improved Unarmed Strike, Stunning Fist, base attack bonus +2	+1d6 damage on unarmed attacks
Fleet of Foot	Dex 15, Run	Make one direction change during a run or charge
Flick of the Wrist	Dex 17, Sleight of Hand 5 ranks, Quick Draw	Cause opponent to be flat-footed for one attack
Flying Kick	Str 13, Jump 4 ranks, Improved Unarmed Strike, Power Attack	+1d12 damage on unarmed attacks when charging
Freezing the Lifeblood[1]	Wis 17, Improved Unarmed Strike, Stunning Fist, base attack bonus +10	Paralyze opponent with unarmed strike
Greater Resiliency	Damage reduction ability	Increase damage reduction by +1
Greater Two-Weapon Defense[1]	Dex 19, Improved Two-Weapon Fighting, Two-Weapon Defense, Two-Weapon Fighting, base attack bonus +11	Gain shield bonus when fighting with two weapons
Hamstring	Sneak attack ability, base attack bonus +4	Trade 2d6 sneak attack damage to cut opponent's speed in half
Hold the Line	Combat Reflexes, base attack bonus +2	Make attack of opportunity against charging foe
Improved Buckler Defense[1]	Shield Proficiency	Apply buckler's shield bonus to AC while using off-hand weapon
Improved Combat Expertise[1]	Int 13, Combat Expertise, base attack bonus +6	Reduce your attack bonus to improve your AC
Improved Familiar	Ability to acquire a new familiar, compatible alignment, sufficient arcane spellcaster level and base attack bonus	Gain a more combat-oriented familiar
Improved Favored Enemy	Favored enemy ability, base attack bonus +5	+3 bonus on damage against favored enemies
Improved Mounted Archery[1]	Ride 1 rank, Mounted Archery, Mounted Combat	Reduce or eliminate attack penalties with ranged weapon while mounted
Improved Rapid Shot[1]	Manyshot, Point Blank Shot, Rapid Shot	Ignore –2 penalty when using Rapid Shot
Improved Toughness[1]	Base Fortitude save bonus +2	Gain hp equal to your current HD
Improved Two-Weapon Defense[1]	Dex 17, Two-Weapon Defense, Two-Weapon Fighting, base attack bonus +6	Gain shield bonus when fighting with two weapons
Improved Weapon Familiarity[1]	Base attack bonus +1	Racial weapons are martial, not exotic
Instantaneous Rage	Rage or frenzy ability	Rage even when it isn't your turn
Intimidating Rage	Rage or frenzy ability	Cause single foe within 30 feet to become shaken
Karmic Strike	Dex 13, Combat Expertise, Dodge	Take –4 penalty to AC to make attack of opportunity against melee opponent that hits you

Kiai Shout	Cha 13, base attack bonus +1	Affected opponents become shaken for 1d6 rounds
Greater Kiai Shout	Cha 13, Kiai Shout, base attack bonus +9	Foes who hear your shout may panic
Monkey Grip	Base attack bonus +1	Use larger melee weapons at −2 penalty
Pain Touch	Wis 15, Stunning Fist, base attack bonus +2	Stunned opponents become nauseated for 1 round
Phalanx Fighting[1]	Proficiency with a heavy shield, base attack bonus +1	Bonus to AC and Reflex saves while fighting in shield wall
Pin Shield	Two-Weapon Fighting, base attack bonus +4	Render opponent's shield useless temporarily
Power Critical[1, 4]	Weapon Focus with weapon, base attack bonus +4	+4 bonus to confirm critical with one weapon
Prone Attack[1]	Dex 15, Lightning Reflexes, base attack bonus +2	Attack while prone at no penalty and stand up
Ranged Disarm[1, 2]	Dex 15, Point Blank Shot, Precise Shot, base attack bonus +5	Use ranged weapon to disarm foe within 30 feet
Ranged Pin[1]	Dex 15, Point Blank Shot, Precise Shot, base attack bonus +5	Use ranged weapon to grapple foe within 30 feet
Ranged Sunder[1]	Str 13, Point Blank Shot, Precise Shot, Ranged Pin, base attack bonus +5	Use ranged weapon to sunder foe's weapon at reduced damage penalty
Rapid Stunning[1, 3]	Combat Reflexes, Stunning Fist, base attack bonus +6	Use one additional stunning attack per round
Roundabout Kick	Str 15, Improved Unarmed Strike, Power Attack	Additional unarmed attack against opponent on which you have just scored a critical hit
Sharp-Shooting[1]	Point Blank Shot, Precise Shot, base attack bonus +3	Halve opponent's cover bonus
Shield Charge[1]	Improved Shield Bash, base attack bonus +3	Free trip attack with shield during charge
Shield Slam[1]	Improved Shield Bash, Shield Charge, base attack bonus +6	Use shield to daze opponent
Swarmfighting	Small size, Dex 13, base attack bonus +1	Occupy same square as other swarmfighting ally, gain +1 morale bonus per ally (up to Dex bonus)
Throw Anything	Dex 15, proficiency with weapon, base attack bonus +2	Throw melee weapon with no penalty
Weakening Touch[1]	Wis 17, Improved Unarmed Strike, Stunning Fist, base attack bonus +2	Cause foe's Strength to drop by 6 for 1 minute
Zen Archery	Wis 13, base attack bonus +1	Use Wis instead of Dex for ranged attacks

1 A fighter may select this feat as one of his fighter bonus feats.
2 You can take this feat multiple times. Its effects do not stack. Each time you take the feat, it applies to a new weapon.
3 You can take this feat multiple times. Its effects stack.
4 You can take this feat multiple times. Its effects stack if you take the feat more than once for the same weapon.

tiate is a devastating archer, and the frenzied berserker takes barbarian rage to the next level. (All three of these prestige classes are among those described in Chapter 2 of this book.)

If you're interested in a specific character ideal—even if you may change your mind later—look at prestige classes that might serve that purpose. Some of them give you the feats you want as class abilities, while others have requirements that suggest feats you might want to select. Even if you decide, for example, not to be an Order of the Bow initiate, it's hard to argue that its prerequisite feats—Point Blank Shot, Precise Shot, Rapid Shot, and Weapon Focus (longbow, shortbow, or the composite version of either)—don't make good choices for any sort of archery-oriented character.

Utilize "free feats" (those that your PC gets regardless of whether he meets the prerequisites) and bonus feat lists when you can. If you create a character with many bonus feats on the lists of classes your character will take, use the feats every character gets at 1st, 3rd, 6th, and subsequent levels to fill out other needs. There are plenty of feats a fighter might want that don't appear on his list of bonus feats.

Observe Your DM

Every Dungeon Master has a tendency to run a certain type of campaign. If your DM likes to theme his campaign around particular types of villains—such as marauding giants, a cabal of evil wizards, or an unholy alliance between a lich lord and its blackguard henchmen—you should find out which feats (and which class choices) work best in that campaign. If you're going to be fighting a lot of giants, for example, worry less about accuracy than damage potential (giants tend to have low ACs relative to their Challenge Ratings, but lots of hit points).

Also, check how your DM runs combat. Some DMs can't help but play even the dumbest monsters "smart." They avoid giving player characters attacks of opportunity, for example, making the selection of the Combat Reflexes feat a less satisfying choice. On the other hand, feats that allow the player to take advantage of the higher number of attacks of opportunity provided by the Combat Reflexes feat—feats such as Defensive Throw or Hold the Line may turn an unsatisfying choice into an advantageous one. This isn't about "tricking" your DM, but rather about coming up with strategies that make the game fun and challenging for both of you.

GENERAL FEATS

The feats described in the following section supplement the general feats in the *Player's Handbook*. Table 3–1 summarizes the prerequisites and benefits of all these feats and indicates which ones can be taken as bonus feats by a fighter.

ARCANE STRIKE [GENERAL]

You can channel arcane energy into your melee attacks.

Prerequisites: Ability to cast 3rd-level arcane spells, base attack bonus +4.

Benefit: When you activate this feat (a free action that does not provoke an attack of opportunity), you can channel arcane energy into a melee weapon, your unarmed strike, or natural weapons. You must sacrifice one of your spells for the day (of 1st level or higher) to do this, but you gain a bonus on all your attack rolls for 1 round equal to the level of the spell sacrificed, as well as extra damage equal to 1d4 points × the level of the spell sacrificed. The bonus you add to your attack rolls from this feat cannot be greater than your base attack bonus.

For example, Yarren the bladesinger has a base attack bonus of +11 and the ability to cast 4th-level arcane spells. On his turn, he chooses to sacrifice one of his 4th-level spells for the day, marking it off as if he had cast it. Until his next turn, Yarren gains an extra +4 bonus on his attack rolls and an extra 4d4 points of damage with a single melee weapon of his choice (his rapier).

ARTERIAL STRIKE [GENERAL]

Your sneak attacks target large blood vessels, leaving wounds that cause massive blood loss.

Prerequisites: Sneak attack ability, base attack bonus +4.

Benefit: If you hit with a sneak attack, you may choose to forgo +1d6 of extra sneak attack damage to deliver a wound that won't stop bleeding. Each wound caused in this manner saps an extra 1 point of damage per round from the victim, until the victim receives the benefit of a DC 15 Heal check or any *cure* spell or other magical healing. Wounds from multiple arterial strikes result in cumulative bleeding loss (two successful arterial strikes cause an extra 2 points of damage per round until healed). You may deliver only one bleeding wound per successful sneak attack.

AXIOMATIC STRIKE [GENERAL]

You can turn your fist into an instrument of law.

Prerequisites: *Ki* strike (lawful), Stunning Fist.

Benefit: Against a chaotic opponent, you can make an unarmed attack that does an extra 2d6 points of damage. You must declare that you are using this feat before you make your attack roll (thus, a failed attack ruins the attempt). Each attempt counts as one of your uses of the Stunning Fist feat for the day. Creatures immune to stunning can be affected by this extra damage.

An elf uses the Arcane Strike feat to deal extra damage to an otyugh.

CLEVER WRESTLING [GENERAL]

You have a better than normal chance to escape or wriggle free from a big creature's grapple or pin.

Prerequisites: Small or Medium size, Improved Unarmed Strike.

Benefit: When your opponent is larger than Medium, you gain a circumstance bonus on your grapple check to escape a grapple or pin. The size of the bonus depends on your opponent's size, according to the following table.

Opponent Size	Bonus
Large	+2
Huge	+4
Gargantuan	+6
Colossal	+8

CLOSE-QUARTERS FIGHTING [GENERAL]

You are skilled at fighting at close range and resisting grapple attempts.

Prerequisites: Base attack bonus +3.

Benefit: You gain an attack of opportunity whenever an enemy attempts to grapple you, even if the enemy has a feat or special ability that would normally bypass the attack. If you deal damage with this attack, the enemy fails to start the grapple unless it has the Improved Grapple feat or a special ability such as improved grab. If the enemy has such an ability, you may add the damage you deal as a bonus on your opposed check to resist being grappled. This feat does not give you extra attacks of opportunity during a round or allow you to make an attack of opportunity when you would be denied one for being surprised, helpless, or in a similar situation.

For example, an ogre attempts to grapple Tordek. Tordek gains an attack of opportunity, hits, and causes damage. Since the ogre does not have any sort of grappling special ability or feat, it fails to start a grapple. Then an ankheg—a creature with the improved grab special ability—attempts to grapple Tordek. He takes an attack of opportunity, hits, and deals 10 points of damage to the creature. Tordek then adds +10 to his opposed check to resist being grappled.

Normal: Creatures with Improved Grapple, improved grab, or similar feats or special abilities do not provoke attacks of opportunity when they attempt to start a grapple.

Special: A fighter may select Close-Quarters Fighting as one of his fighter bonus feats.

DASH [GENERAL]

You can move faster than normal.

Benefit: If you are wearing light armor or no armor and are carrying a light load, your speed is 5 feet faster.

DEFENSIVE STRIKE [GENERAL]

You can turn a strong defense into a powerful offense.

Prerequisites: Dex 13, Int 13, Combat Expertise, Dodge.

Benefit: If an opponent attacks you and misses while you are using the total defense action, you can attack that opponent on your next turn with a +4 bonus on your attack roll. You gain no bonus against an opponent that does not attack you or against an opponent that attacks and hits you.

Special: A fighter may select Defensive Strike as one of his fighter bonus feats.

DEFENSIVE THROW [GENERAL]

You can use your opponent's weight, strength, and momentum against her, deflecting her attack and throwing her to the ground.

Prerequisites: Dex 13, Combat Reflexes, Dodge, Improved Trip, Improved Unarmed Strike.

Benefit: If the opponent you have chosen to use your Dodge feat against attacks you and misses, you can make an immediate trip attack against that opponent. This attempt counts against your allowed attacks of opportunity in the round.

DESTRUCTIVE RAGE [GENERAL]

You can shatter barriers and objects when enraged.

Prerequisites: Rage or frenzy ability.

Benefit: While you are in a rage or frenzy, you gain a +8 bonus on any Strength checks you make to break down doors or break inanimate, immobile objects.

EARTH'S EMBRACE [GENERAL]

You can crush opponents when you grapple them.

Prerequisites: Str 15, Improved Grapple or improved grab, Improved Unarmed Strike.

Benefit: While grappling, if you pin your opponent, you deal an extra 1d12 points of damage in each round that you maintain the pin. You must hold your opponent immobile as normal (with an opposed grapple check), but you must also remain immobile, giving opponents (other than the one you're pinning) a +4 bonus on attack rolls against you (but you are not helpless). You do not gain this extra damage against creatures that are immune to critical hits.

Normal: You may deal normal damage to a pinned opponent by making a successful grapple check.

EAGLE CLAW ATTACK [GENERAL]

Your superior insight allows you to strike objects with impressive force.

Prerequisites: Wis 13, Improved Sunder, Improved Unarmed Strike.

Benefit: When you make an unarmed strike against an object, you may add your Wisdom bonus to the damage dealt to the object.

EXTEND RAGE [GENERAL]

You are able to maintain your rage longer than most.

Prerequisites: Rage or frenzy ability.

Benefit: Each of the uses of your rage or frenzy ability lasts an additional 5 rounds beyond its normal duration.

Special: You can take this feat multiple times. Its effects stack.

Normal: When you are flanked, the flanking opponents receive a +2 bonus on their attack rolls against you.

EXTRA RAGE [GENERAL]

You may rage more frequently than normal.

Prerequisites: Rage or frenzy ability.

Benefit: You rage or frenzy two more times per day than you otherwise could.

Special: You can take this feat multiple times. Its effects stack.

EXTRA SMITING [GENERAL]

You can make more smite attacks.

Prerequisites: Smite ability, base attack bonus +4.

Benefit: When you take this feat, you gain two extra attempts to smite per day. Use whatever smite ability you have (the paladin's smite evil ability or the hunter of the dead's ability to smite undead, for example).

Special: You can take this feat multiple times. Its effects stack.

EXTRA STUNNING [GENERAL]

You gain extra stunning attacks.

Prerequisites: Stunning Fist, base attack bonus +2.

Benefit: You gain the ability to make three extra stunning attacks per day.

Special: You can take this feat multiple times. Its effects stack.

EYES IN THE BACK OF YOUR HEAD [GENERAL]

Your superior battle sense helps minimize the threat of flanking attacks.

Prerequisites: Wis 13, base attack bonus +1.

Benefit: Attackers do not gain the usual +2 bonus on their attack rolls when flanking you. This feat grants no effect whenever you are attacked without benefit of your Dexterity modifier to Armor Class, such as when you are flat-footed. You may still be sneak attacked when flanked.

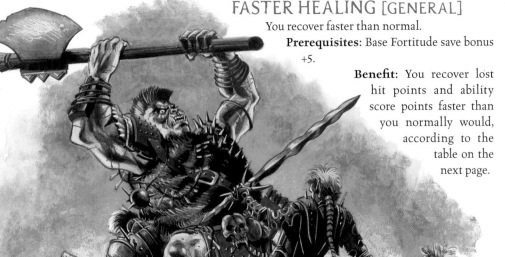

FASTER HEALING [GENERAL]

You recover faster than normal.

Prerequisites: Base Fortitude save bonus +5.

Benefit: You recover lost hit points and ability score points faster than you normally would, according to the table on the next page.

Thanks to the Extend Rage feat, this barbarian is almost invincible.

FAVORED POWER ATTACK [GENERAL]

You are able to deal more damage against your favored enemies.

Prerequisites: Favored enemy ability, Power Attack, base attack bonus +4.

Benefit: When you use the Power Attack feat against a favored enemy, you may subtract a number from your melee attack rolls and add twice that number to your melee damage rolls. If you attack with a weapon in two hands, add three times the number. The normal restrictions of the Power Attack feat apply.

FISTS OF IRON [GENERAL]

You have learned the secrets of imbuing your unarmed attacks with extra force.

Prerequisites: Improved Unarmed Strike, Stunning Fist, base attack bonus +2.

Benefit: Declare that you are using this feat before you make your attack roll (thus, a missed attack roll ruins the attempt). You deal an extra 1d6 points of damage when you make a successful unarmed attack. Each attempt counts as one of your uses of the Stunning Fist feat for the day.

FLEET OF FOOT [GENERAL]

You run nimbly, able to turn corners without losing momentum.

Prerequisites: Dex 15, Run.

Benefit: When running or charging, you can make a single direction change of 90 degrees or less. You can't use this feat in medium or heavy armor, or if you're carrying a medium or heavier load. If you are charging, you must move in a straight line for 10 feet (2 squares) after the turn to maintain the charge.

Normal: Without this feat you can run or charge only in a straight line.

FLICK OF THE WRIST [GENERAL]

With a single motion, you can draw a light weapon and make a devastating attack.

Prerequisites: Dex 17, Sleight of Hand 5 ranks, Quick Draw.

Benefit: If you draw a light weapon and make a melee attack with it in the same round, you catch your opponent flat-footed (for the purpose of this attack only). You may use this feat only once per round and once per opponent during any single combat encounter.

FLYING KICK [GENERAL]

You literally leap into battle, dealing devastating damage.

Prerequisites: Str 13, Jump 4 ranks, Improved Unarmed Strike, Power Attack.

Benefit: When fighting unarmed and using the charge action, you deal an extra 1d12 points of damage with your unarmed attack.

FREEZING THE LIFEBLOOD [GENERAL]

You can paralyze a humanoid opponent with an unarmed attack.

Prerequisites: Wis 17, Improved Unarmed Strike, Stunning Fist, base attack bonus +10.

Benefit: Declare that you are using this feat before you make your attack roll (thus, a missed attack roll ruins the attempt). Against a humanoid opponent, you can make an unarmed attack that deals no damage but has a chance of paralyzing your target. If your attack is successful, your target must attempt a Fortitude saving throw (DC 10 + 1/2 your character level + your Wis modifier). If the target fails this saving throw, it is paralyzed for 1d4+1 rounds. Each attempt to paralyze an opponent counts as one of your uses of the Stunning Fist feat for the day. Creatures immune to stunning cannot be paralyzed in this manner.

Special: A fighter may select Freezing the Lifeblood as one of his fighter bonus feats.

GREATER KIAI SHOUT [GENERAL]

Your kiai shout can panic your opponents.

Prerequisites: Cha 13, Kiai Shout, base attack bonus +9.

Benefit: When you make a kiai shout, your opponents are panicked for 2d6 rounds unless they succeed on Will saves (DC 10 + 1/2 your character level + your Cha modifier). The kiai shout affects only opponents with fewer Hit Dice or levels than you have.

GREATER RESILIENCY [GENERAL]

Your extraordinary resilience to damage increases.

Prerequisites: Damage reduction as a class feature or innate ability.

Benefit: Your damage reduction increases by 1. If it would normally rise thereafter with level, it does so at its previous rate, adding the +1 normally. For example, a 13th-level barbarian has damage reduction 3/–. By taking this feat, he raises it to 4/–. When he reaches 16th level, his damage reduction becomes 5/– and at 19th level, it becomes 6/–. You may not take this feat more than once. This feat has no effect on the type of weapon or damage that overcomes your damage reduction. If you have more than one form of damage reduction, choose which to increase when you take this feat.

HIT POINTS RECOVERED PER CHARACTER LEVEL PER DAY

	With Faster Healing	With Faster Healing and Long-Term Care from a Successful Heal Check	Normal	Normal and Long-Term Care from a Successful Heal Check
Strenuous activity	1	2	0	0
Light activity	1.5	3	1	2
Complete bed rest	2	4	1.5	3

ABILITY SCORE POINTS RECOVERED PER DAY

	With Faster Healing	With Faster Healing and Long-Term Care from a Successful Heal Check	Normal	Normal and Long-Term Care from a Successful Heal Check
Strenuous activity	2	3	0	0
Light activity	2	3	1	2
Complete bed rest	2	3	2	4

GREATER TWO-WEAPON DEFENSE [GENERAL]

When fighting with two weapons, your defenses are extraordinarily strong.

Prerequisites: Dex 19, Improved Two-Weapon Defense, Two-Weapon Defense, Two-Weapon Fighting, base attack bonus +11.

Benefit: When wielding two weapons (not including natural weapons or unarmed strikes), you gain a +3 shield bonus to your AC.

When you are fighting defensively or using the total defense action, this shield bonus increases to +6.

Special: A fighter may select Greater Two-Weapon Defense as one of his fighter bonus feats.

HAMSTRING [GENERAL]

You can wound your opponents' legs, hampering their movement.

Prerequisites: Sneak attack ability, base attack bonus +4.

Benefit: If you hit with a melee sneak attack, you may choose to forgo 2d6 points of extra sneak attack damage to reduce your opponent's base speed by half. This speed reduction ends after 24 hours have passed or a successful DC 15 Heal check or the application of any *cure* spell or other magical healing is made. Creatures immune to sneak attack damage and creatures with no legs or more than four legs can't be slowed down with a hamstring attack. It takes two successful hamstring attacks to affect quadrupeds. Other speeds (fly, burrow, and so on) aren't affected. You may use this ability once per round.

HOLD THE LINE [GENERAL]

You are trained in defensive techniques against charging opponents.

Prerequisites: Combat Reflexes, base attack bonus +2.

Benefit: You may make an attack of opportunity against a charging opponent who enters an area you threaten. Your attack of opportunity happens immediately before the charge attack is resolved.

Normal: You only get an attack of opportunity against a character that exits a square you threaten.

IMPROVED BUCKLER DEFENSE [GENERAL]

You can attack with an off-hand weapon while retaining a buckler's shield bonus to your Armor Class.

Prerequisite: Shield Proficiency.

Benefit: When you attack with a weapon in your off hand, you may still apply your buckler's shield bonus to your Armor Class.

Normal: Without this feat, a character wielding a buckler who attacks with an off-hand weapon loses the buckler's shield bonus to AC until his or her next turn.

Special: A fighter may select Improved Buckler Defense as one of his fighter bonus feats.

IMPROVED COMBAT EXPERTISE [GENERAL]

You have mastered the art of defense in combat.

Prerequisites: Int 13, Combat Expertise, base attack bonus +6.

Benefit: When you use the Combat Expertise feat to improve your Armor Class, the number you subtract from your attack roll and add to your AC can be any number that does not exceed your base attack bonus.

Normal: With Combat Expertise, the number can be no greater than +5.

Special: A fighter may select Improved Combat Expertise as one of his fighter bonus feats.

IMPROVED FAMILIAR [GENERAL]

This feat allows spellcasters to acquire a new familiar from a nonstandard list, but only when they could normally acquire a new familiar (see Familiars, page 52 of the *Player's Handbook*). This feat was originally presented on page 200 of the *Dungeon Master's Guide*; the description here provides new alternatives for arcane spellcasters who want familiars to stand beside them in battle.

Prerequisite: Ability to acquire a new familiar, compatible alignment, sufficiently high arcane spellcaster level, and base attack bonus.

Benefit: When choosing a familiar, the creatures listed below are also available to the spellcaster. The spellcaster may choose a familiar with an alignment up to one step away on each of the alignment axes (lawful through chaotic, good through evil). For example, a chaotic good spellcaster could acquire a neutral familiar. A lawful neutral spellcaster could acquire a neutral good familiar. The spellcaster must have at least the arcane spellcaster level and base attack bonus indicated below in order to acquire the familiar.

Familiar	Alignment	Arcane Spellcaster Level	Base Attack Bonus
Krenshar	Neutral	3rd	+3
Worg	Neutral evil	3rd	+3
Blink dog	Lawful good	5th	+5
Hell hound	Lawful evil	5th	+5
Hippogriff	Neutral	7th	+7
Howler	Chaotic evil	7th	+7
Winter wolf	Neutral evil	7th	+7

Improved familiars otherwise use the rules presented on pages 52 and 53 of the *Player's Handbook*.

Granted Abilities: In addition to their own special qualities, all familiars grant their masters the Alertness feat, the benefit of an empathic link, and the ability to share spells with the familiar.

Improved Evasion (Ex): If a familiar is exposed to any effect that normally allows it to attempt a Reflex saving throw for half damage, it takes no damage with a successful saving throw and only half damage on a failed save.

IMPROVED FAVORED ENEMY [GENERAL]

You know how to hit your favored enemies where it hurts.

Prerequisites: Favored enemy ability, base attack bonus +5.

Benefit: You deal an extra 3 points of damage to your favored enemies. This benefit stacks with any existing favored enemy bonus gained from another class.

IMPROVED MOUNTED ARCHERY [GENERAL]

You can make ranged attacks from a mount almost as well as you can from the ground.

Prerequisites: Ride 1 rank, Mounted Archery, Mounted Combat.

Benefit: The penalty you take when using a ranged weapon if your mount is taking a double move is eliminated, and the penalty for using a ranged weapon when your mount is running is lessened from –4 to –2. You can attack at any time during your mount's move.

Special: A fighter may select Improved Mounted Archery as one of his fighter bonus feats.

IMPROVED RAPID SHOT [GENERAL]

You are an expert at firing weapons with exceptional speed.

Prerequisites: Manyshot, Point Blank Shot, Rapid Shot.

Benefit: When using the Rapid Shot feat, you may ignore the –2 penalty on all your ranged attack rolls.

Special: A fighter may select Improved Rapid Shot as one of his fighter bonus feats.

IMPROVED TOUGHNESS [GENERAL]

You are significantly tougher than normal.

Prerequisite: Base Fortitude save bonus +2.

Benefit: You gain a number of hit points equal to your current Hit Dice. Each time you gain a HD (such as by gaining a level), you gain 1 additional hit point. If you lose a HD (such as by losing a level), you lose 1 hit point permanently.

Special: A fighter may select Improved Toughness as one of his fighter bonus feats.

IMPROVED TWO-WEAPON DEFENSE [GENERAL]

You gain a significant defensive advantage while fighting with two weapons.

Prerequisites: Dex 17, Two-Weapon Defense, Two-Weapon Fighting, base attack bonus +6.

Benefit: When wielding two weapons (not including natural weapons or unarmed strikes), you gain a +2 shield bonus to your Armor Class.

When you are fighting defensively or using the total defense action, this shield bonus increases to +4.

Special: A fighter may select Improved Two-Weapon Defense as one of his fighter bonus feats.

IMPROVED WEAPON FAMILIARITY [GENERAL]

You are familiar with all exotic weapons common to your people.

Prerequisite: Base attack bonus +1.

Benefit: You can treat all the exotic weapons associated with your race as martial weapons rather than as exotic weapons. A weapon is treated as being associated with a race if the race's name appears as part of the weapon's name, such as the elven thinblade (see Chapter 4 of this book) or the dwarven urgrosh.

Normal: Without this feat, you must select the Exotic Weapon Proficiency feat (or have the appropriate weapon

This gnome's worg familiar will fight alongside its master in combat.

Ambush!!!

familiarity as a racial trait) to eliminate the nonproficiency penalty you take when wielding an exotic weapon associated with your race.

Special: A fighter may select Improved Weapon Familiarity as one of his fighter bonus feats.

INSTANTANEOUS RAGE [GENERAL]

You activate your rage instantly.

Prerequisites: Rage or frenzy ability.

Benefit: Your rage begins at any time you wish, even when it's not your turn or when you're surprised. You can activate your rage as a free action in response to another's action. Thus, you can gain the benefits of rage in time to prevent or ameliorate an undesirable event. For example, you can choose to enter a rage when an enemy attacks you, or casts a spell at you (to gain the benefits of a higher Constitution or your bonus on Will saves) before you know the results of the attack. You must be aware of the attack, but you may be flat-footed.

Normal: You enter a rage only during your turn.

INTIMIDATING RAGE [GENERAL]

Your rage engenders fear in your opponents.

Prerequisites: Rage or frenzy ability.

Benefit: While you are raging, you designate a single foe within 30 feet of you that you can attempt to demoralize as a free action (see the Intimidate skill, page 76 of the *Player's Handbook*). A foe that you successfully demoralize remains shaken for as long as you continue to rage. You may only use this feat against a single foe in any particular encounter.

KARMIC STRIKE [GENERAL]

You have learned to strike when your opponent is most vulnerable—the same instant your opponent strikes you.

Prerequisites: Dex 13, Combat Expertise, Dodge.

Benefit: You can make an attack of opportunity against an opponent that hits you in melee. On your action, you choose to take a −4 penalty to your Armor Class in exchange for the ability to make an attack of opportunity against any creature that makes a successful melee attack or melee touch attack against you. The opponent that hits you must be in your threatened area, and this feat does not grant you more attacks of opportunity than you are normally allowed in a round. You specify on your turn that you are activating this feat, and the change to your Armor Class and your ability to make these special attacks of opportunity last until your next turn.

KIAI SHOUT [GENERAL]

You can bellow forth a shout that strikes terror into your enemies.

Prerequisites: Cha 13, base attack bonus +1.

Benefit: Making a kiai shout is a standard action. Opponents who can hear your shout and who are within 30 feet of you may become shaken for 1d6 rounds. The kiai shout affects only opponents with fewer Hit Dice or levels than you have. An opponent in the affected area can resist the effect with a successful Will save (DC 10 + 1/2 your character level + your Cha modifier). You can use the benefit of this feat three times per day.

MONKEY GRIP [GENERAL]

You are able to use a larger weapon than other people your size.

Prerequisite: Base attack bonus +1.

Benefit: You can use melee weapons one size category larger than you are with a –2 penalty on the attack roll, but the amount of effort it takes you to use the weapon does not change. For instance, a Large longsword (a one-handed weapon for a Large creature) is considered a two-handed weapon for a Medium creature that does not have this feat. For a Medium creature that has this feat, it is still considered a one-handed weapon. You can wield a larger light weapon as a light weapon, or a larger two-handed weapon in two hands. You cannot wield a larger weapon in your off hand, and you cannot use this feat with a double weapon.

Normal: You can use a melee weapon one size category larger than you are with a –2 penalty on the attack roll, and the amount of effort it takes to use the weapon increases. A larger light weapon is considered a one-handed weapon, a larger one-handed weapon is considered a two-handed weapon, and you cannot use a larger two-handed weapon at all.

PAIN TOUCH [GENERAL]

You cause intense pain in an opponent with a successful stunning attack.

Prerequisites: Wis 15, Stunning Fist, base attack bonus +2.

Benefit: Victims of a successful stunning attack are subject to such debilitating pain that they are nauseated for 1 round following the round they are stunned. Creatures that are immune to stunning attacks are also immune to the effect of this feat, as are any creatures that are more than one size category larger than the feat user.

PHALANX FIGHTING [GENERAL]

You are trained in fighting in close formation with your allies.

Prerequisites: Proficiency with a heavy shield, base attack bonus +1.

Benefit: If you are using a heavy shield and a light weapon, you gain a +1 bonus to your Armor Class. In addition, if you are within 5 feet of an ally who is also using a heavy shield and light weapon and who also has this feat, you may form a shield wall. A shield wall provides an extra +2 bonus to AC and a +1 bonus on Reflex saves to all eligible characters participating in the shield wall. For example, a single character with this feat gains a +1 bonus to his AC. If two or more characters who all know this feat are adjacent, they each gain an extra +2 bonus to AC (for a total of +3) and a +1 bonus on Reflex saves.

Special: A fighter may select Phalanx Fighting as one of his fighter bonus feats.

PIN SHIELD [GENERAL]

You know how to get inside your opponent's guard by pinning his shield out of the way.

Prerequisites: Two-Weapon Fighting, base attack bonus +4.

Benefit: This feat can be used only when fighting against an opponent who is using a shield and who is your size or one size category bigger or smaller than you. When making a full attack action, you may give up all your off-hand attacks. If you do, you momentarily pin your opponent's shield with your off-hand weapon, and all your remaining attacks during the round are made with your primary weapon (with the normal penalties for fighting with two weapons), and your foe gains no Armor Class benefit from her shield until the end of your action. You cannot use this feat if you are fighting with only one weapon.

POWER CRITICAL [GENERAL]

Choose one weapon, such as a longsword or a greataxe. With that weapon, you know how to hit where it hurts.

Prerequisites: Weapon Focus with weapon, base attack bonus +4.

Benefit: When using the weapon you selected, you gain a +4 bonus on the roll to confirm a threat.

Special: A fighter may select Power Critical as one of his fighter bonus feats.

You can gain Power Critical multiple times. Each time you take the feat, it may be with a different weapon or the same weapon. If you take it with the same weapon, the effects of the feats stack.

PRONE ATTACK [GENERAL]

You can attack from a prone position without penalty.

Prerequisites: Dex 15, Lightning Reflexes, base attack bonus +2.

Benefit: You can make an attack from the prone position and take no penalty on your attack roll. If your attack roll is successful, you may regain your feet immediately as a free action. Opponents gain no bonus on melee attacks against you while you are prone.

Special: A fighter may select Prone Attack as one of his fighter bonus feats.

RANGED DISARM [GENERAL]

You can disarm a foe from a distance.

Prerequisites: Dex 15, Point Blank Shot, Precise Shot, base attack bonus +5.

Benefit: Choose one type of ranged weapon with which you are proficient. You can make a disarm attempt with this weapon as long as your target is within 30 feet.

Special: A fighter may select Ranged Disarm as one of his fighter bonus feats.

You can gain this feat multiple times. Its effects do not stack. Each time you take the feat, it applies to a new ranged weapon.

When using this feat, a character gains no benefit from the Improved Disarm feat.

RANGED PIN [GENERAL]

You can perform a ranged grapple attempt against an opponent not adjacent to you.

Prerequisites: Dex 15, Point Blank Shot, Precise Shot, base attack bonus +5.

Benefit: You can perform a ranged grapple attempt against an opponent by pinning a bit of its clothing to a nearby surface. The target must be within 5 feet of a wall, tree, or other surface in which a thrown weapon or projectile can be stuck and must be wearing some sort of clothing, armor, or other accoutrement. You must succeed on a ranged attack (not a ranged touch attack) and then win an opposed grapple check (your size modifier and the target's size modifiers still apply). To break free, the victim must make a DC 15 Strength check or a DC 15 Escape Artist check as a standard action.

Special: A fighter may select Ranged Pin as one of his fighter bonus feats.

When using this feat, a character gains no benefit from the Improved Grapple feat.

RANGED SUNDER [GENERAL]

You can attack an opponent's weapon from a distance.

Prerequisites: Str 13, Point Blank Shot, Precise Shot, base attack bonus +5.

Benefit: When attacking objects, you deal full damage (instead of half damage) with slashing or bludgeoning ranged weapons. You can make ranged sunder attempts with piercing weapons, such as arrows, but you only deal half damage; divide the damage dealt by 2 before applying the object's hardness. (See the sunder special attack on page 158 of the *Player's Handbook*, as well as page 166 for the hardness of common substances and items.) You must be within 30 feet of your opponent to make a ranged sunder attempt.

Normal: Objects take half damage from ranged weapons (other than siege engines and the like). You can only sunder with a melee attack using a slashing or bludgeoning weapon.

Special: A fighter may select Ranged Sunder as one of his fighter bonus feats.

When using this feat, a character gains no benefit from the Improved Sunder feat.

RAPID STUNNING [GENERAL]

You can use your stunning attacks in rapid succession.

Prerequisites: Combat Reflexes, Stunning Fist, base attack bonus +6.

This halfling monk is never really down because he has the Prone Attack feat.

Benefit: You may use one additional stunning attack (or other special attack that counts against your daily limit of stunning attacks) per round.

Normal: You may only attempt a stunning attack (or any other special attack that counts against your daily limit of stunning attacks) once per round.

Special: A fighter may select Rapid Stunning as one of his fighter bonus feats.

A character can take this feat multiple times. Its effects stack.

ROUNDABOUT KICK [GENERAL]

You can follow up on a particularly powerful unarmed attack with a mighty kick, spinning in a complete circle before landing the kick.

Prerequisites: Str 15, Improved Unarmed Strike, Power Attack.

Benefit: If you score a critical hit on an unarmed attack, you can immediately make an additional unarmed attack against the same opponent, using the same attack bonus that you used for the critical hit roll. For example, Ember the 15th-level monk can make three unarmed attacks in a round, at base attack bonuses of +11, +6, and +1. If she scores a critical hit on her second attack, she can make an additional attack using her +6 base attack bonus. She then makes her third attack (at +1) as normal.

The dwarven defender gains an advantage.

SHARP-SHOOTING [GENERAL]

Your skill with ranged weapons lets you score hits others would miss due to an opponent's cover.

Prerequisites: Point Blank Shot, Precise Shot, base attack bonus +3.

Benefit: Your targets only receive a +2 bonus to Armor Class due to cover. This feat has no effect against foes with no cover or total cover.

Normal: Cover normally gives a +4 bonus to AC.

Special: A fighter may select Sharp-Shooting as one of his fighter bonus feats.

SHIELD CHARGE [GENERAL]

You deal extra damage if you use your shield as a weapon when charging.

Prerequisites: Improved Shield Bash, base attack bonus +3.

Benefit: If you hit an opponent with your shield as part of a charge action, in addition to dealing damage normally, you may make a trip attack without provoking an attack of opportunity. If you lose, the defender does not get to try to trip you in return.

Special: A fighter may select Shield Charge as one of his fighter bonus feats.

SHIELD SLAM [GENERAL]

You can use your shield to daze your opponent.

Prerequisites: Improved Shield Bash, Shield Charge, base attack bonus +6.

Benefit: As a full-round action or as a charge action, you may make an attack with your shield against an opponent. If you hit, you force the target damaged by this attack to make a Fortitude saving throw (DC 10 + 1/2 your character level + your Str modifier) addition to dealing damage normally. A defender who fails this saving throw is dazed for 1 round (until just before your next action). Constructs, oozes, plants, undead, incorporeal creatures, and creatures immune to critical hits cannot be dazed.

Special: A fighter may select Shield Slam as one of his fighter bonus feats.

SWARMFIGHTING [GENERAL]

You and allies with this feat can coordinate melee attacks against a single target and are adept at fighting side by side in close quarters.

Prerequisites: Small size, Dex 13, base attack bonus +1.

Benefit: You can occupy the same 5-foot square in combat with any other allied Small creature that also possesses the Swarmfighting feat at no penalty. When you engage a Medium or larger creature in melee, and at least one other ally with the Swarmfighting feat threatens the target, you gain a +1 morale bonus on the attack roll. This bonus increases by +1 for each additional ally beyond the first with the Swarmfighting feat that threatens the same target. The total morale bonus imparted to your attack roll cannot exceed your Dexterity bonus.

THROW ANYTHING [GENERAL]

In your hands, any weapon becomes a deadly ranged weapon.

Illus. by J. Jarvis

Prerequisites: Dex 15, proficiency with weapon, base attack bonus +2.

Benefit: You can throw a melee weapon you are proficient with as if it were a ranged weapon. The range increment of weapons used in conjunction with this feat is 10 feet.

Normal: You can't throw a melee weapon without taking a –4 penalty unless it has a range increment (such as a hand axe or a dagger).

WEAKENING TOUCH [GENERAL]

You can temporarily weaken an opponent with your unarmed strike.

Prerequisites: Wis 17, Improved Unarmed Strike, Stunning Fist, base attack bonus +2.

Benefit: Declare that you are using this feat before you make your attack roll (thus, a missed attack roll ruins the attempt). You can make an unarmed attack that deals no damage, but instead applies a –6 penalty to the target's Strength score for 1 minute. Multiple weakening touches delivered on the same target are not cumulative. Each attempt to deliver a weakening touch counts as one of your Stunning Fist attacks for the day. Creatures with immunity to stun effects cannot be affected by this feat.

Special: A fighter may select Weakening Touch as one of his fighter bonus feats.

ZEN ARCHERY [GENERAL]

Your intuition guides your hand when you use a ranged weapon.

Prerequisites: Wis 13, base attack bonus +1.

Benefit: You can use your Wisdom modifier instead of your Dexterity modifier when making a ranged attack roll.

DIVINE FEATS

In keeping with the idea of expanding the options of all classes, the feats in this category share characteristics that make them unavailable to single-class fighters. First, they all have as a prerequisite the ability to turn or rebuke undead. Thus, they are open to clerics, paladins of 3rd level or higher, and a member of any prestige class or any creature that has that ability.

Second, the force that powers a divine feat is the ability to channel positive or negative energy to turn or rebuke undead. Each use of a divine feat costs a character a minimum of one turn/rebuke attempt from her number of attempts each day. If you don't have any turn/rebuke attempts left, you can't use a divine feat. Turning or rebuking undead is a standard action (unless you have a special ability that says otherwise). These feats often take a standard action to activate, but may require other types of actions as specified. Regardless, you may activate only one divine feat (or use the ability to turn or rebuke undead once) per round, though overlapping durations may allow you the benefits of more than one divine feat at a time.

Third, turning or rebuking undead is a supernatural ability and a standard action that does not provoke an attack of opportunity and counts as an attack. Activating a divine feat is also a supernatural ability and does not provoke an attack of opportunity unless otherwise specified in the feat description. Activating a divine feat is not considered an attack unless the feat's activation could be the direct cause of damage to a target. Sacred Vengeance, for example, adds 2d6 points of damage to all your melee attacks, but does not directly deal damage to an opponent upon its activation. It is not itself an attack.

Paladins in particular should consider these feats. Because the paladin's turning ability remains behind the cleric's throughout the paladin's career, a paladin who chooses one or two divine feats has more options than just rebuking undead.

DIVINE CLEANSING [DIVINE]

You can channel energy to improve your allies' ability to resist attacks against their vitality and health.

Prerequisites: Turn or rebuke undead ability.

Benefit: As a standard action, you can spend one of your turn or rebuke undead attempts to grant all allies (including yourself) within a 60-foot burst a +2 sacred bonus on Fortitude saving throws for a number of rounds equal to your Charisma modifier.

DIVINE MIGHT [DIVINE]

You can channel energy to increase the damage you deal in combat.

Prerequisites: Str 13, turn or rebuke undead ability, Power Attack.

Benefit: As a free action, spend one of your turn or rebuke undead attempts to add your Charisma bonus to your weapon damage for 1 full round.

DIVINE RESISTANCE [DIVINE]

You can channel energy to temporarily reduce damage you and your allies take from some sources.

Prerequisites: Turn or rebuke undead ability, Divine Cleansing.

Benefit: As a standard action, spend one of your turn or rebuke undead attempts to imbue all allies within a 60-foot burst (including yourself) with resistance to cold 5, electricity 5, and fire 5. This resistance does not stack with similar resistances, such as those granted by spells or special abilities. The protection lasts for a number of rounds equal to your Charisma modifier.

DIVINE SHIELD [DIVINE]

You can channel energy to make your shield more effective for either offense or defense.

Prerequisites: Turn or rebuke undead ability, proficiency with a shield.

This paladin's Divine Resistance feat partially protects her and her allies from fire damage.

TABLE 3–2: DIVINE FEATS

Feat	Prerequisites	Benefit
Divine Cleansing	Turn or rebuke undead ability	Gain +2 sacred bonus on Fortitude saves
Divine Resistance	Turn or rebuke undead ability, Divine Cleansing	Gain resistance to cold 5, electricity 5, and fire 5
Divine Might	Str 13, turn or rebuke undead ability, Power Attack	Add Cha bonus to weapon damage
Divine Shield	Turn or rebuke undead ability, proficiency with a shield	Add Cha bonus as sacred bonus to your shield's defense
Divine Vigor	Turn or rebuke undead ability	Increase base speed by 10 ft., gain +2 hp/level
Sacred Vengeance	Turn or rebuke undead ability	+2d6 points of damage on melee attacks against undead

Benefit: As a standard action, spend one of your turn/rebuke undead attempts to channel energy into your shield, granting it a bonus equal to your Charisma modifier. This bonus applies to the shield's bonus to Armor Class and lasts for a number of rounds equal to half your character level.

DIVINE VIGOR [DIVINE]

You can channel energy to increase your speed and durability.

Prerequisites: Turn or rebuke undead ability.

Benefit: As a standard action, spend one of your turn or rebuke undead attempts to increase your base speed by 10 feet and gain +2 temporary hit points per character level. These effects last a number of minutes equal to your Charisma modifier.

SACRED VENGEANCE [DIVINE]

You can channel energy to deal extra damage against undead in melee.

Prerequisites: Turn or rebuke undead ability.

Benefit: As a free action, spend one of your turn undead attempts to add 2d6 points of damage to all your successful melee attacks against undead until the end of the current round.

TACTICAL FEATS

Feats with the tactical descriptor allow characters to perform a number of powerful attacks.

If you're playing a character who has a tactical feat, it's your responsibility to keep track of the actions you're performing as you set up the maneuver that the feat enables you to perform. It's also a good idea to briefly mention to the DM that you're working toward performing a tactical maneuver; a remark along the lines of "I attack the troll, using Combat Expertise to the maximum, and that's the first step in a tactical maneuver" is appropriate.

Some of the tactical feats refer to the first round, second round, and so on. These terms refer to the timing of the maneuver, not the battle as a whole. You don't have to use Combat Expertise in the first round of combat to begin a tactical maneuver, for example; the round in which you use Combat Expertise is considered the first round of the maneuver.

CAVALRY CHARGER [TACTICAL]

Fighting from the back of a steed is second nature to you.

Prerequisites: Mounted Combat, Spirited Charge, Trample, base attack bonus +6.

Benefit: The Cavalry Charger feat enables the use of three tactical maneuvers.

Unhorse: To use this maneuver, you must be mounted and charge a mounted foe. If your charge attack hits, you may

---

BEHIND THE CURTAIN: TACTICAL FEATS

Tactical feats are more complicated than most other feats, because they cover multiple situations and often require some setup on the part of the player character. So why bother?

Tactical feats are a good way to offer bonuses for situations that don't come up often enough to warrant regular feats. Players understand that their characters only get a precious few feats over the course of their careers, and they want to make sure every feat counts. A fighter can count on his Weapon Focus feat making a difference in almost every combat. A feat that requires you to fight defensively for several rounds in a row might not matter—and players probably won't choose such a feat because they know it's too situational. However, by combining three situational advantages in a single tactical feat, you make the package deal a more compelling choice. You provide big rewards for unusual

situations rather than a smaller reward for a common situation.

A second, related reason to employ tactical feats is to encourage a broader range of combat maneuvers. Combat in the D&D game can sometimes devolve into a ceaseless litany of "I try to hit him again." Tactical feats, on the other hand, often involve movement, bull rushes, power attacks, and other special activities. They reward clever play and teamwork as players think strategically, setting up the situations that grant them big bonuses. But there's an element of risk involved, because the bad guys (intentionally or not) often thwart such plans.

If you design your own tactical feats, take care to keep them somewhat rare in your game. In general, characters shouldn't have more than two or three tactical feats, because six to nine special situations are a lot to keep track of. Tactical feats should be spice—they shouldn't be the main course.

This knight uses the Cavalry Charger feat to make a fell trample against a squad of orcs.

TABLE 3–3: TACTICAL FEATS

Feat	Prerequisites	Benefit
Cavalry Charger[1]	Mounted Combat, Spirited Charge, Trample, base attack bonus +6	See feat description
Combat Brute[1]	Improved Sunder, Power Attack, base attack bonus +6	See feat description
Elusive Target	Dodge, Mobility, base attack bonus +6	See feat description
Formation Expert[1]	Base attack bonus +6	See feat description
Giantbane[1]	Medium or smaller size, Tumble 5 ranks, base attack bonus +6	See feat description
Raptor School	Wis 13, Jump 5 ranks, base attack bonus +6	See feat description
Shock Trooper[1]	Improved Bull Rush, Power Attack, base attack bonus +6	See feat description
Sun School	Flurry of blows ability, base attack bonus +4	See feat description

1 A fighter may select this feat as one of his fighter bonus feats.

make a free bull rush attempt. If the bull rush attempt succeeds, you move your foe normally, but his mount remains where it was.

Leaping Charge: To use this maneuver, you must be mounted and charge a foe at least one size category smaller than your mount. Make a Ride check at the conclusion of the move portion of the charge action. Prior to making the roll, determine the DC of the check: either DC 10 for a chance to deal 2 extra points of damage or DC 20 for a chance to deal 4 extra points of damage. If you fail this Ride check, you miss your target (no attack roll) and if you fail this Ride check by 5 or more, you miss your target and fall off your mount, landing in a square adjacent to the mount's space.

Fell Trample: You can make mounted overrun attempts against more than one foe, resolving each attempt according to the rules on page 157 and 158 of the *Player's Handbook.* Your mount gets a hoof attack against each foe you successfully overrun.

Special: A fighter may select Cavalry Charger as one of his fighter bonus feats.

COMBAT BRUTE [TACTICAL]

You employ strength and leverage to great effect in battle.

Prerequisites: Improved Sunder, Power Attack, base attack bonus +6.

Benefit: The Combat Brute feat enables the use of three tactical maneuvers.

Advancing Blows: To use this maneuver, you must make a successful bull rush attempt against a foe. During the next round, all your attacks against that foe gain a +1 bonus on attack and damage rolls for each square your bull rush moved that foe. For example, if you pushed an orc back 10 (2 squares) feet with a bull rush, you would gain a +2 bonus on attack and damage rolls against that orc on the following round.

Sundering Cleave: To use this maneuver, you must destroy a foe's weapon or shield with a successful sunder attempt (see page 158 of the *Player's Handbook*). If you do so, you gain an immediate additional melee attack against the foe. The additional attack is with the same weapon and at the same attack bonus as the attack that destroyed the weapon or shield.

Momentum Swing: To use this maneuver, you must charge a foe in the first round, and you must make an attack using your Power Attack feat in the second round. The penalty you

take on your attack roll must be –5 or worse. Your attacks during the second round gain a bonus equal to your attack roll penalty × 1-1/2, or × 3 if you're using a two-handed weapon or a one-handed weapon wielded in two hands. For instance, if you choose to take a –6 penalty on your attack roll, you can deal an extra 9 points of damage, or an extra 18 points if you're using a two-handed weapon or a one-handed weapon wielded in two hands.

Special: A fighter may select Combat Brute as one of his fighter bonus feats.

ELUSIVE TARGET [TACTICAL]

Trying to land a blow against you can be a maddening experience.

Prerequisites: Dodge, Mobility, base attack bonus +6.

Benefit: The Elusive Target feat enables the use of three tactical maneuvers.

Negate Power Attack: To use this maneuver, you must designate a specific foe to be affected by your Dodge feat. If that foe uses the Power Attack feat against you, the foe gains no bonus on the damage roll but still takes the corresponding penalty on the attack roll.

Diverting Defense: To use this maneuver, you must be flanked and you must designate one of the flanking attackers to be affected by your Dodge feat. The first attack of the round from the designated attacker automatically misses you and may strike the other flanking foe instead; the attacking creature makes an attack roll normally, and its ally is considered flat-footed. If the designated attacker is making a full attack against you, its second and subsequent attacks function normally.

Cause Overreach: To use this maneuver, you must provoke an attack of opportunity from a foe by moving out of a threatened square. If the foe misses you, you can make a free trip attempt against this foe, and the foe does not get a chance to trip you if your attempt fails.

FORMATION EXPERT [TACTICAL]

You are trained at fighting in ranks and files.

Prerequisites: Base attack bonus +6.

Benefit: The Formation Expert feat enables the use of three tactical maneuvers. You gain the benefit of the feat even if you are fighting in formation with allies that do not have this feat.

Lock Shields: To use this maneuver, you must have a ready shield, and adjacent allies on opposite sides of you must have ready shields. You gain a +1 bonus to Armor Class.

Step into the Breach: To use this maneuver, you must be within a single move of an ally who falls in combat, and an ally must occupy every square between you and the fallen comrade. You can immediately take a single move action (as if you had readied an action to do so) to move into the square the fallen ally occupies.

Wall of Polearms: To use this maneuver, you must be wielding a shortspear, longspear, trident, glaive, guisarme, halberd, or ranseur, and you must have adjacent allies wielding weapons identical to yours on opposite sides of you. You gain a +2 bonus on attack rolls.

Special: A fighter may select Formation Expert as one of his fighter bonus feats.

fully ducked underneath your foe). If there is no unoccupied square on the opposite side of the foe or you fail the Tumble check, you remain in the square you are in and have failed to duck underneath your foe.

Death from Below: To use this maneuver, you must have successfully used the duck underneath maneuver. You may make an immediate single attack against the foe you ducked underneath. That foe is treated as flat-footed, and you gain a +4 bonus on your attack roll.

Climb Aboard: To use this maneuver, you must move adjacent to a foe at least two size categories larger than you. In the following round, you may make a DC 10 Climb check as a free action to clamber onto the creature's back or limbs (you move into one of the squares the creature occupies). The creature you're standing on takes a −4 penalty on attack rolls against you, because it can strike at you only awkwardly. If the creature moves during its action, you move along with it. The

A pair of half-orcs thwart the spellcasting plans of their night hag opponent.

creature can try to shake you off by making a grapple check opposed by your Climb check. If the creature succeeds, you wind up in a random adjacent square.

Special: A fighter may select Giantbane as one of his fighter bonus feats.

RAPTOR SCHOOL [TACTICAL]

You know martial arts techniques inspired by hunting birds.

Prerequisites: Wis 13, Jump 5 ranks, base attack bonus +6.

Benefit: The Raptor School feat enables the use of three tactical maneuvers.

Eagle's Swoop: To use this maneuver, you must charge a foe or jump down on your enemy from at least 10 feet up (see

GIANTBANE [TACTICAL]

You are trained in fighting foes larger than you are.

Prerequisites: Medium or smaller size, Tumble 5 ranks, base attack bonus +6.

Benefit: The Giantbane feat enables the use of three tactical maneuvers.

Duck Underneath: To use this maneuver, you must have taken a total defense action, then have been attacked by a foe at least two size categories larger than you. You gain a +4 dodge bonus to your Armor Class, which stacks with the bonus for total defense. If that foe misses you, on your next turn, as a free action, you may make a DC 15 Tumble check. If the check succeeds, you move immediately to any unoccupied square on the opposite side of the foe (having success-

page 77 of the *Player's Handbook*). Make a Jump check as a free action immediately before your next attack. Prior to making the roll, determine the DC of the check: either DC 15 for a chance to deal 2 extra points of damage or DC 25 for a chance to deal 4 extra points of damage. If you fail this Jump check, you miss your target, and if you fail this Jump check by 5 or more, you fall prone in an adjacent square.

Falcon's Feathers: To use this maneuver, you must be wearing a cloak. As a standard action, you can whip the cloak around you in a distracting fashion. Make an attempt to feint in combat (see page 68 of the *Player's Handbook*), using your base attack bonus instead of your Bluff modifier. If you succeed, your target is treated as flat-footed for the next melee attack you make against it.

Hawk's Eye: To use this maneuver, you must spend at least 1 full round observing your foe. While doing so, you can take no other actions. The next melee attack you make against your foe gains a +2 bonus on the attack and damage rolls for every round you have just spent observing the foe, to a maximum bonus of +6 (for 3 consecutive full rounds of observation). If the target of your observation attacks you while you're observing, or if you don't make the melee attack within 3 rounds of the end of your observation, you don't get the benefit of the feat.

SHOCK TROOPER [TACTICAL]

You are adept at breaking up formations of soldiers when you rush into battle.

Prerequisites: Improved Bull Rush, Power Attack, base attack bonus +6.

Benefit: The Shock Trooper feat enables the use of three tactical maneuvers.

Directed Bull Rush: To use this maneuver, you must make a successful bull rush attempt as part of a charge. For every square you push your foe back, you may also push that foe one square to the left or right.

Domino Rush: To use this maneuver, you must make a successful bull rush attempt that forces a foe into the same square as another foe. You may make a free trip attempt against both foes at the same time, and neither foe gets a chance to trip you if your attempt fails.

Heedless Charge: To use this maneuver, you must charge and make the attack at the end of the charge using your Power Attack feat. The penalty you take on your attack roll must be −5 or worse. In addition to normal charge modifiers (which give you a −2 penalty to AC and a +2 bonus on the attack roll), you can assign any portion of the attack roll penalty from Power Attack to your Armor Class instead, up to a maximum equal to your base attack bonus.

Special: A fighter may select Shock Trooper as one of his fighter bonus feats.

SUN SCHOOL [TACTICAL]

You have learned a number of esoteric martial arts techniques inspired by the sun.

Prerequisites: Flurry of blows ability, base attack bonus +4.

Benefit: The Sun School feat enables the use of three tactical maneuvers.

Inexorable Progress of Dawn: To use this maneuver, you must hit the same foe with the first two unarmed attacks from a flurry of blows. If you do, your foe must move back 5 feet, and you may move 5 feet forward if you wish. This movement does not provoke an attack of opportunity for either character.

Blinding Sun of Noon: To use this maneuver, you must successfully stun the same foe with an unarmed attack two rounds in a row. In addition to being stunned, that enemy is confused for 1d4 rounds thereafter.

Flash of Sunset: To use this maneuver, you must move adjacent to a foe instantaneously, as with a dimension door spell or the monk's abundant step class feature. If you do so, you can immediately make a single attack at your highest attack bonus against that foe.

WEAPON STYLE FEATS

The most famous martial characters are renowned for their distinctive styles, combinations of favored weapons and exotic maneuvers that are as unique as a signature. Many fighters discover how to use their strength to best effect by learning Power Attack, Cleave, and Improved Sunder, or study the pure art of swordsmanship by learning Combat Expertise and Improved Disarm—but in all the kingdom, there may be only a single master of the Crescent Moon technique.

A weapon style feat is one that provides a benefit that draws upon a number of specific feats, and that often requires the use of specific weapons.

ANVIL OF THUNDER [STYLE]

You have mastered the style of fighting with hammer and axe at the same time, and have learned to deal thunderous blows with this unique pairing of weapons.

Prerequisites: Str 13, Improved Sunder, Power Attack, Two-Weapon Fighting, Weapon Focus (warhammer or light hammer), Weapon Focus (battleaxe, handaxe, or dwarven waraxe).

Benefit: If you hit the same creature with both your axe and your hammer in the same round, it must make a Fortitude saving throw (DC 10 + 1/2 your character level + your Str modifier) or be dazed for 1 round.

BEAR FANG [STYLE]

You have mastered the fierce style of fighting with axe and dagger at the same time. You can bring the fight to close quarters in the blink of an eye.

Prerequisites: Str 15, Power Attack, Two-Weapon Fighting, Weapon Focus (dagger), Weapon Focus (battleaxe, handaxe, or dwarven waraxe).

TABLE 3–4: WEAPON STYLE FEATS

Feat	Prerequisites	Benefit
Anvil of Thunder	Str 13, Improved Sunder, Power Attack, Two-Weapon Fighting, Weapon Focus (warhammer or light hammer), Weapon Focus (battleaxe, handaxe, or dwarven waraxe)	Target hit with both axe and hammer becomes dazed if it fails Fortitude save
Bear Fang	Str 15, Power Attack, Two-Weapon Fighting, Weapon Focus (dagger), Weapon Focus (battleaxe, handaxe, or dwarven waraxe)	Free grapple attempt against target hit with both dagger and axe
Crescent Moon	Improved Disarm, Improved Two-Weapon Fighting, Two-Weapon Fighting, Weapon Focus (dagger), Weapon Focus (bastard sword, longsword, scimitar, or short sword)	Free disarm attempt against target hit with both dagger and sword
Hammer's Edge	Str 15, Improved Bull Rush, Two-Weapon Fighting, Weapon Focus (bastard sword, longsword, or scimitar), Weapon Focus (warhammer or light hammer)	Target hit with both sword and hammer falls prone if it fails Fortitude save
High Sword Low Axe	Improved Trip, Two-Weapon Fighting, Weapon Focus (bastard sword, longsword, scimitar, or short sword), Weapon Focus (battleaxe, handaxe, or dwarven waraxe)	Free trip attempt against target hit with both sword and axe
Lightning Mace	Combat Reflexes, Two-Weapon Fighting, Weapon Focus (light mace)	Gain extra attack after scoring threat while wielding two light maces
Net and Trident	Dex 15, Exotic Weapon Proficiency (net), Two-Weapon Fighting, Weapon Focus (trident)	Make combined attack with net and trident
Quick Staff	Combat Expertise, Dodge, Two-Weapon Fighting, Weapon Focus (quarterstaff)	Gain extra dodge bonus when wielding quarterstaff
Spinning Halberd	Combat Reflexes, Two-Weapon Fighting, Weapon Focus (halberd)	Gain dodge bonus and extra attack when making full attack with halberd
Three Mountains	Str 13, Cleave, Improved Bull Rush, Power Attack, Weapon Focus (heavy mace, morningstar, or greatclub)	Target hit twice with mace, morningstar, or greatclub becomes nauseated if it fails Fortitude save

Benefit: If you hit a creature with both your axe and your dagger in the same round, you deal normal damage with both weapons, and you can choose to immediately attempt to start a grapple as a free action without provoking an attack of opportunity, as if you had the improved grab ability. No initial touch attack is required.

If you succeed on your grapple attempt, you drop your axe, but you immediately gain an additional attack against your grappled foe with your dagger at your highest base attack bonus (with the normal −4 penalty for attacking in a grapple). In subsequent rounds, you can use the dagger to attack while grappling at the normal penalty.

CRESCENT MOON [STYLE]

You have mastered the style of fighting with sword and dagger. You know how to twist an opponent's weapons from its grasp with a single graceful motion while using your two weapons together.

Prerequisites: Improved Disarm, Improved Two-Weapon Fighting, Two-Weapon Fighting, Weapon Focus (dagger), Weapon Focus (bastard sword, longsword, scimitar, or short sword).

Benefit: If you hit the same creature with both your sword and your dagger in the same round, you may make an immediate disarm attempt as a free action.

HAMMER'S EDGE [STYLE]

You are a master of the style of fighting with a hammer and sword at the same time, and have learned to hammer your foes into the ground with your tremendous blows.

Prerequisites: Str 15, Improved Bull Rush, Two-Weapon Fighting, Weapon Focus (bastard sword, longsword, or scimitar), Weapon Focus (warhammer or light hammer).

Benefit: If you hit the same creature with both your sword and your hammer in the same round, it must make a Fortitude saving throw (DC 10 + 1/2 your character level + your Str modifier) or fall prone.

HIGH SWORD LOW AXE [STYLE]

You have mastered the style of fighting with sword and axe at the same time, and have learned to use this unusual pairing of weapons to pull your opponents off their feet.

Prerequisites: Improved Trip, Two-Weapon Fighting, Weapon Focus (bastard sword, longsword, scimitar or shortsword), Weapon Focus (battleaxe, handaxe, or dwarven waraxe).

Benefit: If you hit the same creature with both your sword and your axe in the same round, you may make a free trip attempt against that foe. (If you succeed, you may immediately use your Improved Trip feat to gain an additional attack against your foe.)

LIGHTNING MACE [STYLE]

You are a master of fighting with two maces at the same time, and have learned to strike your foes with lightning speed.

Prerequisites: Combat Reflexes, Two-Weapon Fighting, Weapon Focus (light mace).

Benefit: Whenever you roll a threat on an attack roll while using a light mace in each hand, you gain an additional attack at that same attack bonus.

NET AND TRIDENT [STYLE]

You are a master of fighting with the net and the trident, and have learned to quickly follow up a successful net throw with a deadly jab of the trident.

Prerequisites: Dex 15, Exotic Weapon Proficiency (net), Two-Weapon Fighting, Weapon Focus (trident).

Benefit: As a full-round action, you can make a combined attack with your net and trident. First, you throw your net; if you hit and successfully control your foe by winning the opposed Strength check, you may immediately take a 5-foot step toward your opponent and make a full attack with your trident.

QUICK STAFF [STYLE]

You have mastered the style of fighting with a quarterstaff, and have learned special maneuvers that complement this unique weapon.

Prerequisites: Combat Expertise, Dodge, Two-Weapon Fighting, Weapon Focus (quarterstaff).

Benefit: When you use Combat Expertise to gain a dodge bonus while wielding a quarterstaff, you gain a dodge bonus 2 points higher than the penalty you take on your attack rolls. For example, if you take a –1 penalty on your attack rolls, you gain a +3 dodge bonus to your AC.

SPINNING HALBERD [STYLE]

You have mastered the style of fighting with a halberd, and can use all parts of the weapon—blade, spike, hook, or butt—to strike devastating blows.

Prerequisites: Combat Reflexes, Two-Weapon Fighting, Weapon Focus (halberd).

Benefit: When you make a full attack with your halberd, you gain a +1 dodge bonus to your Armor Class as well as an additional attack with the weapon at a –5 penalty. This attack deals points of bludgeoning damage equal to 1d6 + 1/2 your Strength modifier.

THREE MOUNTAINS [STYLE]

You are a master of fighting with powerful bludgeoning weapons.

Prerequisites: Str 13, Cleave, Improved Bull Rush, Power Attack, Weapon Focus (heavy mace, morningstar, or greatclub).

Benefit: If you strike the same creature twice in the same round with your heavy mace, morningstar, or greatclub, it must make a Fortitude saving throw (DC 10 + 1/2 your character level + your Str modifier) or be nauseated by the pain for 1 round.

NEW SPELLS

This section contains descriptions of new domains mentioned in Chapter 4 (see The Warrior Pantheon) and a selection of new divine spells and new hexblade spells (for the hexblade character class detailed in Chapter 1).

All the new divine spells detailed here—*cloak of bravery*, *greater cloak of bravery*, *lion's roar*, and *valiant fury*—are domain spells of the Courage domain (described above). *Cloak of bravery* is also a new spell for clerics and paladins.

Of the new hexblade spells detailed here, augment familiar is also a new spell for sorcerers and wizards; cursed blade is also a new spell for assassins; and phantom threat is also a new spell for bards.

NEW DOMAINS

Each domain described below includes notes on how to add it to the pantheon of deities presented in the *Player's Handbook* if the DM so chooses.

Courage Domain

Deities: Valkar. At the DM's option, this domain may also be available to the following deities from the *Player's Handbook*: Heironeous, Yondalla.

Granted Power: You radiate an aura of courage that grants all allies within 10 feet (including yourself) a +4 morale bonus on saving throws against fear effects. This supernatural ability functions while you are conscious, but not if you are unconscious or dead.

Courage Domain Spells

1 **Remove Fear:** Suppresses fear or gives +4 on saves against fear for one subject + one per four levels.
2 **Aid:** +1 on attack rolls and saves against fear, 1d8 temporary hp +1/level (max. +10).
3 **Cloak of Bravery***: You and your allies gain a bonus on saves against fear.
4 **Heroism:** Gives +2 bonus on attack rolls, saves, skill checks.
5 **Valiant Fury***: +4 Str, Con; +2 Will saves; extra attack; cures 1d8 hp +1/level (max. +20).
6 **Heroes' Feast:** Food for one creature/level cures and grants combat bonuses.
7 **Heroism, Greater:** Gives +4 bonus on attack rolls, saves, skill checks; immunity to fear; temporary hp.
8 **Lion's Roar***: Deals 1d8 points of damage per two levels to enemies; allies get +1 on attacks and saves against fear, plus temporary hp.
9 **Cloak of Bravery, Greater***: You and your allies become immune to fear and get +2 bonus on attacks.
* New spell described later in this chapter.

Fate Domain

Deities: Lyris. At the DM's option, this domain may also be available to the following deities from the *Player's Handbook*: Nerull, Obad-Hai.

Granted Power: You gain the uncanny dodge ability, allowing you to retain your Dexterity bonus to AC (if any) even if caught flat-footed or struck by an invisible attacker. However, you still lose your Dexterity bonus to AC if immobilized. If you have another class that gives you uncanny dodge, your cleric levels add to that class's level for determining when you gain the improved uncanny dodge class feature (see page 26 of the *Player's Handbook*).

Fate Domain Spells
1 **True Strike:** +20 on your next attack roll.
2 **Augury** ^{M F}: Learns whether an action will be good or bad.
3 **Bestow Curse:** –6 to an ability score; –4 on attack rolls, saves, and checks; or 50% chance of losing each action.
4 **Status:** Monitors condition, position of allies.
5 **Mark of Justice:** Designates action that will trigger *curse* on subject.
6 **Geas/Quest:** As *lesser geas*, plus it affects any creature.
7 **Vision** ^{M X}: As *legend lore*, but quicker and strenuous.
8 **Mind Blank:** Subject is immune to mental/emotional magic and scrying.
9 **Foresight:** "Sixth sense" warns of impending danger.

Nobility Domain
Deities: Altua. At the DM's option, this domain may also be available to the following deities from the *Player's Handbook*: Heironeous, Pelor.

Granted Power: You have the spell-like ability to inspire allies, giving them a +2 morale bonus on saving throws, attack and damage rolls, ability checks, and skill checks. Allies must be able to hear you speak for 1 round. Using this ability is a standard action. It lasts a number of rounds equal to your Charisma bonus and can be used once per day.

Nobility Domain Spells
1 **Divine Favor:** You gain +1 per three levels on attack and damage rolls.
2 **Enthrall:** Captivates all within 100 ft. + 10 ft./level.
3 **Magic Vestment:** Armor or shield gains +1 enhancement per four levels.
4 **Discern Lies:** Reveals deliberate falsehoods.
5 **Command, Greater:** As *command*, but affects one subject/level.
6 **Geas/Quest:** As *lesser geas*, plus it affects any creature.
7 **Repulsion:** Creatures can't approach you.
8 **Demand:** As *sending*, plus you can send *suggestion*.
9 **Storm of Vengeance:** Storm rains acid, lightning, and hail.

Planning Domain
Deities: Halmyr. At the DM's option, this domain may also be available to the following deities from the *Player's Handbook*: Boccob, Vecna, Wee Jas.

Granted Power: You gain Extend Spell as a bonus feat.

Planning Domain Spells
1 **Deathwatch:** Reveals how near death subjects within 30 ft. are.

2 **Augury** ^{M F}: Learns whether an action will be good or bad.
3 **Clairaudience/Clairvoyance:** Hear or see at a distance for 1 min./level.
4 **Status:** Monitors condition, position of allies.
5 **Detect Scrying:** Alerts you to magical eavesdropping.
6 **Heroes' Feast:** Food for one creature/level cures and grants combat bonuses.
7 **Scrying, Greater:** As *scrying*, but faster and longer.
8 **Discern Location:** Reveals exact location of creature or object.
9 **Time Stop:** You act freely for 1d4+1 rounds.

Tyranny Domain
Deities: Typhos. At the DM's option, this domain may also be available to the following deities from the *Player's Handbook*: Hextor, Vecna, Wee Jas.

Granted Power: Add +1 to the save DC of any compulsion spell you cast.

Tyranny Domain Spells
1 **Command:** One subject obeys selected command for 1 round.
2 **Enthrall:** Captivates all within 100 ft. + 10 ft./level.
3 **Discern Lies:** Reveals deliberate falsehoods.
4 **Fear:** Subjects within cone flee for 1 round/level.
5 **Command, Greater:** As *command*, but affects one subject/level.
6 **Geas/Quest:** As *lesser geas*, plus it affects any creature.
7 **Bigby's Grasping Hand:** Hand provides cover, pushes, or grapples.
8 **Charm Monster, Mass:** As *charm monster*, but all within 30 ft.
9 **Dominate Monster:** As *dominate person*, but any creature.

HEXBLADE SPELLS
In the following list, an asterisk (*) after a spell name indicates a new spell described later in this chapter.

1st-Level Hexblade Spells
Alarm: Wards an area for 2 hours/level.
Arcane Mark: Inscribes a personal rune (visible or invisible).
Augment Familiar*: Your familiar becomes more powerful.
Cause Fear: One creature of 5 HD or less flees for 1d4 rounds.
Charm Person: Makes one person your friend.
Detect Magic: Detects spells and magic items within 60 ft.
Disguise Self: Changes your appearance.
Entropic Shield: Ranged attacks against you have 20% miss chance.
Expeditious Retreat: Your speed increases by 30 ft.
Identify^M: Determines properties of magic item.

Light: Object shines like a torch.

Magic Weapon: Weapon gains +1 bonus.

Mount: Summons riding horse for 2 hours/level.

Nystul's Magic Aura: Alters object's magic aura.

Phantom Threat*: Subject thinks it's flanked.

Prestidigitation: Performs minor tricks.

Protection from Chaos/Evil/Good/Law: +2 to AC and saves, counter mind control, hedge out elementals and outsiders.

Read Magic: Read scrolls and spellbooks.

Sleep: Puts 4 HD of creatures into magical slumber.

Tasha's Hideous Laughter: Subject loses actions for 1 round/level.

Undetectable Alignment: Conceals alignment for 24 hours.

Unseen Servant: Invisible force obeys your commands.

2nd-Level Hexblade Spells

Alter Self: Assume form of a similar creature.

Blindness/Deafness: Makes subject blind or deaf.

Bull's Strength: Subject gains +4 to Str for 1 min./level.

Darkness: 20-ft. radius of supernatural shadow.

Eagle's Splendor: Subject gains +4 to Cha for 1 min./level.

Enthrall: Captivates all within 100 ft. + 10 ft./level.

False Life: Gain 1d10 temporary hp +1/level (max. +10).

Glitterdust: Blinds creatures, outlines invisible creatures.

Invisibility: Subject is invisible for 1 min./level or until it attacks.

Mirror Image: Creates decoy duplicates of you (1d4 +1 per three levels, max 8).

Protection from Arrows: Subject immune to most ranged attacks.

Pyrotechnics: Turns fire into blinding light or choking smoke.

Rage: Gives +2 to Str and Con, +1 on Will saves, −2 to AC.

Resist Energy: Ignores first 10 (or more) points of damage/attack from specified energy type.

See Invisibility: Reveals invisible creatures or objects.

Spider Climb: Grants ability to walk on walls and ceilings.

Suggestion: Compels subject to follow stated course of action.

Summon Swarm: Summons swarm of bats, rats, or spiders.

Touch of Idiocy: Subject takes 1d6 points of Int, Wis, and Cha damage.

3rd-Level Hexblade Spells

Arcane Sight: Magical auras become visible to you.

Charm Monster: Makes monster believe it is your ally.

Confusion: Subjects behave oddly for 1 round/level.

Deep Slumber: Puts 10 HD of creatures to sleep.

Dispel Magic: Cancels magical spells and effects.

Hound of Doom*: Creates shadowy protector.

Invisibility Sphere: Makes everyone within 10 ft. invisible.

Magic Weapon, Greater: +1/four levels (max. +5).

NondetectionM**:** Hides subject from divination, scrying.

Phantom Steed: Magic horse appears for 1 hour/level.

Poison: Touch deals 1d10 points of Con damage, repeats in 1 min.

Protection from Energy: Absorb 12 points/level of damage from one kind of energy.

Repel Vermin: Insects, spiders, and other vermin stay 10 ft. away.

Slow: One subject/level takes only one action/round, −2 to AC and attack rolls.

Stinking Cloud: Nauseating vapors, 1 round/level.

Vampiric Touch: Touch deals 1d6 points of damage/two levels; caster gains damage as hp.

Wind Wall: Deflects arrows, smaller creatures, and gases.

4th-Level Hexblade Spells

Baleful Polymorph: Transforms subject into harmless animal.

Break Enchantment: Frees subjects from enchantments, alterations, curses, and petrification.

Contact Other Plane: Lets you ask question of extraplanar entity.

Cursed Blade*: Wounds dealt by weapon can't be healed without *remove curse*.

Detect Scrying: Alerts you of magical eavesdropping.

Dimension Door: Teleports you short distance.

Dominate Person: Controls humanoid telepathically.

Enervation: Subject gains 1d4 negative levels.

Fear: Subjects within cone flee for 1 round/level.

Invisibility, Greater: As *invisibility*, but subject can attack and stay invisible.

Phantasmal Killer: Fearsome illusion kills subject or deals 3d6 points of damage.

Polymorph: Gives one willing subject a new form.

ScryingF**:** Spies on subject from a distance.

Sending: Delivers short message anywhere, instantly.

Solid Fog: Blocks vision and slows movement.

NEW SPELL DESCRIPTIONS

The new spells herein are presented in alphabetical order.

Augment Familiar

Transmutation

Level: Sor/Wiz 2, Hexblade 1

Components: V, S

Casting Time: 1 action

Range: Close (25 ft. + 5 ft./2 levels)

Target: Your familiar

Duration: Concentration + 1 round/level

Saving Throw: Fortitude negates (harmless)

Spell Resistance: Yes (harmless)

This spell grants your familiar a +4 enhancement bonus to Strength, Dexterity and Constitution, damage reduction 5/magic, and a +2 resistance bonus on saving throws.

Cloak of Bravery

Abjuration [Mind-Affecting]
Level: Clr 3, Courage 3, Pal 2
Components: V, S
Casting Time: 1 action
Range: 60 ft.
Area: 60-ft.-radius emanation centered on you
Duration: 10 minutes/level
Saving Throw: Will negates (harmless)
Spell Resistance: Yes (harmless)

All allies within the emanation (including you) gain a morale bonus on saves against fear effects equal to your caster level (to a maximum of +10 at 10th level).

Cloak of Bravery, Greater

Abjuration [Mind-Affecting]
Level: Courage 9
Range: 1 mile; see text
Area: 1-mile-radius emanation centered on you
Duration: 1 hour/level

As *cloak of bravery*, except all allies within the emanation (including you) are immune to fear effects and gain a +2 morale bonus on attack rolls. Allies who don't have line of sight to you are unaffected.

Cursed Blade

Necromancy
Level: Assassin 4, Hexblade 4
Components: V
Casting Time: 1 action
Range: Touch
Target: One melee weapon
Duration: 1 minute/level
Saving Throw: None
Spell Resistance: No

A weapon affected by this spell deals wounds that can't be healed in the usual fashion. Any damage dealt by the weapon (not including damage from special weapon properties such as flaming, holy, wounding, and so on) cannot be cured by any means until the damaged individual has received a *remove curse* spell (or some other effect that neutralizes a curse).

If a creature is slain by a weapon that is under the effect of this spell, it can't be raised from the dead unless a *remove curse* spell (or similar effect) is cast on the body or a *true resurrection* spell is used.

Hound of Doom

Illusion (Shadow)
Level: Hexblade 3
Components: V, S
Casting Time: 1 round
Range: Close (25 ft. + 5 ft./2 levels)

The augment familiar spell turns a tiny cat into a formidable combatant.

Effect: Shadowy hound
Duration: 1 minute/level (D) or until destroyed
Saving Throw: None
Spell Resistance: No

You shape the essence of the Plane of Shadow to create a powerful doglike companion that serves you loyally for the duration of the spell. The *hound of doom* has the statistics of a dire wolf (see page 65 of the *Monster Manual*) with the following adjustments: It gains a deflection bonus to Armor Class equal to your Charisma bonus, its hit points when created are equal to your full normal hit points, and it uses your base attack bonus instead of its own (adding its +7 bonus from Strength and –1 penalty from size as normal).

You can command a *hound of doom* as a move action just as if it were fully trained to perform all the tricks listed in the Handle Animal skill (see page 74 of the *Player's Handbook*).

If a *hound of doom*'s hit points are reduced to 0, it is destroyed. A *hound of doom* is treated as a magical beast for the purpose of spells and effects, but it can also be dispelled. You can only have one *hound of doom* in existence at a time. If you cast a second *hound of doom* spell while the first is still active, the first hound is instantly dispelled.

Lion's Roar

Evocation [Sonic]
Level: Courage 8
Components: V, S, DF
Casting Time: 1 action
Range: 120 ft.
Area: 120-ft.-radius burst centered on you
Duration: Instantaneous or 1 minute/level
Saving Throw: Fortitude partial or Will negates (harmless); see text
Spell Resistance: Yes or Yes (harmless); see text

You emit a titanic roar that deals 1d8 points of sonic damage per two caster levels to all enemies within the spell's area and stuns them for 1 round. A successful Fortitude save halves the damage and negates the stunning effect.

In addition, all allies within the spell's area gain a +1 morale bonus on attack rolls and saves against fear effects, plus temporary hit points equal to 1d8 + caster level (to a maximum of 1d8+20 temporary hit points at caster level 20th).

Phantom Threat

Illusion (Phantasm) [Mind-Affecting]
Level: Brd 1, Hexblade 1
Components: V, S
Casting Time: 1 action
Range: Close (25 ft. + 5 ft./2 levels)
Target: One creature
Duration: 1 round/level
Saving Throw: Will negates
Spell Resistance: Yes

You create the sensation in the subject's mind that he is threatened by more foes than he actually faces. Though the subject doesn't actually perceive any additional enemies (and thus doesn't waste any attacks on the phantasm), a creature affected by this spell is considered flanked, even if not threatened by other creatures. No amount of convincing by others can help the victim of this spell avoid its effect—only a successful saving throw against the spell when initially cast can help the target.

Valiant Fury

Transmutation
Level: Courage 5
Components: V, S, DF
Casting Time: 1 action
Range: Close (25 ft. + 5 ft./2 levels)
Target: One living creature
Duration: 1 round/level
Saving Throw: Will negates (harmless)
Spell Resistance: Yes (harmless)

The affected creature gains a +4 morale bonus to Strength and Constitution and a +2 morale bonus on Will saves.

In addition, when making a full attack, the affected creature may make one additional attack with any weapon he is holding. The attack is made using the creature's full base attack bonus, plus any modifiers appropriate to the situation. (This effect is not cumulative with similar effects, such as that provided by the *haste* spell, nor does it actually grant an extra action, so you can't use it to cast a second spell or otherwise take an extra action in the round.)

GUARDIAN FAMILIARS

Few arcane spellcasters are top-notch martial characters as well. Obviously, most use spells to compensate for their weakness in a combat situation. Some arcane spellcasters may also build themselves guardian familiars—construct companions that fight on their behalf. While guardian familiars lack the versatility of other familiars, one of these creatures can be an effective bodyguard for an otherwise fragile wizard or sorcerer.

ACQUIRING A GUARDIAN FAMILIAR

Getting a guardian familiar is a two-step process. First, a spellcaster of sufficiently high level (see the table below) must build the construct in a process similar to wondrous item creation, expending the gold, experience points, and time described in each entry below. Then the character must bind the completed construct to her with the Improved Familiar feat (described earlier in this chapter and also on page 200 of the *Dungeon Master's Guide*). The various guardian familiars, and the minimum level an arcane spellcaster must be to create one, are as follows:

Familiar	Arcane Spellcaster Level
Spark guardian	7th
Gauntlet guardian	9th
Blade guardian	11th

Unlike other familiars, guardian familiars retain their own hit points if they're higher than one-half of the master's total. Their effective HD is the master's character level or the guardian familiar's HD, whichever is greater. They lack the improved evasion and empathic link abilities that most other familiars possess, and they don't confer the Alertness feat on their master. They respond to the master's verbal commands, and they understand any language the master knew when she created the guardian familiar. Because they are mindless constructs, they don't get smarter as the master attains higher levels. Guardian familiars never speak.

If a guardian familiar dies, its master does not have to wait a year and a day to replace it (as is the case with normal familiars). However, a character cannot start to build a new guardian familiar if he or she already possesses one.

SPARK GUARDIAN

Tiny Construct
Hit Dice: 2d10 (11 hp)
Initiative: +0
Speed: 20 ft. (4 squares), fly 20 ft. (good)
Armor Class: 18 (+2 size, +2 Dex, +4 natural), touch 14, flat-footed 16
Base Attack/Grapple: +1/−8*
Attack: Talons +2* melee (1d2−1) or sparks +5 ranged (2d6 electricity)
Full Attack: Talons +3* melee (1d2−1) or sparks +5 ranged (2d6 electricity)
Space/Reach: 2-1/2 ft./ 2-1/2 ft.
Special Attacks: —
Special Qualities:
  Construct traits, damage reduction 5/−, darkvision 60 ft., fast healing 1, find master, low-light vision
Saves: Fort +0, Ref +2, Will +0
Abilities: Str 8, Dex 14, Con —, Int —, Wis 10, Cha 1
Environment: Any
Organization: Solitary
Challenge Rating: 3
Treasure: None
Alignment: Always neutral
Advancement: 3–4 HD (Tiny); 5–6 HD (Small)
* Because it's usually a familiar, a spark guardian has the same base attack bonus as its master. A spark guardian applies its Dexterity modifier, not its Strength modifier, as a bonus on its melee attack roll.

This copper-colored creature looks like a toy hunting bird, with obviously mechanical wings and a strangely glowing beak.

Spark guardians are mechanical birds that shoot sparks at anyone who threatens their master.

Spark guardians are the most basic type of guardian familiar. They usually circle above their master, shooting sparks out of their beaks at enemies. If it isn't undertaking a specific task for its master, a spark guardian flies nearby, prepared to defend its master with its spark attack.

A spark guardian is the size of a songbird or an owl, but it weighs about 10 pounds.

Combat

Spark guardians know that they're ill-equipped for melee combat. Instead, they do their best to remain out of enemies' range, flinging sparks at them from above.

Sparks (Su): The spark guardian's sparks have a range increment of 100 feet.

Find Master (Su): No matter the distance, as long as it is on the same plane, a spark guardian can find its master.

Construction

A spark guardian is built from wood, leather, and copper. The materials cost 2,000 gp. The guardian's master may assemble the body or hire someone else to do the job. Creating the body requires a DC 16 Profession (engineering) check. After the body is sculpted, the spark guardian is animated through an extended magical ritual that requires a specially prepared laboratory or workroom, similar to an alchemist's laboratory and costing 500 gp to establish. If the creator is personally constructing the creature's body, the building and the ritual can be performed together.

A spark guardian with more than 2 Hit Dice can be created, but each additional Hit Die adds 1,000 gp to the market price, and the price increases by 5,000 gp if the creature's size increases to Medium, modifying the cost to create accordingly.

Caster Level: 7th; Prerequisites: Craft Construct (see page 303 of the Monster Manual), lightning bolt, locate creature, minor creation; Market Price: 10,000 gp; Cost to Create: 7,000 gp + 400 XP.

A spark guardian

GAUNTLET GUARDIAN

Small Construct

Hit Dice: 4d10+10 (32 hp)

Initiative: +0

Speed: 20 ft.

Armor Class: 19 (+1 size, +1 Dex, +7 natural), touch 12, flat-footed 18

Base Attack/Grapple: +3/+4*

Attack: Slam +9* melee (1d6+5)

Full Attack: 2 slams +9* melee (1d6+5)

Space/Reach: 5 ft./5 ft.

Special Attacks: —

Special Qualities: Construct traits, damage reduction 5/–, darkvision 60 ft., fast healing 1, find master, low-light vision, *spell storing*

Saves: Fort +1, Ref +2, Will +1

Abilities: Str 20, Dex 12, Con —, Int —, Wis 10, Cha 1

Environment: Any

Organization: Solitary

Challenge Rating: 4

Treasure: None

Alignment: Always neutral

Advancement: 5–8 HD (Small); 9–12 HD (Medium)

* Because it's usually a familiar, a gauntlet guardian has the same base attack bonus as its master.

This squat construct has a barrel-shaped chest and relatively spindly legs. Its forearms are massive pistons ending in oversized, spiked gauntlets.

Gaunlet guardians are created by wizards and sorcerers to be implacable, frightening bodyguards. They perform that task very well; they punch anyone who gets in their master's way.

Gauntlet guardians can handle detailed tactical plans, sentry duty, and similar tasks. Unless ordered not to, a gauntlet guardian focuses its attacks on anyone who attacked its master.

A gauntlet guardian is almost 4 feet tall and weighs more than 200 pounds.

Combat

Gauntlet guardians aren't exactly subtle. They simply move adjacent to their foes and start pummeling with their immense fists.

Find Master (Su): No matter the distance, as long as it is on the same plane, a gauntlet guardian can find its master.

Spell Storing (Sp): A gauntlet guardian can store one spell of 2nd level or lower that is cast into it by another creature. It uses this spell when commanded or when a predetermined situation arises. Once this spell is used, it can store another spell (or the same spell).

A gauntlet guardian

Construction

A gauntlet guardian is built from brass, stone, and steel. The materials cost 3,000 gp. The guardian's master may assemble the body or hire someone else to do the job. Creating the body requires a DC 16 Profession (engineering) check. After the body is sculpted, the gauntlet guardian is animated through an extended magical ritual that requires a specially prepared laboratory or workroom, similar to an alchemist's laboratory and costing 500 gp to establish. If the creator is personally constructing the creature's body, the building and the ritual can be performed together.

A gauntlet guardian with more than 4 Hit Dice can be created, but each additional Hit Die adds 2,000 gp to the market price, and the price increases by 10,000 gp if the creature's size increases to Medium, modifying the cost to create accordingly.

Caster Level: 9th; *Prerequisites:* Craft Construct (see page 303 of the *Monster Manual*), *fabricate, locate creature, stone shape; Market Price:* 20,000 gp; *Cost to Create:* 11,500 gp + 800 XP.

BLADE GUARDIAN

Medium Construct

Hit Dice: 8d10+20 (64 hp)

Initiative: +0

Speed: 20 ft.

Armor Class: 20 (+10 natural), touch 10, flat-footed 20

Base Attack/Grapple: +6/+13*

Attack: Claw +13 melee* (1d6+7)

Full Attack: 2 claws +13 melee* (1d6+7)

Space/Reach: 5 ft./5 ft.

Special Attacks: —

Special Qualities: Construct type, damage reduction 5/–, darkvision 60 ft., fast healing 1, find master, guard, low-light vision, *spell storing*

Saves: Fort +2, Ref +2, Will +2

Abilities: Str 24, Dex 10, Con —, Int —, Wis 10, Cha 1

Environment: Any

Organization: Solitary

Challenge Rating: 6

Treasure: None

Alignment: Always neutral
Advancement: 9–13 HD (Medium); 14–24 HD (Large)
* Because it's usually a familiar, a blade guardian has the same base attack bonus as its master.

This human-shaped creature of metal is covered in spikes. Where its hands should be are instead two whirling blades.

When they are created, blade guardians are forever tied to their masters with a familiar's bond. Unlike the general assistance that most familiars provide, blade guardians exist only to fight on their master's behalf.

A blade guardian is capable of carrying out complex tasks that involve combat in some way. If it's not carrying out a specific command, it stays near its master, attacking anyone who attacks her.

A blade guardian is some 6 feet tall and weighs more than 400 pounds.

Combat

Blade guardians are relentless combatants, striking at foes with their whirling blade-arms and rarely straying far from their masters.

Find Master (Su): No matter the distance, as long as it is on the same plane, a blade guardian can find its master.

Guard (Ex): A blade guardian moves swiftly to defend its master by its side, blocking blows and disrupting foes. All attacks against the master take a –2 penalty if the blade guardian is adjacent.

Spell Storing **(Sp):** A blade guardian can store one spell of 3rd level or lower that is cast into it by another creature. It uses this spell when commanded or when a predetermined situation arises. Once this spell is used, it can store another spell (or the same spell).

Construction

A blade guardian is built from wood, silver, stone, and steel. The materials cost 4,000 gp. The guardian's master may assemble the body or hire someone to do the job. Creating the body requires a DC 16 Profession (engineering) check. After the body is sculpted, the blade guardian is animated through an extended magical ritual that requires a specially prepared laboratory or workroom, similar to an alchemist's laboratory and costing 500 gp to establish. If the creator is personally constructing the creature's body, the building and the ritual can be performed together.

A blade guardian with more than 8 Hit Dice can be created, but each additional Hit Die adds 3,000 gp to the market price, and the price increases by 15,000 gp if the creature's size increases to Large, modifying the cost to create accordingly.

Caster Level: 11th; Prerequisites: Craft Construct (see page 303 of the *Monster Manual*), *fabricate, locate creature, Tenser's transformation*; Market Price: 30,000 gp; Cost to Create: 18,000 gp + 1,200 XP.

A blade guardian

Illus. by W. England

SKILLS

The following skill descriptions supplement those found in the *Player's Handbook*.

PERFORM (WEAPON DRILL) (Cha)

You are skilled in quick, flashy movements of a weapon and can put on a display that shows off your prowess in combat.

This category of the Perform skill covers any sort of weapon display, such as twirling a sword or flipping a dagger from hand to hand. Despite the skill's name, you can use it when unarmed by demonstrating difficult martial arts techniques or shadow boxing against an imaginary opponent.

Check: Unlike other categories of the Perform skill, your prowess with the weapon (indicated by your base attack bonus) is an important factor in how good your Perform (weapon drill) skill is. Apply half your base attack bonus (rounded down) as a circumstance bonus on Perform (weapon drill) checks. Your Charisma modifier also applies, as with any Perform check. If you aren't proficient with the weapon you're using, you take the –4 nonproficiency penalty on Perform (weapon drill) checks.

Action: Varies. If you're performing to earn money in public, a weapon drill requires at least 4 hours of 20-minute performances, with breaks in between. If you're demonstrating your skill or trying to impress the crowd at a gladiator match (see Chapter 4 of this book), the performance is a standard action.

Try Again: Yes, but as with other uses of the Perform skill, subsequent attempts after a failure increase the DC of the Perform check by 2 for each previous failure.

Special: The following feats each grant a +2 bonus on relevant Perform (weapon drill) checks: Combat Expertise, Greater Weapon Focus, Quick Draw, Two-Weapon Fighting, Weapon Focus, and Whirlwind Attack.

A bard cannot use Perform (weapon drill) checks to perform his bardic music abilities (*inspire courage, fascinate,* and so on).

KNOWLEDGE

Several categories of knowledge can be useful to a martial character.

Check: In addition to the checks described in the *Player's Handbook,* the following aspects of the Knowledge skill may prove useful.

Architecture and Engineering: If you have a good vantage point to view an enemy stronghold, a DC 20 Knowledge (architecture and engineering) check reveals a weak aspect of the defense. For every 5 points by which your check results exceeds the DC, the DM can give you another strategy tip for assaulting the fortress. If you have an accurate map of the stronghold, you gain a +5 circumstance bonus on the check.

History: With a successful DC 15 Knowledge (history) check, you know the basics of how a particular army organizes itself. For example, a successful check reveals that bugbears include a shaman in every 20-soldier platoon, or that elf generals often ride with the cavalry.

If you're standing on or near a historic battlefield, you can recall the details of the battle fought there with a DC 20 Knowledge (history) check. You know, for example, that the dwarves of the Brass Hills defeated the orc hordes by starting an avalanche on the hills to your left, and that most of the surviving orcs retreated into the lava tubes somewhere ahead.

Local: A DC 10 Knowledge (local) check is sufficient to identify a military unit or noble's family by its heraldry, if the unit or the family hails from the local area. A Knowledge (nobility and royalty) check is required to identify the heraldry from far-off lands.

Nobility and Royalty: A Knowledge (nobility and royalty) check tells you something about the heraldry of far-off lands. A DC 25 check tells you what part of the world (down to the province or city) a heraldic design comes from. A DC 30 check tells you the name of the military unit or the noble family.

Action: Usually none. In most cases, making a Knowledge check doesn't take an action—you simply know the answer or you don't.

Try Again: No. The check represents what you know, and thinking about a topic a second time doesn't let you know something that you never learned in the first place.

Synergy: There are no bonuses for skill synergy specific to the Knowledge checks described above, but the *Player's Handbook* describes many bonuses that apply to the Knowledge skill in general.

Untrained: An untrained Knowledge check is simply an Intelligence check. Without actual training, you know only common knowledge (DC 10 or lower).

SLEIGHT OF HAND

If you palm a dagger in combat, you can surprise your opponent when it suddenly appears in your hand.

Check: For this technique to work, you must be armed with a dagger, must have the Quick Draw feat, and must be holding nothing in your off hand. You must fight the same foe for at least 2 consecutive rounds to get your opponent used to the idea that you have nothing in your off hand. At the beginning of your turn in the third round, make a Sleight of Hand check opposed by your opponent's Spot check. If you succeed, your foe is considered flat-footed for the next single attack you make with the dagger.

Action: Unlike other uses of the Sleight of Hand skill, it's a free action to put the dagger in your hand because you have the Quick Draw feat.

Try Again: No. Whether your Sleight of Hand check succeeds or fails, no foe will fall for the same trick from you twice in the same combat.

Special: If you have the Deft Hands feat, you get a +2 bonus on Sleight of Hand checks.

Synergy: If you have 5 or more ranks in Bluff, you get a +2 bonus on Sleight of Hand checks.

Most fantasy sagas are replete with massive armies stretching across the horizon, clashing in battles that involve tens of thousands of soldiers. The D&D game is focused on small groups of characters, but such grand battles can make an exciting backdrop for adventures. Low-level characters might be foot soldiers, facing off against a horde of orcs determined to loot and burn more civilized lands. Mid- to high-level characters could be elite commandos and shock troops, taking on missions behind enemy lines to capture or destroy key installations. Because the battlefield is a turbulent place, the characters can be thrust into new situations and new dangers at a moment's notice.

Whether you plan to make warfare central to your D&D game or an occasional diversion, decide what a grand battle looks like in your campaign.

TWO VIEWS OF FANTASY WARFARE

The D&D game is clearly rooted in the medieval warfare tradition. Soldiers wear chainmail or plate armor, and they wield weapons such as swords and bows. Knights gallop across the battlefield on horses, and catapults bombard castle walls. Yet, the presence of fantastic creatures and magic sup-

ports a more modern kind of warfare, in which flying creatures provide air support, soldiers use camouflage or magic to hide themselves from enemies, and spells that affect a large area can devastate clusters of troops.

It's useful to think of D&D warfare as a continuum with historical medieval warfare on one end and modern warfare on the other end. Before you take your D&D game to the battlefield, decide where on that continuum you want your battles to be.

HISTORICAL WARFARE

Medieval armies marched in rank and file for a simple reason. In a world without radios, accurate maps, and global positioning systems, marching in one organized group was the only way to make sure every soldier made it to the battlefield and followed orders once there. Amid the din of battle, soldiers have to be able to hear the shouted orders of their commanders, so they couldn't spread out very much.

Because historical armies marched in rows and columns, obtaining cover and concealment is next to impossible. Battlefields are often large plains, because only in such places can each general stay in contact with the army's units. Camouflage isn't an issue, so armies wear colorful uniforms and carry standards identifying their unit to make it easy to tell friend from foe. Generals send runners with new orders to units, and because the units are easy to identify and reach, those orders are likely to reach subordinate commanders. Catapults are the only artillery weapons, and they're rare sights except during castle sieges. Horse-mounted cavalry was a powerful force on the battlefield, because it could reach the critical ground in a battle quickly. The high walls and arrow slits of a castle provide excellent protect for the defending army; a siege against a well-supplied stronghold can go on for years.

The biggest advantage to historical warfare is that it feels properly epic, with row after row of grim-faced soldiers marching in lockstep toward the enemy. Castles and knights are central to battles in the medieval tradition, and unit tactics respect the difficulties of communication, navigation, and command.

Historical warfare doesn't always interact well with magic or monsters. A single *fireball* can devastate large groups of marching troops, and high-CR monsters can wade through column after column of foot soldiers with impunity. Traditional castles are hard to defend against enemies who can fly or teleport.

If you want your D&D battles to include a strong historical element, use feats such as Hold the Line and Phalanx Fighting to bolster the effectiveness of soldiers in formation. Have soldiers prepare for spells that affect a large area by thinning out their ranks with the disperse maneuver (see Historical Tactics, below). Make flying creatures and monsters with magical abilities rare on the battlefield.

Historical Tactics

Soldiers marching in rows and columns commonly employ the following techniques to increase their effectiveness on the battlefield.

Arrow Volley: If at least ten archers are in a contiguous group (each one adjacent to at least one other), they can loose a high, arcing volley of arrows as a full-round action. Rather than aiming at a specific target, they concentrate their arrows in a specific area, hoping to hit whatever's there. Because they fire in such a high arc, they can ignore any concealment and cover that's not essentially a roof.

The commander of the archers (generally an officer or veteran soldier) makes a special attack roll using only his base attack bonus, Intelligence modifier, and range increment penalty. If the attack hits, arrows land in the target squares, which must have the same shape as the archers in the group. For example, if two rows of five archers each hit with an arrow volley, arrows land in a two-square by five-square area.

If the arrow volley misses its intended target, it still lands somewhere. Refer to the diagram on page 158 of the *Player's Handbook* to determine the misdirection of the attack.

Any creature in a square where an arrow lands must succeed on a DC 15 Reflex save or take damage from the arrow. Because each arrow expends much of its energy getting to the high point in its flight, an archer's Strength bonus doesn't apply to the damage roll even if the archer is wielding a composite bow.

Set for Charge: A halberd, longspear, spear, trident, or dwarven urgrosh can be set against a charge as a readied action. If a charging foe moves into a threatened square, the soldier who set against the charge makes an attack (with the charging foe taking a –2 penalty to AC) that deals double damage on a successful hit. If a noncharging foe moves into a threatened square, the soldier who set against the charge can still make an attack but won't deal double damage.

A formation can have spears, tridents, halberds, or dwarven urgroshes in the first rank and longspears (which have reach) in the second row to get double coverage on the squares just in front of the formation. In such a case, the charging creatures gain a +4 bonus to Armor Class against the longspears in the second row because the soldiers in the front row give the charging creatures cover.

Phalanx: A formation of soldiers advancing under a hail of ranged attacks may raise their shields to protect themselves at the cost of speed and attack capability. To do this, the soldiers all take the total defense action (see page 142 of the *Player's Handbook*). Soldiers on the outer edge of the formation gain a +4 bonus to Armor Class and ones on the inside gain a +8 bonus (+4 for total defense and +4 for the cover their fellow soldiers provide them).

Disperse: If soldiers in rank-and-file formation are concerned about spells that affect a large area, they sometimes advance at their speed every round, then ready an action in order to disperse if they hear a command to do so. The commander, and sometimes scouts deployed ahead of the formation, can ready an action to give the disperse command if they see a spellcaster or monster that might be about to use such a spell.

When a formation disperses, soldiers on its perimeter make a single move away from the center of the formation, and everyone else moves to a space not adjacent to any other soldier. This dispersal can help to reduce the casualties from a *fireball*, *ice storm*, or other spell that affects a large area.

This tactic is effective, but it comes with a cost: The formation can't move twice its speed each round. This disadvantage may expose the formation to more danger, either from ranged attacks or from melee attacks made by enemies that overtake the soldiers.

MODERN-INSPIRED WARFARE

It's not hard to imagine a different means of waging war. By replacing technology with magic and monsters, D&D armies can employ tactics and techniques that wouldn't be out of place on the 21st-century battlefield. A band of elf rangers might hug the tree line on the edge of the forest, seeking concealment and cover among the trees. Every squad of soldiers might have a cleric to act as medic, a rogue sniper, and a sorcerer to provide fire support with *lightning bolts*. Dragons can provide combat air patrols. Teleporting monsters function as paratroopers, suddenly appearing

A horde of orcs mounts a charge against a phalanx of dwarves who are braced for the attack.

behind enemy lines or seizing important objectives. *Whispering wind* and *message* spells can provide instantaneous communication between battlefield commanders.

Powerful monsters and magic rule the modern-inspired battlefield. Giants and other big monsters are the D&D equivalent of tanks: fast, frightening, and built to absorb a lot of punishment. Low-level foot soldiers tend to dig in, relying on cover and concealment to protect them. Foot soldiers also disperse more widely and use ranged attacks more often; even fifty 1st-level warriors can't bring down a giant in melee, but they can wear it down with arrows, and if they're spread out, the giant won't kill more than a few of them each round.

Castles and other strongholds are harder to defend, especially against an enemy who can fly, teleport, or use magic to turn your fortress walls to mud. Thus, underground strongholds (dungeons, in other words) are popular, because they can't be attacked from above, and enemies who don't know their layouts can't teleport into them.

The advantage of modern-inspired warfare is that it's familiar to players, and it rewards smart tactics and the tools that mid- to high-level characters have at their disposal. The Dungeon Master can take material from countless war movies and real-life battles for adventure ideas. Combat has a great deal of variety because the warfare embraces fantastic monsters and powerful spells.

Modern-inspired warfare can be very deadly to low-level characters because the battlefield is rich with powerful monsters and magic. A single *fireball* that deals 5d6 points of damage kills almost every 1st-level character, as does a frost giant marauding through the front lines. A modern-style battle also lacks some of the grandeur of a historical set-piece battle. To an observer, the modern-inspired battlefield is a seemingly deserted place; everyone is dug in or hiding, because standing out in the open makes you an inviting target.

Modern-Inspired Tactics

Magic, monsters, and high-level characters can combine in all sorts of clever ways on the battlefield. The following tactics are representative of warfare in a high-fantasy battle in the modern style.

Aerial Recon: Giant eagles have a Spot modifier of +15, so they make excellent scouts, circling the battlefield at great altitude to watch troop movements. A giant eagle can fly higher than 300 feet still and have a better than even chance of spotting a Huge creature (or 10 Medium creatures moving as a unit). Unless the creatures on the ground are specifically scanning the sky for the giant eagle, it takes a DC 26 Spot check to notice the eagle at that height.

Clerical Medics: For half the price of a suit of full plate armor, a 1st-level cleric can be equipped with a fully charged *wand of cure light wounds*. Such a cleric typically prepares *bless* (to use before battle) and *entropic shield* and *sanctuary* to keep him safe while he runs, wand in hand, from wounded soldier to wounded soldier.

Fire Support: A squad of infantry often includes one or more spellcasters who can bring arcane firepower to bear on the battle. A 4th-level sorcerer, for example, can cast four *scorching ray* spells and have plenty of *mage armor* and *shield* spells in reserve to protect himself. Equip him with a *wand of magic missile* (750 gp) and three scrolls of *fireball* (375 gp each), and you have the sorcerous equivalent of a machine gun and rocket launcher—and it costs less to equip the sorcerer than a typical knight.

Specialized Troops: Sahuagin make effective marines; they can establish a beachhead in enemy territory by swimming ashore at night and slaughtering the coastal guard, and they can swarm a ship at anchor, attacking the crew or simply bull rushing them off the deck to be eaten by waiting sharks. Barghests can use *dimension door* once per day to instantly move up to 640 feet and are effective trackers, so they can function as paratroopers of a sort and seize key objectives in advance of the main army.

Blitzkrieg: With a speed of 50 feet, winter wolves are as fast as all but the fastest horses. They have a strong melee attack and a breath weapon that's effective against massed troops, so winter wolves can often punch a hole in a defensive line that slower troops can then exploit.

Behind Enemy Lines: A team of 4th-level bards can easily slip behind enemy lines by using *invisibility* or *alter self* (perhaps in conjunction with Bluff, Disguise, and Diplomacy checks). Once in the enemy rear, they can use *detect thoughts* or *suggestion* to gather intelligence and an *animal messenger* spell to report what they have learned back to headquarters.

A MERCENARY CAMPAIGN

Traditional D&D campaigns feature site-based adventures prominently. PCs typically explore a dungeon, fight the evil creatures they find there, and carry the treasure back to civilization. It's also possible to build an entire campaign around the PCs as part of a larger military organization. Rather than exploring dungeons, they fight the enemy on the battlefield, undertaking dangerous missions that might mean victory or defeat for the larger army.

Many such campaigns have the characters as part of a mercenary outfit or guerrilla organization rather than as part of the regular army, because it's easier to imagine that a human sorcerer, two dwarf fighter/rogues, and a half-elf druid would be assigned the same mission in a military organization that prizes flexibility. Low-level characters begin as foot soldiers, and they become specialists as they rise in level. Eventually, they may become an elite unit, earning the admiration of their comrades and inspiring fear in the enemy. Some PCs may rise through the ranks to have an army at their command.

A mercenary campaign is a good choice if your players enjoy the tactical challenges that D&D combat offers. It promises plenty of action and danger, and the players never lack for a good fight. Players often enjoy planning their military operations, then seeing them come to fruition on the battlefield. The PCs usually know who the bad guys are and where they can be found. Many players appreciate the rewards beyond better equipment and experience points, hoping to earn higher ranks, posting to better units, and decorations for valor and success.

You don't have to change much about your D&D game; the game's use of the word "campaign" to describe a series of related adventures has its roots in wargaming and military history. Combat is central to the game rules. The Challenge Rating system works just as well on the battlefield as it does in the dungeon. Some differences do exist between a mercenary campaign and a traditional one, however.

Clarity of Purpose: Many DMs devote a lot of effort to developing character hooks to draw the PCs into an adventure and convince them to risk danger. In a mercenary campaign, the PCs know that they're being paid to fight. In short, the DM doesn't need to convince the characters to come to the battlefield, because they're already there, and they know what they're expected to do.

Following Orders: It's easy to start an adventure in a mercenary campaign by simply having a superior officer show up and order the PCs into battle. But some players chafe at following detailed orders because they miss out on planning the operation themselves, while others expect the NPC in command to direct their every action. Adventures work best if the superior officer simply identifies the objective, such as "seize that stronghold" or "defend that hill," leaving the details of the mission to the PCs. This mission flexibility is another reason why less formal organizations such as mercenary companies are a good choice for PCs.

The DM shouldn't force characters to slavishly follow orders. The consequences for disobeying an order should match the circumstances and importance of the order in the first place, unless the DM has a particular reason for being harsh or lenient. Did the characters fail to take the hill because two of the four PCs were gravely wounded? Most commanders call it a failed mission and leave it at that. Did the PCs teleport into the city to shop when they should have been defending the castle walls? Have the commander devise a suitable punishment.

War Has Its Own Tempo: When PCs explore a dungeon, they're free to leave when they're wounded, rest for a few days, and return on their own schedule. When the characters undertake a military mission, other units—and potentially the whole army—might depend on the characters achieving their objective at a certain time. The time pressure makes the PCs' job more difficult, but being "on the clock" can add urgency and excitement to the adventure. Time pressure is a challenge like any other, and the DM should account for it when planning a military adventure.

Conversely, most wars are interrupted by lulls in the fighting as the armies refit for their next operation, train new soldiers, and wait for a move from the enemy. By including some downtime during a war, the DM can give PCs time to create

magic items and research spells without feeling like they're missing something.

The Army's Behind You: Because the PCs are assigned missions with timetables, they have less freedom than they would in a traditional campaign. Because they're part of a large organization, they can rely on a lot more support than a small band of dungeon delvers has at its disposal. If the PCs' mission is important, smart commanders devote more resources to it.

NPCs are often assigned to assist the PCs. A cleric may act as a medic, or a ranger as a guide and scout. Perhaps a dragon provides air support for a mission, or a group of gnome illusionists distracts the enemy before the PCs attack. The characters might also be given equipment or spells important to their mission. Mid-level PCs facing a vampire spawn army might be temporarily issued *maces of disruption*. Low-level characters asked to sneak into an enemy outpost might have extended *invisibility* spells cast on them before they move out.

Even if the characters weren't assigned extra help for their mission, they might be able to get assistance in the middle of the battle if their plans go awry. If the PCs are pinned down at the edge of the forest, a *whispering wind* message back to headquarters could call for another unit to bombard the enemy with catapult stones.

Rank Matters, to a Point: It's natural that as characters gain experience and attain levels, their status in the military improves as well. Promotions can be an effective extra reward for the successful completion of a mission, and players generally appreciate the privileges of rank—even simple things such as being saluted by NPCs.

Issues of rank and authority can make the game less fun if they're not handled carefully. Some players of high-level PCs may resent taking orders from superior officers who clearly aren't as personally powerful as they are. You can minimize this problem if the generals identify broad objectives such as "disrupt supplies to the gnoll army" and let the PCs figure out how to pull it off. Looking at it from the generals' perspective, they have every reason to treat the high-level PCs gingerly, as long as they get results.

Rank can also become divisive if some PCs wind up in command of other PCs. As long as the higher-ranking PC consults with the other PCs and doesn't just pull rank on them, this situation doesn't need to become a problem. However, if one player feels like he can order other players around whenever he wants, that's a recipe for trouble at the game table. The easiest way to avoid this problem, of course, is to keep all the PCs at the same rank. As long as the players police themselves and don't abuse their authority with other players, a difference in rank won't be a problem.

NPCs, of course, are fair game. Many players take great glee in ordering around NPCs and shouting like drill sergeants. Giving the PCs that authority is an important part of a mercenary campaign, because it emphasizes that everyone in the military—PC and NPC alike—is playing by the same rules. Players are more likely to accept orders when they see NPCs accepting orders from them.

The PCs Turn the Tide of Battle: A small band of 1st-level characters can't change the outcome of a battle involving thousands of combatants. If it's a band of 15th-level characters, though, it's a different story. The fighter can wade into battle against dozens of low-level opponents with impunity, the rogue can effortlessly sneak into the enemy headquarters and eliminate the command staff, and the cleric and wizard can bring down fire from the sky and render an entire company unseen.

As their characters gain levels, players increasingly expect their efforts to be reflected in the overall outcome of the battle, if not the war. It's obviously unrealistic to play out a battle involving thousands of creatures, only four of whom are PCs. By the time the characters reach middle levels, the DM should have the PCs' success or failure impact the larger war effort at least some of the time.

An easy way for the DM to have the PCs affect the larger battle is to assign them an important mission. Then the DM develops a list of a half-dozen possible outcomes and lets the players' relative success or failure determine which one actually occurs.

For example, say the PCs' mission during an upcoming battle is to infiltrate the enemy's rear echelons and attack the enemy headquarters. The possible outcomes might be these:

PCs Kill or Capture Enemy Command Staff: The enemy army's southern flank collapses, and it has to retreat beyond the river with heavy casualties. Captured command staff members reveal important plans, which the characters can thwart in a subsequent adventure.

PCs Force Enemy Command Staff to Abandon HQ: The enemy army's southern flank loses contact with the rest of the army because its command was disrupted. Surrounded, the units that comprise the enemy's southern flank take heavy casualties or surrender. The rest of the enemy army wavers, but holds its position for now.

PCs Fight Enemy Command Staff but Don't Seize HQ: The enemy army advances, except for its southern flank, which didn't get orders to do so because the commanders were busy fighting the PCs. The enemy army wins the day, but is spread out and vulnerable to counterattack.

PCs Fail to Reach HQ but Disrupt Enemy Rear: The enemy army wins the day, taking some territory but not pushing ahead. Instead, it rests, reorganizes, and begins planning its next move.

A team of player characters "infiltrates" a tent full of enemy commanders.

Table 4–1: Missions

d%	Orders
01–05	Seize and hold a terrain feature (such as a hill, ford, or mountain pass).
06–10	Drive off enemies holding a terrain feature.
11–15	Reconnoiter a terrain feature.
16–20	Defend a terrain feature.
21–25	Seize and hold a defensive structure (such as a wall, trench, or stronghold).
26–30	Destroy a defensive structure.
31–35	Reconnoiter a defensive structure.
36–40	Defend a defensive structure.
41–45	Disrupt enemy supply system (such as caravans or armories).
46–50	Guard friendly supply system.
51–55	Deliver supplies to friendly unit.
56–60	Attack enemy command structure (such as HQs, officers, or communications).
61–65	Guard friendly command structure.
66–70	Deliver orders to friendly unit.
71–75	Patrol specific area.
76–80	Attack specific enemy unit.
81–85	Rescue friendly unit in trouble.
86–90	Provide distraction for another mission.
91–95	Perform noncombat duty (train, recruit, provide honor guard, and so on.).
96–100	Redeploy to different part of the front.

Table 4–2: Complications

d%	Complication
01–05	Objective has moved to new location.
06–10	Objective is hidden, possibly with magic.
11–15	Objective is heavily guarded.
16–20	It's a trap! Enemy lies in wait around false objective.
21–25	Intelligence failure (map is wrong, objective doesn't exist, and so on).
26–30	In mid-mission, friendly unit requests aid.
31–35	In mid-mission, commander issues new orders.
36–40	Tempting enemy target presents itself elsewhere.
41–45	Weather turns foul (see Table 3–23, page 94 of the *Dungeon Master's Guide*).
46–50	Friendly units engage in unrelated mission nearby.
51–55	Enemy units engage in unrelated mission nearby.
56–60	PCs caught in crossfire between friendly and enemy units.
61–65	Objective overrun by main force of enemy army.
66–70	Timetable of mission changed.
71–75	PCs' support or relief never shows up.
76–80	PCs receive conflicting or garbled orders.
81–85	Friendly army retreats, leaving PCs exposed.
86–90	PCs face unusual enemy unit (such as monsters or high-level NPCs).
91–95	Friendly unit mistakenly attacks PCs.
96–100	Enemy forces counterattack PCs' position.

PCs Fail to Reach Enemy Rear: The PCs' army retreats by noon, and the enemy army captures or surrounds some units. The PCs might get orders to attempt a rescue.

PCs Are Captured or Pinned Down in Enemy Territory: The enemy army advances rapidly, exploiting major gaps in the lines of the PCs' army. The PCs must extricate themselves from their desperate situation and reach friendly territory before the next major assault.

While the list above has PC success paralleling the army's success, that shouldn't always be the case. Sometimes the PCs' army loses a fight despite the characters' best efforts, and sometimes the army succeeds even if the characters' mission fails. In this case, the possible outcomes describe varying degrees of success or failure. The players shouldn't feel like the DM is writing the story of the war to match their personal victories, but they should feel like things would have been worse but for the PCs' presence.

Treasure or Gear: In a traditional dungeon-based campaign, characters get treasure by defeating monsters and use it to buy equipment that makes them more powerful. A lot less treasure tends to be lying around in a mercenary campaign. The characters are being paid if they're mercenaries, and they can take some gear from the bodies of fallen or captured enemies. Because they're not facing creatures in their lairs, they may fall behind the character wealth by level figures given on Table 5–1, page 135 of the *Dungeon Master's Guide*.

The DM can make up for this deficiency by having the army issue the characters more and better gear as they attain higher levels. Superior equipment can also be supplied for particularly dangerous missions. In most cases, the DM can even let players ask for specific items through the army's requisition system (which, depending on the army, could be anything from an entire bureaucracy to Grizzlehook the dwarf smith back at headquarters). They won't always get exactly what they want, of course, but the DM can ensure that they get the gear they have earned on the battlefield.

Table 4–3: Support

d%	Type of Support
01–05	Artillery support at specific time (catapults or area-effect spells).
06–10	Artillery support when requested.
11–15	Artillery support on continuous basis.
16–20	Air insertion (with monsters or magic).
21–25	Air extraction.
26–30	Air support (flying creatures or NPCs) at specific time.
31–35	Air support when requested.
36–40	Air support on continuous basis.
41–45	Shock troops at specific time (heavy infantry, giants, and so on).
46–50	Shock troopers when requested.
51–55	Fast cavalry at specific time (mounted knights, bugbears on howlers, and so on).
56–60	Fast cavalry when requested.
61–65	Clerical healing.
66–70	Bardic inspiration.
71–75	Ranger or druid scouting.
76–80	Magical distraction.
81–85	Magical insertion.
86–90	Magical extraction.
91–95	Magical stealth.
96–100	Magical divination/communication.

Note that some support options (such as magic- and monster-dependent ones) are more appropriate in modern-inspired campaigns than historical ones.

As the players get used to the requisition system, they won't waste time collecting every last weapon from dead enemies because they know that they will receive a just reward in the form of periodic equipment upgrades. Like real soldiers, the characters may still grab souvenirs and valuable items from fallen enemies.

MERCENARY MINI-ADVENTURES

The DM can roll or choose from the previous tables to launch an adventure centered on a mission the PCs must carry out. Once you have one mission and one or more complications and support units, you have the seeds of your next D&D session.

For example, a DM for 4th-level PCs might roll 04 on the mission table, 99 and 53 on the complication table, and 84 and 51 on the support table. For that evening's D&D game, the adventure centers on an assault on a riverbank tower guarded by gnolls. The DM sketches a map of the tower and populates it with gnolls and hyenas. Before they move out, characters are offered support in the form of magical stealth (*invisibility* spells, in this case) to sneak up on the tower, but they will have to deal with the hyenas, which have the scent ability.

The DM uses the two complications in the second part of the adventure. Once they have taken the tower, the PCs see bugbear skirmishers about to ambush a friendly patrol across the river. The PCs have to choose between guarding the tower and helping their allies. Finally, the DM plans to introduce waves of gnolls trying to retake the tower (in EL 4 groups). The characters must hold out long enough for unicorn-riding elves to relieve them shortly after dawn.

SPORTING COMBAT

Combat is ordinarily a deadly business, but its action and danger appeal to many spectators. Many fantasy cultures have developed sports and diversions that put the warrior's skills to use. Jousts, gladiatorial matches, and archery contests are perhaps the most common examples of combat-inspired sports, but in a diverse fantasy world there are countless others.

Sporting combat is a good way for characters to earn experience points in nonlethal (or at least less lethal) settings, and winning a contest can enhance a character's reputation. A recent winner of a sporting combat generally gets a bonus (+2 for routine contests and +4 for championship events) to improve an NPC's attitude if the NPC saw the victory. Many sporting combats come with prizes (cash, jewelry, or art objects) as well.

Each type of competition described below includes a suggested experience point award for winning a sporting combat. These awards are appropriate if such events are only occasional occurrences in your campaign. If your D&D game relies heavily on nonlethal sporting events, you may want to develop your own rules for advancing in level. In most cam-

paigns, characters shouldn't be able to attain levels simply by winning archery contests at the viscount's estate.

JOUSTS

In a traditional joust, two knights on horseback charge each other with blunted lances, separated by a rail that divides two parallel tracks. When they meet in the middle, they clash with great momentum and force, then continue down the track on their side of the rail. They repeat the process until one knight yields or is knocked from the saddle. A great deal of pageantry and ritual accompanies most jousts, and colorful heraldry, dress, or banners often identify knights.

Because the jousters are running full-tilt at one another with blunted weapons, jousts function differently from mounted combat. Initiative isn't necessary; during each pass, each knight simply makes a special attack with the blunted lance, and the results of both attacks are resolved simultaneously. Each knight makes an attack roll normally; if it hits, the knight can also attempt to unhorse the rider (treat as a trip attack) or make a sunder attempt against the enemy's weapon or shield. Neither the trip attempt nor the sunder attempt provokes an attack of opportunity. A successful blow deals lance damage (doubled because the knights are both charging), but it's nonlethal damage. A knight with the Ride-By Attack feat gains a +4 bonus on attack rolls during a joust.

In some versions of a joust, a knight can continue with a blunted longsword if he loses his lance. Such a longsword deals nonlethal damage and can make the free sunder attempt described above, but not the trip attack.

The most obvious variation on the traditional joust is simply to use real lances and attack with lethal force. This functions exactly as normal mounted combat, except that a knight can still make a free trip or sunder attempt if his attack hits (the momentum of two opposing charges makes these special attacks possible, not the prowess of the knights). Another variant is to use steeds other than horses, including such exotic choices as worgs, hippogriffs, dire boars, or pegasi. The githyanki have jousts riding red dragons, and the dragons themselves attack each other during each pass.

Because they're most likely to have a steed and ranks in Ride—not to mention the diplomatic skills to put the victor's bonus on NPC attitudes to good use—paladin PCs are most likely to be drawn into a joust. Fighters have the skills and feats to make good jousters, as do barbarians and rangers, though the latter two classes have a hard time riding and fighting in heavy armor. Other classes lack the horsemanship or proficiency with the lance to make effective jousters, but they can help a combatant in other ways. Clerics can cast beneficial spells on steed and rider, for example, while a bard can use music to inspire a knight. Given enough imagination, any PC can be effective in a joust. The sight of a wizard mounted on a *phantom steed* with a glowing *Mordenkainen's sword* floating at her side gives pause to even a confident knight.

Illus. by W. England

The arena is littered with victims, but the spectators—and the triumphant winner—are having a good time.

To award experience for jousts, calculate the Challenge Rating of the rival knight normally, but award only half the usual XP award because a joust is both less lethal and less likely to force the character to expend significant resources. Only the actual combatant receives the experience points, unless another character in the party helped in a significant way or cast important spells on the knight's behalf.

GLADIATORIAL MATCHES

Some cultures have built massive arenas where thousands gather to watch armed gladiators fight in bloody battle, while other societies gather around pits, rings, and other informal structures to watch (and usually wager on) fights. Because organizers of gladiator matches want to provide entertainment, they frequently introduce rules to make the fight last longer than a few rounds. Unless they're used as a means of public execution, gladiatorial fights don't usually result in the death of the loser.

The most common gladiatorial match is a one-on-one fight between two lightly armed foes. Armor is rarely issued to the combatants, because the spectators want to be able to see each wound. Magic items are likewise prohibited, because they tend to make matches end quickly. If spellcasting is allowed, it's typically restricted to flashy evocations and conjurations.

Gladiators and the Crowd

A gladiatorial fight follows the normal rules for combat in the D&D game, with one exception: The presence of the crowd can inspire or demoralize a gladiator.

Treat the crowd as a single NPC, and use its attitude toward each gladiator to track the morale bonus or penalty he receives. If the crowd is friendly toward a gladiator, that gladiator gets a +1 morale bonus on attack and damage rolls. If the crowd is helpful, the gladiator gets a +2 morale bonus on attack and damage rolls. An indifferent or unfriendly crowd confers no bonus or penalty, but a crowd that's hostile to a gladiator confers a –1 penalty on attack and damage rolls.

Unless a particular gladiator is exceptionally well known, the crowd starts indifferent to both combatants. Each gladiator typically makes a Perform (weapon drill) check (see the section on skills near the end of Chapter 3) before the fight begins, using the check result in an attempt to influence the crowd (as described under Influencing NPC Attitudes on page 72 of the *Player's Handbook*). Once the fight begins, only certain actions change the crowd's attitude, as described in the table below. Note that the crowd's attitude toward each gladiator is tracked separately. It's possible for two inept gladiators to both be loathed by the spectators, and two veteran gladiators can both have the crowd on its feet cheering them on.

TABLE 4–4: GLADIATOR CROWD REACTION

Situation	Check	Consequence[1]
Gladiator rolls natural 1 on attack roll	—	Attitude toward gladiator worsens
Gladiator confirms critical hit	—	Attitude toward gladiator improves
Successful feint in combat	Bluff vs. Sense Motive[2]	Attitude toward opponent worsens
Successful demoralize opponent	Intimidate vs. level check[2]	Attitude toward opponent worsens
Successful tumble through enemy square	DC 25 Tumble	Attitude toward you improves
Successful Perform (weapon drill) check	DC 20 Perform	Attitude toward you improves
Destroy opponent's weapon	See sunder rules	Attitude toward you improves
Trip opponent	See trip rules	Attitude toward you improves[3]
Disarm opponent	See disarm rules	Attitude toward you improves[3]
Pin an opponent	See grapple rules	Attitude toward you improves, attitude toward opponent worsens
Bull rush opponent 10 feet[4]	See bull rush rules	Attitude toward you improves
Gladiator caught cheating	—	Attitude toward gladiator worsens by two steps

1 All attitude changes are one step (for example, indifferent to unfriendly) unless otherwise noted.
2 Special modifiers apply to this check. See the appropriate skill description in the *Player's Handbook*.
3 If you are tripped or disarmed yourself in a failed attempt, the attitude toward you worsens.
4 If you fall prone during a failed attempt, the attitude toward you worsens.

In more exotic gladiatorial matches, there may be other ways to influence the crowd. In a match featuring gladiators on horseback, for example, being knocked from the saddle might worsen the crowd's attitude toward you by one step. If the crowd is composed of mind flayers, a successful coup de grace that reveals your opponent's brains may improve the crowd's attitude by two steps.

While one-on-one gladiator contests are the most common, team matches are also popular (and may be more convenient, because all PCs can participate). One common variation pits a single Large or Huge creature against a team of smaller gladiators. Occasionally, a gladiatorial match includes mounted combat or ranged combat.

It's also commonplace for match organizers to add terrain elements to make a fight more memorable or deadly. Sometimes two gladiators fight atop tall platforms, attempting to bull rush each other to their doom. Some organizers hide weapons all over the arena, leading to a mad scramble as the gladiators arm themselves. Sometimes a maze or stockade is built inside the arena, although spectators will not likely pay to attend a gladiator match they can't see.

To award experience for gladiator matches, calculate the Encounter Level for the match normally, but cut the experience point award by 25% to 50% if the match's equipment or rules make it less lethal than a normal combat. If the match is deliberately unfair (which usually happens only when the match serves as punishment), increase the experience point award for the underdog by up to 25%.

ARCHERY CONTESTS

Whether they use a bow in warfare or for hunting, good archers relish the chance to test their mettle against their peers. Unlike jousts and gladiatorial matches, archery contests require very little in the way of extra equipment—although the archery tests favored by the nobility sometimes include elaborate mannequins as targets.

In the simplest form of archery contest, a round target divided into three concentric sections is placed 150 feet away. The outermost section of the target is Tiny (AC 7), the next section in is Diminutive (AC 9), and the inner bullseye is Fine (AC 13). Each archer gets five arrows, earning 4 points for every hit in the bullseye, 2 points for every hit in the outer circle, and 1 point for every arrow that hits the edge of the target. Compare the attack roll against each of the three Armor Classes in turn, from the bullseye outward. If two or more archers are tied with the most points once everyone has had a turn, the targets are moved to 250 feet away and the tied archers each shoot five arrows again. If they're still tied, they each shoot five arrows at a target 350 feet away. If they're still tied after that, contest organizers typically declare a tie or settle the matter with arrows fired at moving targets.

It's possible—but exceedingly difficult—to hit and split an arrow that's already lodged in the bullseye. Such an arrow has an AC of 35.

The most common variation is to arrange a moving target; mounting the target on a wagon or swinging it like a pendulum from a tree limb are two simple ways to increase the difficulty. Either technique increases the AC of the targets by 5. Elf archers play a game where one identifies a far-off Fine target, typically a fluttering leaf or swaying branch. Each other archer fires an arrow as quickly as possible, rolling initiative to see who goes first. The elves then walk over and examine the target, and whoever hit the target first or came the closest if they all missed (the highest attack roll) chooses the next target. The drow play a similar game, but they use fleeing goblins as targets.

To award experience for an archery contest, treat it as an encounter with a creature of a CR equal to the best NPC archer, and cut the award by 50% to account for the lack of danger. Only the winner earns experience points.

CONJURERS' CHESS

This elaborate contest pits two spellcasters against each other in a test of their ability to summon fighting creatures from other planes. It requires that the spellcasters be able to cast *summon monster* spells numerous times and that they be able to communicate with the called creatures. Accordingly, it's the province of mid- to high-level conjurers, not an entertainment for the masses.

The two spellcasters agree to a number of calling rounds (four is typical) and a time limit (1 minute is common, although lower-level casters sometimes opt for 30 seconds). The spellcasters move to opposite corners of the chessboard (a 10-by-10-square area on the battle grid).

At the start of each of the calling rounds, a referee rolls a die (usually a d4 or d6) and calls out a number. The two conjurers each cast a *summon monster* spell, choosing a monster from the list that corresponds to that number. For example, if the referee rolls a 4, the conjurers can summon any monster from the *summon monster IV* list. They need not cast *summon monster IV*, however; they could cast *summon monster V* to get 1d3 monsters or *summon monster VI* to get 1d4+1 monsters. Any summoned monster must appear adjacent to the conjurer who summoned it, or as close to that conjurer as possible.

In subsequent calling rounds, two things happen: The conjurers cast *summon monster* again, based on a new die roll from the referee, and monsters summoned in previous calling rounds may move one square in any direction. Each conjurer is responsible for directing the summoned monsters, and if they ever move more than one square per round or leave the grid, that conjurer forfeits the contest.

If opposing monsters wind up in the same square, they fight at the direction of their summoner. Once the calling rounds are over, the conjurers continue to direct their creatures until the time limit is reached. At that point, whichever conjurer has creatures in the most squares of the grid is the winner.

The most common variation on conjurer's chess is to change the die rolled by the referee, the number of calling rounds, or the time limit. To award experience for a successful game of conjurer's chess, base the award on the CR of the opponent, and reduce the award by 50% to account for the lack of danger.

ALABASTER CUP

The Alabaster Cup is an example of the multievent sporting contests that occur over the course of several days at many a noble villa. Originally designed as a series of tests for would-be knights of the realm, the Alabaster Cup has evolved into an annual event that draws hopeful combatants from near and far.

The contest consists of seven events held over three days. A young noblewoman—typically an unmarried daughter of the noble who hosts the event—sits before a low table with a dozen alabaster goblets: one for each contestant. After each event, she drops three platinum coins in the winner's cup, two coins in the runner-up's cup, and one coin in the third-place contestant's cup. Then she takes half the coins out of the last-place finisher's cup (if that cup has any coins).

The first day begins with an archery contest (as described above). Then contestants run an obstacle course that winds its way around the estate, featuring walls to climb, pits to jump, and narrow beams to cross. Finally, they have a single-elimination wrestling match—you lose if you're rendered unconscious or pinned.

On the second day, the contestants have a single-elimination jousting tournament in the morning. At noon, they are sent out into a nearby forest with orders to bring back an elusive albino dire boar for the evening's banquet. After the banquet is the strangest event of all—the noblewoman says to each contestant in turn, "Impress me." She awards coins at her sole discretion.

At noon on the final day, the contestants gather for the final event: a single-elimination dueling tournament worth twice the usual number of coins. Characters can have any nonmagical equipment they like except for ranged weapons. They can cast spells as long as they don't do so before the duel begins. Each duel lasts for exactly 1 minute and is fully lethal, but both duelists have *shield other* cast on them by NPC clerics before the fight begins. You lose the duel if you yield to your opponent, fall unconscious, or have taken more damage than your opponent when the minute is up (in the judgment of the host, who has a keen eye for wounds).

After another banquet, the noblewoman counts the coins in each alabaster goblet, then declares a winner. The contestant with the most coins gets to keep the cup (worth 1,000 gp, although it's considered unlucky to sell it) and has the right to be called Champion of the Alabaster Cup.

To award experience for the events in the Alabaster Cup, treat each day's events as a single encounter with an EL equal to a normal encounter with the significant NPC contestants. As long as a character has more coins at day's end than she started with, he or she earns experience points for that day.

MAGIC ITEMS

The following magic items and special materials supplement those described in Chapter 7 of the *Dungeon Master's Guide*.

NEW ARMOR SPECIAL ABILITIES

Anti-Impact: Armor with the anti-impact quality is designed to cushion the blow from massive blunt traumas. Anti-impact armor doesn't give extra protection against weapon damage (beyond its AC bonus), but bludgeoning damage that affects all or most of the entire body (such as constriction and falling damage) is halved.

Faint Abjuration; CL 4th; Craft Magic Arms and Armor, *feather fall*; Price +2,000 gp.

Axeblock: This armor is magically enhanced to turn away slashing weapons such as axes and most swords. The wearer gains damage reduction 5/bludgeoning or piercing.

If a single shield or suit of armor has two of the three blocking armor qualities (axeblock, hammerblock, and spearblock), it grants its owner just 5 points of damage reduction by whatever damage type appears twice. For example, a +1 *chain shirt* with the axeblock (DR 5/bludgeoning or piercing) and hammerblock (DR 5/piercing or slashing) special abilities only provides DR 5/piercing.

Moderate abjuration; CL 11th; Craft Magic Arms and Armor, *polymorph any object*; Price +2 bonus.

Hammerblock: Armor with this quality functions the same as axeblock armor, except that it provides damage reduction of 5/piercing or slashing.

Moderate abjuration; CL 11th; Craft Magic Arms and Armor, *polymorph any object*; Price +2 bonus.

Spearblock: Armor with this quality functions the same as axeblock armor, except that it provides damage reduction of 5/bludgeoning or slashing.

Moderate abjuration; CL 11th; Craft Magic Arms and Armor, *polymorph any object*; Price +2 bonus.

NEW SPECIFIC ARMOR DESCRIPTIONS

Armor of the Unending Hunt: This mithral +2 *chainmail* armor was built by the elves for rangers on long-range patrols. In addition to its protective qualities, it provides the wearer with immunity to fatigue and exhaustion.

Moderate Abjuration; CL 8th; Craft Magic Arms and Armor, *restoration*; Price 21,500 gp; Cost 10,900 gp + 848 XP; Weight 20 lb.

NEW WEAPON SPECIAL ABILITIES

The following weapon special abilities supplement those found in the *Dungeon Master's Guide.*

Blood Seeking: Weapons with the blood seeking ability often have strange-looking sights on them. Ammunition fired from blood seeking weapons flies around cover if necessary to strike a living creature, negating any bonus to Armor Class the target might have due to intervening cover. The shooter can even fire at a target with full cover, but she must know the target is there, there must be an unobstructed path for the ammunition to reach the target, and the target still has total concealment (and thus a 50% miss chance). The blood seeking ability doesn't function against plants, oozes, undead, and constructs.

Moderate divination; CL 9th; Craft Magic Arms and Armor, *arcane eye*; Price +1 bonus.

Armor of the unending hunt

Deflecting: If you're wielding a deflecting weapon of your size or one size larger, you can try to knock projectiles aimed at you out of the air. Once per round when you would normally be hit by a ranged weapon, you may make a DC 20 Reflex saving throw (if the ranged weapon has a magical enhancement bonus, the DC increases by that amount). If you succeed, the ranged weapon or projectile deflects away harmlessly. You must be aware of the attack and not flat-footed. Only melee weapons can have this ability.

Faint transmutation; CL 5th; Craft Magic Arms and Armor, *entropic shield*; Price +1 bonus.

Disarming: This weapon ability functions differently depending on whether it's applied to a melee weapon or a ranged weapon. If applied to a melee weapon, the disarming ability eliminates the opponent's bonuses for both weapon size and two-handed weapons. If applied to a ranged weapon, the disarming ability makes possible a disarm attack; you can shoot a weapon out of someone's hand. The relative weapon sizes don't matter for a ranged disarm attempt, but the defender gains a +4 bonus for wielding a weapon in two hands.

Moderate transmutation; CL 11th; Craft Magic Arms and Armor, *telekinesis*; Price +2 bonus.

Exit Wound: Weapons with the exit wound ability propel their ammunition entirely through living targets they hit. This effect deals an extra 1d6 points of damage. The weapon or projectile continues in a straight line beyond the original target. Targets in that path are attacked using the same attack roll as the original target; these additional targets gain a +4 bonus to AC for each previous target in the path. When an exit wound weapon or projectile hits an object, it stops. The exit wound ability can be applied to any ranged weapon; projectile weapons so enhanced bestow the ability on their ammunition.

Moderate transmutation; CL 8th; Craft Magic Arms and Armor, *Melf's acid arrow*; Price +2 bonus.

Explosive: Always slightly warm to the touch, weapons with the explosive ability deal extra damage to anyone near the intended target. Each successful hit with an explosive weapon deals 2d4 points of damage to all targets in a 5-foot burst (Reflex DC 15 half), including the original target. The explosive ability can be applied to any melee weapon (though the wielder may be subject to the extra damage) or ranged weapon. Projectile weapons so enhanced bestow the explosive ability on their ammunition.

Moderate transmutation; CL 10th; Craft Magic Arms and Armor, *shatter*; Price +2 bonus (+3 bonus for ranged weapons).

Knockback: Knockback weapons often emit a low, almost inaudible hum when drawn. Whenever a knockback weapon hits its target, it initiates a bull rush attack in addition to dealing normal damage. To resolve the bull rush attempt, treat the projectile as a Medium creature with a +8 Strength bonus. The projectile doesn't provoke an attack of opportunity, and it always tries to push the target as far back as possible. Only ranged weapons can have the knockback ability, and they bestow it on their ammunition.

Moderate evocation; CL 11th; Craft Magic Arms and Armor, *Bigby's forceful hand*; Price +3 bonus.

Last Resort: A melee weapon (usually a dagger) with the last resort ability is particularly effective in a grapple. Its wielder doesn't take the −4 penalty for attacking with a weapon while grappling, and the weapon deals an extra 1d6 points of damage in a grapple for every size category the target is bigger than the wielder. For example, a halfling armed with a *+1 last resort dagger* would deal an extra 2d6 points of damage when being grappled by an ogre.

Moderate transmutation; CL 7th; Craft Magic Arms and Armor, *freedom of movement*; Price +1 bonus.

NEW SPECIFIC WEAPON DESCRIPTIONS

The following weapons supplement those found in Chapter 7 of the *Dungeon Master's Guide.*

Burrowing Arrow: This +1 arrow sticks into its target on a successful hit and embeds itself in the wound. A *burrowing arrow* must be pulled out before natural healing can occur, and this removal deals a further 1d8 points of damage. If the target receives magical healing, the *burrowing arrow* immediately deals 1d8 points of damage as the magic forces it out of the wound.

Faint necromancy; CL 4th; Craft Magic Arms and Armor, *inflict light wounds*; Price 167 gp; Cost 87 gp + 6 XP.

Lance of the Last Rider: Whenever the wielder of this *+1 lance* charges a mounted foe from the back of a steed, the weapon allows a free bull rush attempt on a successful hit. If the bull rush attempt succeeds, the enemy rider moves back, but the enemy's mount stays where it is.

Faint transmutation; CL 5th; Craft Magic Arms and Armor, *bull's strength*; Price 8,306 gp; Cost 4,306 gp + 320 XP.

Oglien's Final Answer: This *+2 spiked chain* has a glittering sheen, but most spellcasters don't identify it as magic due to the persistent *nondetection* effect on it. A DC 25 Spellcraft check is required for a spellcaster to detect the magic of *Oglien's final answer*. The weapon gives its wielder a +5 bonus on Perform (weapon drill) checks. (See the section on skills near the end of Chapter 3.) Oglien, a noted gladiator from a bygone age, used his "final answer" to get an edge in the arena. Since his death, the weapon has passed from gladiator to gladiator, with many unaware of its magical nature.

Moderate transmutation and abjuration; CL 10th; Craft Magic Arms and Armor, *nondetection*; Price 26,325 gp; Cost 13,325 gp + 1,040 XP.

NEW WONDROUS ITEMS

The following wondrous items supplement those found in Chapter 7 of the *Dungeon Master's Guide.*

Bracers of Dawn: These bejeweled bracers have a miniscule lens-and-dial contraption mounted on the exterior of one bracer of the pair. When the dial is turned to the left, the bracers appear normal. When the wearer turns the dial to the middle position (a move action), a beam of light emerges from the lens, illuminating the surroundings as a bullseye lantern. Four times per day, the wearer can turn the dial to the right position as a standard action and aim the lens at a target, unleashing a beam of *searing light* that deals 3d8 points of damage to most creatures, 6d6 points of damage to undead, and 6d8 points of damage to creatures with light sensitivity. The dial returns to the middle position after each *searing light*. Even though only one of the pair contains the lens-and-dial apparatus, both bracers must be worn for the magic to be effective.

Bracers of dawn

Moderate evocation, CL 6th; Craft Wondrous Item, *searing light*; Price 26,000 gp; Weight 1 lb.

Gauntlet of the Dwarven Forge: This iron gauntlet extends to the elbow and is always cool to its wearer's touch. When its command word is spoken, a *gauntlet of the dwarven forge* glows red-hot for 10 rounds, illuminating everything within 10 feet as if by torchlight. Anyone else touched by the gauntlet during this time takes 1d6+10 points of fire damage. The wearer of a *gauntlet of the dwarven forge* takes half damage from fire-based attacks while the gauntlet is glowing. Fire attacks that allow Reflex saves for half damage deal the wearer no damage if he makes his save.

Moderate evocation; CL 10th; Craft Wondrous Item, *fire shield*; Price 24,000 gp; Weight 3 lb.

Gauntlet of Lassitude: This leather glove bound in brass magically transforms to match the hand shape of its owner, and thus it can be worn on either hand. With a successful melee touch attack, the *gauntlet of lassitude* slows the target for 5 rounds (Will DC 14 negates).

Faint transmutation; CL 5th; Craft Wondrous Item, *slow*; Price 27,000 gp; Weight 2 lb.

Gauntlet of Utterdeath: This spiked gauntlet of jet-black steel smells faintly of brimstone. If the wearer succeeds on a melee touch attack, the target must make a DC 20 Fortitude save or be reduced to a pile of smoldering cinders. If the Fortitude save succeeds, the target instead takes 10d6 points of damage. A *gauntlet of utterdeath* is usable three times per day.

Strong necromancy; CL 13th; Craft Wondrous Item, *destruction*; Price 96,000 gp; Weight 2 lb.

Sacred Scabbard: This item has a variable appearance. When first found, there is a 25% chance it looks like a dagger sheath, a 25% chance it looks like an axe case, and a 50% chance it looks like some sort of sword sheath. A user quickly discovers, however, that a *sacred scabbard* can change shape to fit whatever dagger, sword, or axe is touched to it, even making allowances for double weapons. This scabbard keeps any weapon carried in it clean and sharp. In addition, up to three times per day, the user may place a weapon in the scabbard, utter a command word, and invoke *bless weapon* on the weapon inside.

Faint transmutation; CL 4th; Craft Wondrous Item, *bless weapon*; Price 4,400 gp; Weight 1 lb.

Standard of Courage: For a *standard of courage* to be effective, it must be affixed to a two-handed hafted weapon such as a halberd or a lance. The bearer of the standard and any allies within 30 feet of the item gain a +4 morale bonus against fear effects.

Faint abjuration; CL 5th; Craft Wondrous Item, *remove fear*; Price 15,000 gp; Weight 1 lb.

Standard of Heroism: This standard functions as a *standard of courage*, except that the standard bearer and any allies within 30 feet of the item gain a +2 morale bonus on attack rolls, saves, and skill checks.

Faint enchantment and abjuration; CL 5th; Craft Wondrous Item, *heroism*, *remove fear*; Price 40,000 gp; Weight 1 lb.

Standard of No Retreat: This standard functions as a *standard of courage*, except that it also prevents outward extradimensional travel within 30 feet, just as if creatures were subjected to a *dimensional anchor* spell. Creatures trying to flee from the standard's area must succeed on a DC 19 Will save, or their attempt to flee fails. A *standard of no retreat* doesn't prevent creatures from using extradimensional travel to enter the area, just to leave it. Summoned creatures within the standard's area still disappear when the spell that brought them here ends.

Moderate abjuration; CL 11th; Craft Wondrous Item, *dimensional anchor*, *remove fear*; Price 145,000 gp; Weight 1 lb.

NEW SPECIAL MATERIALS

The following special materials supplement those found in Chapter 7 of the *Dungeon Master's Guide*. Except for double weapons, a particular object can be made of only one special material.

Pandemonic Silver: Mined from thin veins of ore on the plane of Pandemonium, pandemonic silver has all the properties of alchemical silver (see page 284 of the *Dungeon Master's Guide*). In addition, a thin, unearthly scream issues forth from a bladed weapon made of pandemonic silver whenever it's unsheathed in at least a light breeze. This scream is a sonic, mind-affecting compulsion that is a fear effect. Other than the wielder, those within 30 feet who hear the scream must succeed on a Will save or cower for 1d4 rounds. The DC of the Will save depends on the strength of the wind, as indicated on the table below.

Wind Force	Save DC
Light (0–10 mph)	10
Moderate (11–20 mph)	13
Strong (21–30 mph)	16
Severe (31–50 mph)	19
Windstorm (51–74 mph)	22
Hurricane (75–154 mph)	25
Tornado (175–300 mph)	28

Pandemonic silver can be used to coat the striking surface of any slashing or piercing weapon made of steel. The cost of the weapon increases as shown below.

Type of Pandemonic Silver Item	Item Cost Modifier
Light slashing or piercing weapon	+9,000 gp
One-handed slashing or piercing weapon, or one head of a slashing or piercing double weapon	+11,000 gp
Two-handed slashing or piercing weapon, or both heads of a sladhing or piercing double weapon	+13,000 gp

Susalian Chainweave: Made by a technique known only to the greatest elven armorsmiths, susalian chainweave is an elaborate system of chainmail links knitted together to provide additional protection against some blows. When an attack with a slashing or bludgeoning weapon hits a character wearing susalian chainweave, the armor stiffens at the point of contact and disperses the force of the attack. This quality gives the wearer damage reduction 3/piercing as long as the susalian chainweave armor is worn.

Type of Susalian Chainweave Item	Item Cost Modifier
Light armor	+28,000 gp
Medium armor	+35,000 gp
Heavy armor	+42,000 gp

Thinaun: This dark, glittering steel alloy holds an attraction to souls recently released from their bodies. Obviously, this has application for melee weapons. If a thinaun melee weapon is touching a creature when it dies, that creature's soul is sucked into the weapon rather than passing on to its final reward. The soul remains in the thinaun weapon until the weapon is destroyed or another creature dies while touching the thinaun weapon (the new soul displaces the old one). *Raise dead, resurrection*, and similar spells won't bring back a creature whose soul is trapped by a thinaun weapon unless the caster has the weapon in his possession. Because the soul is nearby, fewer material components are required for such spells: *Reincarnation, raise dead, resurrection,* and *true resurrection* require half as much of the relevant material component (unguents or diamonds) to cast if the soul is within a thinaun weapon.

A thinaun weapon captures a soul from anyone killed while touching the weapon. This means that if the thinaun weapon's wielder dies, her weapon captures her soul.

Only melee weapons made primarily of metal can be crafted as thinaun weapons.

Type of Thinaun Item	Item Cost Modifier
Light weapon	+10,000 gp
One-handed weapon, or one head of a double weapon	+15,000 gp
Two-handed weapon, or both heads of a double weapon	+20,000 gp

WARRIORS IN THE CAMPAIGN

This section covers a wide range of topics appropriate to any campaign that features (or even just includes) martial characters, including tips for warrior-oriented campaigns, exotic and improvised weapons, organizations for warriors, epic-level warriors, and a warrior's interactions with the deities of the campaign's pantheon.

WARRIOR CAMPAIGNS

For an interesting twist on the traditional DUNGEONS & DRAGONS experience, try putting away the spellbooks and holy symbols to play a warrior-oriented campaign. In this type of campaign, most characters in the party focus on combat-related classes: barbarian, fighter, paladin, and ranger, and to a lesser extent, monk and rogue.

By definition, a warrior-oriented campaign tends to be low in magic. This simple term can have a variety of meanings, depending on the DM's vision of the campaign world. Spellcasting may be difficult, rare, or simply unknown; magic items may be rare or expensive; and anything other than slow, natural healing may be tough to come by.

SPELLCASTING

The simplest way to create a warrior-oriented campaign is to prohibit PCs from taking levels in a spellcasting class, but allow for the occasional NPC spellcaster. The key here is to avoid making the players feel inferior to your NPCs by limiting their exposure to spellcasting characters. If the PCs meet a spellcaster on every adventure, they're likely to wonder why they can't pursue the same options.

Alternatively, the DM may choose to eliminate spellcasters from his world. In such a world, no character—PC or NPC—can take any levels in a spellcasting class (for this purpose, defined as bard, cleric, druid, sorcerer, or wizard), and even other classes that would normally gain spells (paladin and ranger) do not gain any spell slots. At the DM's option, he may choose to grant paladins and rangers alternative class features to make up for this loss (see the Variant Classes section at the end of Chapter 1).

When populating a community (see pages 137–139 of the *Dungeon Master's Guide*) in a setting without spellcasters, replace any bards that might be present with rogues, any druids with rangers (or with barbarians if in a particularly savage or uncivilized area), any sorcerers with monks, and any wizards with fighters. Replace 25% of the clerics with paladins, and the other 75% with fighters.

Assuming the DM doesn't simply ban spellcasting classes to player characters, he may instead limit the PCs' access to such classes. One method of doing so is to restrict the number of class levels that any character may take in a spellcasting class. For instance, any character might be limited to no more than half his total character levels in a spellcasting class (bard, cleric, druid, sorcerer, or wizard). No character could begin play as a 1st-level bard, cleric, druid, sorcerer, or wizard. In this campaign, paladins and rangers retain their normal spellcasting abilities.

Another method of limiting access to potent spells is to treat the spellcasting classes much like prestige classes. Any character wishing to begin gaining levels as a spellcaster must first be at least a 3rd-level character with 3 ranks each in Spellcraft and an appropriate Knowledge skill (arcana for bards, sorcerers, or wizards; religion for clerics; nature for druids). This requirement ensures that such characters are significantly behind the power curve of a traditional single-classed spellcaster, but have other talents to fall back on in times of need.

MAGIC ITEMS

Part and parcel of a low-magic world is the scarcity of magic items. Even if spellcasters are present in the world, it's unlikely that they traffic in magic items to the degree assumed by the *Dungeon Master's Guide*. Talk to your DM to determine what exactly "low magic" means in terms of magic items, and plan accordingly.

For example, even in a low-magic setting, you may be able to purchase minor items, such as potions or the occasional scroll, from the local alchemist or hedge wizard. Particularly if you don't have a cleric or other healer, a few curing potions can give you a big edge.

Another important issue is magic weapons and armor. While you may be able to survive with only masterwork equipment for a while, you may eventually run into opponents resistant to your weapons or the type of damage they deal. Check with your DM to see if magic weapons even exist in the campaign—such items may be rare heirlooms, relics of a bygone era, or treasured artifacts, or they may just be extraordinarily expensive to create (double, triple, or even 10 times the normal cost to create).

SURVIVING IN A WARRIOR CAMPAIGN

The fighter's most precious resource is his supply of hit points. In no uncertain terms, a fighter's hit points measure his ability to continue doing what he does best: fight. Without hit points, it doesn't matter how strong or fast you are, because you have lost the fight.

A wise fighter manages this resource carefully, and in a warrior campaign, this becomes even more important (since there probably isn't a cleric around when you need one). In general, managing your hit points comes down to two things: saving them until needed, and restoring them when lost.

Saving Hit Points

In a typical party, a fighter can often avoid dealing with the enemy's minions because the wizard takes them out with spells such as *sleep* or *fireball*. This tactical advantage lets the fighter save his precious hit points until he really needs them (the battle with the big bad guy). Without the artillery support provided by spellcasters, the fighter is likely to face significantly more (and longer) melee combats with his enemies, resulting in a greater depletion of hit points. Here are some ways of avoiding or solving that problem in a fighter-heavy group.

Stay Alert: While no amount of preparation or feat selection can ensure that you are never caught flat-footed, every time you avoid giving up a surprise round or a sneak attack to a foe, you have gained an edge. Make sure somebody in the group—such as the barbarian or ranger—has a high initiative modifier (Improved Initiative is key) and a good Spot or Listen modifier.

Keep Your Distance: The reason that 1st-level wizards prefer *magic missile* to *shocking grasp* is that the former lets them hit opponents from a long way away. Learn this lesson well. Most characters in your group should carry a bow, or failing that, a loaded crossbow, when trudging through the dungeon. (If you have a big enough group, you can afford to have at least one character who specializes in ranged combat.) Assuming you aren't ambushed, chances are you will be able to get off at least one shot at your opponent before melee begins. While the few points of damage dealt by that shot may not seem impressive when compared to your average sword- or axe-swing, those may be the few points that keep the monster from getting another full attack against you later in the encounter. In fact, in most fights, the longer you stay out of melee range, the better your chances of success. The exception, of course, is if your opponent has better ranged attacks than you.

Smaller Fights Are Better: Though a sorcerer may complain about only having two bugbears to incinerate with his *fireball*, the fewer opponents faced by a fighter simultaneously, the better. In most rounds, you can only damage a very limited number of opponents (unlike a typical spellcaster), but many opponents might be able to damage you. Never let an enemy escape (he's probably going for reinforcements), and never let

an enemy shout a warning. If one of the goblins carries a horn, take him out first. If there's a big drum in the middle of the guard post, put an arrow through it right away.

Neutralize Spellcasters: A typical fighter's Achilles' heel is his tendency to fail Will and Reflex saves. While a failed Reflex save isn't likely to cost you the battle—only more of those precious hit points—a failed Will save can turn the tide in a moment. If your enemies include a spellcaster, focus your efforts on him right away. It's probably worth provoking an attack of opportunity to charge past the minions of the evil cleric or necromancer just to get in a position to prevent him from blasting you with his spells. Failing that, use your bow or crossbow (see above) to chase him off. A particularly potent tactic against a spellcaster is to ready an action to attack him just as he casts a spell (including a 5-foot-step to follow him if he tries to step back out of melee). While this may cost you some attacks (since you're potentially giving up a full attack in exchange for a single readied attack), a hit forces a pretty tough Concentration check from the spellcaster to succeed in casting the spell. Most spellcasters, facing this situation, prefer to run away rather than stay and be pummeled.

Avoid Unnecessary Fights: Just because a half-dozen orcs are standing between you and the entrance to the enemy's fortress doesn't mean you have to fight them now, or ever. Despite the oft-repeated advice never to leave enemies behind you, if you do your job right, an enemy avoided now can easily become an enemy avoided forever. Do you really think those orcs are going to stick around to fight you after you have defeated their master and set the castle ablaze? Just because you can fight the orcs doesn't mean you should. Even though the result of the fight seems a foregone conclusion, all one of those orcs needs to do is score a key critical hit to make the fight much more costly than you had anticipated.

Restoring Hit Points

Despite the fighter's best efforts, he must inevitably take some damage. This brings up a big concern for any fighter-heavy group: Namely, who's providing the healing? Without a cleric (or at least a druid), it's tough for characters to replenish the hit points they use up in combat. Consider any or all the following options for your warrior-oriented campaign, assuming they're available.

Take Care of Yourself: Each character must be much more self-reliant when it comes to healing. If possible, every PC should carry around a supply of potions of various *cure* spells. If you don't have enough potions to restore you from 0 hit points to full normal hit points (assuming average rolls), you're taking a serious chance that you won't be around to see the end of the adventure. Of course, some classes have an edge in this regard. Both the monk and the paladin have some limited supernatural healing capabilities, and the paladin and ranger have healing spells available as they attain higher levels.

Use All Available Resources: An often-overlooked option for rangers and paladins is to stock up on wands of *cure* spells. Since both classes have *cure light wounds*, *cure moderate wounds*, and *cure serious wounds* on their spell lists, they can use wands of these spells without difficulty, even before they can actually cast the spells. While a *wand of cure light wounds* isn't likely to save the day in the middle of a pitched battle, once the fighting stops it's a cheap way to get rid of a lot of damage. Assuming average rolls, a *wand of cure light wounds* (market price 750 gp) heals about 275 points of damage before it's exhausted. That's less than 3 gp per hit point, which is the best deal available. Despite the value of the cheaper wands, however, consider picking up a *wand of cure serious wounds* as soon as you can afford it for quicker fixes. (Of course, this option may not be available in a low-magic setting.)

Multiclass: Multiclass fighter/clerics, barbarian/druids, and the like gain access to spellcasting, scrolls, and wands just as rangers and paladins do. Even a single level of bard or rogue allows you to invest heavily in the Use Magic Device skill, which lets you use the scrolls, wands, or staffs that a cleric might otherwise wield.

Rest: When all else fails, take time off from fighting. Every day of rest is another few hit points for the next battle. Make sure you have at least one character with some ranks in the Heal skill—long-term care dramatically reduces the downtime between adventures forced by lost hit points.

WARRIOR ORGANIZATIONS

The six organizations presented here are appropriate for just about any DUNGEONS & DRAGONS campaign. Each one is tied to a specific prestige class presented in Chapter 2 of this book, allowing you to give those classes a rich background in your world.

ISE ZUMI MONASTERY

The tradition of the tattooed monk comes from the Ise Zumi Monastery, hidden high in the mountains. Here, the order of tattooed monks trains newcomers in their mysteries while seeking personal enlightenment.

Most monks who live at the Ise Zumi Monastery are ascetic in their outlook, preferring quiet solitude to the complex life of the outside world. Though many more worldly monks have trained here and visit from time to time, such individuals spend more time away from the monastery than in residence.

To join the monastery, one must merely be of lawful alignment and display a devotion to achieving enlightenment while avoiding temptation. Typically, this display of devotion involves a three-day ritual in which one must deny oneself temptations appealing to the five senses. Those who would learn the mysteries of the tattooed monk prestige class must meet more stringent requirements (see the tattooed monk prestige class in Chapter 2).

In addition to the obvious benefits of becoming a tattooed monk, the Ise Zumi Monastery is a repository of religious lore from a wide variety of races and cultures. One can only guess at the ancient secrets that lie deep in the monastery's basements.

Sample Member

Mesehti Taharqa received his training at the Ise Zumi Monastery but soon found that he could not stomach the ascetic lifestyle of his mentors. Instead, he struck out to explore the world, reasoning that the more he knew of its temptations, the better prepared he would be to resist them.

He still visits the monastery from time to time, and could easily encounter a PC undergoing training there.

The Ise Zumi Monastery

Mesehti is quick to advise such characters that the ascetic life practiced in the monastery is ill-equipped to handle the temptations of the outside world, and urges any tattooed monk PC to widen her horizons. He enjoys the company of other dedicated souls, but feels threatened when he isn't the center of attention. An incautious PC could easily find Mesehti's attitude shifting from that of friendly advisor to jealous rival.

Mesehti Taharqa: Male human monk 5/tattooed monk 6; CR 11; Medium humanoid; HD 5d8 plus 6d8 plus 3; hp 56; Init +6; Spd 60 ft.; AC 21, touch 19, flat-footed 19; Base Atk +7; Grp +8; Atk +10 melee (1d10+1, unarmed strike); Full Atk +10/+5 melee (1d10+1, unarmed strike) or +8/+8/+3 (1d10+1, unarmed strike); SA flurry of blows, *ki* strike (magic), lion tattoo; SQ crab tattoo, evasion, purity of body, slow fall 20 ft., still mind, white mask tattoo; SV Fort +9, Ref +11, Will +14; AL LN; Str 13, Dex 14, Con 10, Int 12, Wis 21, Cha 8.

Skills and Feats: Bluff +16, Escape Artist +16, Knowledge (religion) +9, Listen +19, Move Silently +8, Tumble +16; Deflect Arrows, Endurance, Improved Grapple, Improved Initiative, Improved Unarmed Strike, Toughness, Weapon Finesse, Weapon Focus (unarmed strike).

Flurry of Blows (Ex): Mesehti may use a full attack action to make one extra attack per round with an unarmed strike or a special monk weapon at his highest base attack bonus, but this attack and each other attack made in that round take a −1 penalty apiece. This penalty applies for 1 round, so it affects attacks of opportunity Mesehti might make before his next action. If armed with a kama, nunchaku, or siangham, Mesehti can make the extra attack either with that weapon or unarmed. If armed with two such weapons, he uses one for his regular attack(s) and the other for the extra attack. In any case, his damage bonus on the attack with his off hand is not reduced.

Ki Strike (Su): Mesehti's unarmed strike can deal damage to a creature with damage reduction as if the blow were made with a magic weapon.

Lion Tattoo (Su): This tattoo gives Mesehti the ability to smite a foe, gaining a +4 bonus on a single melee attack and a +5 bonus on the damage roll if the attack hits. He can make a smite attempt up to three times per day.

Crab Tattoo (Su): This tattoo provides Mesehti with damage reduction 6/magic.

Evasion (Ex): If Mesehti is exposed to any effect that normally allows him to attempt a Reflex saving throw for half damage, he takes no damage with a successful saving throw.

Purity of Body (Ex): Mesehti has immunity to all diseases except for magical diseases such as mummy rot and lycanthropy.

Slow Fall (Ex): When within arm's reach of a wall, Mesehti can use it to slow his descent while falling. He takes damage as if the fall were 20 feet shorter than it actually is.

Still Mind (Ex): +2 bonus on saving throws against spells and effects from the enchantment school.

White Mask Tattoo (Su): Mesehti is immune to *detect thoughts, detect lies,* and any attempt to magically discern his alignment. He gains a +10 bonus on all Bluff checks (included in the above statistics).

Possessions: Periapt of Wisdom +4, bracers of armor +2, potion of cure serious wounds, 250 gp.

THE KNIGHT PROTECTORS

Less an organization than a variety of individuals who share a code of conduct, the knight protectors are dedicated to the preservation (and restoration) of the ideals of honor, chivalry, and courage. The protectors think of themselves as the last remnants of a formerly great order of knights, but actually may come from a variety of backgrounds. Usually, they come from defunct orders of chivalry or the service of fallen lords who aspired to good works but fell short in some way. Those who take up the mantle of knight protector hope for the return of "better days," and they believe they can hasten that process and repair society's ills by living their lives as paragons of their venerable chivalric code.

The knight protectors have no official hierarchy or admission procedure. Unlike most knightly orders, declaring oneself a knight protector requires no time of service, proof of worthiness, or oath of allegiance, except to the code of conduct shared by others in the order. The knights police their own, however, and a knight protector who does not deserve that title eventually finds himself in conflict with more devout members, who look upon such hypocrisy as a high crime against their ideals. A knight who unwillingly or unknowingly violates the code, or violates it willingly in the belief that doing so contributes to an act of greater good, may redeem himself by undertaking and completing a quest or other dangerous mission assigned by more senior knights. A protector who willingly and knowingly violates this code for no adequate reason is no longer considered one of the order, and is shunned (if not despised or even hunted) by other knight protectors.

Sample Member

Joris Welker was once a proud member of a great order of paladins. Over time, he came to believe that his fellows were too slow to battle corruption or moral weakness in others, preferring charity to order. Joris struggled with this dilemma for many months. When called upon to serve a local duke he knew to be morally bankrupt, Joris refused to obey, but lied to his superiors about the reason. Though they did not know the truth, his superiors recognized the lie (as well as the disrespect for authority) and banished Joris from their order. In search of a new code to follow, Joris encountered a knight protector who taught him the beliefs of the group. Now, Joris roams the land in search of corruption and moral decay to fight against. He allies with PCs with similar goals, and proudly tells anyone interested about his new fellows and their mission in life.

Joris Welker: Male half-elf ex-paladin 6/knight protector 3; CR 8*; Medium humanoid; HD 6d10+12 plus 3d10+6; hp 72; Init +1; Spd 20 ft.; AC 25, touch 12, flat-footed 24; Base Atk +9; Grp +11; Atk +12/+7 melee (1d8+3/19–20, *+1 longsword*, or 1d8+2/×3, masterwork lance); SA supreme cleave; SQ best effort +2, defensive stance +2, shining beacon; SV Fort +8, Ref +4, Will +7; AL LN; Str 14, Dex 13, Con 14, Int 10, Wis 11, Cha 16.

*Ad hoc CR adjustment due to lack of paladin abilities.

Skills and Feats: Diplomacy +13, Gather Information +5, Knowledge (nobility and royalty) +4, Listen +1, Ride +7, Search +1, Spot +5; Cleave, Great Cleave, Iron Will^B, Power Attack, Mounted Combat, Trample.

Supreme Cleave (Ex): Joris can take a 5-foot step between attacks when using the Cleave or Great Cleave feat.

Best Effort (Ex): Joris can add a +2 bonus to any skill check once per day.

Defensive Stance (Ex): Joris can transfer up to 2 points of Armor Class to an ally within 5 feet, reducing his AC by the same amount.

Shining Beacon (Su): All of Joris's allies within 10 feet gain a +4 morale bonus on saves against fear effects. If Joris is paralyzed, unconscious, or otherwise rendered helpless, his allies lose this bonus.

Possessions: +1 full plate armor, +2 heavy steel shield, +1 longsword, ring of protection +1, masterwork lance, heavy warhorse with chain barding, 27 gp.

ORDER OF THE BOW

The Order of the Bow teaches that one's true character can be determined through one's archery. Practicing a form of archery simply called the Way of the Bow, the members of the order search for truth, patience, and beauty through commitment, diligent practice, and spiritual sincerity. Its origins are unclear, and some scholars claim it originated among the elves, but regardless, it has spread to many sentient races.

The Way of the Bow is a spiritual art. By learning it, the archer learns about himself. By improving in the Way of the Bow, the archer improves himself.

Even with these shared goals, each follower of the Way of the Bow sees archery in different manners. Some see archery as spiritual self-improvement, while others believe it to be a philosophical art. They may employ it as a religious ceremony, practice it as a way of life, or simply see the art of killing by the bow as an important talent in a dangerous world. As they are wont to say, the Way of the Bow is always a little more than what you make of it.

Pure skill is not enough to join this organization; only those truly dedicated to the Way of the Bow can become an initiate of the order (see the Order of the Bow Initiate prestige class in Chapter 2).

Sample Member

Chanticleer Winterwood had wanted to become an Order of the Bow Initiate since before he even knew of such a group.

As long as he's been walking, Chanticleer has had a bow in his hands, and it's as much a part of him as his fingers or toes. During his adventures in a great human metropolis, he learned of the order and its teachings, and wasted no time in proving his worth. Today, aided by his loyal companion Quilaembril Straylight (male elf cleric 7), Chanticleer wanders the land in search of ways to test his talents against the forces of evil and tyranny. He can be an enigmatic ally to the PCs, a mentor to a young archer, or a deadly foe to those who wrong him.

Chanticleer Winterwood: Male elf fighter 5/Order of the Bow initiate 4; CR 9; Medium humanoid; HD 5d10+5 plus 4d8+4; hp 59; Init +4; Spd 30 ft.; AC 18, touch 14, flat-footed 14; Base Atk +9; Grp +11; Atk +16 ranged (1d8+5, *+1 shock composite longbow* [+2 Str bonus]) or +12 melee (1d8+3, *+1 longsword*); Full Atk +16/+11 ranged (1d8+5, *+1 shock composite longbow* [+2 Str bonus]) or +14/+14/+9 ranged (1d8+5, *+1 shock composite longbow* [+2 Str bonus]) or +12/+7 melee (1d8+3, *+1 longsword*); SA ranged precision +2d8; SQ close combat shot; SV Fort +6, Ref +9, Will +4; AL CG; Str 14, Dex 18, Con 12, Int 10, Wis 8, Cha 12.

Skills and Feats: Climb +7, Craft (bowyer) +5, Knowledge (religion) +2, Listen +1, Search +2, Spot +10; Dodge, Greater Weapon Focus (longbow), Mobility, Point Blank Shot, Precise Shot, Rapid Shot, Weapon Focus (longbow), Weapon Specialization (longbow).

Close Combat Shot (Ex): Chanticleer can attack with a ranged weapon while in a threatened square without provoking an attack of opportunity.

Ranged Precision (Ex): As a standard action, Chanticleer may make a single precisely aimed attack with a ranged weapon, dealing an extra 2d8 points of damage if the attack hits. When making a ranged precision attack, Chanticleer must be within 30 feet of his target. A ranged precision attack only works against living creatures with discernible anatomies. Any creature that is immune to critical hits (including undead, constructs, oozes, plants, and incorporeal creatures) is not vulnerable to a ranged precision attack.

Possessions: Mithral chain shirt, *+1 shock composite longbow* (+2 Str bonus), 20 arrows, *+1 longsword*, potion of haste, 47 gp.

ORDER OF THE CHALICE

The Order of the Chalice is a holy order of virtuous knights sworn to a noble quest: the extermination of demonkind. Held to the highest standards of law, good, and nobility, the knights of this order are everything one might associate with the word "paladin"—paragons of virtue, pure of heart, perfect in valor, cultured and refined, pious and devoted, and too often, arrogant and vain.

The Order of the Chalice takes its name from a holy relic guarded by the order's highest leaders—an ornate silver cup said to have caught the blood of a solar while it fought a demon prince. The chalice is rich in holy powers, or so the tales say, but more important, it is a constant source of inspiration to the knights of the order as they pursue their difficult mission.

The order is a devoutly lawful good organization, and its members offer prayers to Heironeous (or a similar lawful good deity of honor and valor if you don't use Heironeous in your campaign) at every gathering. However, characters who hold other lawful good deities as patrons are welcome in the order, as long as they do not balk at offering prayers to the order's patron deity as well.

True to its alignment, the Order of the Chalice is rigidly hierarchical in organization. At its head are the nine Masters of the Chalice, whose greatest responsibility is safeguarding the holy chalice itself. Each Master of the Chalice (typically a character of at least 10th level) has command over nine Chalice Marshals (usually 7th- to 10th-level characters, each marshal has authority over nine Chalice Commanders (typically 5th- to 8th-level characters), and each commander leads nine Chalice Sergeants (who generally range from 3rd to 6th level).

Most knights of the order prepare from youth for this high calling, serving as squires to older, more experienced knights while they learn about the responsibilities of knighthood. After a minimum of five years of unquestioning service, the squire is evaluated by a council of nine senior knights, largely based on testimony given by the squire's knightly master. If this evaluation is favorable, the squire is elevated to the status of quester and is now a 1st-level character (usually a paladin, but occasionally a ranger, cleric, or other class). Player characters who begin their adventuring careers as members of the Order of the Chalice are typically of this rank.

It is possible to join the order as a quester without undergoing this time of preparation, but such a character must meet minimum qualifications similar to (but less stringent than) those required by the knight of the Chalice prestige class, including a lawful good alignment, 4 ranks of Knowledge (religion), 2 ranks of Knowledge (the planes), and either the ability to cast divine spells (including *protection from evil*), the ability to smite evil, or a favored enemy of evil outsiders.

Most questers aim to qualify as a knight in full standing, which requires the character to meet the full requirements necessary to gain levels in the knight of the chalice prestige class. Once these qualifications are met, the quester returns to the knightly council and presents evidence of her accomplishments. Assuming the council approves the quester's admission into the order, the quester spends a night in prayer and fasting, then takes the solemn vows of the order at daybreak, becoming a knight in full standing. At any point thereafter, the character may begin taking levels in the knight of the chalice prestige class.

In addition to the general principles of paladinhood and lawful good alignment described in the *Player's Handbook*, the Order of the Chalice demands that its members swear to a stricter code of conduct. Knights of the Chalice must be chaste and celibate, must never defile their bodies by touch-

ing a corpse, and must always place the extermination of a demon above all other priorities. Failure to adhere to this code of conduct can result in censure or even expulsion from the order.

Sample Member

Colette Daumier is a newly admitted knight in the order, after long years as a quester fighting demons. She is eager to prove her worth, boldly launching into battle against demons and other evil foes. She can serve as an ally of good-aligned PCs (particularly of a quester or other new knight of the order), a recruiter for the order, or as a vigorous enemy of evil characters.

Colette Daumier: Female human paladin 7/ranger 1/knight of the Chalice 1; CR 9; Medium humanoid; HD 6d10+6 plus 2d8+2 plus 1d10+1; hp 61; Init +3; Spd 20 ft.; AC 22, touch 9, flat-footed 22; Base Atk +9; Grp +12; Atk +14 melee (1d8+3/×3, masterwork cold iron warhammer) or +13 melee (1d4+4/19–20, *+1 dagger*); Full Atk +14/+9 melee (1d8+3/×3, masterwork cold iron warhammer) or +13/+8 melee (1d4+4/19–20, *+1 dagger*); SA fiendslaying +1/+1d6, smite evil 5/day, turn undead 5/day; SQ aura of courage, aura of good, *detect evil*, divine grace, divine health, favored enemy evil outsiders +2, lay on hands, *remove disease*; SV Fort +12, Ref +6, Will +6; AL LG; Str 17, Dex 8, Con 12, Int 10, Wis 13, Cha 14.

Skills and Feats: Bluff +2, Concentration +11, Intimidate +5, Knowledge (religion) +10, Knowledge (the planes) +5, Listen +3, Spot +3, Survival +8; Alertness, Improved Initiative, Iron Will, Weapon Focus (warhammer).

Fiendslaying (Ex): As a member of the knight of the Chalice prestige class, Colette has a +1 bonus on attack rolls against evil outsiders. On a successful attack, she deals an extra 1d6 points of damage. She also has a +1 competence bonus on Intimidate, Listen, Sense Motive, and Spot checks against evil outsiders, and a +1 bonus on Will saving throws and opposed ability checks against evil outsiders.

Smite Evil (Su): Colette may attempt to smite evil with one normal melee attack. She adds +2 to her attack roll and deals an extra 7 points of damage. Smiting a creature that is not evil has no effect but uses the ability for that day.

Turn Undead (Su): As a 4th-level cleric.

Aura of Courage (Su): Colette is immune to fear (magical or otherwise). Allies within 10 feet of her gain a +4 morale bonus on saving throws against fear effects.

Aura of Good (Ex): Colette's aura of good (see the *detect good* spell) is equal to that of a 7th-level cleric.

Detect Evil (Sp): At will, as the spell of the same name.

Divine Grace (Su): Colette gains a +2 bonus on saving throws (already figured into the above statistics).

Divine Health (Ex): Colette is immune to all diseases, including magical diseases such as mummy rot and lycanthropy.

Favored Enemy (Ex): From her experience as a ranger, Colette gains a +2 bonus on her Bluff, Listen, Sense Motive,

Spot, and Survival checks when using these skills against evil outsiders. She gets the same bonus on weapon damage rolls against evil outsiders.

Lay on Hands (Su): Colette can cure 14 hit points of wounds per day.

Remove Disease (Sp): As the spell, once per week.

Paladin Spells Prepared (2; save DC 11 + spell level): 1st—*bless weapon, protection from evil.*

Possessions: +2 *full plate armor*, +1 *heavy steel shield*, masterwork cold iron warhammer, +1 *dagger, ring of sustenance*, 45 gp.

PURPLE DRAGONS

The Purple Dragons is an army of disciplined, loyal soldiers dedicated to the service of a noble king. They are widely respected for their skill and heroism in battle, and enjoy a proud tradition dating back many generations.

Membership in the Purple Dragons is open to anyone willing to pledge service to the king. After a minimal amount of training to ensure the applicant's dedication and aptitude, the new member receives his initial assignment based on his skill set. Some are assigned to active duty in the standing army, while others might be designated as a skirmisher, a scout, or even part of an independent detachment of elite soldiers taking part in specific missions against the forces of evil.

Most terms of service in the Purple Dragons last a minimum of five years, though many enjoy lifetime careers in the organization. Particularly gifted individuals may even become Purple Dragon knights, who are often responsible for leading forces of soldiers. (See the prestige class in Chapter 2 for more information.)

Sample Member

Thorvald is a scout and skirmisher with the Purple Dragons. He aims to become a Purple Dragon knight, and speaks of his dream with anyone who listens. He knows that he has the talents to join the ranks of the knights, but has yet to prove himself to his superiors. If he encountered a PC Purple Dragon knight, he would seek desperately to impress that individual, perhaps even throwing himself into a situation above his head.

Thorvald: Male dwarf fighter 2/ranger 3; CR 5; Medium humanoid; HD 2d10+4 plus 3d8+6; hp 38; Init +6; Spd 20 ft.; AC 16, touch 12, flat-footed 14; Base Atk +5; Grp +6; Atk +7 melee (1d8+1, masterwork battleaxe) or +7 ranged (1d6+2, +1 *composite shortbow* [+1 Str bonus]); Full Atk +7 melee (1d8+1, masterwork battleaxe) or +7 ranged (1d6+2, +1 *composite shortbow* [+1 Str bonus]) or +5/+5 ranged (1d6+2, +1 *composite shortbow* [+1 Str bonus]); SA —; SQ dwarf traits, favored enemy goblinoids +2, wild empathy +4; SV Fort +9, Ref +6, Will +1; AL LN; Str 13, Dex 15, Con 14, Int 10, Wis 8, Cha 12.

Skills and Feats: Climb +2, Hide +7, Intimidate +3, Listen +5, Move Silently +7, Ride +8, Spot +5, Survival +5; Endurance,

Improved Initiative, Mounted Combat, Negotiator, Point Blank Shot, Rapid Shot, Track.

Dwarf Traits (Ex): +4 bonus on ability checks to resist being bull rushed or tripped; +2 bonus on saving throws against poison, spells, and spell-like effects; +1 bonus on attack rolls against orcs and goblinoids; +4 bonus to AC against giants; +2 bonus on Appraise or Craft checks related to stone or metal.

Favored Enemy (Ex): Thorvald gains a +2 bonus on his Bluff, Listen, Sense Motive, Spot, and Survival checks when using these skills against goblinoids. He gets the same bonus on weapon damage rolls against goblinoids.

Wild Empathy (Ex): Thorvald can improve the attitude of an animal in the same way a Diplomacy check can improve the attitude of a sentient being. He rolls 1d20+4, or 1d20 if attempting to influence a magical beast with an Intelligence score of 1 or 2.

Possessions: Masterwork chain shirt, *cloak of resistance +1*, masterwork battleaxe, +1 *composite shortbow* (+1 Str bonus), 10 arrows, 10 silvered arrows, 25 pp.

THE RAVAGERS

Some of the most thoroughly evil and foul acts the world has ever known can be laid squarely at the feet of the Ravagers, a tight-knit group of deadly marauders. Fortunately for the more civilized areas of the world, the total number of individual Ravagers remains small. However, these unrepentant slayers make up in sheer ferocity what they lack in numbers. Gathering in warbands having as few as three members to as many as two dozen, they strike without warning, descending on unsuspecting towns, villages, and hamlets, and sometimes even upon isolated farmsteads or traveling caravans. Their violent depredations are made all the more horrible by the fact that their principal motives seem to be maiming and killing, rather than theft or kidnapping or some other more understandable (if equally detestable) reason.

The Ravagers lead a seminomadic existence, establishing more or less permanent encampments hidden away in the wilderness and other remote areas, from which they plan their savage raids. They occasionally enter towns and cities in which they know a secret temple dedicated to Erythnul (or a similar deity of slaughter) can be found, often receiving supplies and equipment from the local clergy, and sometimes even special assignments. Those unfortunate enough to come across a Ravager encampment usually meet the same fate as the Ravagers' intended victims.

The Ravagers need not recruit new members, for they know that the infamy of their deeds inevitably attracts those who have lost any reverence for life. Hatred, malice, and bitterness toward all other folk are the core of the Ravagers' beliefs and behaviors. Among their number are found some of the most irredeemable and vile persons ever to walk under the sun. Soldiers who betrayed their country and oaths for profit, kidnappers who murdered their victims though the ransom was paid in full, mass murderers whose crimes are too heinous to describe; these people the Ravagers accept into their warbands eagerly, for they are the ideal candidates to carry chaos and destruction into the world.

When a prospective member approaches a warband and makes his intention to join known, the Ravagers attack him en masse. If the newcomer holds his own for a predetermined period of time (usually between 3 and 10 rounds, depending on the size of the warband and the relative ruthlessness of the leader), he earns a place among the Ravagers, at least for the time being. At some later (and seemingly random) point, the leader of the warband chooses a random member to meet the initiate in single melee combat, no holds barred with the exception of spell casting, for they firmly believe that any Ravager should be able to win a place through force of arms alone. If the newcomer wins—the fight is always to the death—he is subjected to the final segment of his initiation: the fire sacrifice. (Erythnul or the appropriate deity of your campaign automatically resurrects members losing the combat to an initiate and who fought according the Ravagers' code.)

While the candidate waits on his knees, praying to Erythnul to fill his heart with hate and malice, other members of the warband acquire a suitable sacrificial victim (preferably human, but in a pinch any humanoid will do). The would-be Ravager must sacrifice the victim in accordance with the unholy rites of Erythnul, which involve bloodletting followed by burning the sacrifice alive. Following this cruel and horrific act, the warband applies a distinctively repulsive set of tattoos to the applicant's face, which forever marks him as a Ravager. Once the ceremony is complete, the only escape is in death. (The DM should feel free to make the Ravager initiation ceremony as morally and ethically repulsive and physically arduous as her imagination, and her playing group's shared sense of good taste, allows.)

To join the Ravagers means leaving behind all that is good and decent. No redeeming features of this organization or its members exist. Those who seek to join their number should be prepared to participate fully in their divine mission of wanton malice, or face destruction at the hands of their fellows. The Ravagers work best in a campaign not adversely affected by an atmosphere that is grimmer, perhaps even oppressive, than the norm, since the inclusion and presence of the Ravagers may lead to just such conditions.

Sample Member

Zyera was raised by a group of monks dedicated to Wee Jas, and for a time she managed to fit in with the order. Though she found great fulfillment in her studies of death, her inner struggles against the lawful nature of the order increased after maturity, and she eventually lashed out at her adopted family, both spiritually and physically. An outcast, she wandered in search of a purpose until hearing of the Ravagers. (Ironically, Zyera's parents were themselves slain by the Ravagers many years earlier, resulting in the orphan finding a home with the monks.) Since surviving her initiation, Zyera has proven her savage ferocity many

An honorable samurai faces down a band of ravagers.

times to her fellows. She revels in the destruction spread by the Ravagers, and would make an excellent recurring enemy for good-aligned PCs.

Zyera: Female half-orc ex-monk 4/fighter 2/ravager 4; CR 10, Medium humanoid; HD 4d8+8 plus 2d10+4 plus 4d10+8; hp 74; Init +1; Spd 40 ft.; AC 16, touch 13, flat-footed 15; Base Atk +9; Grp +14; Atk +14 melee (1d8+5, unarmed strike) or +11 ranged (1d2+6, +1 *shuriken*); Full Atk +14/+9 melee (1d8+5, unarmed strike) or +12/+12/+7 melee (1d8+5, unarmed strike) or +11/+6 ranged (1d2+6, +1 *shuriken*) or +9/+9/+4 ranged (1d2+6, +1 *shuriken*); SA cruelest cut 2/day, flurry of blows, *ki* strike (magic), pain touch 2/day; SQ aura of fear, evasion, slow fall 20 ft., still mind; SV Fort +13, Ref +6, Will +7; AL NE; Str 20, Dex 12, Con 14, Int 8, Wis 14, Cha 6.

Skills and Feats: Intimidate +1, Knowledge (religion) +3, Move Silently +13, Survival +6; Combat Reflexes, Diehard, Endurance, Improved Sunder, Power Attack, Stunning Fist.

Cruelest Cut (Ex): If Zyera declares ahe is using cruelest cut before making an attack, and the attack strikes successfully, she deals an extra 1d4 points of temporary Constitution damage.

Flurry of Blows (Ex): Zyera may use a full attack action to make one extra attack per round with an unarmed strike or a special monk weapon at her highest base attack bonus, but this attack and each other attack made in that round take a –1 penalty apiece. This penalty applies for 1 round, so it affects attacks of opportunity Zyera might make before her next action. If armed with a kama, nunchaku, or siangham, Zyera can make the extra attack either with that weapon or unarmed. If armed with two such weapons, she uses one for her regular attack(s) and the other for the extra attack. In any case, her damage bonus on the attack with his off hand is not reduced.

Ki Strike (Su): Zyera's unarmed strike can deal damage to a creature with damage reduction as if the blow were made with a magic weapon.

Pain Touch (Su): Zyera's melee touch attack deals 1d8+4 points of damage. She can also use pain touch through a melee weapon, dealing 1d4+4 points of damage.

Aura of Fear (Su): Enemies within 10 feet of Zyera take a –2 morale penalty on all saving throws for as long as they remain within range.

Evasion (Ex): If Zyera is exposed to any effect that normally allows her to attempt a Reflex saving throw for half damage, she takes no damage with a successful saving throw.

Slow Fall (Ex): When within arm's reach of a wall, Kyera can use it to slow her descent while falling. She takes damage as if the fall were 20 feet shorter than it actually is.

Still Mind (Ex): +2 bonus on saving throws against spells and effects from the enchantment school.

Possessions: Bracers of armor +3, 12 +1 shuriken, gauntlets of ogre power, boots of elvenkind, 21 sp.

Unlike the typical divinely oriented character, a combat-minded character's link to his deity is less based on "what powers my deity grants me" and more based on "to whom I pay respect and homage for my victories." A fighter doesn't worship a deity to gain spells or other special abilities, he worships a deity because he believes that such worship brings him good luck in battle or protects him from ill favor.

For this reason, such a character's choice of deity (or deities) to venerate is simultaneously less important and more important than the same choice made by a cleric. On one hand, since the choice isn't likely to affect the character's capabilities in a fight, some players might simply blow off the decision. "My fighter worships whichever deity provides my healing" is a common statement by such a player.

But that mentality ignores the great roleplaying opportunities provided by your choice of patron deity. Sure, it's easy for a warrior to say that he doesn't care about deities, but how believable is that in a world where the powers of the deities are in plain view for all to see? It's much more likely that any character would see one or more deities as his patron(s), paying respect, worshiping, or even sacrificing in their names.

USING THE DEITIES FROM THE PLAYER'S HANDBOOK

The following material provides some insight into why a fighter might select a deity from the *Player's Handbook* as his patron, and what type of fighters each deity tends to attract. For the uncommon and rare patron deities, each entry also includes brief notes on how to tweak that deity to make it more appealing to warriors (or more appropriate in a warrior-oriented campaign).

Each deity's alignment is given in parentheses after its name, but remember that nonclerics can revere any deity, regardless of the character's alignment.

Common Fighter Patron Deities

Erythnul (CE) is a popular choice of evil fighters and barbarians, particularly among the more savage races. As a deity of slaughter, Erythnul rarely draws worshipers from those fighters who follow strict martial codes or belong to regimented armies. A fighter who reveres Erythnul lives only to deal out death and mayhem, and grows impatient when prevented from doing so for extended periods. Erythnul's worshipers typically have high Constitution scores, the better to increase their staying power in a fight.

Heironeous (LG) is the best patron deity for any fighter who holds chivalry and valor as high ideals. Paladins obviously fall into this category, but any good or lawful fighter or monk could easily find much to respect in the teachings of Heironeous. Such characters would tend to fight at the forefront of the battle, leading the charge against tyranny and injustice. They are often proud and outspoken, and may have a high Charisma score. Consider adding the Courage and Nobility domains (see Chapter 3) to the list of domains that Heironeous grants access to.

Hextor (LE) is the evil mirror to Heironeous, promoting conflict and destruction. Many blackguards worship Hextor, as do evil fighters and monks. These characters prefer to lead the fight against freedom and good, preferring action to subtlety. They often have high Charisma scores. Consider adding the Tyranny domain (see Chapter 3) to the list of domains that Hextor grants access to.

The worship of Kord (CG) attracts those who appreciate physical prowess and athleticism, including both barbarians and fighters. Even warriors who profess not to worship any deity may subconsciously ask Kord to grant his favor in a contest of muscle or stamina. Such characters chafe in settings where strength can't win the day, often growing impatient with diplomatic functions or other interactions. In addition to high Strength scores, worshipers of Kord often have good Constitution scores.

St. Cuthbert (LN) draws many worshipers who believe in the authority of law and order, and who share his dedication to punishing transgressors. Paladins, monks, and lawful fighters and rangers all make fine followers of St. Cuthbert. His worshipers tend to be single-minded in their approach to life, and may have a very black-and-white view of things. Such characters often have high Wisdom scores.

Uncommon Fighter Patron Deities

Ehlonna (CG) is often worshiped by rangers and archers, as well as by elves, gnomes, half-elves, and halflings. Some barbarians, particularly those who feel close to the natural world of the forest, also choose the deity of the woodlands as a patron deity. Worshipers of Ehlonna are usually good and tend to be very protective of the woodlands, and may have high Wisdom scores. Consider adding archery to Ehlonna's portfolio to make her more appropriate for a warrior-oriented campaign.

Fharlanghn (N) isn't usually associated with warriors, but any wandering sellsword must pay at least some homage to the deity of roads. A fighter who worships Fharlanghn probably doesn't like to stay in one place for very long, preferring the open road even to a comfortable home. A fighter who worships Fharlanghn may have a high Dexterity score. Consider adding mercenaries to Fharlanghn's portfolio to make him more appropriate for a warrior-oriented campaign.

Like his rival Ehlonna, Obad-Hai (N) attracts the worship of rangers, barbarians, and other nature-minded characters. Those who revere Obad-Hai live in harmony with nature and often have high Wisdom scores, making them more like their rivals than they might care to admit. Some of Obad-Hai's more dedicated followers take it upon themselves not only to protect nature, but also to seek retribution against those who abuse it. Consider adding retribution to Obad-Hai's portfolio and the Fate domain (see Chapter 3) to the list of domains he grants access to to make him more appropriate for a warrior-oriented campaign.

Olidammara (CN) is an excellent patron deity for swashbucklers and other martial characters who survive on wit and skill as much as physical prowess. Such characters often have good Charisma or Dexterity scores, and may have levels of bard or rogue to take better advantage of their strength of personality. Consider adding dueling to Olidammara's portfolio to make him more appropriate for a warrior-oriented campaign.

Pelor (NG), as a stalwart adversary of evil, is venerated by good-aligned martial characters of all classes, from barbarians to paladins. What's more, since all fighters need frequent healing, it's a rare fighter who doesn't know at least one prayer of thanks to offer the Shining One. Fighters who revere Pelor tend to be helpful and friendly, particularly to those in need. They typically have good Wisdom or Charisma scores. Pelor's portfolio includes strength, and is thus perfectly appropriate for a warrior-oriented campaign. Consider adding the Nobility domain (see Chapter 3) to the list of domains that Pelor grants access to.

Rare Fighter Patron Deities

Boccob (N) might well be the most unusual patron deity for a fighter, barbarian, or other martial character. As the deity of magic and knowledge, Boccob would seem singularly inappropriate as the deity of a character devoted to combat. However, a particularly intelligent fighter might pay respect to Boccob the Uncaring, as could a neutral mercenary warmaster. Of course, multiclass fighters with arcane spellcasting ability would also have reason to venerate Boccob. A fighter who worships Boccob may care little about why (or for whom) he swings his sword, as long as the job keeps him comfortably supported. Such characters typically have a high Intelligence score. Consider adding strategy to Boccob's portfolio and the Planning domain (see Chapter 3) to the list of domains Boccob grants access to to make him more appropriate for fighter-oriented campaigns.

Nerull (NE) is typically associated with necromancers and assassins, but also counts blackguards and other purely evil martial characters among his flock. Above all else, fighters who worship Nerull work to deliver merciless death to all who live. Such characters often gain levels of rogue to enhance their murderous abilities. Fighters who choose Nerull as a patron deity seek only to conquer and destroy their opponents, and often have above-average Wisdom scores. To increase Nerull's appropriateness for warrior-oriented campaigns, consider adding conquest to his portfolio and the Fate domain (see Chapter 3) to the list of domains he grants access to.

Vecna (NE), like Boccob, has far more worshipers among magic-wielding characters than among martial characters. However, fighters with secrets to protect may find themselves offering a more than occasional prayer to the Whispered One, and some go so far as to give this deity their full allegiance. Fighters who worship Vecna often have good Intelligence scores and tend to be quiet, private individuals, rarely trust-

TABLE 4–5: THE WARRIOR PANTHEON

Name	Alignment	Domains	Weapon	Portfolio
Altua (F)	Lawful good	Good, Law, Nobility*, War	Longsword	Honor, nobility
Syreth (M)	Neutral good	Good, Healing, Protection	Heavy mace	Protection, community
Valkar (M)	Chaotic good	Chaos, Courage*, Good, Strength	Battle axe	Courage
Halmyr (M)	Lawful neutral	Law, Planning*, War	Rapier	Strategy, skill
Lyris (F)	Neutral	Fate*, Luck, War	Warhammer	Victory, fate
Konkresh (M)	Chaotic neutral	Chaos, Destruction, Strength	Greatclub	Brute force
Typhos (M)	Lawful evil	Evil, Law, Tyranny*, War	Greatsword	Tyranny
Sulerain (F)	Neutral evil	Death, Destruction, Evil	Greataxe	Slaughter
Nadirech (M)	Chaotic evil	Chaos, Evil, Luck, Trickery	Short sword	Cowardice, trickery

*New domain described in Chapter 3 of this book.

Deities by Race

Race	Deities
Human	By class and alignment
Dwarf	Altua or by class and alignment
Elf	Valkar or by class and alignment
Gnome	Halmyr, Syreth, or by class and alignment
Goblin	Nadirech or by class and alignment
Half-elf	Valkar or by class and alignment
Halfling	Syreth, Valkar or by class and alignment
Hobgoblin	Typhos or by class and alignment
Kobold	Nadirech or by class and alignment
Orc or half-orc	Konkresh or by class and alignment

Deities by Class

Class	Deities (Alignment)
Barbarian	Valkar (CG), Konkresh (CN), Sulerain (NE)
Bard	Altua (LG), Valkar (CG), Lyris (N), Nadirech (CE)
Cleric	Any
Druid	Syreth (NG), Lyris (N), Konkresh (CN), Sulerain (NE)
Fighter	Any
Monk	Altua (LG), Halmyr (LN), Typhos (LE)
Paladin	Altua (LG)
Ranger	Syreth (NG), Valkar (CG), Sulerain (NE)
Rogue	Valkar (CG), Halmyr (LN), Nadirech (CE)
Sorcerer	Valkar (CG), Konkresh (CN)
Wizard (any)	Halmyr (LN)
Abjurer	Syreth (NG)
Diviner	Lyris (N)
Enchanter	Typhos (LE)
Illusionist	Nadirech (CE)
Necromancer	Sulerain (NE)

ing anyone with their plots and schemes. Consider adding domination to Vecna's portfolio and the Planning or Tyranny domains (or both; see Chapter 3) to the list of domains he grants access to to make him more appropriate for warrior-oriented campaigns.

Wee Jas (LN), another deity who oversees magic, doesn't attract many fighters to her worship. Those few who select her as a patron are often strict taskmasters, typically belonging to a disciplined, hierarchical organization (such as a military force). They are obedient to superiors and demand similar attitudes of those beneath them. They often have high Charisma scores. Consider adding discipline to the portfolio of Wee Jas and the Planning or Tyranny domains (see Chapter 3) to the list of domains she grants access to to make her more appropriate for a fighter-oriented campaign.

Race-Specific Deities

Corellon Larethian (CG) is the patron deity of most elf fighters and rangers, but typically is revered by only a small number of nonelves. However, in a more racially integrated campaign, Corellon could easily become a common choice of rangers and fighters of many races, particularly those who favor the sword or the bow. Fighters who worship Corellon tend to be self-reliant, and often have high Dexterity scores. Consider adding swordplay and archery to Corellon's port-

folio to make him more appropriate for racially integrated warrior-oriented campaigns.

Among gnomes, there are few who follow the path of combat to exclusion, and thus Garl Glittergold (NG) doesn't count many fighters among his worshipers. Much more common are fighters or rangers who also have levels of rogue or bard, and who tend to appreciate Garl's love of wit. In a racially integrated campaign, nongnomes who share similar likes might well find Garl an appropriate patron. Fighters who worship Garl Glittergold appreciate a good joke and may also be accomplished craftsmen, but they never forget the lessons of vigilance taught by their patron deity. They frequently have high Intelligence scores. Consider adding vigilance to Garl's portfolio to make him more appropriate for a racially integrated warrior-oriented campaign.

Gruumsh (CE) draws most of his worshipers from among orcs and half-orcs, but any fighter who believes that might makes right can find much to appreciate in the one-eyed deity's teachings. Fighters who worship Gruumsh have no mercy for the weak, believing that only those able to defend their lands and possessions have any right to them. They may have high Charisma scores, the better to intimidate their enemies and lead followers. Gruumsh's portfolio includes war, and is thus perfectly suited to a martial campaign.

Moradin (LG), like Gruumsh, is both a deity of his people and of war, and he fits well into a warrior-oriented campaign. In a racially integrated setting, many nondwarves would likely be drawn to the banner of the Soul Forger. Fighters who worship Moradin are stoic and tenacious, and tend to have good Constitution scores.

Yondalla (LG) is a protector goddess. In a racially integrated campaign, any fighter responsible for the defense of a community or similar group of innocents might choose Yondalla as a patron deity. Her worshipers are kind-hearted to those they guard, but stalwart and ruthless against their enemies. Since her portfolio includes protection, it is appropriate for a warrior-oriented campaign. Consider adding the Courage domain (see Chapter 3) to the list of domains that Yondalla grants access to.

THE WARRIOR PANTHEON

In a warrior-oriented setting, it's natural to assume that the deities looking down on the activities below would have portfolios that reflect the world. The pantheon of deities described in this section is designed for a world in which martial combat is the rule of the day. You can use the entire pantheon as the religious structure of your world, or add one or more to the list of deities already present in your campaign, either augmenting or replacing the deities of war and combat you're currently using. Basic information about these deities is summarized on Table 4–5: The Warrior Pantheon.

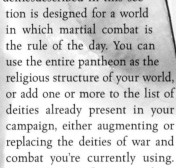

Symbol of Altua

Altua

The deity of honor and nobility, Altua guards the Sacred Tenets of Warfare by which all civilized races engage in battle. Her worshipers include paladins, good fighters and monks, and a number of knightly orders. Altua's clerics pray for spells at sunrise.

Syreth

Also known as the Guardian, Syreth protects those in need. Her worshipers include good fighters and rangers, as well as anyone dedicated to guarding others. She grants spells to her clerics at dusk—the better to protect the community through the long, dark night.

Symbol of Syreth

Valkar

Symbol of Valkar

The deity of courage, Valkar, is a favorite of good barbarians, bards, fighters, and rogues. He rewards bravery in battle, but can be fickle to those who choose discretion over valor. His clerics pray for spells at midnight, when courage is most needed.

Symbol of Halmyr

Halmyr

The deity of strategy and skill in warfare, Halmyr is patient and thoughtful in all things. He looks kindly upon those who use planning and forethought in their endeavors. Many generals and warlords offer up a prayer to Halmyr on the evening before a battle. Lawful characters of many classes, particularly fighters, monks, rogues, and even some wizards revere him. Halmyr's clerics pray for spells at dusk.

Lyris

As the deity of both victory and fate, Lyris has two aspects. To the bold, she symbolizes the inevitability of victory. Others see her as controlling the great wheel of fate, which promises that each person shall receive his or her just rewards (or punishments) in the afterlife. The clerics of Lyris pray for spells at noon, the "balance point" of the day.

Symbol of Lyris

Konkresh

The deity of brute force, Konkresh is the brother of Halmyr. The two couldn't be more diametrically opposed in their outlook—where Halmyr is patient, Konkresh is rash; Halmyr rewards skill, while Konkresh believes only in strength. Konkresh is a favorite deity of barbarians and of druids who favor the savage aspect of nature. His clerics pray for spells at dawn.

Typhos

The deity of tyranny, Typhos is the sworn enemy of all freedom-loving people. He is the patron of those who believe that the best method of rulership is total domination, including evil fighters, blackguards, and evil enchanters. He grants spells to his clerics at dawn.

Sulerain

The deity of death and slaughter, Sulerain is often called the Grim Lady. She is pleased only by destruction and loss of life—the greater the loss, the better. Her worshipers include assassins, evil necromancers, and anyone else attracted by the power of death. Sulerain's clerics pray for spells at dusk, called "the dying of the sun."

Nadirech

Also known as the Shunned One, Nadirech is called the deity of cowardice by some and the god of trickery and luck by others. Followers of Valkar deride Nadirech's worshipers for their lack of valor, while the faithful of Lyris dispute Nadirech's claim to be a deity of luck. The clerics of Nadirech pray for spells at midnight, and usually in secrecy.

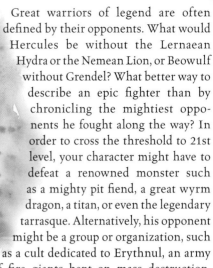

Symbol of Kohresh

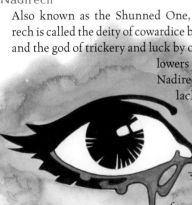

Symbol of Sulerain

Symbol of Typhos

THE EPIC WARRIOR

The *Player's Handbook* establishes 20th level as the limit to a character's power and experience. The *Dungeon Master's Guide*, however, provides rules for going beyond that limit to 21st level and onward. Such characters are called epic-level characters and use slightly modified rules to govern their interactions.

This section addresses some issues relevant to epic martial characters, from becoming an epic-level character, to advancing to epic levels in prestige classes, to new epic feats.

BECOMING AN EPIC-LEVEL WARRIOR

The passage from everyday hero to epic hero isn't a given in all games. Every DM has his own opinions about how (or if) to incorporate epic-level characters into the campaign. Assuming that your campaign offers characters the opportunity to attain 21st level, this section provides some advice for the player of a martial character and the DM to use when approaching that point.

Symbol of Nadirech

Great warriors of legend are often defined by their opponents. What would Hercules be without the Lernaean Hydra or the Nemean Lion, or Beowulf without Grendel? What better way to describe an epic fighter than by chronicling the mightiest opponents he fought along the way? In order to cross the threshold to 21st level, your character might have to defeat a renowned monster such as a mighty pit fiend, a great wyrm dragon, a titan, or even the legendary tarrasque. Alternatively, his opponent might be a group or organization, such as a cult dedicated to Erythnul, an army of fire giants bent on mass destruction, or an enclave of mind flayers intending to take over the kingdom's capital.

In other cases, epic warriors are best symbolized by a great achievement. The assembling of the Argonauts and their quest for the Golden Fleece marks Jason as a legendary hero, and Alexander the Great is remembered throughout history for his great conquests. Appropriate legendary achievements for a warrior might be to lead an army of paladins and angels against the gates of Hell, to free a kingdom (or even an entire plane) from tyrannical rule, or to restore the balance of life upset by necromantic forces from another reality.

A third mark of a legendary warrior is his weapon. From Roland's Durandal, to King Arthur's Excalibur, to the blade wielded by Vecna's traitorous lieutenant Kas, a great weapon becomes inextricably linked with its owner. To achieve epic levels, your fighter may have to wield a legendary weapon. This weapon might be an artifact, such as the *Mace of Cuthbert* or the *Sword of Kas*, or it might simply be an extraordinarily powerful nonartifact, such as an intelligent *holy avenger*, a *+5 vorpal greataxe* named Deathbringer, or any other unique weapon. In a low-magic campaign, even a relatively weak item might fill the bill, as long as it carried special significance in the world. Regardless, the weapon should be a special item, something that you couldn't just find lying around (or buy off the shelf). You might have to construct the weapon yourself (perhaps with the help of powerful allies), recover it from a long-forgotten tomb, or take it from its current wielder.

EPIC-LEVEL PRESTIGE-CLASS CHARACTERS

The *Dungeon Master's Guide* has information on advancing characters of the basic classes beyond 20th level (see Epic Characters, beginning on page 206). You can also advance beyond 10th level in a prestige class that already offers ten levels, but only if your character level is already 20th or higher. You cannot advance in a prestige class with fewer than ten levels beyond the maximum level indicated for that class, regardless of your character level.

When an epic-level character advances beyond 10th level in a prestige class, he follows all the rules presented in the *Dungeon Master's Guide*. (Many of those rules are repeated or summarized later in this section, for convenience.) In addition, you must create an epic-level progression for the prestige class, just as the *Dungeon Master's Guide* presents epic-level progressions for the classes from the *Player's Handbook*. Many, but not all, class features continue to accumulate after 10th level. The following guidelines describe how to create an epic prestige class progression, and are followed by a sample epic progression for the frenzied berserker prestige class (presented in Chapter 2 of this book).

—Class-related base save bonuses and base attack bonus don't increase after 20th level. Instead, use Table 6–18: Epic Save and Epic Attack Bonuses, page 206 of the *Dungeon Master's Guide*, to determine the character's epic bonus on saving throws and attack rolls.

—You continue to gain Hit Dice and skill points as normal beyond 10th level.

—Generally speaking, any class feature that uses your class level as part of a mathematical formula, such as a loremaster's lore check, continues to increase as normal by class level. However, any prestige class feature that calculates a save DC using the class level (such as the assassin's death attack) should add only half the character's class levels above 10th. Thus, a 24th-level assassin's death attack would have a

save DC of 27 + Int modifier (10 + class level up to 10th + 1/2 class levels above 10th). Without this adjustment, the save DC for epic-level character prestige class abilities increase at a much faster rate than those of normal class abilities.

—For spellcasters, your caster level continues to increase after 10th level at the same rate it did during the first ten levels of your prestige class. Thus, a 13th-level loremaster adds 13 to his caster level derived from another class to determine total caster level. However, your spells per day don't increase after character level 20th.

—The powers of familiars, special mounts, and fiendish servants continue to increase as their masters gain levels, if they're based on a formula that includes the character's level.

—Any class features that increase or accumulate as part of a repeated pattern also continue to increase or accumulate after 10th level at the same rate. An exception to this rule is any bonus feat progression granted as a class feature. If you get bonus feats as part of a class feature, these do not increase with epic levels. Instead, these classes get a new bonus feat progression (which varies from class to class; see below).

—In addition to the class features retained from nonepic levels, each class gains a bonus feat every two, three, four, or five levels beyond 10th. This benefit augments each class's progression of class features, because not all classes otherwise improve class features after 10th level. These bonus feats are in addition to the feat that every character gets every three levels.

—You don't gain any new class features, because there aren't any new class features described for these levels. Class features with a progression that slows or stops before 10th level and features that have a limited list of options do not improve as you gain epic levels. Likewise, class features that are gained only at a single level do not improve.

BEHIND THE CURTAIN: EPIC LEVELS AND PRESTIGE CLASSES

The epic rules allow you to go beyond the normal level limit in a prestige class, but only if it is a ten-level class. Why can't you add levels to a prestige class with fewer than ten levels?

It's Too Easy: Maxing out a ten-level prestige class takes a lot of time and effort, detracting significantly from your pursuit of other classes. But after maxing out a prestige class with only five levels, for instance, you haven't necessarily taken more than a short detour from your main class or classes.

It's Not Significant Enough: Characters with ten levels in the blackguard prestige class undoubtedly think of themselves as blackguards, regardless of the fact that they also have ten levels in one or more other classes. If you have taken fewer than ten

levels in a prestige class, those levels represent a smaller fraction of your character's identity.

It's Hard to Build an Epic Progression: With only a few levels to guide you, it's hard to determine what an appropriate progression of class features would be for the class. The rate of improvement of a special ability might be too fast to extrapolate over an infinite number of levels, or there might simply be too few class features to build a unique epic progression.

That said, if your DM wants to allow a character to gain epic levels in a prestige class with fewer than ten levels in its progression, that's okay. Work together with your DM to create an epic progression for the class (see Behind the Curtain: Building an Epic Progression on page 210 of the *Dungeon Master's Guide*).

Sample Epic Prestige Class Progression: The Epic Frenzied Berserker

Few mortal beings can surpass the destructive capabilities of the epic frenzied berserker.

Hit Die: d12.

Skill Points at Each Additional Level: 2 + Int modifier.

Frenzy: An epic frenzied berserker may enter a frenzy one additional time per day for every two levels gained after 9th (6/day at 11th, 7/day at 13th, and so forth).

Inspire Frenzy: An epic frenzied berserker may use this ability one additional time per day for every two levels gained after 10th (4/day at 12th, 5/day at 14th, and so on).

Bonus Feats: An epic frenzied berserker gains a bonus feat every three levels beyond 10th (13th, 16th, 19th, and so on).

EPIC FEATS

The feats below are only available to epic-level characters; that is, characters of at least 21st level. The version of a feat described here supersedes any previously published version of that feat.

Armor Skin [Epic]

Your skin becomes like armor.

Benefit: You gain a +1 natural armor bonus to Armor Class, or your existing natural armor bonus increases by +1.

Special: A character can gain this feat multiple times. Its effects stack.

Combat Archery [Epic]

You can fire a bow in melee safely.

Prerequisites: Dodge, Mobility, Point Blank Shot.

Benefit: You do not provoke attacks of opportunity when firing a bow.

Normal: Without this feat, you provoke attacks of opportunity from all opponents who threaten you whenever you use a bow.

Combat Insight [Epic]

Your keen intellect allows you to place melee attacks where they will deal the most damage.

Prerequisites: Combat Expertise, Epic Prowess, base attack bonus +15.

Benefit: When wielding a melee weapon, add your Intelligence modifier rather than your Strength modifier to the weapon's damage rolls.

Damage Reduction [Epic]

You can shrug off some damage from attacks.

Prerequisites: Con 21.

Benefit: You gain damage reduction 3/–. This benefit doesn't stack with damage reduction granted by magic items or nonpermanent magical effects, but it does stack with damage reduction granted by permanent magical effects, class features, or this feat itself.

Special: A character can gain this feat multiple times. Each time you gain the feat, your damage reduction increases by 3.

Epic Combat Expertise [Epic]

You have extraordinary talent at using your combat skill for defense.

Prerequisites: Int 19, Combat Expertise, base attack bonus +21.

Benefit: When you use the attack action or full attack action in melee, you can take a penalty of as much as –5 on your attack rolls and add the same number (+5 or less) as a dodge bonus to your Armor Class and to the Armor Class of an adjacent friendly creature. The changes to attack rolls and Armor Class last until your next action.

The effect of this feat supersedes the effect of the Combat Expertise feat; you can't use both feats simultaneously to gain two dodge bonuses.

Epic Prowess [Epic]

You have great skill in combat.

Benefit: Gain a +1 bonus on all attack rolls.

Special: A character can gain this feat multiple times. Its effects stack.

Epic Toughness [Epic]

You are preternaturally tough.

Benefit: You gain +30 hit points.

Special: A character can gain this feat multiple times. Its effects stack.

Epic Weapon Focus [Epic]

You are especially good at using one chosen type of weapon.

Prerequisite: Greater Weapon Focus and Weapon Focus with the weapon chosen.

Benefit: Add a +2 bonus on all attack rolls you make using the selected weapon. This bonus stacks with other bonuses on attack rolls, including the bonuses from Weapon Focus and Greater Weapon Focus.

Special: A character can gain this feat multiple times. Its effects do not stack. Each time you take the feat, it applies to a different type of weapon.

Epic Sunder [Epic]

You deal extra damage when attacking objects.

Prerequisites: Str 25, Epic Prowess, Improved Sunder, Power Attack.

Benefit: When attacking an object, you may double any extra damage derived from Strength. When attempting to break an object with sudden force rather than dealing damage, you gain a +4 bonus on your Strength check.

Legendary Rider [Epic]

You can ride a mount in combat with ease, even bareback.

Prerequisite: Ride 24 ranks.

Benefit: You don't take a penalty on Ride checks when riding a mount without a saddle (bareback). You never need to make a Ride check to control a mount in combat (and even controlling a mount not trained for combat doesn't require an action).

Normal: Without this feat, you take a −5 penalty on Ride checks without a saddle, and you must make a Ride check to control a mount in combat (and controlling a mount not trained for combat requires a move action).

Illus. by J. Jarvis

With the Wield Oversized Weapon feat, this halfling can hold her own against a frost giant.

Perfect Two-Weapon Fighting [Epic]

You can attack with your off-hand weapon as frequently as with your primary weapon.

Prerequisites: Dex 25, Greater Two-Weapon Fighting, Improved Two-Weapon Fighting, Two-Weapon Fighting.

Benefit: When making a full attack, you can make as many attacks with your off-hand weapon as with your primary weapon, using the same base attack bonus. For example, a character with this feat and a base attack bonus of +18/+13/+8/+3 could make four attacks per round with his primary weapon and four attacks per round with his off-hand weapon, using the sazme set of base attack bonuses. You still take the normal penalties for fighting with two weapons.

Normal: Without this feat, you can only make a single attack with an off-hand weapon during a full attack (or two attacks with an off-hand weapon if you have Improved Two-Weapon Fighting, or three attacks with an off-hand weapon if you have Greater Two-Weapon Fighting).

Wield Oversized Weapon [Epic]

You can use larger than normal weapons with ease.

Prerequisites: Str 25, Monkey Grip*, base attack bonus +21.

Benefit: You can treat any weapon as if it were one size category smaller than normal and one category "lighter" for the purpose of determining the amount of effort it takes to wield. For instance, a halfling with this feat could wield a Medium short sword as a Small light weapon, or a human could wield an ogre's Large greatclub as a Medium two-handed weapon. The weapon still deals its normal amount of damage.

Normal: You may only wield weapons of your size without penalty.

*New feat described in Chapter 3 of this book.

A WARRIOR AND HIS WEAPONS

In most cases, a warrior is defined by his choice of weapons. A barbarian wielding a greataxe presents a very different test of skill than a fighter with twin short swords, a ranger with a composite longbow, or a paladin with a longsword and shield. Even a monk, who often doesn't wield a weapon in the truest sense, is herself a living weapon that presents special challenges to opponents.

Most fighters tend to choose a limited group of favorite weapons at a relatively low level, investing feats (such as Weapon Focus or Exotic Weapon Proficiency) and gold (in the form of magical enhancements) into these weapons. Before too long, a fighter has made a reputation for fighting in a certain way, and that style almost certainly reflects his weapon choice. More than most characters, the fighter chooses a style and generally sticks to it. It's a rare fighter, for instance, who sets aside a career of sword-and-shield combat for a two-handed weapon, but a wizard or druid can change her spell selection every day. On top of that, most fighters can't easily change weapons during a battle, so specializing in a weapon with a limited niche of usefulness (such as a reach weapon or a ranged weapon) can put you at a disadvantage when that isn't the right weapon for the job (such as fighting in a cramped dungeon corridor).

All this makes the fighter's choice of weapon an extraordinarily important one. By 8th level, most combat-minded characters have spent at least two feats on a specific weapon (Weapon Focus and Improved Critical), and possibly three or more. The last thing a fighter wants to worry about is whether he's going to find out that this weapon he's spent so much effort mastering isn't the right choice.

So how can you be sure you're making the right choice? There's no perfect answer, but there are some guidelines to consider when picking your weapon.

If You Have It, Flaunt It: If you have a high Strength, there's no better weapon than a two-handed weapon to deal out truly massive amounts of damage. This option sacrifices some Armor Class (since you can't carry a shield), so you may need to rely on a good Dexterity (for extra points of AC) or a high Constitution (for more hit points). Similarly, the high-Strength fighter with a composite longbow built to his specifications puts the crossbow user to shame.

Hide Your Weaknesses: If you have a low Strength but a high Dexterity, don't fight with a big weapon. Instead, use a light weapon (or better yet, a rapier) with Weapon Finesse as a cheap way of dramatically improving your attack roll. If your Dexterity modifier is at least 2 points higher than your Strength modifier, Weapon Finesse is better than Weapon Focus. Sure, you're giving up some damage potential by using a lighter weapon, but in most situations you would rather be hitting more often and dealing slightly less damage than hitting less often and dealing slightly more damage.

A low-Dexterity character may need the extra bonus to Armor Class provided by heavy armor and a shield, putting two-handed weapons and two-weapon fighting out of reach. This character should focus on getting the biggest one-handed weapon he can, such as a bastard sword or a dwarven waraxe.

Look at Your Feats: Many feats lend themselves to being used with certain types of weapons. For instance, Power Attack is much more potent with a two-handed weapon than with a one-handed weapon, and is useless with a light weapon. A character with Two-Weapon Fighting should wield the same light weapon in both hands to reduce penalties and maximize bonuses from other feats. If you have Combat Reflexes, carry a reach weapon to widen your range of threatened squares (and thus make more attacks of opportunity). Spring Attack is much more useful to a character wielding a single big weapon (such as a bastard sword or a greataxe) than a character wielding two light weapons, since you only get to make one attack during any round that you use Spring Attack. Quick Draw lets you change between weapons easily, allowing you a wider range of options in any given fight.

Go with Your Heart: Some fighters insist that a weapon with a bigger threat range (such as a longsword or, better yet, a scimitar) is preferable to a weapon with a bigger critical multiplier (such as a battleaxe or a heavy pick) because it's "more reliable." On the other hand, a triple-damage critical hit by a raging barbarian with a greataxe may end the fight before it begins. In the end, the choice of wide threat range versus big multiplier depends a lot on whether you prefer to slog along steadily, dealing out double-damage critical hits on a regular basis, or swing the fight wildly on the rare occasion of a triple-damage critical hit. Both are fine choices, but you should pick the one that suits your temperament.

EXOTIC WEAPONS

As stated above, a fighter's choice of weapon says a great deal about his tactics and combat style. Those who use exotic weapons—whether a whip, dire flail, or one of the weapons described below—consciously differentiate themselves from the rank-and-file sword- and axe-swingers. The fighter swinging a spiked chain or lajatang says to his opponents, "I am different from others you have fought, and your previous experience did not prepare you for what I am capable of doing to you." Sometimes, that's all the edge you need.

Weapon Familiarity

Some races are associated with specific exotic weapons, such as dwarves and the dwarven waraxe. The *Player's Handbook* grants weapon familiarity to these races, allowing them to treat certain exotic weapons as martial weapons. With the limited number of race-specific exotic weapons in the *Player's Handbook*, this doesn't give any one race an unfair advantage. However, if you introduce more race-specific exotic weapons, such as the ones included in this book, the advantage increases in significance.

To compensate, consider limiting the number of exotic weapons that a given character of that race can treat as familiar to no more than the number of weapons associated with the race in the *Player's Handbook* (or in the *Monster Manual* for orcs). Thus, a given dwarf fighter might be able to treat

TABLE 4–6: NEW EXOTIC WEAPONS

Exotic Weapon	Cost	Dmg (S)	Dmg (M)	Critical	Range Increment	Weight[1]	Type
Light Melee Weapons							
Buckler-axe, dwarven	20 gp	1d4	1d6	×3	—	4 lb.	Slashing
Lightblade, elven	50 gp	1d4	1d6	18–20/×2	—	1 lb.	Piercing
Tortoise blade, gnome	10 gp	1d4	1d6	19–20/×2	—	3 lb.	Piercing
One-Handed Melee Weapons							
Maul	15 gp	1d8	1d10	×3	—	20 lb.	Bludgeoning
Pick, dire	30 gp	1d6	1d8	×4	—	12 lb.	Piercing
Scourge	20 gp	1d6	1d8	×2	—	2 lb.	Slashing
Thinblade, elven	100 gp	1d6	1d8	18–20/×2	—	3 lb.	Piercing
Warmace	25 gp	1d10	1d12	×2	—	10 lb.	Bludgeoning
Two-Handed Melee Weapons							
Greatspear[4]	25 gp	1d10	2d6	×3	10 ft.	9 lb.	Piercing
Hammer, double[5]	70 gp	1d6/1d6	1d8/1d8	×3	—	18 lb.	Bludgeoning
Lajatang[5]	90 gp	1d6/1d6	1d8/1d8	×2	—	7 lb.	Slashing
Mancatcher[4]	20 gp	1d3[3]	1d4[3]	×2	—	8 lb.	Bludgeoning
Poleaxe, heavy[4]	20 gp	1d10	2d6	×3	—	15 lb.	Piercing or slashing[2]
Ranged Weapons							
Blowgun, greater	15 gp	1d2	1d3	×2	10 ft.	2 lb.	Piercing
Darts (10)	1 gp	—	—	—	—	1/2 lb.	—
Bolas, barbed	10 gp	1d3	1d4	×2	10 ft.	3 lb.	Piercing
Boomerang	10 gp	1d3[3]	1d4[3]	×2	20 ft.	2 lb.	Bludgeoning
Greatbow	150 gp	1d8	1d10	×3	120 ft.	6 lb.	Piercing
Greatbow, composite	200 gp	1d8	1d10	×3	130 ft.	6 lb.	Piercing

1 Weight figures are for Medium weapons. A Small weapon weighs half as much, and a Large weapon weighs twice as much.
2 The weapon deals either piercing damage or slashing damage (player's choice at time of attack).
3 The weapon deals nonlethal damage rather than lethal damage.
4 Reach weapon.
5 Double weapon.

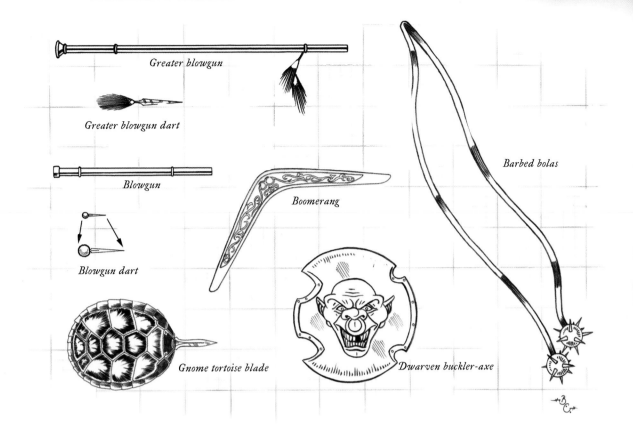

Greater blowgun

Greater blowgun dart

Blowgun

Blowgun dart

Gnome tortoise blade

Boomerang

Dwarven buckler-axe

Barbed bolas

the dwarven waraxe and the dwarven buckler-axe (a new weapon described here) as martial weapons, but would have to treat the dwarven urgrosh as an exotic weapon. A gnome ranger could treat the gnome hooked hammer or the gnome tortoise blade (a new weapon) as a martial weapon, but not both. An elf fighter can't treat any exotic weapons as martial weapons, since elves don't have weapon familiarity with any exotic weapons according to the *Player's Handbook*. Characters who wish to master all their race's exotic weapons can select the Improved Weapon Familiarity feat described in Chapter 3 of this book.

If the character must choose which exotic weapons to treat as martial weapons, this decision should be made the first time the character gains proficiency in all martial weapons (at 1st level for a barbarian, fighter, paladin, or ranger, or the first time a character gains a level in any of those classes or any prestige class that grants proficiency in all martial weapons). Once the decision is made, it can't be changed; however, the DM may allow characters to change their decisions if new race-specific exotic weapons are later introduced to the game.

Even if a character treats an exotic weapon as a martial weapon thanks to weapon familiarity, it is still treated as an exotic weapon for the purpose of qualifying for feats, prestige classes, or other benefits that require the character to be skilled in the use of an exotic weapon.

EXOTIC WEAPON DESCRIPTIONS

The weapons on Table 4–6 are described below, along with any special options the wielder has for their use.

Blowgun, Greater: Like its smaller cousin (see page 145 of the *Dungeon Master's Guide*), the greater blowgun is often used to deliver poison. The darts it fires are larger than blowgun needles, but smaller than a thrown dart. These darts deal damage in addition to delivering poison. A greater blowgun requires two hands to use or reload. Loading a blowgun is a move action that provokes attacks of opportunity.

A greater blowgun has a maximum range of five range increments.

Bolas, Barbed: This weapon is similar to a normal set of bolas, except that its weighted balls are studded with hooked barbs and thus deal lethal (not nonlethal) damage. Because the barbed bolas can wrap around an enemy's leg or other limb, you can use this weapon to make a ranged trip attack against an opponent. You can't be tripped during your own trip attempt when using a set of barbed bolas.

For purposes of weapon proficiency and similar feats, barbed bolas are treated as if they were bolas. Thus, if you have Exotic Weapon Proficiency (bolas), you are also proficient with barbed bolas.

Boomerang: The boomerang is a curved throwing stick that returns to its thrower if it misses its target. To catch a returning boomerang, the thrower must make an attack roll (as if he were throwing the boomerang) and hit AC

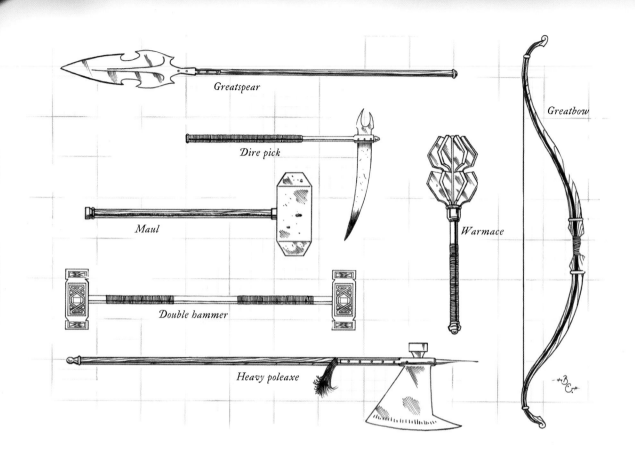

Greatspear

Dire pick

Maul

Warmace

Greatbow

Double hammer

Heavy poleaxe

10. Failure indicates the boomerang lands in a randomly determined square adjacent to the thrower (if the thrower is proficient) or 1d4 squares away in a random direction (if not proficient).

Buckler-Axe, Dwarven: At first glance the dwarven buckler-axe appears similar to a standard buckler, but this weapon has enlarged bladelike edges at its top and bottom, allowing the wielder to swing it like an axe. Thus, in addition to its obvious protective qualities, it proves a capable off-hand weapon or emergency weapon when disarmed.

A dwarven buckler-axe grants its wielder a +1 shield bonus to Armor Class. As with any shield, when you attack with a dwarven buckler-axe, you do not get the shield bonus to your AC.

The buckler-axe also provides a –1 armor check penalty and incurs a 5% arcane spell failure chance for its wielder. Like a spiked shield, a buckler-axe can be enhanced as a weapon, as a shield, or both, but such enhancements must be paid for and applied separately.

Dart, Blowgun: A blowgun dart resembles a lightweight, undersized arrow. You don't apply your Strength modifier to damage with a blowgun dart. A blowgun dart can't effectively be used as a melee weapon. Blowgun darts come in a leather pouch that holds 10 darts. A dart that hits its target is destroyed; one that misses has a 50% chance to be destroyed or lost.

Greatbow: You need at least two hands to use a bow, regardless of its size. A greatbow sized for a Medium character is 6 feet or more in length when strung. A greatbow is too unwieldy to use while mounted. Like other bows, if you have a penalty for low Strength, apply it to damage rolls when using a greatbow. If you have a bonus for high Strength, you can apply it to damage rolls when you use a composite greatbow (see below) but not a regular greatbow.

Greatbow, Composite: You need at least two hands to use a bow, regardless of its size. A composite greatbow is too unwieldy to use while mounted. A composite greatbow sized for a Medium character is 6 feet or more in length when strung. Composite greatbows follow all of the normal rules for composite bows, including strength ratings. Each point of Strength bonus granted by the bow adds 200 gp to the cost.

Greatspear: This broad-bladed spear has a long, flat blade, and is too heavy to wield properly without proficiency.

Hammer, Double: A double hammer is a double weapon. You can fight with it as if fighting with two weapons, but if you do, you incur all the normal attack penalties associated with fighting with two weapons as if you were attacking with a one-handed weapon and a light weapon. (See page 160 of the *Player's Handbook* for details on fighting with two weapons.)

Lajatang: The lajatang is a staff with a crescent-shaped blade at each end. A lajatang is a double weapon. You can fight with it as if fighting with two weapons, but if you do, you incur all the normal attack penalties associated with fighting with two weapons: a one-handed weapon and a light weapon (see page 160 of the *Player's Handbook*).

A monk who is proficient with the lajatang can treat it as a special monk weapon, as described in the monk class description (page 40 of the *Player's Handbook*). Each end counts as a separate weapon for the purpose of the flurry of blows ability, similar to how the quarterstaff works.

Lightblade, Elven: This rapierlike weapon is the size of a short sword, but weighs only as much as a dagger. Dexterous elf fighters and rogues favor it. Its thin, flexible blade slips easily into the seams of armor or between the ribs of a foe. Some elf nobles carry a lightblade—often decorated with intricate filigree and tiny gemstones—as a sign of their station, even if they aren't proficient in its use.

Mancatcher: City guards and others who prefer to capture their opponents unharmed use the mancatcher. A wielder who hits a target of its size or one size category smaller than it with a mancatcher can immediately attempt to grapple (as a free action) without provoking an attack of opportunity. Any grapple check you make using a mancatcher includes the mancatcher's enhancement bonus (if any) and any other bonuses you might have on attack rolls with the weapon (such

as from the Weapon Focus feat). If you grapple a target with a mancatcher, you are considered grappling, but unless your target can reach you, he can't attempt to attack you, damage you, or pin you. You can escape the grapple automatically by releasing the target as a standard action.

In addition to the normal options available to a grappler, the wielder of a mancatcher can attempt to force his target to the ground (the equivalent of a trip attack, though no attack roll is necessary). The mancatcher is a reach weapon and cannot be used against adjacent opponents.

Maul: A maul is too large to use in one hand without special training (the appropriate Exotic Weapon Proficiency feat). A character can use a maul two-handed as a martial weapon.

Pick, Dire: A dire pick resembles a heavy pick, but with a longer shaft and a more massive head. A dire pick is too large to use in one hand without special training (the appropriate Exotic Weapon Proficiency feat). A character can use a dire pick two-handed as a martial weapon.

Poleaxe, Heavy: A heavy poleaxe has reach; you can strike opponents 10 feet away with it, but you can't use it against an adjacent foe. Normally, you strike with the heavy poleaxe's axe head, but the spike on the end is useful against charging opponents. If you use a ready action to set a heavy poleaxe against a charge, you deal double damage if you score a hit against a charging creature.

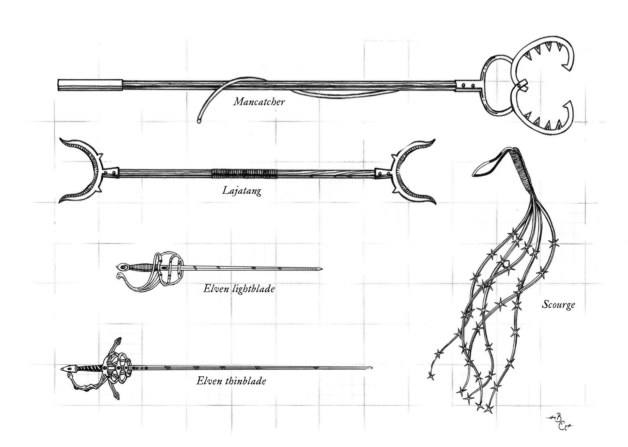

Mancatcher

Lajatang

Elven lightblade

Elven thinblade

Scourge

Scourge: This multitailed, barbed whip is often dipped in a poison delivered via injury. You get a +2 bonus on your opposed attack roll when attempting to disarm an opponent (including the roll to keep from being disarmed if the attack fails) with this weapon.

Thinblade, Elven: This rapierlike weapon is the size of a longsword, but much lighter. Dexterous elf fighters and rogues favor it. Its thin, flexible blade slips easily into the seams of armor, or between the ribs of an enemy.

You can use the Weapon Finesse feat to apply your Dexterity modifier instead of your Strength modifier to attack rolls with an elven thinblade.

Tortoise Blade, Gnome: This contraption is designed to be used by a gnome in his or her off hand. It is particularly useful in cramped tunnels or warrens where swinging a weapon is difficult or impossible. It looks like a turtle shell strapped to the wielder's wrist, with a daggerlike blade jutting out where the wielder's fingers should be.

A tortoise blade grants a +1 shield bonus to Armor Class. As with any shield, when you attack with a tortoise blade you do not get the shield bonus to your AC.

A tortoise blade also provides a –1 armor check penalty and incurs a 5% arcane spell failure chance for its wielder. Like a spiked shield, a tortoise blade can be enhanced as a weapon, as a shield, or both, but such enhancements must be paid for and applied separately.

Warmace: Anyone wielding a warmace takes a –1 penalty to Armor Class because the weight of the weapon makes it difficult to recover quickly from swinging it. A warmace is too large to use in one hand without special training (the appropriate Exotic Weapon Proficiency feat). A character can use a warmace two-handed as a martial weapon.

PRIMITIVE WEAPONS

Many so-called exotic weapons are weapons more common to primitive cultures, such as Stone Age humans. To reflect that fact, the DM could allow primitive cultures (or even some of the more savage races, such as lizardfolk) to treat blowguns as simple weapons and any or all the following exotic weapons as martial weapons: bolas, barbed bolas, boomerang, greater blowgun, and net. As a tradeoff, you could rule that such races treat bows and crossbows (of all sorts) as exotic weapons. If you want to play such a character, work out a fair balance with your DM.

IMPROVISED WEAPONS

As detailed in the *Player's Handbook*, objects not crafted to be used as weapons may nonetheless find use in combat. This is most true in the stereotypical tavern brawl, but any time a character can't or doesn't want to use a weapon, he needs to know how effective the closest object is in a fight.

Any creature using an improvised weapon—from a broken bottle to a barstool—in a fight is considered to be nonproficient with it and thus takes a –4 penalty on attack rolls made with it. An improvised weapon scores a threat (a possible critical hit) on a natural roll of 20 and deals double damage on a critical hit. An improvised thrown weapon has a range increment of 10 feet.

What about fighting with ladders, wagon wheels, or coils of rope? In the hands of a determined (or desperate) individual, these oddly shaped objects offer a wide variety of options in combat. Of course, you must still deal with the –4 penalty on attack rolls made with such a weapon, but sometimes you have to make use of what's available!

Bull Rush: If you perform a bull rush while carrying a big, sturdy object (such as a bench or table), you add a +2 bonus on your Strength check to push back the defender.

Defense: Objects with lots of surface area (such as tables) grant you a +2 shield bonus to Armor Class (or a +4 shield bonus to AC if you use the total defense action), but require two hands to use.

Disarm: Any object with a lot of protrusions (such as a chair or a broken wagon wheel) or that can easily ensnare objects (such as a cloak or a ladder) grants the wielder a +2 bonus on opposed attack rolls made to disarm an enemy (including the roll to avoid being disarmed if such an attempt fails).

Entangle: Any sheetlike flexible object (such as a carpet or tapestry) can entangle an opponent with a successful ranged touch attack. An entangled creature takes a –2 penalty on attack rolls and a –4 penalty to Dexterity, can move at only half speed, cannot run or charge, and may have difficulty casting

How do you get to be the last one standing? Practice, practice, practice. . . .

spells (see the Concentration skill description, page 69 of the *Player's Handbook*). Escaping from such an object requires a standard action and a DC 10 Escape Artist check. These objects are treated as two-handed weapons.

Reach: Long objects (such as ladders) have reach, allowing a Small or Medium character to strike at opponents up to 10 feet away (but not at adjacent foes). These objects are treated as two-handed weapons.

Trip: An object with protrusions at the end (such as a hat rack or a barstool) or that can wrap around a leg (such as a chain) can be used to make trip attempts. If you are tripped during your own trip attempt, you can drop the improvised weapon to avoid being tripped.

Improvised Weapon Damage

Most improvised weapons deal between 1d3 and 1d6 points of damage (usually bludgeoning, but possibly piercing or slashing). For more guidance on how much damage an improvised weapon deals, see Table 4–7: Improvised Weapon Damage. For every additional 200 pounds of an object's weight beyond 400 pounds, it deals an additional 1d6 points of damage if used as an improvised weapon.

If an object weighs up to 2 pounds, a Medium character can treat it as a light weapon. Objects weighing between 2 and 10 pounds are one-handed weapons for Medium charac-

ters, and objects weighing 11 to 50 pounds are two-handed weapons. Halve these numbers for every size category below Medium, and double them for every size category above Medium.

TABLE 4–7: IMPROVISED WEAPON DAMAGE

Object Weight	Damage[1]	Examples
Less than 2 lb.[2]	1d3	Mug, torch
2 lb.–5 lb.	1d4	Lantern, manacles
6 lb.–10 lb.	1d6	Chair, shovel
11 lb.–25 lb.	1d8	Ladder, small table
26 lb.–50 lb.	2d6	Barrel (empty)
51 lb.–100 lb.	3d6	Chest (full), big table
101 lb.–200 lb.	4d6	Cart
201 lb.–400 lb.	5d6	Wagon

1 A sharp object deals damage as an object of twice its weight. For instance, a broken bottle (1 lb.) deals 1d4 points of damage, not 1d3. Conversely, a soft or malleable object, such as a gourd, deals damage as an object of half its weight, and the damage is nonlethal.

2 If an item has no weight worth noting, it doesn't deal any damage when used as a weapon.

SMARTER

Wade into combat knowing what it takes to survive—anytime, anywhere. With expanded rules for head-to-head skirmishing and mass battles, the *Miniatures Handbook* is reinforced with new base classes, feats, spells, prestige classes, and monsters—so you can really put up a fight. Pick one up and charge right in.

PLAY MORE